Entertaining Politics

Communication, Media, and Politics

Series Editor
Robert E. Denton, Jr., Virginia Tech

This series features a range of work dealing with the role and function of communication in the realm of politics, broadly defined. Including general academic books and texts for use in graduate and advanced undergraduate courses, the series encompasses humanistic, critical, historical, and empirical studies in political communication in the United States. Primary subject areas include campaigns and elections, media, and political institutions. Communication, Media, and Politics books will be of interest to students, teachers, and scholars of political communication from the disciplines of communication, rhetorical studies, political science, journalism, and political sociology.

Recent Titles in the Series

Entertaining Politics

Satiric Television and Political Engagement

Second Edition

Jeffrey P. Jones

ROWMAN & LITTLEFIELD PUBLISHERS, INC.
Lanham • Boulder • New York • Toronto • Plymouth, UK

ROWMAN & LITTLEFIELD PUBLISHERS, INC.

Published in the United States of America
by Rowman & Littlefield Publishers, Inc.
A wholly owned subsidary of The Rowman & Littlefield Publishing Group, Inc.
4501 Forbes Boulevard, Suite 200, Lanham, Maryland 20706
www.rowmanlittlefield.com

Estover Road
Plymouth PL6 7PY
United Kingdom

British Library Cataloguing in Publication Information Available

Library of Congress Cataloging-in-Publication Data:

Jones, Jeffrey P., 1963–
   Entertaining politics : satiric television and political engagement / Jeffrey P.
Jones. — 2nd ed.
      p. cm. — (Communication, media, and politics)
   Previous edition cataloged under title.
   Includes bibliographical references and index.
   ISBN 978-0-7425-6527-2 (cloth : alk. paper) — ISBN 978-0-7425-6528-9
(pbk. : alk. paper) — ISBN 978-0-7425-6529-6 (electronic)
   1. Television in politics—United States. 2. Television and politics—United
States. 3. Television talk shows—United States. 4. Political satire, American. I.
Entertaining politics. II. Title.
   HE8700.76.U6J663 2010
   306.20973—dc22   2009026299

Printed in the United States of America

♾ ™ The paper used in this publication meets the minimum requirements of
American National Standard for Information Sciences—Permanence of Paper
for Printed Library Materials, ANSI/NISO Z39.48-1992.

In memory of my mother,
Grace Preiss Jones
Amazing Grace!

Humour is the only test of gravity, and gravity of humour; for a subject which will not bear raillery is suspicious, and a jest which will not bear serious examination is false wit.

—Aristotle

Contents

Preface to the Second Edition

Entertaining Politics appeared around Election Day in 2004, but was written amidst a bizarre presidential sex scandal and impeachment, across the even more bizarre 2000 presidential election outcome, the shocking terrorist attacks of 9/11, and the subsequent wars in Afghanistan and Iraq. As a genre (or subgenre, depending on how one sees it), political entertainment television began in the tranquil, if overly partisan years of the early to mid 1990s. When the book went to press, however, the programs and hosts that constituted the genre were faced with what can be seen in hindsight to have been a minor crisis of American democracy brought on by the Imperial Presidency of George W. Bush. The primary issues addressed in the first edition, therefore, look somewhat quaint in retrospect.

Nevertheless, what seemed clear at that time was that television's relationship to politics was undergoing a transformation. New political entertainment talk shows were appearing that presented a challenge to the privileged position of traditional public affairs talk shows—especially those programmed by network news divisions. These pundit shows featured experts or political insiders, but their insistence that viewers engage politics based on their inside-the-beltway thinking often made political programming seem inaccessible, predictable, or distant from the daily lives of viewers. What was appearing in entertainment television, however, was a brand of hybrid talk that blended entertainment and politics in newly creative ways, including the use of humor and a vernacular approach to politics as its central draw. In the process, these shows were establishing an alternative to both the staid entertainment and political brands that dominated television talk. The programs extended politics into popular culture (and vice versa) and offered a different means of making sense of politics in the process.

What is more, audiences welcomed these new outsider voices (much to the chagrin of Washington elites) as legitimate commentators on politics. The question the first edition tried to address, then, was what exactly were these shows contributing to American political life, and how the answer to that question might address the normative claims by critics that this programming was detrimental to democracy because of its supposedly unholy blending of entertainment with the serious business of politics/democracy.

Since that time, much has changed, both within the genre as well as in the world. The primary characters that composed the narrative of the first edition of this book were Bill Maher, Dennis Miller, and Jon Stewart. Maher's role as the most prominent and visible comedian-commentator and weeknight talk show host diminished when he left a broadcast network and moved to subscription television with a once-a-week show. Dennis Miller left the air, finding it hard to stay employed after experiencing what looked like a right-wing conversion experience after 9/11 and seemingly losing his sense of humor in the process. Jon Stewart, who early on characterized himself as one of the guys in the back of the room lobbing spitballs, over time had assumed a court jester role in the early years of the Bush administration. While an aggressive, in-your-face comic like Maher was fired for his supposedly unpatriotic commentary, Stewart adroitly used his satiric humor to poke, prod, and critique King George and his administration's brazen and ruthless yet incompetently waged "War on Terror" without Stewart losing his head.

Two weeks prior to the publication of this book's first edition, Stewart assumed a new public role when he appeared on CNN's pundit talk show *Crossfire* and lambasted the program's hosts in a very serious but cringe-inducing manner for "hurting America," transforming political talk into spectacle, and making politics into a theatrical joke. If not a shot heard round the world, he certainly announced that this comedian—whose job was to satirize the absurdity of public life—didn't find politics a laughing matter when performed by news networks that had abrogated their public responsibility. After that October surprise and the reelection of Bush, Stewart's *Daily Show* continued to garner critical acclaim for being one of the few programs on television that consistently offered a critical perspective on the ever-shocking activities of the Bush administration, as well as the news media whose job it was to keep governmental abuse of power in check. By the following summer, Stewart had removed the guest couch on his program's set, added a chair more conducive to serious interviews, and began hosting an array of authors, journalists, politicians, and bureaucrats—all of whom were there to help make sense of the confusing and frustrating events and governmental actions that seemed to appear daily. *The Daily Show* became a serious (though humorous) arena for interrogating power, and in the process, Stewart left the jester persona behind. In short, Stewart and *The Daily*

Show became Exhibit A for the ways in which political entertainment television (especially the satirical kind) could play a positive, important, and critical role in communicating politics, especially in the seeming absence of such from traditional news media.

What also transpired between editions was the addition of another critical voice within the genre—comedian Stephen Colbert, who expanded a persona crafted during his years as a *Daily Show* correspondent into a parody of a bloviated right-wing talk show host on his own program, *The Colbert Report.* Colbert too announced the seriousness of the genre and its location as a place for substantive political commentary and critique when he appeared as the featured entertainment at the White House Correspondents' Association Dinner in 2006. Colbert performed in character, and as should have been expected after his parodic characterization of the inanity of right-wing thinking on his program, he took the president and press corps to task as President Bush grimly looked on. Colbert became an almost overnight sensation as the video of his performance spread quickly across the Internet by viewers hungry for just such a critique. In sum, here then was Exhibit B of how the power of satire and parody could play an important role in enunciating critiques that were difficult to articulate (or be effective) in other ways.

With this successful maturation of the genre, there has been a more general public and critical acceptance of entertaining political programming as a legitimate location for public discourse. The more pressing and contentious question today, though, is whether such programming substitutes for news and older forms of political information, especially for younger citizens, and if so, whether that is a dangerous thing. Journalists, scholars, and other cultural critics have perpetuated the claim that young people "get their news" from comedy-entertainment programs, with the fear that if this is true, they are missing vitally important information central to an engaged citizenship by not attending to traditional forums for news. But what if such programming is actually an alternative form of reporting—another way of producing useful, informative, or meaningful materials with just as much value to citizens as that provided by television news? Are such criticisms of the genre merited in that case? And what if citizens maintain a meaningful relationship with the genre, using it for forms of civic engagement beyond simple information acquisition? Central to this critique as well is the assumption that satirical and parodic programming, by donning a faux premise, are therefore trafficking in falsities because the fake cannot, by definition, be "real," and therefore anything said in that format must simply not be true. But what if the fake is actually just a mode for accessing reality in different ways? What if the fake can actually produce a more realistic picture of the world by stepping outside the traditional (and accepted) means for encoding reality that were established through the conventions of news?

These are questions that now dog the genre, and ones that this book is dedicated to addressing. The intensified presence of Jon Stewart and the addition of Stephen Colbert are also examined for the central role they now play in interrogating public life from a satirical and humorous perspective. For as we have also seen in the intervening years, abuses of power and privilege can easily continue unabated. Through the months in which this edition was penned, Jon Stewart and his staff turned their attention to the remarkably poor job the news media had performed in reporting on the Wall Street activities that led to the economic meltdown of 2008–2009. If not the first, Stewart was certainly the most prominent television commentator to turn a critical eye and extended attention to the subject, and his confrontations with CNBC and NBC could not have been more extraordinary for workers receiving pink slips and those who wondered why their retirement accounts were suddenly worth 30 percent less. In short, entertaining political television has become much more than simply a pluralist addition of vernacular talk about politics. It offers a critical voice for citizens interested in taking measure of the powerful, especially in a period in which much of television news media have seemingly abandoned that job.

Norfolk, Virginia
June 1, 2009

Acknowledgments

Many people have contributed to the writing of this book, for which I am very grateful. Thanks to Dean Chandra DeSilva and the College of Arts and Letters at Old Dominion University for a sabbatical research leave through which I acquired time to tackle this project. My department chair, Gary Edgerton, and departmental colleagues in Communication and Theatre Arts, also deserve thanks for their continued interest and support, as do Michelle Falck, Jennifer Mullen, and Steve Daniels in the Office of University Relations.

Numerous colleagues across the fields of media studies and political communication have contributed to the writing of this book in various ways, and deserve heartfelt thanks. These include Jonathan Gray, Ethan Thompson, Geoffrey Baym, Danna Young, Amber Day, Cornel Sandvoss, Christian Christensen, Amanda Lotz, Jason Mittell, Serra Tinic, Barbie Zelizer, Matthew Bernstein, Kristina Riegert, Sue Collins, Liesbet van Zoonen, Avi Santo, Tim Anderson, Dana Heller, Michael Delli Carpini, Peter Dahlgren, Toby Miller, Bob Denton, Rod Hart, Sharon Strover, Bob Jensen, John Downing, and Karin Wahl-Jorgensen. Very special thanks go to my academic heroes, mentors, and intellectual inspirations, Horace Newcomb and John Hartley. I could not be more privileged to count two of television studies' most important scholars as my friends, from whom I have learned many things, and with whom I've enjoyed many a laugh and wonderful conversations.

I am also indebted to the staffs at Comedy Central, *The Daily Show*, *The Colbert Report*, and *Real Time/Politically Incorrect* for their support of this project through its many phases. This includes Tony Fox, Mat Mahoney, James Kailor, Jon Stewart, Stephen Colbert, Bill Maher, Scott Carter, Chris

Kelly and Sheila Griffiths, without whose early assistance this book would not have been possible. I also extend gratitude to my dear friends Seble Dawit, Angelo Robinson, and Kyle Nicholas for their continued support and good cheer, and my students Elizabeth Aucamp, Kat Ely, Courtney Childers, Maria Lopresto, Angela Sexton, Amy Lutz-Sexton, among others, for their spirited discussions, intelligent conversation, and support and interest in this project throughout.

Special thanks also goes to my loving and dedicated family, including my lovely wife Shana and precious son Andrew, for all they do to keep me sane and happy, and my father, Allen Jones, who greatly shaped my interests in politics and laughter. Finally, much love goes to my wonderful, sweet, and recently departed mother, Grace Jones, for whom this book and the hard work it represents is dedicated.

The publisher and I would like to acknowledge Helgref Publishers, University Press of Kentucky, Routledge, New York University Press, and Rowman & Littlefield for permission to reprint sections originally published in the following chapters and articles:

- "Pop Goes the Campaign: The Repopularization of Politics in Election 2008," in *The 2008 Presidential Campaign: A Communication Perspective*, ed. Robert E. Denton, Jr. (Lanham, MD: Rowman & Littlefield, 2009), 170–90.
- "Vox Populi as Cable Programming Strategy." *Journal of Popular Film & Television* 31 (Spring 2003): 18–28.
- "Comedy Talk Shows," in *The Essential HBO Reader*, eds. Gary R. Edgerton and Jeffrey P. Jones (Lexington: University Press of Kentucky, 2008), 172–82.
- "Believable Fictions: Redactional Culture and the Will to Truthiness," in *The Changing Faces of Journalism: Tabloidization, Technology and Truthiness*, ed. Barbie Zelizer (New York: Routledge, 2009), 127–43.
- "Forums for Citizenship in Popular Culture," in *Politics, Discourse and American Society: New Agendas*, eds. Roderick P. Hart and Bartholomew H. Sparrow (Lanham, Md.: Rowman & Littlefield, 2001), 193–210.
- "'Fake' News Versus 'Real' News as Sources of Political Information: *The Daily Show* and Postmodern Political Reality," in *Politicotainment: Television's Take on the Real*, ed. Kristina Riegert (New York: Peter Lang Publishers, 2007), 129–49.

I

TELEVISION AND POLITICS TODAY

1

The Changing Face of Politics on Television

Late in the 2008 presidential campaign, Cindy McCain, wife of Republican presidential nominee Senator John McCain, complained to supporters about the rough treatment she and her husband received during a media interview. "They picked our bones clean," she exclaimed. She wasn't complaining, however, about an encounter with traditional venues for political journalism such as *Meet the Press* or the *New York Times*. Instead she was referring to a joint appearance by the McCains on ABC's entertainment talk show *The View*. Although the program is crafted in the morning-talk-show mold of light talk and easygoing banter by female hosts for predominantly female viewers, *The View* turned out to be anything but soft-edged in the 2008 election season. The five cohosts routinely debated each other and visiting political guests (including the Obamas and the Clintons) with pointed questions and rebuttals.

Following the McCain campaign's release of two ads that included blatantly false accusations about his opponent, comedian cohost Joy Behar confronted the senator directly on the veracity of the ads' claims. "You know that those two ads are untrue, they're lies, and yet you at the end of it say, 'I approve this message.' Do you really approve them?" *New York Times* opinion columnist Frank Rich contextualized the importance of the exchange when he wrote, "You know the press is impotent at unmasking this Truthiness when the hardest-hitting interrogation McCain has yet faced on television came on *The View*." Rich went on to proclaim sardonically that Behar was the "new Edward R. Murrow" of a defunct news culture.

Around the same time, little-known Alaska governor and Republican vice-presidential hopeful Sarah Palin gave her first interviews to major news organizations since being nominated. Following interviews with *ABC World*

News's Charlie Gibson and *CBS Evening News*'s Katie Couric, the long-running NBC sketch comedy show *Saturday Night Live* (*SNL*) became one of the most influential sites of public commentary on Palin's embarrassing performances. While traditional forums for political discourse on television such as network and cable talk shows debated the merits of Palin's interviews from their predictable partisan positions, it was comedian Tina Fey's spot-on parody of Palin's performance in these journalistic encounters that captured the most prescient interpretation. Fey, who naturally bears a striking resemblance to the governor, was able to parody Palin's interview with Couric by, in one instance, simply repeating much of what Palin actually said in the interview with slight derivations for comic relief. In so doing, Fey and *SNL* transported the viewer out of the serious context associated with journalism—one that offered the viewer little recourse beyond befuddlement or disbelief—and recontextualized the encounter through a comedic lens, thereby granting the viewer a different perspective from which to view the event. Steve Linstead makes this point well when he argues, "Humor can have great impact in the world by having its content transposed and defined as serious, but also by transposing real-world content into the humorous frame, and defining it as humorous in an indelible and irreversible way. Its impact may be more effectively destructive in this way than through the more tortuous channels of negotiation and construction."[1] The power of satire as a tool with which to scrutinize its comedic subjects allowed the comedian to strip the encounter bare and offer up the essence of the situation instead—a governor who was a political novice and intellectual lightweight seeking to charm her way through a campaign and into an office that she was ill-prepared to fill.

In a presidential campaign of historic proportions, the sketch comedy parodies of *Saturday Night Live* and the entertainment talk of *The View* played an important role in mediating the relationship between candidates and voters. While the McCain-Palin campaign and the news media were simultaneously attempting to "define" Sarah Palin for the voting public, *SNL* took this nationally unknown politician and through its satirical commentary on news footage, cemented a largely negative and damning public perception of the candidate.[2] Similarly, when the hosts of *The View* took what was supposed to be a "safe" campaign appearance designed to appeal to women and turned it into a hard-nosed grilling over honor and fairness, an infotainment forum not only became a venue through which a politician was directly held to account for his questionable public actions, but also demonstrated the freedom such venues have to engage in discourse that other forums shy away from. Popular media outlets discovered that political content could be its hottest commodity. *The View* broke viewership records, while *SNL* recorded ratings numbers it hadn't seen since 1994.[3] In so doing, these shows produced a centrifugal push of political information (and perhaps even primed citizen interest) to sectors of the polity that may not regularly attend to the traditional venues of electoral politics and its narratives. What is also demonstrated is that entertainment media hosts and writers can operate outside the structural norms and unwritten rules that typically govern the interactions between news media, candidates, and campaign staffs. In popular culture, those interactions can be unscripted, more aggressive or critical than journalism, and often more far-reaching, moving from serious to humorous and back again in seconds. As such, popular culture forums offered fresh and alternative perspectives from which to assess candidates and their campaigns.

For the purposes of this book, these events from the 2008 election also direct our attention to the role that entertainment television now plays in contemporary political communication more broadly, a role that has greatly increased in recent years. Popular culture has become one of the more open and free-flowing arenas for communication about politics.[4] Whereas newspapers, news magazines, television news, and public affairs talk shows have traditionally served as primary arbiters of information and commentary about politics (often in very predictable ways), entertainment media can arguably now play just as significant a role. As the news media continue to falter economically and lose status (both culturally and politically) as the primary agents and venues for the conduct of politics through media, entertainment television has offered viable and at times important alternative forums for political discussion, information, and critique. Indeed, "new political television" (as I label it here), along with the content and user-centered practices now available through the Internet, has been central to citizen reassessment of the authority and legitimacy of journalism and its affiliated practices in the conduct of public affairs.[5] This book explores the role that new political television has played in the questioning and critique of traditional forms of politics on television, what it offers to citizens instead, and how and why citizens have responded favorably. At the core here is an argument about entertainment television's role in shaping political culture—what it contributes to new ways of thinking about both politics and television. But such new ways of thinking did not arrive overnight.

A TRANSFORMED PROGRAMMING LANDSCAPE

A cursory look at the last two decades of political programming on television demonstrates an array of political content that has appeared across numerous television channels. Politics is now packaged in a variety of formats and genres beyond news and documentary, including talk shows, dramas, sitcoms (including animated sitcoms), fake news and pundit shows, sketch comedy, and even reality programming. The conventional lines that once segregated the "serious" from the "entertaining" in television programming are largely now eroded, and the location for where institutional politics resides within and across those lines is varied. The daily and nightly sense-making of political events is processed in new ways by new voices, and rarely operates by the previous assumptions that guided televised political discourse for much of the medium's history.

For decades, television broadcast networks maintained an artificial separation between politics and popular culture, specifically assigning public affairs programming to news divisions while entertainment—the preponderance of network programming—was managed by different divisions. Politics was found primarily in newscasts, Sunday morning talk shows, and documentaries, but much less so in other genres. Such strict segregation helped the networks call attention to the specific areas of programming that could be used to justify claims of serving the public interest, a requirement necessary for the broadcast licensure in the United States. It also assured network executives that nothing too controversial would interfere with their primary business interest: the delivery of the largest mass audience possible to advertisers accrued through entertainment programming. Through forced segregation, therefore, network executives construed politics in reductive terms—minimally engaging, focused on the delivery of information about political elites, primarily handled by "experts," employing a grave and serious tone. Politics, television executives told the viewing public, is an "eat-your-peas" endeavor. Although the history of American television contains notable exceptions, the overall result was an artificial separation of politics from other forms of programming (and how these forms can make sense of politics through alternative narratives), but also from cultural life in general. This separation began to be erased, however, with the advent of competition from cable and its challenge to the network oligopoly in the post-network era.[6]

The first sustained blurring between the generic lines of political news and entertainment programming was seen in a significant fashion in the 1992 presidential campaign when candidates began appearing frequently on entertainment talk shows, largely on cable (such as *Larry King Live*) and those programs offered through syndication (such as *The Phil Donahue Show*). Critics were aghast at what they considered a degradation of the electoral process, proclaiming this the "entertainmentization" of politics.[7] Audiences, however, reveled in these new venues for political information, as they were invited to engage directly with the candidates via telephone or as studio audience members.[8] With increasingly intense competition arising in the television marketplace in the 1990s, politics gained currency as a programming strategy for cable producers who were seeking distinctive original programming and who recognized that audiences just might be attracted to alternative forms of political discussion, information, and entertainment. Entertainment cable channels such as Comedy Central, MTV, Court TV, Bravo, and HBO, as well as the cable news channels MSNBC, Fox News, CNN, and CNBC, attempted a variety of political programming alternatives that addressed varied viewer interests and pleasures in politics.[9]

Comedy Central is perhaps the most notable and groundbreaking channel in this regard. In an attempt to establish itself as a location for more than sitcom reruns and stand-up comedians, the network began to brand itself by offering original programming based on topical humor. Their slogan, "same world, different take," signaled that they would apply a new approach to genres such as talk, news, and animation. From 1993–1996, the network offered its groundbreaking roundtable political discussion show *Politically Incorrect*, hosted by comedian Bill Maher. The show violated the norms of traditional political talk on television by featuring Maher seated among four guests who were typically not experts on politics discussing politics—indeed, their lack of expertise was largely the show's premise and draw.[10] The producers aimed to create the feel of a televised cocktail party by structuring debates about current events amongst notable guests from numerous areas of public life, including television, politics, sports, film, music, interest groups, radio, publishing, and others. By including such

Politically Incorrect taping in Washington, D.C., in 2000. Courtesy of Politically Incorrect with Bill Maher.

non-experts, the show introduced a commonsense form of discourse on politics that was allowed to veer more freely into humorous (and at times racy) talk, both of which were outside the norm of conventional talk about politics on television.[11] The show was enough of a success that it was picked up by ABC in 1997, where it ran until 2002, when Maher was essentially fired for his politically incorrect talk about the events of September 11, 2001.

In 1997, the network introduced *South Park*, an animated sitcom featuring a crew of four potty-mouthed kids in a nondescript Colorado town who engage an array of social and political situations, all of which serve as a vehicle for the scorched-earth approach to satire by creators Matt Stone and Trey Parker, seemingly appealing to liberals, conservatives, and every stripe of cynic and skeptic in-between.[12] The show has skewered numerous politicians, including Hillary Clinton, Gary Condit, George W. Bush, Saddam Hussein, Barack Obama, and UK Prime Minister Gordon Brown, as well as an array of political issues. In April 2001, Comedy Central turned to Stone and Parker again to offer the short-lived *That's My Bush*, a sitcom that ridiculed a moronically portrayed President George W. Bush and his wife shortly after he assumed office. The show was a parody of the typical home and office sitcoms, yet was set in the White House and with most of the jokes at Bush's expense. The network followed this six years later—effectively "bookending" the Bush presidency—with another animated sitcom, *Lil' Bush*. This program envisioned Bush and his inner circle of advisors (Lil' Cheney, Lil' Rummy, Lil' Condi) as petulant, evil, and idiotic fifth graders running amok in the world. Far from simply using Bush as a motif to achieve sophomoric humor, the program instead offered a blistering attack on the Bush administration's policies, ranging from nuclear proliferation and sound science to attacks on gay rights and the Iraq War. Both shows demonstrated that a cable network was willing to take on a sitting president through serialized narrative programming, and do so in brutal and damning fashion.[13]

Although the network began offering its faux news program *The Daily Show* in 1996, it wouldn't be until 1999 that the program began to take on a more political bent with the arrival of its new host, Jon Stewart. As discussed in later chapters, *The Daily Show*—cast as a fake news program, complete with anchor and reporters—became a hit by offering critiques of both politics and the television news media. The show began building a loyal following (and garnering much critical acclaim) after the events of September 11, 2001. As the Bush administration took advantage of patriotic fervor to advance an aggressive and highly questionable (if not also illegal) series of domestic and foreign policy initiatives, *The Daily Show* became a location for some of the most consistent and insistent questioning of not only the administration's policies, but also its information management techniques and the compliant news media that aided and abetted those efforts. After the reelection of George W. Bush in 2004, the program spawned a successful spin-off around the faux conservative persona of show reporter Stephen Colbert. In 2005, the *Colbert Report* premiered with Colbert starring as bloviated right-wing talk show host in the vein of Fox News's Bill O'Reilly. Here too the network offered a program that simultaneously deconstructed conservative media and politicians through humorous and parodic critiques. In sum, Comedy Central has been one of the main creative forces in television—cable or broadcast—for political and social satire.

Subscription cable television channels such as HBO and Showtime have also produced a variety of creative programming centered on politics. HBO has offered groundbreaking talk shows that have blended the political and entertainment genres of traditional late-night talk television, including the pioneering *Dennis Miller Live* (1994–2002), as well as *The Chris Rock Show* (1997–2000) and *Real Time with Bill Maher* (2003–present; discussed in subsequent chapters).[14] In 2003, the network produced a video-vérité, documentary-style show called *K Street* that centered on a make-believe Washington lobbying firm. The show featured a mixture of actors and real-life politicos such as consultants James Carville and Mary Matalin, but also included cameos by lawmakers such as Senators John McCain, Hillary Clinton, and Orrin Hatch.[15] The show was commercially unsuccessful, but it did feature an important arena of politics as its narrative center—one that has rarely been featured on television.

For its part, Showtime aired a reality program called *American Candidate* during the 2004 election cycle. Produced by R. J. Cutler (*The War Room*), the show featured a group of citizen contestants who competed in a campaign to be president of the United States.[16] Cutler's stated intention was to "comment on the [political] process" by showing "how the sausage is made."[17] Despite what some might see as a trivialization of politics, the reality show nevertheless did offer a dose of pluralism by discussing issues that rarely find their way onto television (such as animal rights), while also offering up candidates who were not beholden to the rigid ideological or partisan categories that typically dominate political campaigns. In sum, the subscription channels have demonstrated that they are willing to take programming risks that the networks rarely would and, in the process, expand our understanding of how democracy can be viewed and understood through alternative narratives about politics.

By the turn of the new millennium, prime-time network television programming with government institutions as the central theme or setting (traditionally a formula for ratings death) included three shows on the CIA, one on the FBI, one on the White House, two on the Supreme Court, one on City Hall, two on the U.S. armed forces, and one on an American embassy.[18] Two of those shows—*The West Wing* and *24*—became enormous hits, arguably for different reasons. As numerous critics have pointed out, Aaron Sorkin's *The West Wing* was a liberal Democratic fantasy, offering a narrative that featured an honest, fair, and ethical Democratic president, a salve for many Democrats still smarting from the humiliation and party damage caused by President Bill Clinton's reckless behavior, baby boomer narcissism, and conservative politics.[19] Oddly enough, as the show's narrative evolved in its final two seasons (2004–2006), it also presaged and paralleled the story line of what would occur in the 2008 presidential contest between Barack Obama and John McCain by featuring a youthful minority Democratic candidate (in this case, a Latino) in a race with a straight-talking, old-guard Republican senator opponent.[20] The show *24* also mirrored political reality by featuring a CIA agent who would stop at nothing to thwart terrorists. In the process, the show became a vehicle for graphic displays of the Bush administration's real-life policies regarding torture and the audience's vicarious pleasure in seeing the bad guys cry.[21]

One additional network program of note is *Saturday Night Live*, the late-night weekend sketch comedy show that has aired since 1975 on NBC. Through the years, the show has had a spotty track record as a place for consistent high-quality late-night comedy, tending of late to "go political" primarily in presidential election years. For many cultural critics, however, *SNL* is *the* place for satirical political commentary during an election. Elsewhere I have criticized *SNL*'s political humor for failing to adequately live up to the true potential of political satire as a discourse of critique.[22] The central weakness is that the show's preferred form of political humor focuses more on the personal characteristics of politicians (such as Dana Carvey making fun of George H. W. Bush's strange lexical ticks) than their policies or approach to power. There are moments, however—such as the 2008 presidential election discussed previously, but also in 2000—when the show produced stinging satirical critiques that have affected public deliberation about the election and/or candidates, becoming "water-cooler" moments as well as widely circulated video clips that are replayed across numerous media channels.[23] In 2008, the program even became part of the official campaign when Democratic hopeful Hillary Clinton seized on a skit that suggested press favoritism toward Barack Obama and used it as rhetorical ammunition against her rival and the journalist-moderators during a Democratic debate.

This is one example of how the political world has embraced this encroachment of entertainment television into politics. But presidential candidates also regularly appear on *Saturday Night Live* during campaign seasons, even participating in jokes at their own expense. Such was the case in 2008 when Sarah Palin, after being ridiculed mercilessly, appeared on the show but had to sit smiling at the "Weekend Update" anchor desk while the show's actors engaged in a damning rap song about her. Similarly, John McCain stood beside Tina Fey (caricaturing Sarah Palin) and nervously laughed at the jokes made about his running mate, including her overspending on clothes and her "going rogue" by secretly trying to sell a "Palin in 2012" T-shirt to the audience behind McCain's back. Subjects that would either be ignored or ignite McCain's famous temper if brought up by the press were treated here simply as things worth chuckling about.

Almost all major political candidates routinely appear on talk shows across all television dayparts (that is, morning, afternoon, and late-night). A study by the Center for Media and Public Affairs reported that the presidential candidates in the 2008 campaign (including those running in the primaries) made 110 appearances on late-night talk shows alone, far surpassing the 25 counted in the 2004 election.[24] Politicians and their media consultants see these programs as forums through which the candidate can address hard-to-reach audiences, show their more "human" side (including their ability to be good-humored and self-deprecating), while typically experiencing an interview that steers clear of controversial matters and doesn't engage in tough questioning.[25] As we have seen with the example of *The View*, however, this assumption of "safety" is increasingly a questionable one. Indeed, during the 2008 election, when John McCain made a last-minute cancellation of a scheduled appearance on *The Late Show with David*

Tina Fey "going rogue" as Vice Presidential-hopeful Sarah Palin on Saturday Night Live's *final presidential skit of the 2008 presidential campaign while Republican Presidential Candidate John McCain sheepishly looks on. AP/Wide World Photos.*

Letterman (and then turned up giving a news interview instead), the host proceeded to harass and mock the candidate for the rest of the program, then for two more weeks. When McCain finally appeared weeks later to offer a mea culpa, Letterman proceeded to ask about every uncomfortable issue that was dogging the flailing campaign. Far from the smooth sailing through the waters of entertainment media that McCain had hoped for, the campaign instead experienced a public relations nightmare.[26] Picking a television news interview over an entertainment talk show turned out, in hindsight, to be the wrong choice.

Beyond the campaign trail, politicians are also learning that entertainment television can also serve the purposes of governance—that is, as an alternative means for "selling" policies or positions to the mass public. The Bush administration, for instance, undertook several unconventional means for addressing the American people in the aftermath of the 9/11 terrorist attacks. The FBI sought leads or tips on twenty-two terrorist suspects via a special edition of *America's Most Wanted*, the program dedicated to catching criminals by enlisting the viewing audience's assistance.[27] The Pentagon then attempted to explain the concept and workings of military tribunals via the CBS dramatic program *JAG*, providing more details and explanations of the workings of such tribunals to the program's scriptwriters than that offered to reporters.[28] Finally, the State Department sought diplomacy with young citizens of the world by sending Colin Powell to appear in a live "town hall" meeting on MTV's "Be Heard," fielding questions from young adults in seven countries.[29] The administration obviously recognized the power and potential benefits in circumventing traditional channels of communication (namely, journalists and news networks) to speak directly to American and global citizens through a variety of entertainment programming.

Finally, the tremendous growth of broadband and the availability of streaming and archived video on the Internet have unleashed television programming from the confines of the set and network schedules. Citizens can now experience television content "on-demand" (when and where they want to watch) through sites such as YouTube, Hulu, TV.com, Fancast, Joost, network-owned websites, or even through blogs and social networking sites such as Facebook, as television content is increasingly shared by users themselves. Every episode of *The Daily Show with Jon Stewart*, for instance, is archived on Comedy Central's website (as is most of Colbert's shows); *The Late Show with David Letterman* uses a YouTube channel to distribute excerpts from the show (what the show's staff consider to be its nightly best "water-cooler moments").[30] The point here is that much of the new political television programming described in this book is now widely available on the Internet. Thus, access to new forms of engaging politics is also increased through new distribution avenues, not just the production decisions of programmers. Furthermore, citizens themselves are now empowered to participate in the production of political video content—repurposing news interviews or other "serious" political content for their own political critiques and commentaries through video mash-ups and other remediated materials. It is in this convergence—between producer and consumer, politics and popular culture, and across once distinctive technologies—that Henry Jenkins foresees the potential for a reinvigoration of democratic citizenship.[31]

In summary, entertaining political programming is now an integral component of American political culture, and at times, is even included in the formal processes of electoral politics and governance. The first edition of this book argued that the boundaries between "serious" political media and "entertainment" media had become substantially blurred. Yet, as we have just seen, to continue to speak of such "blurred boundaries" makes little sense. Given the previous discussion, where exactly does political communication start and cultural exchange end? At what point is political practice these days simply a cultural act, in both creation and consumption? In fact, this book challenges the rigid binary construction of "entertainment" and "information," arguing that such a dichotomy obscures the array of interactions that citizens have with political programming forms, engagements that cannot be captured by such limited categorization. Political communication and popular culture are now thoroughly integrated and intertwined, and at times, mutually constituting. We should focus our attention, then, on how popular culture gives shape, form, and meaning to politics in ways that traditional avenues of political communication do not, as well as how it provides multiple avenues through which politics is attended to and made sense of by citizen-audiences in their daily lives. A focus on "boundaries" or "segregation" must give way to the realization that entertaining political forms of TV programming are active participants in shaping the micro and macro dimensions of politics, political communication, and political culture.

ENTERTAINING POLITICS AND ITS CRITICS

Yet these changes in the media-politics landscape can still be derided and dismissed by claims that entertainment culture has polluted the important business of democracy. Because it is quite easy to view politicians and the entertainment industry with cynical disdain, it is also tempting to let normative desires overcome serious analysis of the changes that are occurring and the effect of such changes on political culture. To label the changes outlined so far "entertaining politics"—as I have done in the title of this book—is to risk the scorn of numerous academic and cultural critics who have decried the encroachment of television, celebrity, and entertainment into politics. Critics often lay the blame for increased interactions between politics and entertainment (and the supposed detrimental "effects" that result) at the feet of television, a medium that is often seen as inherently harmful.

For instance, Robert Putnam's problem with television is ontological—citizens have forgotten the importance of social connections and the benefits those connections have in producing a rich, democratic polity because we have divorced ourselves from each other through our isolated acts of watching entertainment television.[32] For Neil Postman, the problem is epistemological—television is an inferior (even dangerous) means of knowing the arena of politics. Due to the technological biases of electronic communication (as opposed to his privileging the written word), television offers little more than amusement, entertainment, and distraction because the medium is incapable of helping us think in any other way.[33] For Roderick Hart, the problem is phenomenological—television is a cynical medium that may encourage us to feel engaged or empowered politically, but ultimately such feelings are false and temporal, certainly not residual or behavioral.[34] These critics maintain a certain normative standard of rational-critical discourse that should be found (although rarely is) in the public sphere of television. The changes in mediated politics noted previously, therefore, are likely to be viewed skeptically by those who find these popular critiques of television affirming.

These criticisms are faulty, however, in several important regards, the first being the long history of association between entertainment and politics. Politics is drama, and as such has always had entertainment value for individuals, communities, and the nation.[35] Politicians are showmen, and they depend upon similar rhetorical and performative tools and techniques that show-business hucksters use to create and sustain their audience.[36] Second, politics is increasingly crafted through and for media spectatorship, and hence the desired separation between media and politics is no longer possible. The conduct of politics is rarely conceived and executed without consideration of the actions themselves as communicative events, including how they will "play" across media channels and forms. And third, such criticisms are rarely built upon analyses of actual audiences. Critics freely make claims about entertainment television's supposed detrimental effects on democracy, but they almost never conduct or refer to direct studies of audiences to prove their point.[37] The study offered here asks that we interrogate this conjoining of politics and popular culture by engaging in intensive scrutiny of exactly what is occurring and why. To do so, we must recognize that the medium of television is a multifaceted communication medium that allows for numerous performative, rhetorical, perceptive, and disseminative positions for presenting, understanding, celebrating, and critiquing politics. We must also be aware of the multivocality of media texts, as well as attempt to understand the complex readings and relationships that audiences make and have with television, including their abilities to negotiate, appropriate, employ, and appreciate many different types of programming forms that include politics.

"Entertaining politics" suggests a double meaning: one is that television producers, audiences, and politicians have shown their desire or willingness to entertain politics in newly creative ways. As we have just seen, politics is a subject area that is more frequently examined through myriad televisual formulations. Two, "entertaining politics" highlights the fact that politics can be pleasurable, and that engaging or contemplating it need not always be the equivalent of swallowing bitter medicine. Politics is naturally interesting, dramatic, strange, unpredictable, frustrating, outrageous, and downright hilarious in ways that far exceed the reductive formulations of politics as horse races, policy maneuvers, and palace court intrigue that journalistic and "insider" presentations of politics tend to emphasize.[38] What the success of these new forms of political programming suggests is that television now explores multiple avenues for presenting politics in imaginative ways, treatments that can offer voices, positions, perspectives, and critiques not found in traditional political television. It also suggests that audiences are receptive to, if not also hungry for, political programming that is meaningful and engaging to them—programming that connects with their interests and concerns, provides new ways of thinking about politics, criticizes that which needs scrutiny, and speaks to them through accessible and pleasurable means.

NEW POLITICAL TELEVISION

To this point, we have highlighted the numerous ways in which entertainment television now programs politics. This book, however, focuses on only two areas for closer inspection—political entertainment talk shows and fake news programs. The reasons for this focus are twofold. First, as the previous discussion suggests (and is explored further in chapter 3), talk and news have traditionally been the primary means through which television has dealt with and made sense of politics—and to some extent, still does on a daily basis. How entertainment television contributes to, rewrites, and even directly challenges these generic forms of political communication is of utmost importance for understanding both the former and the latter. It is in this regard that I have designated these shows "new political television," as they have refashioned television's fundamental relationship to politics by offering something new and creative as an alternative. Furthermore, not only does new political television offer alternative approaches to talk and news, but in so doing also directly challenges the legitimacy and viability of these traditional forms as well as their vaunted place in politics.

Second, entertaining political talk and fake news are also the specific forms of programming from the broad swath mentioned earlier that continue to garner the most critical attention in both the scholarly and popular press.[39] Concurrent with their popularity, though, is the assertion (perhaps even myth) largely propagated by news media that these programs have become substitutes for the older, supposedly more legitimate forms of talk and news, especially among young people. As a result, new political television is seen—directly or by association—as presenting a normative challenge to both democracy and legitimate news programming because of its supposedly inferior ability to inform citizens properly about their government and society. Similarly, the recurrent claim (and perhaps even myth) that entertainment programming—and in particular, satirical, and humorous political programming—celebrates, if not also propagates, political cynicism has yet again accompanied the popularity of programs such as *The Daily Show*.[40] Addressing and analyzing such normative claims, therefore, is imperative if we seek to understand the role this programming now plays in contemporary political life.

The shows that dominate the genre of political entertainment programming are *The Daily Show with Jon Stewart*, *The Colbert Report*, and *Real Time with Bill Maher*. As I will argue, each in their own way defines the form, has been the most commercially and critically successful, has received the most public attention (from the press as well as politicians seeking exposure through such programming), and has had the greatest impact in shaping the ongoing relationship of television to politics, including their impact on other television programs in news and entertainment (such as *Countdown with Keith Olbermann*, for instance, or *The Late Show with David Letterman*). These three shows, along with two sets of programs no longer on the air but with direct connection and relevance to the discussion here (*Politically Incorrect with Bill Maher* and Michael Moore's *TV Nation/The Awful Truth*), are the primary focus of this investigation. To complicate matters, *The Daily Show* and *The Colbert Report* transcend categorical boundaries. They are fake news and pundit shows, respectively, but also engage in serious (or playfully serious) political talk and discussions with guests in the second half of the program. They are hybrid programs that engage what Geoffrey Baym calls "discursive integration," therefore spanning the categories of news and talk (as well as comedy).[41]

Chapter 2 concludes this opening chapter's review of television and politics today by asking us to rethink what engagement with public life means when citizens most often encounter politics through popular media texts, not through physical participation in political/spectacle events or even through the organizations of civil society—both of which have dominated democratic theory (normatively and empirically) as the proper means and modes of civic engagement. The chapter reviews several studies that demonstrate how popular culture is a complex site of citizenship, one that offers narratives that citizens routinely employ in making sense of politics. These studies also show how television can be an important site of engagement with public life, and why we should take it and the narratives that appear there seriously.

Part II examines entertaining political talk as an alternative means of critically discursive engagement with politics. Chapter 3 charts the history of political talk on television, from its beginnings in network news divisions with programming that featured experts or Washington "insiders" to the eventual inclusion of multiple participants, many of whom are non-experts and Washington "outsiders," in the post-network era. The chapter demonstrates the importance of post-network competition in introducing a turn toward "excessive style," resulting in the transformation of cable news into spectacle displays of polemics and opinionated talk. Chapter 4 picks up this history by examining the birth of entertaining political talk on cable in the early 1990s and its development and growth through three phases. The chapter analyzes the historical circumstances that have influenced each phase, as well as how this programming challenges the traditional definitions of political talk and news. The chapter shows how news media's special role and authority as the primary arbiter of public life (what Foucault called society's "regime of truth") is actively challenged by such programming.

Chapter 5 looks more closely at the type and quality of political discussion that emerges from entertaining political programming, comparing talk on such a show (*Politically Incorrect*) with that found on a traditional Sunday morning pundit talk show (*This Week*). The chapter analyzes how political elites and laity employ different means of making sense of politics, and why that matters. Television's pluralist inclusion of alternative public voices, therefore, produces very different "conclusions" about what course of action should be taken in the public arena (in this instance, the impeachment of a president). Chapter 6 rounds out this section by examining the ways in which Jon Stewart's fake news reporting and guest interviews on *The Daily Show* amount to an effort to change the public conversation. It shows how Stewart engages in his own brand of news reporting by prosecuting and interrogating public lies and truth through techniques of video redaction. Stewart's interviews with guests also depart from traditional journalistic practice as he engages in a sincere deliberative exchange aimed at airing agreements and differences of opinion between two people, not engaging in shouting matches or partisan polemics for spectacle display. Though humor might be employed in both, the outcome is that a comedy show has been instrumental in introducing important changes to the public conversation made available through television through its quite serious and earnest insistence on arriving at honest truth.

Part III turns our attention to the "fake news" genre as manifest in programming that challenges the journalistic authority constructed through television newsmagazines, newscasts, and pundit talk shows. In chapter 7, we look at Michael Moore's work on television in the 1990s, the fake newsmagazines *TV Nation* (NBC and FOX), and *The Awful Truth* (Bravo). As an early progenitor of political entertainment television in the United States, Moore's work directly contributed to the stylistics and critiques inherent to the political entertainment genre. Although many people condemn Moore for his left-of-center politics, supposedly unethical production choices, or self-aggrandizement, few seem willing to acknowledge the contributions he has made to a novel performance of politics on television. Here we analyze the techniques he developed, why they are important tools for getting at particular truths while holding the powerful accountable, and how they are still employed by others who produce political entertainment television.

Chapter 8 examines the fake news program *The Daily Show* as a *news* program. It takes the popular though questionable premise that young people today increasingly get their news from late-night comedy programs and asks "so what?" If the premise were true, what type of news or information would they receive? The chapter compares the political reporting of *The Daily Show* with news reports from CNN during the 2004 presidential campaign. The chapter argues that not only does Stewart offer equivalent information in his coverage of particular campaign events, but actually goes much further in helping viewers "add things up," that is, in helping citizens construct meaning from what may seem to be isolated or random events in traditional news reporting. The chapter concludes that *The Daily Show* is "fake" only in that it refuses to make claims to authority and authenticity, as opposed to those claims repeatedly asserted through the techniques and conventions used by news media. Chapter 9 examines the fake pundit show *The Colbert Report*, examining the various segments that comprise this parodic performance, including his interview segments with guests. Through his parodic inversions, Colbert is able to advance a critique of conservative talking points and "truthiness" thinking while also providing a platform through which guests can participate in the critique (either wittingly or unwittingly). The interviews offer a "real/unreal" game for viewers, challenging them to keep up with the moving shell game of "truth." It is this playful parody that allows viewers to constantly question the means through which traditional political talk shows and their opinionated hosts construct political reality.

The final section focuses on audience engagement with new political television, including the claims that this form of television is detrimental to democracy and its viewing publics. Chapter 10 examines audiences for programming from the first and second phases of new political television's history. The chapter questions the normative dichotomies of audiences *versus* citizens, positing instead a model for examining the multiplicity of ways in which political narratives address viewer's needs, interests, tastes, and desires that compose their identities as citizens. To demonstrate, the chapter examines audiences for *Politically Incorrect with Bill Maher* and *The Colbert Report*. *Politically Incorrect* didn't just display political talk, but instigated and facilitated public thinking and discussion of politics by viewers themselves. Furthermore, the analysis demonstrates a crisis in representation, as audiences used their affective attachments to celebrity and popular culture to invigorate and inform their relationship to the public sphere. We then examine fans of *The Colbert Report*, exploring the opportunities and value of "play" and discovery as performative ingredients of citizenship, thereby allowing for viewers' playful creativity in the construction of political meaning.

Chapter 11 concludes the volume by revisiting the major arguments presented throughout, but also entertains three discussions that deserve further critical attention. First, the chapter examines the persistent claim that satire produces cynical citizens, and explains why such a formulation is fundamentally wrong, based on the evidence presented in this book. Second, with the explosion of television shows/clips and user-generated video across the Internet, the chapter tries to come to terms with what such accessibility/availability means for the circulation of the types of thinking advanced by new political television. Third, the discussion examines persistent questions that dog the genre of political entertainment television, in particular, questions of race, gender, and ideology. The chapter interrogates the boundaries of entertaining political talk and fake news—who gets to participate, in what ways, and with what restrictions—in an effort to understand the positioning of entertaining politics within the broader landscape of media and contemporary political culture.

Several persistent themes run through this book. The first is our inability to continue to speak in terms of an entertainment-information dichotomy when examining politics on television. When it comes to the fluid interactions between media and politics, including each one's relationship to audiences and citizens, this division proves arbitrary and artificial, meaningless and misleading. Entertainment-centered or entertainment-derived media are quite capable, as we will see, of providing an array of meaningful materials to address the audience's identities as citizens (not to mention the value that it provides to politicians themselves). Only news media feel the need to perpetuate such a distinction, but that is a need largely built on self-interest in terms of preserving their own vaunted place within the government-citizen axis.

This relates to the second theme of the book: the ways in which new political television leads us to question how news media constitute "reality." Entertaining political talk challenges the taken-for-granted logic of Washington insiders presented in news and traditional political talk shows, offering instead a quite different interpretation of what politics means when such meanings are formulated by political outsiders. Similarly, fake newscasts, fake newsmagazines, and fake pundit talk shows all demonstrate the power of "fake" as a way of reflecting upon the "real." As Jonathan Gray has argued, such programs defamiliarize the codes and conventions that certain programs (such as news media) use to "lay claim to the right to show us the real and to insist that they are real."[42] By imitating (and often mocking) such codes and conventions, new political television holds these authoritative and legitimizing mechanisms up for scrutiny, providing the opportunity for viewers to question the formulas as well as logic upon which they are based. In the process, these programs demonstrate an alternative means for talking about, engaging with, and making sense of political life that is at times at odds with news media's claims to authority and truth. For as Gray argues elsewhere (summarizing Bakhtin), "texts do not take on meaning for any reader in a vacuum. Rather, a reader will always make sense of texts relative to other texts, "socially" or intertextually."[43] The fake may therefore prove more authentic than programming that proclaims itself "real" for no other reason than it eschews such modernist truth claims altogether. These programs use a structured fakeness to produce "news" that is more real*istic* and truth*ful*, even though such programming brands itself as "unreal."

This argument leads us to the third theme: the ways in which new political television has become a powerful means for challenging and questioning the sources of power—both political and economic—that regularly establish political truth and reality in American public life. Politicians and corporate capitalists (which include news media) have fashioned a relationship for constituting truth and reality, yet it is a relationship that may serve the public poorly—as seen most notably in the run-up to the Iraq War (2002–2003) and the near economic collapse of the American economy (2008–2009). It is a structured, publicly visible relationship that both have mastered, but that both also can easily hide behind (as terms such as "objectivity," a "free press," "open government," and so forth represent). Each of the primary actors analyzed in this book— Jon Stewart, Stephen Colbert, Bill Maher, and Michael Moore—offer programming that has challenged this relationship in one way or another. Although such critiques have been around for some time now (Karl Marx, anyone?), new political television has shown how entertaining and seriously playful (and effective) such critiques can be. Satire, parody, and entertaining talk all invite audiences to scrutinize in fresh and enjoyable ways. And as Bakhtin suggests, by comically playing with the political, one can gain a greater sense of ownership over it and, in turn, feel more empowered to engage it. In sum, the new means of engagement may be through entertaining political programming, but it would be foolish to suggest that the entertainment of politics offered there is nothing more than foolery. This book demonstrates how and why that is the case.

2

Rethinking Television's Relationship to Civic Engagement

> If citizens are home watching television or its future counterpart, they cannot be out participating in politics.
>
> —Norman Nie, political scientist

Of the many claims that can be made about media and politics in late modern society, two points are indisputable: one is that television continues to be an enormously popular and powerful cultural presence in American society, and the second is that traditional measures of democratic vitality—voting, political party affiliation, trust in leaders, political knowledge, voluntary activism—all register signals of "decline" (although the revival of electoral participation in the 2006 and 2008 elections in the United States has made a few of these claims questionable). The question, of course, is whether these two things are related; that is, whether television, as the central arena of America's public sphere, is in some way "responsible" for producing detrimental effects on civic participation and engagement. The question of television as a negative social and political influence has, in one form or fashion, dogged the medium almost from its beginnings. In recent years, however, there has been no shortage of scholars and social commentators willing to spill ink (and sell some books) in suggesting a causal link between the two. With alarmist titles such as *Seducing America, Remote and Controlled, The Sound Bite Society, Amusing Ourselves to Death,* and *Life: The Movie,* these authors have trumpeted the dangers they believe television presents to American political and social life.[1]

Robert Putnam's argument concerning our supposed civic disengagement from the body politic—and television's primary role in that withdrawal—has perhaps attracted the most attention. He contends that

21

participation in voluntary civic associations has greatly decreased during the past forty years, and when combined with other data, suggests a weakening of the social bonds (or "social capital") that are crucial in supporting democracy. The thesis works under the catchy yet paradoxical slogan, "Bowling Alone," that neatly sums up the dilemma—how can you engage in a group activity with just one person? Well, you can't—at least not as a "group." So where is everybody instead of participating in life's communal activities? At home watching television. That was the singular conclusion offered in the original journal article that first announced the argument, although by the time of its arrival in book form, Putnam had included other explanatory factors beyond television.[2] Nevertheless, his arguments about television continue to dominate the proposition (at least in political science circles). Here are his conclusions about television's primary role in civic disengagement:

> Americans at the end of the twentieth century were watching more TV, watching it more habitually, more pervasively, and more often alone, and watching more programs that were associated specifically with civic disengagement (*entertainment*, as distinct from news). The onset of these trends coincided exactly with the national decline in social connectedness, and the trends were most marked among the younger generations that are . . . distinctively disengaged. . . . At the very least, television and its electronic cousins are willing accomplices in the civic mystery we have been unraveling, and more likely than not, they are ringleaders.[3]

Putnam admits that his evidence is circumstantial and correlational in this regard, not causational. Yet, to extend the metaphor, he is still willing to assert the conclusion that television—especially entertainment television—is the chief culprit in the crime.[4]

Several scholars have offered rebuttals to Putnam from a variety of intellectual perspectives. From a behavioral perspective, Pippa Norris contends that the civic malaise theory, at least in regard to news media, is wrong, because news programming—in conjunction with political party activities—is actually an activating force for the politically engaged.[5] From a cognitive perspective, Doris Graber mounts a defense of television news programming by arguing that audiovisual materials are quite important in individual learning about politics, and that citizens are therefore engaged with politics when processing political information that appears on television.[6] From a historical perspective, Michael Schudson suggests that theories of decline (such as Putnam's) have ignored the changing norms and practices of American civic culture that have occurred from the nation's founding to the present.[7] Americans have operated under several different models for what constitutes proper behavior by "good citizens," he argues, only one of which is the normative model from which Putnam believes we have strayed (and which Schudson believes we have moved beyond). And from a new media perspective, Henry Jenkins responds specifically to Putnam's nostalgia by arguing that new media platforms such as social networking sites and massively multiplayer video games provide an important means through which media users now obtain the skills necessary to engage in cultural and political participation, crafting in the process what he calls a new form of "participatory culture." He notes, "Game guilds and other kinds of social networks are as central to what we mean by civic engagement in the 21st century as civic organizations were to community life of the 20th century."[8]

What we must first recognize is the state of contemporary citizenship that so frustrates Putnam and others—that daily citizen engagement with politics is more frequently textual than organizational or "participatory" in any traditional sense. For better or worse, the most common and frequent form of political activity—its actual practice—comes, for most people, through their choosing, attending to, processing, and engaging a myriad of media texts about the formal political process of government and political institutions as they conduct their daily routines. Media are our primary points of access to politics, the "space in which politics now chiefly happens for most people" and the place for political encounters that precede, shape, and at times determine further bodily participation (if it is to happen at all).[9] Furthermore, those encounters occur through a panoply of media forms (books, magazines, newspapers, newsletters, billboards and advertisements, direct mail, radio, film, e-mails, websites, blogs, social networking sites, and, of course, cable and network television) and across numerous fictional and nonfictional genres, and constitute what communication scholars call our "media ensemble."[10] Such encounters do much more than provide "information" about political ideas, issues, events, or players. They constitute our mental maps of the political and social world outside our direct experience. They provide a reservoir of images and voices, heroes and villains, sayings and slogans, facts and ideas that we draw upon in making sense of politics. They provide the constituent components of the narratives we construct for organizing, interpreting, explaining, understanding, and adjudicating the realities and illusions we find within the media, but also within our lives. They are ritual encounters with public life that help in our understanding of who and what we are as individuals, a community, a public, and a nation.[11]

But if we recognize that attending to media presentations of politics in all its myriad forms is central to most citizens' daily engagement with politics, it is also helpful to recognize that (perhaps as a result) media are "the center of gravity" for the conduct of politics in general.[12] As Peter Dahlgren argues, "Politics no longer exists as a reality taking place outside the media. . . . Rather, politics is increasingly organized as a media phenomenon, planned and executed for and with the co-operation of the media."[13] Indeed, politics and popular culture are essentially opposite sides of the same coin. John Street argues that for politicians,

> Politics, like popular culture, is about creating an "audience," a people who will laugh at their jokes, understand their fears and share their hopes. Both the popular media and politicians are engaged in creating works of popular fiction which portray credible worlds that resonate with people's experiences. To this extent, therefore, political performance has to be understood in similar terms to those applied to popular culture.[14]

This intertwined relationship and logic of contemporary politics and popular culture includes notions of representation, popularity, "the people," and identity that they both share.[15] Street contends that politicians not only use the arts and techniques of popular culture in instrumental ways, but that in doing so, politicians "are also being changed—in their language and their priorities, and in the way they are 'read' by their citizens."[16]

The point here is that politics is increasingly a textual practice, both in how it is constructed and presented for publics and how it is consumed or "read" by audiences. But as texts, this engagement does not happen in a vacuum. It happens in the swirl of other images, narratives, and ritual practices with which we invest our time and make commitments through all forms of popular culture. And it happens in the context of our primary social relationships—among our families, friends, or colleagues and in our homes, workplaces, or gathering spots. Politics occurs for many people in what one author calls our "media surround": the forms, types, places, and contexts in which media are inserted into our lives.[17] It is this complexity to our relationship with politics via media—its simultaneously private and public nature—that provides a location for reexamining the notion of television's role in civic (dis)engagement.

There are scholars and critics of television who will argue that the cognitive or deliberative dimensions of television viewing—thinking through its content, using it to begin discussions, sharing the content with others—is one thing, but that "nontextual" political behaviors such as the traditional behaviors associated with electoral politics are ultimately of more value (as the epigram so succinctly put it). Upon closer inspection, however, the rudimentary behaviors of citizen participation in electoral politics are not so easily divorced from texts. If I conduct door-to-door canvassing for a party or candidate, for instance, I hand out literature. If I call voters from a phone bank, I use a script. If I give money to a campaign, I supply my credit card information. If I attend a campaign rally, I wave a sign and wear buttons. At what point is a citizen's political behavior ever nontextual? The media experiences I am describing (including television) are simply a set of textual experiences that exists within this spectrum of textual activities listed previously. That should come as no surprise, given the enormous amount of money spent on television advertisements (more texts) during a campaign. And in the era of media convergence, including social networking, streaming video, e-mail, blogging, and so forth, the conception that television is synonymous with passivity is no longer tenable. Although I am arguing that we must recognize the value of popular media as an important relationship that citizens maintain with the world of politics, we should also realize that this textual relationship is only different in kind from the normative ideal of citizen electoral activities. If *The Daily Show*, for instance, became a forum through which people came to think or feel differently about their government in the election cycles between 2004 and 2008 (whether they became more angry or more cynical, more willing to talk politics with others, contribute money, vote, or whatever), then such engagement is arguably just as important as handing out campaign literature to people with an enormously low percentage chance of being registered to vote, much less voting. As citizens, it is unclear why we should value one textual engagement over the other.

The situation I am posing, therefore, extends beyond Putnam and the critics of television noted earlier. What they represent is the broader desire by scholars and social critics to realize a normative ideal of the citizen as a "rational-critical actor" in public life. It is what Schudson calls the "informed citizen" model—a Progressive Era construction of the voter as "independent, informed, public-spirited and above partisanship," and I would add, one who does his or her civic duty by voting and not wasting her time on frivolous matters such as the distractions of mass entertainment.[18] By extension, this model includes the desire to segregate various forms of media practice by citizens. That is, it advocates a strict separation between the "serious" information needed for citizens to be informed, deliberative, interrogational, and empirically reasoning thinkers, and the "entertainment" programming that is threatening because it is supposedly none of these things.

Yet this normative ideal, I contend, is rarely found in the practices of modern citizenry and is an unrealistic standard for the types of behavior that currently hold much interest for many citizens. What's more, it does not represent the multitude of ways in which people exchange, process, and engage political material in their day-to-day lives, ways that just as easily can be crude, limited, dismissive, trivial, playful, and emotional as they can be thoughtful, wide-ranging, generous, complex, rational, serious, and high-minded. Nor does it accurately represent the ways in which people attend to politics—in passing, cursorily, mixed in with other activities, from various media and across numerous subjects. In short, holding onto a conception of citizenship born from a rational-critical standard is perhaps noble, but it is an inappropriate means for assessing the relationship of television to politics. Instead, I agree with Schudson when he argues, "We require a citizenship fit for our own day."[19]

Schudson advances the concept of a "monitorial citizen," one who "engages in environmental surveillance more than information-gathering." As he describes it, "Monitorial citizens scan (rather than read) the information environment in a way so that they may be alerted on a very wide variety of issues for a very wide variety of ends and may be mobilized around those issues in a large variety of ways."[20] These citizenship practices are actually quite similar to the arguments made by media researchers for understanding how media are used in everyday life.[21] For instance, Howard Bausinger contends that there are four ways in which audiences engage media: that we construct and consume a daily "media ensemble"; that we do not always give our full attention and concentration to media as they are used (for instance, we skim while reading, flip while watching television, and scan while listening to radio); that media are incorporated into our daily routines (such as meals, driving, at the dentist's office); and that media usage is not an isolated process but often occurs in the presence of—and under the influence of—other people (for instance, the male's typical control of the television remote).[22]

What this chapter offers, then, is some reflection on contemporary citizenship practices that involve media and popular culture generally—and television specifically—practices that challenge the assumptions held by critics of the medium. I first explore the conditions of our contemporary political culture—our beliefs, attitudes, and behaviors toward political practice that have reconstituted the norms and practices of citizenship. I briefly examine what theorists have posited as a postmodern citizenship in which traditional forms of political engagement and previous relationships with media have changed. I then review several studies that examine the role of television in the lives of citizens (television being the most popular form of media engagement), studies that support the claims made previously regarding media as a constitutional force in maintaining our relationship to political life. These studies exemplify how politics is increasingly seen as a discursive activity, as well as how monitorial citizens behave when their fundamental values have been challenged by what they see and hear on television. The chapter concludes by examining this question: If politics is increasingly a textual practice for citizens, how are television narratives involved in the construction of political "meaning making"? The case is made for television as a pluralist forum of social conversation that offers accessible interpretive procedures for making sense of the world. That argument is linked to the recognition of the importance of popular culture as a central location of our affective commitments in public life, as a familiar site where political life can be made meaningful.

THE VICISSITUDES OF MEDIA AND POLITICAL CULTURE

Peter Dahlgren has offered one of the most concise yet instructive summations of contemporary political practice by citizens, describing what some scholars have called "postmodern politics."[23] This political culture is increasingly marked by a lack of commitment to traditional institutions (such as political parties, labor unions, and civic associations), yet composed of temporary alliances around issues and values linked to everyday life (such as morality, identity, and worldview). These alliances can be associated with new social movements (e.g., environmentalism or the ethical treatment of animals) or "identity politics" (e.g., race, sexuality, gender), but are generally ones that offer more individualistic forms of expression.[24] This approach to politics, Dahlgren notes, is part and parcel of the larger reflexive project of the emergence of "self," an "ongoing process of the shaping and reshaping of identity, in response to the pluralized sets of social forces, cultural currents and personal contexts encountered by individuals."[25] This project of the self results in multiple identities we each maintain—again, one of which is as "citizen" (although, as he notes, that word itself may not resonate with many people).

Citizens increasingly act as bricoleurs in their beliefs and ideological commitments, constructing their own à la carte politics through mixing, and individualizing ad hoc social and political positions. Of course, this can be criticized as a "consumerist" approach to communal life, and indeed is probably shaped by both public and private sector appeals to the public as "consumers" more so than as "citizens."[26] Nevertheless, many citizens are more comfortable constructing their own "frameworks rather than inherit(ing) culturally received 'packages.'"[27] John Gibbins and Bo Reimer see this as a tendency toward direct representation in public life by individuals who value dialogue, discussion, and dissension, and who demand "the voicing of one's view and having it heard." Politics in postmodernity, they argue, is "recognized to be constructed in language; politics *is* language."[28]

Concurrent with these changes have been changes in media that accentuate and perhaps even accelerate these tendencies. We live now, according to Jay Blumler and Michael Gurevitch, in a world of media abundance. As such, the audience has moved beyond its role as simple receptor of top-down political communication as traditionally established by elite gatekeepers (journalists, politicians, experts). Because of technologies such as satellites, the Internet, cable, and video and digital recorders, audiences are now smaller and more fragmented, with more choice and control over what information they do and don't consume, including when and where. With that said, such media abundance also means that it is much easier to "bump up against" the political in one's daily life. Such changes have led to a porous relationship between politics and popular culture, where "politics has undoubtedly broken out of the shells of respect, deference, and distance from people's daily lives in which it had formerly been enclosed. There is now a less identifiable core of what counts in some delimited sense as 'the political.'"[29] There has also been a blossoming of populist media formats with an increased presence of the voices and images of ordinary citizens expressing their political opinions. All of these changes have altered how audiences are addressed by media, therefore affecting what they find politically "interesting, relevant and accessible."[30] The new political communication system that has emerged from this process, Blumler and Gurevitch conclude, results from three root sources:

> A widespread belief that democracy as conventionally interpreted is in trouble and that shortcomings of mainstream media coverage of politics are largely to blame for its "crisis"; the rising tide of populism in cultural, political, and media quarters, which upgrades the value of heeding the views and preferences of ordinary people; and an impression that certain qualities of the new media could be enlisted behind more active forms of political participation.[31]

It is important to note at this point that, in subsequent chapters, we see how these changes are visible at every level of production, content, and consumption of new political television: the lack of commitment to traditional political bodies and the rejection of elite formulations about politics, including the exclusionary language used by experts and political insiders; the mix-and-match approach to political values and ideas by new television commentators and public alike; the populist impulse to project and hear the voices of ordinary people (including oneself) and the usage of new media and communication technologies to achieve this; the small and fragmented yet committed audiences attentive to new offerings in political communication; and the porous nature of politics within and across popular cultural formats.

The question still to be considered now, however, is what we know about audience engagement with television given these changes in political culture and the media landscape. Several studies of audiences suggest that the viewing public's political relationship to television is much more complex than critics of the medium either understand or express.

STUDIES OF TELEVISION AND CITIZENSHIP

Media researcher Kevin Barnhurst has conducted several studies of young people (generally college-level students) and their habits of news consumption.[32] His findings buttress the observation that young people are disconnected from traditional sources of political information—namely, the news. He finds that they generally disdain the displays of political opinion on television news programs, considering them little more than "reality-based variety shows" and something not to be taken seriously. Similarly, he finds that young people largely find newspapers irrelevant to their lives, because newspapers' version of "news" has little meaning within the localities where these young citizens live. As he notes, "The news floats past them, unanchored."[33] Instead, he argues, citizenship for young people is lived from the personal into the public. Their knowledge, understandings, and concerns for public life emanate from personal bonds with family and friends, but also from their personal relationship with popular media. "Their understanding of political life seems primarily discursive," he notes, "existing in the ideas that emerge from local interactions in the presence of the media. Their practical knowledge is rooted in media savvy rather than in the traditional modes of political action."[34] This is why, he notes, young people use "many genres (especially entertainment media) to make sense of the political world."[35] Their understanding of political life as primarily discursive is also seen in their belief that "the essence of political life for them is the expression of opinions and preferences."[36]

Similar results are reported by Michael Delli Carpini and Bruce Williams in their examination of television's effect on how citizens process information and formulate opinions on environmental issues. They conducted a series of focus group discussions with citizens of all ages and found that television is a constituent part of people's understandings of public life, a central reference in their thinking and arguing about political issues. They found that citizens make few distinctions between fictional and nonfictional television, and tend to refer to both in making knowledge claims— even more so than their own personal experiences. Furthermore, people retain an enormous variety and array of television-related personalities in their heads (from Ted Turner, Bill Cosby, and Bob Barker to Sally Struthers, Nadia Comaneci, and Bette Midler), and use these figures as reference when talking politics, almost to the total exclusion of politicians and government officials.[37] That is, rather than explain environmental issues by referencing the politicians who craft or manage regulatory policies, they instead use a repertoire of other figures from popular culture as communal signifiers to make their point. Popular culture, then, clearly comprises many people's constellations of meaning, even in regard to political life.

The narratives of popular culture are significant in their provision of characters, plots, outcomes, and morality tales that can be employed in people's construction of their own narratives about politics. Television not only instigates conversation, then, but in their engagement with it, citizens construct their own opinions or views through these narratives. As Delli Carpini and Williams argue, "Citizens often 'discover' their political views in the give-and-take of discussions with others. Television plays a central role in this process in that it is engaged in an ongoing political conversation: when we turn our set on, we dip into this conversation."[38] And it matters not whether the conversation arises from fictional or nonfictional programming. For viewers, it is all part of the same narrative flow that is "television."

What this study reveals is that the conversation citizens have with television exists in three ways. People talk to television, speaking back to the set (whether alone or in groups), just as television talks to them. Sometimes that conversation is a silent one, but it is a conversation nonetheless.[39] People also talk about television with others (what they have watched there) with great regularity. And people talk with television, using its narratives as part of how the world is to be understood and explained. Delli Carpini and Williams conclude that, "in many ways, television serves as a privileged member in public discourse, one to whom citizens feel an obligation to respond."[40] In other words, television is leading the discussion, or what political communication scholars have generally referred to as the agenda-setting function of media (not what to think, but what to think about). Here, though, the concept should be extended to recognize not just what to talk about, but the impetus to speak about politics publicly at all.

An important study by sociologist Ron Lembo, although not specifically focused on political communication, investigates the ways in which we "think through television." By interviewing and observing television viewers in their homes, his work is focused on examining television's use in everyday life, developing what he refers to as the "sociality of the viewing culture."[41] He contends that the viewing culture "encompasses the formation of attitudes and opinions that emerge from television use and that people may carry around in their heads and draw upon in making sense of themselves and their world, especially the world beyond their own day-to-day experiences."[42]

Lembo investigates the factors that are involved as people engage the medium, and how they go about relating to, accepting, or dismissing what is found there. One of the most important of these factors is the narrative's plausibility: does it ring true with their experiences or understanding of people, situations, and the world, "a world that they know in common with others—family, friends, co-workers"?[43] Like Delli Carpini and Williams, Lembo finds people engaged in a conversation with the medium—either silently, directly to the set, or with other people. When watching with other people, he reports, a comment or criticism tended to set off a series of interactions and extended discussions about the program, other programs, real life, and so on. People associate what they are watching with other aspects of their lives, both textual and "real."[44] As such, people make the choice to be mindfully engaged with television "in a way that is not simply oriented around escaping thoughts of their own real-life circumstances."[45] When they believe narratives are plausible, they incorporate the discourses of television as their own understanding of the world. When not seeing social reality, they see formula, and disengage from what they consider commercial product and manipulated images. Lembo concludes that when people watch television, "they can identify with or be critical of what is presented to them, but, either way, they enter into a process in which they are continually judging, monitoring, and evaluating things."[46] In other words, people engage the medium and what they find there.

Another illuminating study of how audiences engage with politics on television comes from an examination of citizen reactions to the televised hearings and media reports of the Iran-Contra scandal.[47] Using citizen correspondence (both letters and telephone calls) with members of Congress over the matter, historian David Thelen investigates how citizens were mobilized by watching the hearings and news, objecting to or applauding what they saw there, and feeling an immense need to have their voices heard as a result. He summarizes the process viewers took by noting that "viewers talked about what they saw on television with the people around them, and they became so troubled by public officials or journalists that they felt compelled to interrupt them, to add their own voices, and to try to make talk on television more nearly resemble everyday talk."[48] Indeed, Thelen argues that it was a perceived "disconnect" by politicians and journalists from the fundamental principles and values of everyday life that motivated viewers to take action, which usually began in conversation with others first.

Instead of finding the primary places for participation in public life to be large-scale social institutions (such as political parties, pressure groups, churches, unions), Thelen contends that the most meaningful participation in politics now occurs in intimate relationships, the places where people make sense of and actually take part in politics through their conversations.[49] It is here that the viewers in his study found "standards for authenticity and authority, so that those [primary] relationships became powerful sites from which to challenge the construction of the mass media."[50] In turn, they contacted the members of Congress they saw on television in an effort to assert that "the values that shaped their everyday relationships ought to shape the [political] conversation."[51]

It is this intimacy between public and private life that occurs with, through, and because of the medium of television that deserves our attention here. Television is invited into our homes, and the pageantry of public life becomes intimate and accessible. As noted by Barnhurst, citizenship is lived from the personal into the public. Thelen argues that citizens wanted the conversations on television to resemble those that occur in their homes, including the usage of their language, their conversational style, and their value-driven (not issues- or policy-driven) discourse.[52] And he notes that "viewers participated in the hearings, as in real life, not so much in a topic as with a person," wanting desperately to engage in a conversation.[53] He goes on to describe how the articulated desires between private principles,

actions, and behaviors and a specific vision of public life became the motivation for engagement with the actors they found in the national drama. This
particular engagement, in the end, tethers them to the nation and revives the
democratic spirit. The description deserves to be quoted at length:

> The issue at the core of popular participation was whether the trust that people
> sought in their personal relationships could become the kind of bond they
> felt with citizens they did not know and, through them, with their nation and
> government. To help them turn personal trust into public trust and public trust
> into democratic hope, citizens needed someone they could trust to carry their
> vision into government. During the hearings, Americans were thrilled to find
> representatives who spoke for their distinctive worlds instead of to common
> denominators. They needed these people to think as they did, to have access
> to government, and to fight courageously for their views. By their letters they
> tried to draw these people into their personal worlds. They offered their new-
> found champions encouragement, advice, and information just as they did to
> people around them.
>   By defending their values at the hearings their champion encouraged citi-
> zens to feel connected once again to each other and to government. . . . By
> expressing what the writers thought, their champion reconnected them with
> the traditions that mattered most to them. The thrill at hearing their thoughts
> come through the voice of a defender they had brought into their intimate
> worlds—the voice of a fellow citizen—was the thrill of renewed confidence in
> the community.[54]

Thelen concludes that "the core of democracy was the confidence that
their interests, beliefs, and feelings were fully represented in public life."[55]
Citizenship, then, becomes an assertion of one's values that have become
threatened and must be reestablished in a public way. That representation
occurs through texts, through words that are publicly displayed and made
available to all. The creation of texts is perhaps what politics is all about
for the postmodern citizen. As Sonia Livingstone and Peter Lunt argue,
"Political participation as narrowly defined is a minority activity. . . . A
more discursive notion of participation may be as significant for involving
the majority of the public in the fairly undemanding activity of talk and
opinion formation."[56]
One last point from this study deserves mention. Much of what Thelen
reports also corroborates the claims about television audiences made in
the studies cited previously. His study reveals that citizen-viewers: (1) find
much of what journalists and politicians do has little relevance to their
daily lives; (2) are critically engaged with what they find on television
("cheering, modifying, dismissing, or ridiculing");[57] (3) examine content
for plausibility, asking whether it rings true with their experiences and understandings, and whether it is related to the world they share in common
with family and friends; (4) feel an obligation to respond to television

when it doesn't correspond to their realities; and (5) believe that the central political practice available to them is discursive, that is, expressing their political opinions and having them heard publicly.

To summarize these studies in relation to the conception of postmodern citizenship described earlier (including our changed relationships with media), we see from Barnhurst's study that young citizens have a personalized engagement with politics and conceive of political activity as primarily discursive (and populist) in nature ("politics is language"). Media plenitude provides opportunities to brush up against politics in ways that shape these young citizens' understandings of political issues and events. The findings by Delli Carpini and Williams exemplify the fluid boundaries between politics and popular culture as citizens spliced together political meanings from myriad media representations. Furthermore, they contend that the citizenry's political views are not "received" packages but are "discovered" through discursive interactions with television and others in their everyday lives. Lembo's research also emphasizes the ways in which audiences use media as a means of discursive engagement with others. Their activities of judging, critiquing, incorporating, or dismissing media narratives exemplify the bricoleurs at work, constructing meanings that ring true with their experiences. Finally, Thelen's study also highlights an active brigade of citizen-viewers who fashioned the public sphere in the image of their private relationships and discursive interactions.[58] Political action was seen as discursive, driven by personal values, and based on their engagement with the "characters" that media provided and with whom they identified. As such, television narratives brought politics vividly to life (and into their lives), to a place where citizens felt comfortable or emboldened enough to participate.

POLITICAL MEANING AND TELEVISION NARRATIVES

From these studies, then, we see how television serves as a significant source for the public's relationship to politics. For many citizens, politics is a textual practice that exists in the interplay between media representations and the discursive interactions that then occur between television and themselves within their intimate relationships. As a textual practice, however, we should focus our attention on how the "meaning" of politics is produced by citizens through their systematic interpretations of media offerings. As psychologist Jerome Bruner succinctly put it, culture *"gives meaning to action* by situating its underlying intentional states in an interpretive system. It does this by imposing the patterns inherent in the culture's symbolic systems—its language and discourse modes, the forms of logical and narrative explication, and the patterns of mutually dependent communal life."[59]

Obviously, television has become a (if not the) dominant purveyor of communal life through the various languages, discourses, and narratives that citizens ritually attend to now in late modern society. But as Bruner also notes, "What makes a cultural community is not just shared beliefs about what people are like and what the world is like or how things should be valued"—all things that television ritually provides. Instead, "What may be just as important to the coherence of a culture is the existence of interpretive procedures for adjudicating the different construals of reality that are inevitable in any diverse society."[60] Of the languages, discourses, and narratives that television provides, how do we make sense of them, how do we chose what "realities" to believe and which to reject, and on what basis?

The most common interpretive procedure we utilize, Bruner argues, is "common sense" (what he also calls "folk psychology"), a cognitive system "by which people organize their experiences in, knowledge about, and transactions with the social world."[61] In media studies, Antonio Gramsci's writings on common sense have been the most widely employed in examining mass media content. As a Marxist, Gramsci's interest in common sense is how it serves the process of ideological legitimation and maintenance of ruling-class power, or hegemony, a process whereby the ruling class's ideas become normalized assumptions of how the world works. Although it is a particularly helpful approach for examining ideological processes at work in capitalist media systems, that is not the emphasis or approach taken here. I, like Horace Newcomb and Paul Hirsch, do not find such processes of ideological maintenance surprising, because "that is what central storytelling systems do in all societies."[62] Clifford Geertz also examines common sense, but he approaches it as a "cultural system."[63] Geertz has developed perhaps the most useful typology for analyzing common sense in practice, one to which we return in chapter 5.

For the purposes of my argument here, however, Bruner's exploration of common sense as a primary cognitive system for processing social realities has more theoretical significance. He characterizes common sense as a "set of more or less connected, more or less normative descriptions about how human beings 'tick,' what our own and other minds are like, what one can expect situated action to be like, what are possible modes of life, how one commits oneself to them, and so on."[64] What interests me in regard to television, however, is his contention that the organizing principle of common sense is "narrative in nature rather than logical or categorical" or conceptual.[65] It is through narrative that we process "established canonical expectations and the mental management of deviations from such expectations."[66] And this is the crux of the matter: that narrative provides an efficient means through which we establish both the normative and its breach through the stories we tell each other—stories that ultimately link us together in a common culture. The primary currency of television is, of course, narrative—whether it is news, dramas, documentaries, talk shows, home shopping, sports, or weather. Television is heavily invested in leading viewers through the narratives of normal/abnormal, the expected/unexpected, the acceptable/unacceptable, and new political television is awash in such narratives as well.

To argue as I have that much of our current engagement with politics occurs textually is to recognize that part of the process of making meaning of political and social realities will be located in the common sense narratives that television offers. The diversity and array of those narratives matter, as do the voices that are allowed to "speak" within narratives. And those narratives only begin the discussion, which is then continued by audiences as they engage in politics discursively with others. Some of the studies presented above begin to offer a glimpse of how television's narratives play an important role in citizens' engagement with and thinking about politics. As seen in the evidence presented by Thelen, many citizens refused to believe the "stories" that journalists were telling about "Ollie-mania" (the supposed infatuation of the viewing audiences with the charismatic Colonel Oliver North). The narratives that journalists and politicians constructed violated the audience's common sense understandings of politics and the bedrock principles that government was supposed to protect. Therefore, many citizens "spoke back" to the power of media and government by creating their own narratives to set the record straight. Or, as was seen in the study by Delli Carpini and Williams, the focus group participants on environmental issues found the narratives of both fictional and nonfictional television programming equally meaningful and equally significant as referential material in their talking and thinking about politics. Both were narratives that provided an easy means of identification and understanding of political issues in fundamentally human terms.[67]

To argue, however, that television narratives are awash in canonical commonsense understandings that allow people to make sense of the deviations from those norms, we should be careful not to fall into the trap of believing that television is as ideologically monolithic (or hegemonically effective) as scholars and critics on both the left and the right have made it out to be. Its narratives, discourses, and commonsense thinking become a means through which social/political issues and ideological dilemmas are worked through, allowing politics to take a less violent path than many societies experience.[68] As Bruner notes, "In human beings, with their astounding narrative gift, one of the principal forms of peacekeeping is the human gift for presenting, dramatizing, and explicating the mitigating circumstances surrounding conflict-threatening breaches in the ordinariness of life. The objective of such narrative is not to reconcile, not to legitimize, not even to excuse, but rather to explicate."[69]

John Ellis makes a similar argument when he asserts that television produces the social performance of what in psychoanalysis is called "working-through," a "process whereby material is not so much processed into a finished product as continually worried over until it is exhausted."[70] By extension, the same is true for television, he maintains. It "attempts to define, tries out explanations, creates narratives, talks over, makes intelligible, tries to marginalize, harnesses speculation, tries to make fit and, very occasionally, anathematizes."[71] Both of these arguments relate to Newcomb and Hirsch's conception of television as a "cultural forum." The multiplicity of messages and meanings offered by television suggests that television's overall emphasis is "on process rather than product, on discussion rather than indoctrination, on contradiction and confusion rather than coherence."[72] They contend that "television does not present firm ideological conclusions—despite its formal conclusions—so much as it comments on ideological problems."[73] In short, a cultural forum is a place in which it is more important to raise questions than to answer them. To bring the argument full circle by returning to the common sense found in television narratives, social psychologist Michael Billig and colleagues argue that common sense is an important means through which publics think through and discuss deeper "ideological dilemmas" that often lie at the heart of public issues and events.[74] Billig maintains that it is because "a social group's stock of commonsensical beliefs contains contrary elements that argument, and thereby thought, is possible."[75] Here again, common sense is central to public thought, and to envision television as a place where such thinking occurs about politics is to recognize television's central role in the construction of public life.

It is through the narratives of television and popular culture that we give meaning to political action by debating, arguing, mulling over, and working through that which television provides. Television is a site of commonsense applications to politics through its narratives. It is a site that people look to for narratives that fulfill this need, a place to engage and work through the divergence between norms and realities, a place to apply lived experience to the intellectual constructions of state and ideology. News "stories" are a common starting place in the process of television's working through of public issues. News, however, is only the first (incomplete) step because it offers "bits of stories" but few endings. Hence its offerings are incomplete and frustrating to a narratively impatient audience, Ellis argues. Audiences often turn to talk shows next because these shows provide "greater narrative content that news can't provide."[76]

In political communication research, news is and has been the most thoroughly examined area of television, and the analysis of common sense within news narratives was one of the primary points of investigation in early British cultural studies research. More recently, scholars have examined the common sense found in talk show narratives, mainly those of daytime audience participation programming (such as *Oprah* and *Donahue*). The focus has generally centered on talk that pits "experts" versus "laity" on personal and social issues.[77] My investigation (chapter 5) focuses on the commonsense narratives of new political talk shows and on the ways in which this programming offers interpretations of politics that are different from that offered by both news and the pundit variety of political talk shows. These commonsense narratives are produced in shows that exist in relation and response to news and other political talk programming, the latter having lost its appeal for many in the viewing public as a means of supplying sufficient explanations of social reality. As Paolo Carpignano et al. contend, "The present crisis of the public sphere is the result of . . . a crisis of legitimacy of the news as a social institution in its role of dissemination of information about and interpretation of events (i.e., the social construction of public life)."[78] The arrival of alternative political programming more firmly grounded in popular cultural appeals that offer different narratives of public life is, I argue, an important development for citizen engagement with politics on television.

CONCLUSIONS

This discussion began with an assessment of current critiques of television and its supposed role in public disengagement with politics and traditional political institutions. The case has been made that television is instead a quite active source for audience engagement with public life. Politics has increasingly become a discursive behavior for audiences, and that conversation occurs through the articulation of their public and private lives and their media surround. The argument I am making is that we should rethink what engagement with politics means as a result. Thelen also contends that textual activity by citizens (which he notes has greatly increased over the past generation) is perhaps "a much better activity from which to imagine the future of political participation than is a declining activity such as voting or more episodic ones such as strikes, demonstrations, and riots."[79] Finally, Carpignano et al. make the argument best, perhaps, when they offer us a choice: we can think of the reconstitution of the public sphere in terms of revitalization of old political organizations and politics as state management; or "if we conceive of politics today as emanating from social, personal, and environmental concerns, consolidated in the circulation of discursive practices rather than in formal organizations, then a common place that formulates and propagates common senses and metaphors that govern our lives might be at the crossroads of a reconceptualization of collective practices."[80]

The argument here is also addressed to criticisms that the boundaries between politics and entertainment are increasingly blurred, and that the supposed rational thinking that should surround all matters political is becoming subsumed by the entertainment and celebrity values of television and popular culture. My contention, based on the arguments and evidence presented above, is that popular culture—with television as the dominant engine driving it—is our central social practice that does more than offer spectacle, amusement, and distraction (although it certainly provides a bounty of that as well). Popular culture is, as John Street, Lawrence Grossberg, and Simon Frith have all argued, the primary location of our affective commitments in public life, the means through which we articulate our emotions to the wider world.[81] Popular culture is where we link our interests and pleasures to our identities, where we tell stories that are accessible and emotionally meaningful. Popular culture is proximate. It humanizes, simplifies, and embodies complex issues, concepts, and ideas. And to paraphrase Bruner's points about narrative, popular culture (and its narratives) is well fit for reiterating social norms without being didactic, persuading without being confrontational, and teaching without being polemical.[82]

From the studies reviewed previously, it is clear that citizens do not segregate their practices of citizenship into "information" over here, "entertainment" over there. Many manifestations of mediated politics occur through our relationships with popular culture, and it is with popular culture that many citizens are emotionally invested. As Peter Dahlgren notes in regard to the citizenry's needs from media, "Information is necessary, though not sufficient. It must be made meaningful and must be related to previous understandings in order to become knowledge."[83] My argument is that for political life to be meaningful, its presence in venues that we ritually attend to, understand, are comfortable and familiar with, and maintain feelings and commitments to should not necessarily be seen in a negative light. And as will be seen in subsequent chapters, the politically oriented entertainment shows of new political television carry the dual quality of accessible popular culture and meaningful political material. Didactic, confrontational, and polemical is plentifully served up by the John McLaughlins, Bill O'Reillys, and Pat Buchanans of mediated political talk. New political television, I contend, offers something else.

I should warn, however, against any misreading of my argument as simply another populist (and formulaic) reading of audiences and popular culture that has become quite prevalent in cultural studies. That is, one might be tempted to see here an effort to celebrate the audience activities around the "disreputable" medium of television (or the lowbrow practices of popular culture) as being complex, progressive, or liberatory, thereby saving both the audience and the medium from the scorn typically levied by academic and cultural elites. Certainly there is an impetus here to present evidence to address continuing misconceptions about citizens and their relationship to television and politics that still, at this late date, continue to dominate the field of political communication (at least in America) and the discipline of political science. To argue, however, that people's relationship to television and popular culture is more full of meaning, substantive, and publicly constitutional than is often given credit for is not to argue that watching television will "save" democracy or that the masses will necessarily be "empowered" without moving their feet off the coffee table. Rather, the point I wish to advance is the need for a reconceptualization of how our common democratic culture is shaped by popular media and the practices that surround it.

In sum, popular culture can support a civic culture when both producers and audiences make or find programming or other cultural practices politically meaningful and engage them as such. Thus, popular culture is just as capable of shaping and supporting a culture of citizenship as it is of shaping and supporting a culture of consumption. This book explores evidence of those possibilities.

II

ENTERTAINING POLITICAL TALK

3

From Insiders to Outsiders

The Transformation of Political Talk on Television

The airing of political talk on television has always assumed one crucial point: that those doing the talking should have direct "insider" knowledge of what they are talking about. The assumption by television producers has been that "expertise" should be the defining characteristic of who gets to speak—either by politicians who are directly involved, their handlers or strategists, or the journalists and opinion columnists whose job it is to study and report on their activities. The assumption is built on the belief that such speech is designed primarily to inform or educate, not fulfill other functions of political communication. By maintaining such a standard, however, a whole series of logical outcomes follow: that the subjects, issues, and players that properly constitute politics are the self-evident product of this expertise; that audiences are only interested in hearing expert opinions on politics; and that other forms of political discourse do not merit airing in the public sphere that television provides.

Such assumptions of speakers and audiences are, most certainly, the product of a political culture with expectations of an informed citizenry, a culture that has held the conduct of rational political thought as the discursive ideal.[1] They are also the product of a time in which social scientists, journalists, and even philosophers had a more prominent place in the national political dialogue conducted in the press and through mass-circulated magazines and journals prior to the arrival of television. And as various histories of political talk on television remind us, this thinking is the product of the history of network news bureaus that developed the shows, as well as the role and place that journalists felt they occupied as arbiters of political discussion and opinion.[2]

Over three decades later, these assumptions have changed. Although talk by political experts continues to dominate both network and cable political programming, the decade of the 1990s ushered onto the stage new programming and cable channels that explicitly offered new forms of and approaches to political talk on television.[3] In particular, that change has been associated with the addition of talk not by political insiders, but inclusive now of those who position themselves outside the conventional wisdom and sense-making of political elites. These new voices and programming types challenge the assumptions of what constitutes knowledge, who gets to speak, what issues can be addressed, and what is open for criticism.

This chapter charts this evolution by first examining political talk on television from the network era through the first generation of cable programming (to the late 1980s), and then exploring how a series of developments and changes in the economic, political, cultural, and technological realms of American society in the early 1990s provided the fertile soil from which new political programming would grow. Included here is a discussion of the changes in television that resulted from increased competition brought on by cable that lead to new risk-taking, new programming stylistics, and attempts at new relationships with audiences. In particular, cable programmers offered new forms of political talk television, beginning with the populist talk radio–style imitators that featured outsider political voices—at times, those of "disgruntled" citizens, but also including right-wing rabble-rousing. As these new forms of programming failed economically, what rose in its stead was the creation of two new cable news channels (Fox News and MSNBC), both of which lead the way in transforming cable news into channels that primarily feature ideologically driven forms of talk programming rather than older-style forms of traditional television news reporting.

PUNDIT TALK IN THE NETWORK ERA

For much of television's history, political talk programming[4] has grown from the roots of journalism, in particular the practices of interviewing and op-ed writing. The earliest manifestations of this on network television were the shows *Meet the Press* on NBC (1947) and *Face the Nation* on CBS (1954), where newspaper and broadcast journalists interviewed government officials and news makers of the day.[5] The names of these shows, of course, signal the press's understanding of their role as representatives of the public and public interest through their journalistic interrogational style. That tradition lives on today through these shows, but also through descendants such as *Nightline* and *The NewsHour with Jim Lehrer*. Another type of early political talk program is the journalist roundtable discussion, first developed in 1969 through *Agronsky and Company*, hosted by television and radio journalist Martin Agronsky, and broadcast on public television. The show derives from the op-ed journalistic tradition and featured four journalists and Agronsky offering their opinions of the week's news events. The show was based in the belief that because journalists are the closest independent observers of actions occurring in the political arena, they would offer the most informed yet impartial opinion of what was really going on. Agronsky (later renamed *Inside Washington*) became the model upon which programs such as *Washington Week in Review* (1967 on PBS), *The McLaughlin Group* (1982 on PBS), and *The Capital Gang* (1988 on CNN) were formulated.

It is from this type of programming that critics have derisively given the participants the name "pundits," derived from the ancient Sanskrit word meaning "learned man." But as the word made its way into the English language, it became not only a reference for someone who gives authoritative opinions, but is also used in "mocking the pretensions of those who nag politicians through public and widely circulated observations."[6] Rather than simply an annoying gadfly role, critics contend that pundit programs are, in essence, somewhat dangerous, because these journalists tend to spout opinions on all sorts of issues and events that they generally have little knowledge of as reporters (hence, they aren't really expert thinkers, just expert talkers). As Dan Nimmo and James E. Combs contend, "They now constitute a source of opinion-formation and opinion-articulation, agenda-setting and agenda-evaluation, so vast as to make the United States a punditocracy: a nation where the mediation of opinion by important and highly visible media figures is paramount."[7]

The last type of political talk show is somewhat an amalgam of the first two, whereby one or two commentators hold a discussion (rather than an interview) with a guest, thus creating a context in which opinions are freely forthcoming, albeit connected to political actors of the day. The pioneer and, in many ways, defining show in this subgenre is *Firing Line*, a syndicated program first offered by RKO in 1966, featuring the firebrand conservative and founder of the *National Review* William F. Buckley, Jr.[8] Programs of similar structure that have developed over the years include *Crossfire* (1982 on CNN) and, to some extent, *This Week with David Brinkley* (1981 on ABC). On *Firing Line*, Buckley took the concept of televised political debate seriously and would resort to all manner of rhetorical techniques (both fair and out-of-bounds) to win his encounters. Buckley's producer even conceived the show as "an intellectual version of Friday night at the fights."[9] Buckley's take-no-prisoners approach to political discourse, complete with name-calling, physical threats, interruptions, and put-downs, was the presentational model of televised political discourse from which many subsequent programs have drawn.

Indeed, although the typology of shows offered thus far is based on the structural features of the programming and the arrangement of the cast that conducts those discussions, a more fruitful approach might be to chart the lineage of political talk based on the ideological leanings and discursive style that these shows offer. In such a formulation, the logical progression moves from the pedantic style and postwar libertarian brand of conservatism offered by Buckley to the belligerent style and Reagan school of neoconservatism in John McLaughlin, to the inanely blowhard style and rabid right-wing reactionary Bill O'Reilly (*The O'Reilly Factor* on Fox News), the current king of agonistic political talk on cable television. This reformulated lineage also recognizes that the quality of political talk has seen a marked devolution from the days of *Firing Line*, not to mention the ideological triumph of conservatism. Buckley, whom most people (including his archenemies) concede possessed a high level of intelligence, has spawned O'Reilly, who almost single-handedly has shown that a talk-show host need know nothing about anything to hold forth on every issue in stunning ignorance and yet draw the largest audience in cable political talk (and be a bestselling author to boot). And, of course, O'Reilly is simply one of many manifestations of political talk in the rotisserie league of programming now found on the cable channels Fox News, MSNBC, CNN, and CNBC.

Although this review of the genre of pundit-based political talk is cursory, the detailed histories provided by Alan Hirsch, Eric Alterman, and Nimmo and Combs lead to three primary conclusions about the nature of these shows, their participants, and the talk that is offered there.[10] First, and perhaps most importantly, the independent and impartial observer of politics that the journalistic form assumes is, in fact, neither of those things. That is to say, although most pundits retain jobs as columnists for major newspapers and news magazine weeklies, their participation in televised political talk has clearly shown how closely connected to power they are. Indeed, several prominent pundits (or their wives) have been employed in various presidential administrations.[11] Yet they all are active participants in the political sphere, employ an epistemology often called "inside-the-beltway" thinking, and contribute to the conventional wisdom and general circulation of meanings of politics that emanate from the nation's capital. Perhaps more damning is that these pundits are full-scale participants in the spreading of rumors, the settling of scores, and intrabureaucratic power struggles typical of Washington politics.[12] *Media-Week* reporter Alicia Mundy notes the important role that Sunday morning talk shows play in Washington political maneuverings: "These shows aren't mere entertainment, nor are they simply commentary," she writes. "Today, politicians use these shows to make news and to make waves. They use them to send signals to their allies and to the opposition. And they use them to evaluate their own packaging and marketing efforts."[13] In short, these pundits are not commentators on the system—they and their shows *are* the system.

The second, and related, conclusion about television's pundits is that they are not just journalists, but celebrity elites in their own right. As pundit Robert Novak notes, "When I'm recognized now it is as a television celebrity. Not even as a television commentator!"[14] As such, they are guests in the Georgetown social circles and maintain personal friendships with politicians, including many a president. They not only command larger salaries than their nontelevised peers but also parlay their celebrity status into enormous speaking fees on the lecture circuit.[15] In short, they are the visible face of political opinion, and as a result have a vested interest—as all celebrities do—in maintaining that image by staying within the bounds of the celebrity system that created them.[16]

The final and overriding conclusion that can be drawn from pundit television is that its reality belies the argument that those with high levels of political knowledge will offer the highest forms of rational political discourse. What pundit television has clearly shown is that more often than not, their public presentations are pure spectacle. As noted previously, the rhetorical flourishes of Buckley have grown into full-blown circuses on programs like *The McLaughlin Group*, perhaps the flagship show in this regard. Most pundits, regardless of the program on which they appear, have learned the lessons of what makes for good television. Calm, thoughtful, introspective, and compromising demeanors are not among them. Audiences also recognize the spectacle nature of these talk "shows," but the incestuousness of the participants and their banter ultimately limits its audience appeal beyond those who can both keep up with the demands of insider knowledge yet also stomach the bellicose displays of showmanship.[17]

In sum, then, what has become the dominant form of political talk on television does not adhere to the journalistic ideals of objectivity, dispassion, or rational thought from which it was supposedly born. What has developed in its stead are programs that feature celebrity commentators who are intimately connected to power, who participate in a circumscribed system of political thinking, and who construct a discursive spectacle with limited appeal beyond the political cognoscenti or political junkies. Although it has been argued that these programs probably do more in greasing the wheels of the establishment than in informing and educating an electorate, as far as television political talk is concerned, these programs have generally been the only game in town. In turn, the viewing and voting public has received the media's message: "*This* is politics—love it or leave it." Of course, what was shown through the tremendously low levels of voter turnout in the 1988 presidential and 1990 congressional elections was that people were, in fact, leaving it in droves.

Hence, as a series of changes in the political and economic climate began to take hold in the 1980s and early 1990s, television producers recognized the weaknesses in the system and began to offer new forms of political talk programming that they believed audiences were interested in seeing. Any objections that these new forms of political talk programming would be illegitimate because of their using celebrity hosts, or allowing people who were not experts to talk, or producing an entertainment spectacle all seemed moot, because of what pundit television itself had become. Before discussing that programming, however, we must understand the changes in politics, technology, culture, and the economics within the media industries that laid the groundwork for these new types of programs.

CONTEXTUAL CHANGES

The most significant factor in shaping politics and political culture in the 1980s was the election and popularity of Ronald Reagan. As a Hollywood celebrity, he maintained the credentials to effectively communicate his outsider status and his conservative populist mantra that government is not part of the problem—rather, it is the problem. To a great extent, Reagan's popularity was not built on actual policies or programs that benefited the vast majority of Americans who supported him, but rather on his posturing against government as a negative force in American life.[18] By the 1988 presidential election, both Republican and Democratic candidates Pat Robertson and Jesse Jackson attempted to assume Reagan's populist mantle by running "outsider" campaigns.[19] Although unsuccessful in their electoral bids, the populist rhetoric they offered from both the far right and far left would appear again two years later when populist angst became a driving force in several "Throw the Rascals Out" campaigns in the midterm congressional elections.[20] Two years hence, such angst again found its embodiment in Ross Perot's outsider presidential campaign with his "commonsense" approach to government and town hall meetings to find out what "the people" really wanted from government.[21] Perot also led the way in using popular, nonpolitical television talk shows as a primary means of communicating with the public. Indeed, his candidacy was a product of his appearance on *Larry King Live* in which he informed the audience that if the American people wanted to draft him to run, he was willing to finance that effort himself.[22] As the campaign progressed, all of the presidential candidates appeared on similar types of "populist" entertainment talk shows to communicate directly with "the people" as well as to avoid the more confrontational questioning that typically occurred in forums with the press.[23] Yet again, two years later many citizens signed up with Republicans who now joined the populist bandwagon by promising fail-safe legislative guarantees through written "contracts" with the public.[24]

A component of this populist upsurge was the language of "common sense." Citizens and politicians embraced common sense as the Holy Grail of the legitimacy crisis, a cure-all remedy that would supposedly bring san-ity, clarity, and efficiency to out-of-control politicians and bureaucrats.[25] Vice President Al Gore sought to sell his efficiency-in-government report by dressing it up as a voting man's beer commercial—"Common Sense Government: Works Better and Costs Less."[26] The rhetoric of common sense also sought codification by becoming one of the ten commandments of the Republican Party's "Contract With America," including a piece of legislation advanced in Congress known as "The Common Sense Legal Reform Act of 1995."[27]

This same period also witnessed the fluidity between the fields of politics and media. The traditional revolving door between government and industry became much more high-profile. Politicians who once garnered media attention while serving in some capacity as government officials or political candidates became media celebrities after departing government service by working for media corporations that attempted to exploit their celebrity name-value. Oliver North, Mario Cuomo, Ross Perot, Jesse Jackson, Jerry Brown, Susan Molinari, George Stephanopoulos, David Gergen, and Pat Buchanan, among others, all found work in some capacity as on-air personalities. This movement toward "politician as celebrity," however, was simply a continuation of the dwindling loss of public identification with political parties and widespread public emphasis on choosing among politicians as individuals whom they "get to know" through media exposure.[28] As public frustration with government increased, politicians distanced themselves from traditional political structures, posturing as political "outsiders" not beholden to any interest except the mandate of "the people."

In summarizing the changes in the political climate, then, the decade of the 1980s and early 1990s witnessed an intermixing of celebrity and politics, the appeal to commonsensical ways of talking and thinking about politics, and a concurrent upsurge in populist anti-politics by a public that was increasingly finding the political arena repugnant. Audiences therefore tuned in to politicians on entertainment talk shows precisely because these shows did not produce the traditional staid political talk to which they had grown accustomed. Instead, audiences now found that they too were allowed to ask questions of the candidates, and that responses came in a language that was more accessible and commonsensical than the highly cloaked and guarded language of spin offered in other venues.[29]

In the technological realm, political anxiety mixed with social expectations and technological opportunities to produce a degree of populist hope. The 1990s saw the flowering of potentialities developed in the 1980s through the microcomputer and cable television revolutions. The Internet became a commercial, social, and political reality, especially for middle- and upper-class citizens at that time. Expectations of media-driven political change rose amid a rhetoric of technological progress, exemplified by claims of five hundred cable channels, electronic town hall meetings, worldwide communication in the global village, easy access to political information in the form of citizen-centered presidential debates, candidate appearances on phone-in talk shows, congressional e-mail addresses, and the ability to organize and identify with like-minded people in cyberspace.[30] The frontiers of space and time had seemingly been conquered, and the divisions between elite and mass discourse seemingly overcome. Problems associated with recalcitrant politicians and bureaucracies would disappear as people became empowered by new communication technologies to participate in the decisions that govern their lives (or at least to make better and easier choices from the menus provided).[31]

In the cultural realm, citizens waged ideological battles in what is often called the "culture wars."[32] Roughly speaking, the term refers to the prolonged disagreements between liberals and conservatives over issues such as sexual orientation, racial identity, physical access equality, media representations, religion, public morality, and gender relations. These battles have been conducted as much through social institutions or cultural patterns and behaviors (such as media, language, "lifestyle," academia, religion) as through formal politics. The battlegrounds are quite fluid, though, to the point where cultural battles can be waged in political forums (judicial rulings, impeachment hearings, etc.),[33] and political battles may be waged in cultural forums such as talk television. "Political correctness" became the term used by conservatives and moderates alike to derisively chide efforts by liberals and progressives to alter what were seen as harmful, stereotypical, or ideologically loaded practices in society. Political correctness mandated certain behaviors, critics claimed, and resistance to such efforts in a strongly individualistic American society appeared with great frequency in public life, including on television talk shows.

Also in the realm of popular culture came a general displacement of afternoon soap operas with syndicated, issue-oriented talk shows. Although these types of shows had their initial success through male-hosted programs such as *Donahue* and *Geraldo* in the 1980s, it was the success of Oprah Winfrey and a bevy of imitators such as Jenny Jones, Sally Jessy Raphael, and Ricki Lake that led to the enormous expansion of the genre in the early to mid 1990s.[34] As has been examined in numerous scholarly works, these shows typically discuss personal issues such as anorexia, teenage pregnancy, incest, homosexuality, and so on, and involve both experts and laity on stage with the host moderating. Eventually in each program, the audience participates in the discussion, and it is here that scholars have argued that laity has successfully offered challenges to institutionally based expertise.[35] These programs have since grown into what has been called "trash television," featuring guests who appear on the program to reveal bizarre sexual and personal peccadilloes, or who appear so they can "confront" other people in their lives, all for the camera to record and witness as exotic spectacle. The king and queen of trash television, many people widely acknowledge, are hosts Jerry Springer and Ricki Lake.[36]

In the economic realm of media industries, the wisdom of "the people" also became a value that producers realized could be commoditized. Talk radio formats became the godsend of AM stations nationwide as listeners and participants revived a flailing industry with populist political talk. Talk radio host Rush Limbaugh led the way, but a bevy of conservative copycats were also spawned nationwide by Limbaugh's success, such as Ken Hamblin ("The Black Avenger"), G. Gordon Liddy, and Sean Hannity.[37] Trying to model the success of talk radio, as well as tap into the interactive capabilities brought on by the Internet craze, cable television entrepreneurs developed talk television channels and programming strategies that sought to mobilize populist angst by showcasing commonsense commentary of the average person and exploiting interactive technologies to intensify the connection with the viewing audience. CNN developed an hour-long daily program, *TalkBack Live* (1994); MSNBC's precursor was *America's Talking* (1994); Multi-Media/Gannett produced the Talk Channel (1994) (renamed NewsTalk Television in 1995); C-SPAN introduced its morning call-in show, *Washington Journal*; Republican party activists produced National Empowerment Television (1993; renamed America's Voice in 1998), a channel that actually billed itself as explicitly "populist." Around the same time, two comedians stepped forward with shows that featured entertaining political talk in new and unusual formats for both the political and entertainment genre: *Dennis Miller Live* appeared on HBO in 1994, and Comedy Central introduced *Politically Incorrect* in 1993, only to lose it to network television four years later.

In sum, then, by the early 1990s, an environment existed in which populist rhetoric and thinking had become a popular vehicle for addressing political anxiety, where "common sense" became a catchall solution to complex problems, and where political celebrity became the point of public identification with new types of politics that might provide a more appealing solution. This is a social environment where communication technologies offered hope and optimism for overcoming one-way flows of communication from distant forces of bureaucracy and control, thereby giving people greater voice, access, and choice. It is a cultural environment in which political struggles are increasingly played out in cultural forums such as talk shows, and it is an economic environment where media industries competitively struggle to create programs and channels that are cheap to produce, yet innovative and popular with audience tastes. Also important to note here is how interrelated these processes are: disillusionment in politics leads to hopeful answers in technology and new media; frustration with government finds an outlet in culture, including the primary currency in popular culture of "celebrity"; cultural wars become political wars (and vice versa), and hence, attractive content for conflict-driven media programming; technological convergence produces opportunities for political and economic exploitation; economic competition results in new forms of programming related to politics featuring technology.

In understanding the type of political programming that would develop from this context, it is important that we examine in some detail the television industry's specific response to the increased competition brought on by the rapidly expanded offerings made available by cable. That is, it bears asking: What specific measures did programmers take (in particular, for both new and existing cable channels) not only to mark themselves as appealing to audiences, but also to establish different relationships with audiences based on that appeal?

TELEVISUAL STYLE, AUDIENCE PARTICIPATION, AND OUTSIDER TALK

Two major things occurred in the post-network period of the late 1980s and early 1990s that speak to the issues at hand: the television industry's change in programming style to appeal to audiences in new and different ways, and the concomitant popularity of syndicated audience participation shows in afternoon programming and their effect in altering assumptions about such issues as authority, voice, knowledge, and participation in television's presentation of public issues. It is from these two major developments that new political television was formed, leading to a style of political programming inclusive of "outsider" political voices provided by both comedians and the non-expert public itself.

The first of these developmental changes was produced as a result of the rise of competition to the network oligopoly from cable programmers. For the networks, consumers were now able to choose from a broad array of more narrowly defined options on cable for their viewing pleasures (sports, music, news, etc.). For new and existing cable channels, the challenge was to provide some level of interesting and attractive content that would draw viewers away from their former habits of attending to network programming, but also away from other cable competition. In the process, it was necessary to give the network a specific "brand image" in viewers' minds. The increased competition led one network executive in 1993 to state, "It's not business as usual anymore. We have got to find ways to recreate this business so that it will survive into the next decade."[38] In addition to this increased competition, the industry was also experiencing changing production factors such as advances in audiovisual technologies and changing costs of production, both allowing for newer presentational aesthetics and altered appeals to audiences.

John Thornton Caldwell offers perhaps the most thorough and illuminating analysis of the ways in which the industry responded. The means the networks used to fight for survival, he argues, involved an intensive program of innovation and stylistic development. The new look offered is what he calls "televisuality," an aesthetic tendency toward excessive style. "Television moved from a framework that approached broadcasting primarily as a form of word-based rhetoric and transmission," he notes, "to a visually based mythology, framework, and aesthetic based on extreme self-consciousness of style."[39] Style became the subject, the defining practice of television as a means of attaining a distinctive look in the battle for audience share. Excessive style, however, is more than simply a visual phenomenon. Instead, it becomes a means of developing a "look" by individualizing programs in viewers' minds via their distinctive appeal.

A driving force behind the need for this new exhibitionism was the changing relationship between audiences and the televisual product. "The individuation and semiotic heterogeneity evident in televisual excess," he argues, "means that such shows are from the start defined by, and pitched at, niche audiences who are flattered by claims of difference and distinction."[40] These new rules affect both viewers and industry, and the texts that exist between them. Viewers are positioned as savvy and self-conscious televisual consumers by the industry, while the texts "demand a more conscious form of viewer negotiation."[41]

Simultaneous with this reconfiguration of industry perspective was the increasing popularity and multiplicity of syndicated issue-oriented afternoon talk shows, often called audience participation programs. As noted previously, an enormous body of scholarly work has been devoted to exploring these programs and their place in society. What merits our attention here are the conclusions these scholars make in two regards: first, how (through the inclusion of studio audience participation in creating these programs) these shows led the way for audiences to question what constituted "authority" and "expertise" in televised talk about issues of public concern, including questioning who has the right to speak and be heard about such issues; and second, how such programming has eroded the boundaries between the differing programming genres of talk (e.g., the "entertaining" and the "serious"). Paulo Carpignano et al. argue that audience participation programs "problematize the distinction between expert and audience, professional authority and layperson." For them, these shows "constitute a 'contested space' in which new discursive practices are developed in contrast to the traditional modes of political and ideological representation."[42] Through talk that often pits "experts" against "laity," these authors highlight the importance of the studio audiences' (and perhaps the viewing audiences' as well) rejection of the claims offered by authority figures:

> What is expressed is a refusal not of knowledge but of expertise. The talk show rejects the arrogance of a discourse that defines itself on the basis of its difference from common sense. In debate, the authority of the expert is replaced by the authority of a narrative informed by lived experience.[43]

Similarly, in their study of British and American talk shows, Sonia Livingstone and Peter Lunt make an analogous argument by expanding upon Jürgen Habermas's conception of a separation between the life-world and system-world, that is, the differences between the organic knowledge derived from lived lives and that of the specialized knowledge produced within the professionalized and institutionalized logic of "the system." They contend that these shows "adopt an anti-elitist position which implicitly draws on . . . alternative epistemological traditions, offering a revaluation of the life-world, repudiating criticisms of the ordinary person as incompetent or ignorant, questioning the deference traditionally due to experts through their separations from the life-world and their incorporation into the system, and asserting instead the worth of the "common man.""[44] Livingstone and Lunt find these altered patterns to be so substantive that they read into the British media at large a tendency for movement "away from critical exposition and commentary. Letting ordinary people speak for themselves is replacing critically conscious social realism."[45]

The second conclusion from this literature is that contemporary talk shows are a distinctive field of discourse composed of intergeneric and cross-generic features where the boundaries between the "serious" and the "popular" or "entertaining" are increasingly blurred.[46] The reason this is possible, argues Wayne Munson, is that the talk show is a contingent and malleable form of programming—a hybrid, by definition. The talk show, he contends, "combines two communicative paradigms, and like the term itself, the 'talkshow' fuses and seems to reconcile two different, even contradictory, rhetorics. It links conversation, the interpersonal—the pre-modern oral tradition—with the mass-mediated spectacle born of modernity."[47] Within it, there is space for the creation of multiple points of audience identification, as well as the opportunity for programmers to "refresh" the televisual landscape. He argues,

> the talkshow mingles the "professional" or "expert" with the "amateur," the guest or participant who appears by virtue of particular personal experience or simple audience membership. It shrewdly combines the folk and the popular with the mass, the immediate and interpersonal with the mediated, in a productive dialectic that both reflects and constructs an image economy's "voracious need for change and innovation" and for "continually changing the rules, and replacing the scenery," as Andrew Ross puts it.[48]

The result of these changing and recombinatory forms is the fact that the audiences for such programming are increasingly "fragmented." Echoing Caldwell's claim that television producers sought to create new relationships with niche audiences who are flattered by claims of distinction, Andrew Tolson argues that there "is no longer the general 'popular' audience (targeted by mass advertising), but rather it is diversified into cults and cliques, characterized by different kinds of 'knowingness.'"[49]

In short, this literature illuminates features that would also become distinguishing characteristics of new political television. These features include the cross-generic construction of programming, the inclusion of "ordinary voices," the range of diverse positions presented, the challenge to "expert" authority, the informal conversational style, and the usage of a common vernacular and "common sense" thinking about issues and solutions that were traditionally approached through professional languages and knowledge. These features are important in that they offer a qualitatively different approach to the more paternalistic political discourse offered through pundit television. Combined with Caldwell's observations about stylistic excess in post-network television, programmers of the new populist brand of political television (discussed shortly) utilized angry political talk as a stylistic marker, a distinctive presentation of excess wrapped in the gadgetry and buzz of new communication technologies. Furthermore, viewers were flattered by a rhetoric that their voices mattered, and that America was waiting to hear what they had to say. A new relationship was built on viewer activity around the televisual text, rewarding the viewer as an "engaged" citizen as he or she helped construct the programming. Television's search for style, then, its search for a new and different look, actually opened up new modes of discourse and new forms of participation and presentation for political talk on television that had previously been ignored or disregarded.

VOX POP PROGRAMMING

Cable television in the mid-1990s gave birth to a handful of programs and channels offering an eclectic array of programming featuring audience-centered political talk. NBC, Multi-Media/Gannett, CNN, C-SPAN, and the Free Congress Foundation all constructed programs or entire cable channels dedicated to offering an "outsider" political voice in the mode of talk radio.[50] As a cheap form of programming, these groups attempted to ride the waves of success not only of talk radio, but also of the populist rhetoric of the anti-politics/anti-government groundswell and the buzz over new communication technologies. Indeed, cable programmers attempted to access these citizen/viewer dissatisfactions with politics via the promise of communication technologies, thereby allowing programmers to establish both stylistic and content changes relatively inexpensively while providing enormous potential for including its audience within the programming beyond talk radio's disembodied voices. Political commentary and opinions from viewing audiences could become part of the programming via e-mail, faxes, voice mail, phone calls, chat rooms, videoconferencing, and bulletin board systems. The stylish new programming also offered high-tech sets and gadgetry featuring fax machines, screen "crawls," computer screens, video kiosks in malls and shopping centers, and other visual displays of "the people's voice" in action.

As Caldwell argues, competition in the cable marketplace required these distinctive stylistic markers but also required an appeal for new and more significant relationships with viewers. The move to "the people's voice" in cable programming created different temporal and spatial relationships with viewing audiences as networks encouraged viewers to extend their participation in the program prior to, during, and after a particular show's airing by joining in discussions via chat rooms, bulletin boards, e-mail, and voice mail. In short, audiences were tired of elite-centered political and social discourse, cable network executives argued, and therefore were perceived as interested in consuming new forms of talk programming that included their own voices and concerns.

Efforts in this regard include NBC's attempt to exploit synergies between their broadcast and cable properties by creating America's Talking on July 4, 1994, a new channel dedicated to all-talk programming (which became MSNBC two years later). America's Talking (A-T) was NBC's effort to expand the limited talk television concept that it was featuring on CNBC during prime-time hours into an all-talk format. With talk radio's enormous popularity in mind, the network hired Roger Ailes, former Republican Party strategist and the executive producer of Rush Limbaugh's syndicated television program, to head both America's Talking and CNBC. As a result, Ailes brought the impulses he developed with Limbaugh to the new network, offering initial program lineups and an overall channel concept that mirrored the success Limbaugh was having with his "common man" persona and rage-against-the-liberal-system populism.

With programs like *Pork* (about government waste and corruption), *Bugged!* (billed as "primal scream therapy brought to you courtesy of the information superhighway"), and *Am I Nuts?* (about the stresses of everyday life), Ailes sought to construct the network as an outlet for the perceived frustrations viewers were supposedly experiencing with modern life.[51] He also emphasized that the network was "trying to represent real people."[52] A-T sought to position itself on the cutting edge of televisual difference by acting on the assumption that audiences don't passively watch television anymore but instead actively participate in constructing programming. Twelve of A-T's programs incorporated on-line bulletin boards, polling, electronic mail, and chat room services.[53] The linking of technology and populist politics was intended to flatter and involve a certain niche audience, thereby not waiting for an audience to appear, but in many ways attempting to create it.

The same populist impulse was seen in the programming of National Empowerment Television (NET), a small cable channel officially associated with the Free Congress Foundation—a conservative political organization founded by Republican party activist Paul Weyrich. NET launched on December 6, 1993, and was run as a tax-exempt, nonprofit entity. The primary purpose of the channel was not to make a profit, but to impact politics. Its mission was simple: empower people to hold (liberal) political elites accountable. That task would be achieved, they argued, first, by providing programming that would bypass the media elite, presenting their viewers "unbiased" and "truthful" information necessary to see the lies they were being told by mainstream media and elite politicians; and second, by providing the means—interactive call-in programming—through which Americans could "talk back to Washington" and thereby "put government on the defensive."[54] "Our bent is populist," proclaimed Burton Pines, vice chairman of the network. "America has a grievance against Washington. We will be on America's side, not Washington's side."[55] The network sought to empower its viewers (and achieve their loyalty) primarily through its programming, 80 percent of which incorporated viewer call-ins. But as a network that arose alongside the conservative populism of Newt Gingrich et al. and the "Republican Revolution" of 1994, the network found that it could not sustain itself as those forces subsided, and ultimately it declared bankruptcy in January 2000.

One final example of the move toward featuring "outsider" audience voices in cable programming came from CNN. In an effort to bolster its afternoon ratings when no news stories merited extensive coverage, the network introduced *TalkBack Live* on August 22, 1994. *TalkBack* was a one-hour public affairs talk show that aired in the heart of CNN's afternoon schedule (3:00 P.M. EST), and sought the traditional town hall meeting as its romantic corollary. Upon its launch, CNN argued that the program would create a national forum for dialogue, a place to build bridges and seek commonality, a place where publics could interact with policy makers who had power to "change things." Whereas America's Talking incorporated interactive technologies for both stylistic and populist purposes, *TalkBack* embraced a rhetoric of democratic utopianism—technology as a means of reviving democracy, providing access to power, and bringing the nation closer together. "The point is to re-create an old-time town meeting using the most advanced technology to create a connection that I think we lack," said Teya Ryan, the show's executive producer.[56] "People are interested not simply in what the experts have to say, but what their fellow Americans have to say," she noted elsewhere.[57]

Like America's Talking, *TalkBack* would employ numerous technological vehicles to incorporate the lay voice into the program, including phone calls, electronic mail, faxes, videoconferencing, and chat groups. The show's original host, Susan Rook, argued, "This is 'Crossfire' for real people."[58] The studio set was built to visually represent the interactive nature of the program (as well as effectively merge the spheres of business, consumption, and politics into one seamless whole). Constructed in the atrium lobby of CNN Center in downtown Atlanta, the set would seat up to 150 people, including tourists, shoppers, workers, and local residents. In addition to a live audience, the program integrated the voices and messages of viewers at home by including a table in the middle of the set with a ten-line telephone, a fax machine, and computer terminal. Producers off-screen would also integrate viewer opinions and questions via video remotes and on-line comments while allowing faxes to pop out of the machine on stage.[59]

As both the populist and techno-euphoric mood of the country receded substantially by the turn of the century, the overt rhetoric of angry voters, town hall meetings, alienation from Washington, and electronic democracy largely left with it. With *TalkBack Live*'s cancellation on March 7, 2003, only C-SPAN's morning call-in show, *Washington Journal*, has survived as a program solely dedicated to interactive viewer participation centered on politics.[60] What this discussion offers, however, is insight into how cable television programmers attempted to exploit the mood and context of the moment, and in turn challenged the normative conceptions of who gets to speak about politics on television and what will be spoken about. America's Talking, National Empowerment Television, and *TalkBack Live* altered the landscape by insisting that the audience was not simply to be spoken to, but also to be spoken with. The audience was welcomed into the conversation and flattered—not only for what they know, but also for their technological savvy and abilities to connect to information and share it with others. Television had finally asserted that politics isn't just what occurs inside the beltway but rather is also what people make of it in their daily experiences and activities of living. These programs and channels were venues, according to the producers, where citizens could express themselves, connect to power and to each other, and create political change. Each of these three encouraged, to various degrees, an "us versus them" approach in attracting disaffected audiences to political talk—a marked change from the pundits' assumption of a public as a singular "us."[61]

THE TRANSFORMATION OF CABLE NEWS

Perhaps the most substantial and lasting legacy of Vox Pop programming is the stunning success of Roger Ailes and his progenerative influence on the transformation of cable news programming. When America's Talking became MSNBC in 1996, Ailes left the network to become programming chief at Fox News. Whereas he had generally failed to capitalize on efforts to feature conservative, populist, and bombastic rhetoric with *The Rush Limbaugh Show* and America's Talking, here he found success by cloaking it in the mantle of journalistic "objectivity." Featuring overtly conservative talk shows and ideologically biased news reporting, the network nevertheless branded itself "Fair and Balanced." The network also retained its alignment with "the people" from Ailes's Vox Pop days by using slogans such as "we report, you decide" in its promotional materials. In some ways, the network hasn't shied from the conservative label placed on it by critics because it argues that "the American people" believe the news media is liberal, and hence the network is offering a corrective choice.[62]

Since 1996, Fox News, CNN, and MSNBC have been the leading networks featuring political talk programming on cable,[63] largely depending on talk to support the bottom line. The reason, of course, is that hard news reporting is expensive to produce. Though broadcast networks historically absorbed news programming costs (so great a money loser that news divisions were dubbed "loss leaders"), cable news networks don't have that luxury. Hence, as competition between the three quickly ramped up, the networks turned to talk as a cheap means of filling a 24-hour programming schedule.[64] In short, what has occurred is that these "news" channels actually program more hours of talk shows than news.

What Ailes unleashed, then, was a full-frontal attack on the long-running understanding that television news should center on the reporting of information, doing so in a fair, unbiased, and nonpartisan manner. Instead, Fox News showed just how ruthlessly it would pursue audiences and broader conservative ideological dominance by playing on audience fears and desires for retribution following the September 11, 2001, terrorist attacks. It also became the ratings leader by doing so. The political mood of the country had changed from one of know-it-all viewers in a robust America to a public desperate for answers after one of the most puzzling and disturbing events in American history.[65] Placing American flag banners in the corner of each screen, Fox embraced the flag and its own patriotic hubris to establish an emotional connection with viewers by cheerleading the Bush administration's "War on Terror," employing the same "us versus them" rhetoric of the Vox Pop days, only now with a different "enemy." The "people's voice" would be that of Bill O'Reilly, with his rhetoric of "common sense" and his use-and-abuse style with guests who just don't get it. Similarly, the people's voice would also be Geraldo Rivera, the surrogate American qua Fox News reporter rummaging through the caves of Tora Bora, Afghanistan, with a pistol on his hip as he sought to hunt down Osama bin Laden himself! In sum, Fox News may operate under the label of "news," but the excessive style of discursive spectacles (whether through lay or expert voices, screaming hosts, or roving reporters) and the alignment with and flattering of the viewing public (through e-mails and studio audiences, ideological sensibility, or patriotic zeal) is ultimately just political talk programming with a different name.

When the ravages of the Bush years had begun to take hold in the public's mind and the Democratic Party was swept back into legislative power in the fall of 2006, Fox News's ratings generally followed the declining popularity of President Bush and Vice President Dick Cheney in the waning years of their administration. During the 2008 presidential election, in particular, Fox's spectacle performance of Republican Party cheerleading was no match for viewer excitement over two historic candidates for the nomination of the Democratic Party.[66] Beginning in 2007 but rapidly gaining steam in 2008, MSNBC was finally able to craft a successful brand identity by featuring a full line-up of liberal talk show hosts in its prime-time hours with programs such as *Hardball with Chris Matthews, Countdown with Keith Olbermann*, and eventually, *The Rachel Maddow Show*.[67] MSNBC proudly became the location for news viewers' disgust and discontent with the Bush presidency yet also hope for a Democratic administration. It was easy to argue (as some critics did) that MSNBC and Fox had become opposite sides of the same coin in featuring ideological talk that flattered their audiences by tending to the audience's emotions. The turn to partisanship suggested that both were incapable of "reporting" political "reality" fairly and accurately.[68]

Contention over the overt partisanship of the two networks (which both networks maintain only appears in its prime-talk talk programming, not its news reporting) spilled into the presidential contest as Democrats refused to allow Fox News to host a Democratic Party debate due to its perceived biases.[69] Similarly, delegates and party officials at the Republican National Convention openly lashed out at NBC News—the mother network for MSNBC—by arguing that it was tainted by the same liberalism that dominated the cable network.[70] Thus, while all cable news networks greatly benefited from a campaign that attracted an enormous amount of viewer interest (especially CNN), the question remained as to what these ideologically competitive news networks would look like after the intense partisan struggle subsided.[71]

The answer turned out to be more of the same. In the Obama era, Fox News surged back to the top as ratings leader (which it briefly surrendered to CNN during the campaign) by producing a full-throated ideological war on Barack Obama and his administration within days of his assuming office.[72] The network upped the ideological ante by offering a new brand of xenophobic host, Glenn Beck, who eerily summoned a deranged Howard Beale (from the movie *Network*) with his "mad as hell and we're not going to take it anymore" riff on the supposed threat to American society and values posed by the new administration of "socialists" *and* "fascists."[73] Beck quickly became a ratings success by adroitly crafting a potent cocktail of familiar televisual styles, combining the rage of Bill O'Reilly, the emotionalism of televangelist Jimmy Swaggert, the theatrics of Geraldo Rivera, and the salesmanship of a ShamWow infomercial into a hysterical rhetoric of impending doom. What made Fox's move all the more surprising was that Beck didn't appear in the prime-time hours (as with the networks' other overtly ideological talk-show hosts). Instead, he was featured during the traditional daytime news hour—5:00 P.M. (EST).

On MSNBC, liberal host Rachel Maddow, a former Air America Radio host and the first openly lesbian host of a political talk show, attracted a huge following for her prime-time show that was launched concurrent with the election of Barack Obama. Maddow is, in many ways, Glenn Beck's opposite, holding a PhD from Oxford University, and is a self-professed policy wonk who quickly proved herself capable of all manner of political discussions, as perhaps shown best in her interview with Obama where they discussed the finer points of updating America's electrical grid.[74] At CNN, however, the network dipped to fourth in prime-time ratings (behind its own Headline News channel), finding that while its ideological middle-of-the-road approach was favored during election season, it wasn't so popular with routine cable news viewers who tune in nightly for a review of the day's stories through partisan lenses.

In sum, the cable news networks have produced a direct challenge to the traditional definition of television news. Ideology (if not partisanship) is often front and center, while talk and opinion (not reporting) dominates their brands. Rather than using their expanded programming schedule (24-hours, as opposed to the networks' 30-minute newscasts) to offer in-depth reporting, the cable nets have shown that it is partisan talk that draws the largest audience. As with the Vox Pop era, here too the networks' primary political voices are defined by political outsiders—a former Miss America as morning news host on *Fox & Friends* (Gretchen Carlson); radio talk-show personalities transposed to television (Glenn Beck, Sean Hannity, and Rachel Maddow); a former tabloid news anchor (Bill O'Reilly); and a former sports news host (Keith Olbermann)—almost all of whom engage in the excessive style described by John Thornton Caldwell. Furthermore, as the broadcast networks have largely abandoned most coverage of ritual politics outside of major events (such as presidential debates, election night, and State of the Union speeches), the cable news nets have become the primary location for political news coverage on television. In short, it is this transformed conception of what defines "news" that now constitutes the vast majority of daily political programming in the post-network era.

CONCLUSION

What the history of political talk on television demonstrates is that the arbitrary boundaries between political experts and non-experts are now much more fluid, and the variety of ways in which programs intentionally recognize and flatter their audiences have greatly increased from the earlier model of political talk programming. Whether the exaggerated claims of political "empowerment" for viewers by "talking back" to power made by Vox Pop producers in the mid-1990s were ever achieved is questionable. What did occur in the process, however, is a reformulation by television producers and audiences of what counts as desirable and attractive political talk on television. The spectacle performance of agonistic and partisan politics thus took root in the success of these transformed "news" networks. But as the next chapter explores, two entertainment talk shows with politics clearly at the center of the discussions were also born during the Vox Pop era. In many respects, they paved the way for the acceptance of entertaining political programming as a meaningful and alternative form of audience engagement with politics. Such forms of "new political television" would eventually serve as an antidote to the spectacle performance of politics that cable news networks regularly produce. That is, fake news and fake pundit talk would turn out to be the perfect means for addressing and critiquing the excesses of cable news, not to mention rogue politicians and Wall Street bankers.

4

New Political Television

Questioning News Media's Regime of Truth

Every society, Michel Foucault argues, has a "regime of truth" that is composed of "the types of discourse it harbours and causes to function as true; the mechanisms and instances which enable one to distinguish true from false statements, the way in which each is sanctioned; the techniques and procedures which are valorized for obtaining truth; the status of those who are charged with saying what counts as true."[1] For much of the twentieth century, the news industry served as a primary institution in America's regime of truth. The discourse it produced was called "news," based on its supposedly "objective" reporting techniques and procedures designed to convey impartial ideological commitments. This discourse is what society "cause[d] to function as true," and society granted a special status to the news industry as the primary arbiters of truth in public life (especially in regards to politics). This includes their central role in helping formulate a public understanding of political reality through their reporting, but also through the political discourse conducted and moderated in public affairs talk shows. Journalists and reporters were granted special access into the public's homes and into the halls of power, and given special authority in establishing and sanctioning discourses of truth. They often reified that monopoly position by reminding society of the vital role they play in mediating reality, including an indexical relationship to reality, perhaps captured best in their rhetoric of holding a "mirror to the world."

But what happens if that special access and authority are denied? What if nonjournalist media actors began criticizing the premise entirely, showing the weaknesses that are produced through such a system? What if citizens were to demote news from its privileged place in their homes or challenge its monopoly status by turning to other discourses and means of arriving at truth (such as those found on the Internet)? And what if government officials also challenged that monopoly by elevating other sources (such as radio talk show hosts or fake reporters) and including other means for establishing and disseminating truth (i.e., through more proactive information management across media outlets and platforms)? Just such a questioning of journalism's regime of truth, I contend, has been underway for much of the first decade of the twenty-first century, as government authorities, new media actors, and active audiences have all begun challenging (directly or indirectly) journalism's central status in this regard.[2]

This chapter focuses our attention on the ways in which new forms of political entertainment television have not only participated in that challenge but also been the leading players in mounting that challenge on television. As noted in the introductory chapter, the term "new political television" is employed to designate those forms of political entertainment television that have refashioned television's fundamental relationship to politics by contributing to, rewriting, and directly challenging what constitutes political talk and news. This includes the ways in which new political television programs have directly questioned the news media's status as the primary programmer of televised political talk, the integrity of their reportorial techniques for encoding reality, and their credibility as nonpartisan interpreters of politics. The chapter examines the appearance of humorous political talk shows, as well as fake news and talk shows, that have offered alternative means of making sense of political reality while directly and indirectly questioning the vaunted place of journalism as the primary arbiter of political truth for viewing publics.

The development and evolution of political entertainment television has occurred in roughly three phases. The first phase (1993–2001) saw the rise of two groundbreaking humorous political talk shows—*Politically Incorrect with Bill Maher* on Comedy Central and *Dennis Miller Live* on HBO—during the Vox Pop phase of cable innovation described in the previous chapter. These shows were instrumental in bridging the subgenres of late-night entertainment talk and political pundit talk, and in many ways, ignited the current popularity and acceptability of entertaining politics as a programming form on American television. Less commercially successful but politically and satirically important nonetheless was Michael Moore's two fake newsmagazine programs, *TV Nation* and *The Awful Truth*, both of which also appeared during this timeframe. Moore crafted a fine satirical edge with his programs, demonstrating how fake news could be used penetrate the façades of power and make a pointed political critique, all with a laugh and devious smile (discussed in chapter 7).

The second phase (2001–2006) was brought on by a changed political climate resulting from the terrorist attacks of September 11 and the increasing realization of the stark and shocking realities presented by a roguish presidential administration.[3] The humorous political talk shows of the Clinton era left the air and were replaced in cultural significance by a fake news program, *The Daily Show with Jon Stewart*. Fake news proved to be a more appropriate form of satirical television for the critical interrogation of the falsities presented by both the government and television news media, especially at a time in which political speech was policed for its (in)appropriate level of patriotism during wartime. Bill Maher also returned to television, recognizing perhaps that it was time for him to "get real" with his political talk and commentary, launching a talk show called *Real Time*. A fake pundit talk show, *The Colbert Report*, also launched during this time, furthering the popularity and success of the fake news/talk genre. The show set its satirical sights on "truthiness" (emotion as reason) in public life as crafted by right-wing talk show pundits and government authorities.

In the last phase of genre development (2007–present), cable news networks (as well as Comedy Central) have attempted to capitalize on the popularity of the form by offering their own imitations and derivatives of fake news or entertaining political talk such as *The ½ Hour News Hour* (Fox News), *D. L. Hughley Breaks the News* (CNN), *Chocolate News* (Comedy Central), and *Huckabee* (Fox News). What they produced, however, was programming that is fundamentally unrelated to their predecessors. By offering little to no critical perspective, these shows not only represent the worst aspects of television's entertainmentization of public affairs, but also contribute to the continued transformation of cable news into little more than politainment networks. In what is yet another blow to journalism's regime of truth (not to mention integrity), it is instructive to note that this degradation of political talk and commentary has come not from entertainment channels or divisions, but largely at the hands of news media itself.

HUMOROUS POLITICAL TALK

The industrial and contextual forces of the early post-network era described in the previous chapter—intensive competition, excessive style, flattered audiences, cross-genre experimentation, the challenge to expert authority, and the inclusion of outsider or ordinary voices—were also at play when two cable networks, Comedy Central and HBO, made the programming decision to reformulate that mainstay of late-night television, the entertainment talk show. Beginning with *Politically Incorrect* in 1993 on Comedy Central, followed a year later by *Dennis Miller Live* on HBO, both networks were looking for distinctive original programming that would attract viewers, critical attention, and increased cable carriage. In so doing, they turned to two sharp-witted comedians—Bill Maher and Dennis Miller—and granted them the license to bend the inherited rules of entertainment talk and craft a new model by melding politics with humor. The end result was successful programs that ran for nine years each, and in the process, helped ignite a significant change in the relationship between politics and entertainment television, between popular culture and political culture.

Dubbed the "McLaughlin Group on Acid" in its early promotional materials, *Politically Incorrect* was a half-hour program (initially appearing weekly, but increased to five days in its third season) that featured Bill Maher and four non-experts on politics discussing political and social matters of the day. This hybrid political-entertainment talk show featured a no-holds-barred approach to politics designed to live up to the show's name. *Politically Incorrect* was the first signature show for the young comedy network (itself forming in 1991), helping to define the channel beyond its standard fare of stand-up comedy routines, stale B-movies, and sketch comedy reruns. The show featured an array of comedians, actors, and actresses, but also various public persons such as authors, politicians, journalists, activists, and sports and music stars, discussing topics introduced by Maher. The novelty of having famous people, few of whom were political experts, talking about something other than their latest project, was considered its draw for audiences and the guests who increasingly requested to be on the show. The show invited viewers to identify and link names and faces seen in other public forums with the guests' opinions on politics and social issues. As such, the show did not stand apart from other media and cultural offerings. Culture and politics mixed, and audiences were encouraged not to see the arbitrary boundaries traditionally constructed between the two. Instead, audiences could relate these texts to other things that confer meaning in their lives, such as tastes in music and literature, political issues, sources of information, or simple life experiences. Indeed, I argue, it is this type of fundamental conjoining of popular culture and politics that represents the fundamental shift in political programming on television that shows like *Politically Incorrect* (*PI*) helped introduce.

Because the majority of guests were not political experts, they tended to utilize the same means for making sense of public issues as the viewing audience. Specifically, they discussed politics in a language resembling more of what would be found in a bar, basement, or barbershop than what occurs at the National Press Club or on *Meet the Press*—a common vernacular that is accessible and familiar. Furthermore, the guests apply more commonsensical notions to what politics *means* than the conventional elite discourse on television that is largely derived from insider knowledge and concerned with political maneuverings. As social psychologist Michael Billig argues, common sense is a means through which publics think through and discuss deeper "ideological dilemmas" that often lie at the heart of public issues and events.[4] Part of that freedom to think and talk in commonsensical terms is the opportunity to make fun of or satirize both politicians and other guests who "just don't get it." Humor, often lacking on most political talk shows, became an important tool of political critique, especially when political events became absurd or surreal (e.g., the Clinton-Lewinsky scandal and the 2000 presidential election).

Maher made it clear that the program was specifically designed as a response to the type of television talk shows that irritated him. "The genesis for this show," Maher noted, "comes in some ways from my frustration with doing talk shows over the past ten years and always being shoved away from controversial material."[5] When Maher pitched the program idea to producers, therefore, he says he "sold the idea that there wasn't anything that lived up to being a talk show. Talk shows had become boring, publicity-driven promotional shows with one guest at a time. They were missing the two biggest areas of humor: the connection of guests and controversial subjects."[6] Maher wanted a show in which guests would interact with each other, and that interaction would be based on things in life that actually matter.

Like other cable news and talk channels, *PI*'s ratings were best when breaking news or controversial issues had arisen for public discussion. The Oklahoma City bombing and the O. J. Simpson murder trial were favorite topics of discussion for many shows in the early years. The scandal associated with President Clinton's affair with White House intern Monica Lewinsky (and Clinton's subsequent impeachment) dominated much of the conversation in the middle of the show's run. Maher was a persistent and aggressive supporter of Clinton during the controversy, and the subject's mixture of sex and politics proved perfect for entertaining late-night discussions. The discussions on *PI* were unusual, however, because they more closely resembled public opinion on the scandal than the political talk found on most pundit political talk shows during the controversy (the subject of chapter 5). And during the show's final years, it was the terrorist attacks of 9/11 that not only shaped the content but also influenced much of the show's more somber tenor and tone.

The program moved to ABC in January 1997 to become a post-*Nightline* companion show for the network. ABC thought the program would work well because of its topicality and interest in public affairs, while also allowing the network to tap the 18–49 age demographic that advertisers desire in the late-night market (more so than *Nightline*). By jumping from cable to network, the show was able to reach ten times the audience it had on Comedy Central while offering essentially the same show in the same format with little to no interference from network censors. It thereby gave the program (and this new genre of political entertainment television) much greater visibility. From 1999–2000, the show began sporadically featuring a "Citizen Panelist." Fulfilling one of the show's top viewer requests for a "regular" citizen to appear on the panel, Maher and his staff visited cities across the nation conducting tryouts at affiliate stations for a local citizen (the "average Joe or Jane") to win a guest spot on the show. The frequency of such requests seems to represent, along with the popularity of the show itself (which averaged around 3 million viewers), a yearning or desire by viewers to see themselves "represented" in this seemingly free-form version of televised political discourse (as discussed in chapter 10). That is, although viewers appreciated the celebrities and stars that supplied their opinions, they also wanted to see one of "their own" (perhaps even projecting themselves in that role) duke it out with Maher and the others.

In sum, *Politically Incorrect* began as the product of a cable channel's need for an identity in a competitive cable environment and as a comedian's jab at sanitized public discourse in an era of political correctness. But through its nine-year run, the show proved that political talk on television was no longer the exclusive domain of news divisions and broadcast networks, and that elite sources of political content did not necessarily speak to or for many audience members. Highlighting the populist politics popular at the time, the show challenged the notion that only "experts" (e.g., journalists and policy wonks) had the right to talk about politics on television, and overtly highlighted the fact that politics is as much performance and theater as anything else. In the end, *PI* represents the television talk show as a truly combinatory form, a hybrid blend of politics and social issues, humor and serious discourse, comedic monologues and group discussions, celebrities and less well-known public personalities, and lay and elite discourse.

HBO embarked on its own approach to reinventing the comedy talk show with the introduction of *Dennis Miller Live* in 1994. As the subscription network searched for ways to increase its original offerings in the early 1990s, the comedy talk show became a logical vehicle for such experimentation and brand differentiation, providing familiar material to viewing audiences yet also advancing the genre beyond the tired formula of celebrity product pitches, scripted interactions between host and guests, and the ubiquitous house band and musical sidekick. Although the show included such traditional features as a comedic monologue and interviews with celebrity guests, it is there that the relationship to the Steve Allen–Johnny Carson–Jay Leno brand of late-night talk show ends. With no concerns for offending advertisers due to "controversial" political material and no strictures on the language allowed, Dennis Miller went on to develop a successful talk show persona as an opinionated sociopolitical commentator with a no-holds-barred approach to what could or should be said about the state of the world. The result was a show that was opinionated without being predictable, political without being boring, and entertaining without being formulaic.

HBO Downtown Productions, an affiliated production company, helped create *Politically Incorrect* for Comedy Central in 1993, and the mother network subsequently witnessed the critical success of that program. HBO then contracted with comedian Dennis Miller for a 30-minute political comedy talk show airing live on Fridays at 11:30 P.M. Miller had just come off a failed attempt at a syndicated talk show, but was better known for his work on *Saturday Night Live* from 1986 to 1991. *Dennis Miller Live*, which debuted on April 22, 1994, similarly focused on Miller's strengths as a caustic and biting commentator on the day's events. His HBO show brought him out from behind the news and talk show desk. With Miller standing center stage, the show opened with a monologue of comedic material largely based on headline news stories and bizarre news oddities. The lack of regulation on language, though, gave Miller's acerbic wit an added punch due to his notorious potty-mouth. The jokes blended with Miller's strong-willed and pointed commentary with little differentiation between the two. Johnny Carson once said, "I just don't feel Johnny Carson should become a social commentator. . . . If you're a comedian, your job is to make people laugh. You cannot be both serious and funny."[7] Yet Miller took the opposite approach.

This is seen most clearly in the next feature of the program, the five-minute segue between the monologue and the guest interview known as the "rant." Miller began by saying, "Now I don't want to get off on a rant here, but . . .," and then proceeded to soliloquize on that evening's topic of discussion, covering over the course of the show's run topics as disparate as drugs, affirmative action, homosexuality, fame, and civil disobedience. As a once-weekly program, the topics for comment and discussion were broader political and social issues than the daily events or news that composed *Politically Incorrect*. Therefore, Miller's engagement with politics was at an expansive level, removing his commentary from a focus on micro-events to the larger sweeps of political life, giving the rant a more prophetic quality as a result.

Yet Miller built upon a self-described basic level of political intelligence by crafting himself as a savvy and intellectual guy who offered a mix of literary and cultural references that expects a similar level of sophistication and knowledge from the audience. Furthermore, his main point of reference was usually popular culture, not political history. In explaining the battles between the Republican Party and Bill Clinton in the 1990s, for instance, he makes his point by invoking a popular children's cartoon, a Hollywood movie, and a television show from the 1960s:

> But you've got to feel sorry for the Republicans. They're constantly painting fake tunnels on the sides of cliff walls, only to see President Clinton somehow beep-beep right through them. See, Clinton is like the bad guy in *Terminator 2: Judgment Day*, able to assume the shape and voice of his enemies to get what he needs. He appropriated Republican ideas, added a little dash of his inimitable dewy-eyed "Bubba" magic, and presto! The next thing you know, ol' Jed's a millionaire.

After the rant, Miller would bring on a guest to discuss the topic he had just introduced. Sometimes the guest would have a connection to the topic (such as former U.S. Surgeon General Dr. Jocelyn Elders on teen pregnancies) and sometimes the visitor would discuss something entirely different (as with Jon Stewart on bad habits). Although most of the guests were celebrities, they were not appearing to pitch their latest media projects but to talk about the issue at hand. As with the rant, there was no segregation between serious talk (like Oprah) and entertaining talk (like Letterman). And following the populist impulse of alternative talk shows at that time (as well as to signal the show's "liveness"), he even took phone calls from viewers at home.

What Miller ultimately offered the audience was himself as an intelligent and humorous commentator on politics who was unafraid to state openly and honestly how and why he thinks the world is, in his words, fucked up. In the process, he stood both traditional talk show comedy and political punditry on their heads. His signature verbal essay didn't wait for the audience to laugh, didn't care if it offended, wasn't assured that the audience would get it, and wasn't afraid to be politically direct and committed. He treated his audience with respect by assuming they would get it, and that they too are a mix of disappointed yet hopeful citizens. The expletive-laced commentary linked the language of contemporary stand-up comedy found in comedy clubs and on cable television with the late-night talk show, but suggests that both late-night comedy and political punditry could benefit from the real and honest language that curse words seemingly afford in communicating with some audiences.

Miller, like his comic sage predecessors before the creation of television, inverted traditional punditry by contending that a political commentator need not be a master of every subject and that a common sense understanding of right and wrong was all the currency one needed to point out political and social idiocy. Politics is not just a special preserve for those who traffic in insider knowledge and employ a specialized language. Instead, Miller showed that he had enough sense to get the big picture and then translate that into a popular vernacular that audiences could understand. As he used them, the pop culture references are what produce both comedy and clarity, for culture more than politics is ultimately what the audience really knows and understands.[9] As Lawrence Grossberg argues, popular culture is where our affective investments are in late modern culture, the major points of location on our "mattering maps."[10] Finally, the "truth" offered is neither singular nor forced down the viewer's throat. Instead, it is just an opinion, one that viewers are invited to take or leave. And this is perhaps Miller's defining accomplishment as a comedic political commentator—he assumed that audience members cared enough about public life to tune in, were smart enough to know what he is talking about to laugh, would make the connections between the intertwined spheres of public and private life, and then make up their own minds.

Dennis Miller Live finally went dark on August 30, 2002. As a transformative television show, the program demonstrated that substantive conversations could occur in a 30-minute time-slot while still including comedy routines. It also showed that a comedy program could focus on a single topic of discussion with a single guest, and that audiences were interested in political talk from someone other than the inside-the-beltway crowd. Together, *Dennis Miller Live* and *Politically Incorrect* were pioneers in the development and eventual critical acceptance of the merger of entertainment talk shows with political talk. A 1994 article in *Time* magazine that appeared near the beginning of Miller's run and just as Maher's show kicked off its second season pointed out just what these shows could contribute to television:

> In an era when most comedians are too cool to care, here's an odd twist: the two best stand-up comics on TV are the ones who have ventured most boldly into the political arena. Not the easy-to-take, non-partisan "topicality" of Leno and Letterman, but informed, savvy, opinionated comedy about real issues. . . . These two comics read the whole newspaper—not just the funny clippings their writers collect for them. . . . "We will strive," said Miller on his first show, "to be in the vanguard of the movement to irresponsibly blur the line between news and entertainment." Finally, two comedians who actually know the difference.[11]

At that point in their careers, both Maher and Miller did not see themselves as "political" humorists and certainly not experts on politics. But they both insisted that any citizen had the right to talk about political life, even if for entertainment purposes. Furthermore, entertainment talk shows *and* political talk shows, in their estimation, had lost all relevance as meaningful forms of television, with both forms offering scripted and predictable encounters. From Maher's political incorrectness to Miller's rants, both comedians bust open the doors of political talk, challenging normative conceptions of acceptable political discourse, including who exactly was allowed to talk about politics in the first place.

Around the same time as these shows' debut, NBC offered a summer replacement program called *TV Nation* in July, 1994. Written and produced by Michael Moore, the show was cast as a satirical fake newsmagazine program in the vein of *60 Minutes* and *20/20*. It too was a product of television programmers (this time, the broadcast networks NBC and FOX) believing that the populist political impulse of the era could be captured and packaged as entertainment programming. Who better than the self-appointed "everyman" who had made himself a celebrity and commodity in the documentary *Roger & Me* to wage a satirical attack on corporate greed and

government malfeasance? Moore used the fake news genre to address many
of the left-wing issues that were not fully addressed during the conservative
Clinton era (such as gun control, corporate malfeasance, the death penalty,
and health care). Furthermore, Moore's programs called attention to the
ways in which debate, deliberative exchange, and disagreement are easily
repressed by the techniques of public relations. The newsmagazine format
gave license to engage in investigative reporting, while the fake gave license
to satire it. And as we will see (chapter 7), many of its fake reporting and
interview techniques were later employed by other fake news programs that
would follow—namely *The Daily Show* and *The Colbert Report*.

Finally, this era also saw the birth of Comedy Central's *The Daily Show*
(*TDS*) in 1996. First hosted by Craig Kilborn, the program was not focused
initially on news media or politics. Only with the arrival of host Jon Stewart
in 1999 did the program venture more clearly into topical events and political matters. That timing was fortuitous, as the 2000 presidential election
became Stewart's coming out party. *The Daily Show*'s coverage of the election through its "Indecision 2000" segments—including sending faux news
correspondents to the two political party conventions—continued Comedy
Central's interest in mining the political for laughs, dating back to the network's election coverage from 1992. For the first time, however, the show
began to enjoy some level of respectability as a commentator on politics.[12]
When *TDS*'s correspondents received press passes to cover the Republican
National Convention, Bill Hilary, the executive vice president of Comedy
Central, exclaimed in surprise, "People are taking us seriously, even though
we're a comedy show. For the first time, they're saying 'The Daily Show' has
a place in social commentary." Stewart, on the other hand, was less amazed
about his supposed new role: "The whole point of our show is that we're a
fake news organization. What's more appropriate than going to a fake news
event? Everybody knows it's a trade show."[13]

As the campaign became increasingly bizarre—a robotic Al Gore trying
on multiple fake personas and George W. Bush's "subliminable" advertisements and gaffe-laden remarks when moving off script—the fake news
show was handed a wealth of material with which to work satirically.
Although the network had used the moniker "Indecision" in its coverage
of previous presidential elections, the naming could not have been more
appropriate for the surreal outcome that would follow. With concurrent
legitimate and illegitimate ballots (Florida), winners (the electoral college
versus the popular vote), and outcomes (the 5–4 Supreme Court decision
determined along party lines), "reality" increasingly became difficult to
define or locate as the absurdities of the process seemed ever more constructed, arbitrary, and chaotic. Thus, a fake news show became, at times, a
legitimate substitute or supplement to its cousins on the other cable channels. The show's co-executive producer, Madeleine Smithberg, would later

reflect on the show's fortuitous positioning: "Everything (in the campaign) became so absurd that the absurd people became the actual pundits. Jon Stewart is now a kind of recognized, viable pundit."[14] Although Smithberg might have overstated her case at that point, Stewart and *TDS* nevertheless emerged from the 2000 election with an air of respectability from a bewildered and punch-drunk audience who found that the court jester in the corner was making more sense than the traditional institutional voices that typically command center stage and interpretive authority on television. Stewart and the show were in perfect position for what would become a defining moment of the new century less than a year later.

FAUX NEWS MEETS FAKE NEWS

The terrorist attacks of September 11, 2001, were a turning point, obviously, for the American government, citizenry, and political culture, but also affected political entertainment television as well. Bill Maher made comments about the attack that were deemed unpatriotic and controversial, and he essentially lost his job as a result. Maher's fall began when, upon *PI*'s return to the air after a brief hiatus following the attacks, he and conservative panelist Dinesh D'Souza were discussing whether the Bush administration's labeling of the terrorists as "cowards" was an appropriate label. When D'Souza argued that the word was misplaced, Maher agreed saying, "We have been the cowards, lobbing cruise missiles from 2,000 miles away. That's cowardly. Staying in the airplane when it hits the building, say what you want about it, it's not cowardly." Although Maher was referring to American military conduct during the Clinton administration, one radio talk show host used the statement the following day to excoriate Maher as an unpatriotic traitor and called for a boycott of the two advertisements he remembered seeing after the segment. Although Maher attempted to clarify his statements in the days and weeks ahead, seventeen network affiliates eventually dropped the show, and two major advertisers—Sears & Roebucks and Federal Express—dropped their advertising. The comment even elicited a rebuke from White House Press Secretary Ari Fleischer saying that Americans "need to watch what they say" and that "this is not a time for remarks like that." Maher and others have suggested that this event was the final step in the show's demise, as Maher's contract was not renewed and *Politically Incorrect* subsequently went off the air in December 2002.

Dennis Miller, who rarely displayed any sort of political allegiance, much less ideological fervency, was radicalized by the event. His show on HBO ended its run in 2002 as planned, and he moved on to other things (notably, an odd stint with ABC's *Monday Night Football*). But when he returned to talk television in early 2004 with a new, *Politically Incorrect*–style talk show called *Dennis Miller* on CNBC, he had seemingly experienced, as one reporter put it, a right-wing "conversion" that has "led to zealotry" and "seems to have cost him his satiric instincts." He no longer offered the "savage commentaries about social hypocrisy" that he once did where "no one was safe," but instead had become a political partisan who seemed McCarthyesque in his obsession with liberals and liberal thinking (as the enemy within) during a time of war.[15]

The Daily Show with Jon Stewart thus stepped into the political-comedic void, providing more than just needed laughter to a nation traumatized by such brazen actions. Rather, the fake news program became the perfect format for questioning the faux "reality" that was increasingly being created through the manipulations, distortions, and outright lying of the Bush administration and a compliant, sloppy, and sensationalistic news media. This period was marked by a variety of public deceptions and "fake" news emanating from both government and the news media. These include Dan Rather's *60 Minutes II* (false) report on Bush's National Guard records during Bush's service in the Vietnam War; a variety of fabricated stories by *New York Times* reporter Jason Blair; the Bush administration's claims that weapons of mass destruction existed in Iraq (justifying the invasion); top-tiered and well-respected journalists such as Judith Miller (*New York Times*), Tim Russert (NBC), and Bob Woodward (*Washington Post*) playing along with the administration's stories in the run-up to that war; and the Bush administration widespread public relations campaign that paid at least three journalists and a PR firm to promote its policies on education, marriage, and prescription drugs through their reporting, syndicated columns, and fake video news releases.[16]

Furthermore, for over a decade, the nature of what constituted news and news reporting had changed as a result of the fierce competition among cable news outlets.[17] After 9/11, cable news had learned to merge the overly patriotic and sentimental packaging of its music, titles, and graphics that CNN first developed in the Gulf War of 1991 with the louder-brighter-faster graphics and sounds that Fox Sports had developed in its coverage of the NFL. The result was an array of televisual spectacles unlike anything seen in the history of television journalism. Fox News, in particular, darted to the front of the ratings pack with its overt flag-waving and patriotic pandering (as discussed in chapter 3). Stewart was dismayed. In regard to cable news reporting he noted, "They've so destroyed the fine credibility or the fiber that was the trust between the people and what they're hearing on the air."[18] Not only had the reporting become a prime example of the excessive style highlighted by John Thornton Caldwell's notion of televisuality, but it is a viable illustration of Jean Baudrillard's argument that publics are offered simulated reality, even hyperreality—imagery that is realer than real.[19] *The Daily Show* took it as its patriotic duty, so to speak, to parody, satirize, and ridicule these constructed falsities.

A second set of circumstances that greatly affected *TDS*'s content and direction was the Bush administration's "War on Terror" conducted at both the domestic and international levels. From actions by government officials that affected civil liberties domestically (such as illegal wiretapping and the detaining of American citizens as "enemy combatants") to the administration's unilateral decision to invade Iraq in pursuit of nonexistent weapons of mass destruction and "regime change," Stewart and *TDS*'s writers sought to poke holes in the government's legitimizing claims. Stewart was dumbfounded by the Bush administration's willingness to assert boldface lies and expect the public to believe them. He argued at that time,

> This administration, more than any other I've ever seen, is gaslighting us! Literally, it's raining on us, it's cloudy, and they go, "And on this sunny day"—No, it's not sunny. And they say, "Uh—this sunny day," and then you look at the backdrop they've got and it says sunny and they say, "See, sunny?" It's just a lie. They just don't acknowledge it. And by not acknowledging it, what they say becomes true![20]

Illuminating such lies became central to the show's moral mission. "What we try to do," Stewart contends, "is point out the artifice of things, that there's a guy behind the curtain pulling levers."[21]

But it was the confluence of these two forces—masterful information management techniques and fear-mongering by the Bush administration and a television news media that helped facilitate these political deceptions and ruses through its weak reporting and tendency toward patriotic spectacle—that made *TDS* the perfect vehicle for interrogating the truth.[22] Because news media are typically the primary social institution that democracies depend on for keeping a check on power, its abdication of that role left an opening. Thus it made complete sense for a fake *news operation* to step in to play the part (as explored in chapter 6). What is more, by donning the styles, conventions, and practices of a news organization, a simultaneous critique of the failed media practices is built into the form. Not only does the show skewer certain targets (such as politics) in the content of its "reporting," but the form itself demonstrates just how weak, ineffectual, and off-the-mark "real" television news organizations have become. For instance, *TDS* has mastered the art of using existing news footage, taken from the news organizations' own reporting, to offer visual evidence of the duplicity and mendacity of politicians. These can simply include running two video clips back-to-back that reveal the lie, or splicing together a series of misstatements politicians have made across months and years showing changes in position, repeated falsities, or vacuous talking points. The point here is that in doing so, *TDS* repeatedly *demonstrates* through its satire how seldom such basic "fact checking" occurs within real television news organizations, even when they already possess the evidence and means to do so themselves.

Instead of simply repeating what politicians say and, in effect, becoming willing or unwitting conduits for (dis)information, *TDS* has demonstrated how public affairs television can play a role in questioning and poking holes in public rhetoric without insisting that the audience adopt its own truths (beyond "the emperor might not be wearing clothes"). As Stewart has argued, "Our audience can watch without feeling like we're grabbing them by the lapels and shouting, 'This is the truth!' in their faces. Our show is about not knowing what the truth is."[23] Furthermore, Stewart realizes that these spectacle displays of truth manufactured from the interactions of politicians and news media are disorienting and dispiriting to the public. He has argued that one of the primary functions of his show is to provide a means of reorientation through satire. Satire, of course, need not be funny, but it does offer a form of communal evaluation and rebuke. One of the functions of his show, as he sees it, is embedded in this evaluation: "There are times when it's not about making a joke, it's about having to acknowledge what is going on so you can feel like you're still in the same world as everyone else."[24]

Stewart held true to his word when he appeared on the CNN's pundit talk show *Crossfire* on October 15, 2004, and offered an intentionally serious and unfunny critique of just how insidious such insider political talk had become. Hosted by Tucker Carlson and Paul Begala, the program's format featured two political experts with opposing ideological stances who debated each other and their political guests. When Stewart appeared, he immediately launched into his critique of the program, forthrightly telling the hosts to "stop hurting America" because what they do "is not honest. What you do is partisan hackery." Instead, he insisted, "you have a responsibility to the public discourse, and you fail miserably." When Carlson pushed back, suggesting that Stewart had no room to talk because of his supposedly timid questioning of Democratic presidential candidate John Kerry in a recent interview on Stewart's show, Stewart replied, "I didn't realize that...the news organizations look to Comedy Central for their cues on integrity. . . . If your idea of confronting me is that I don't ask hard-hitting enough news questions, we're in bad shape, fellows."[25]

The confrontational exchange between the political outsider and two insiders quickly became legend, as clips of the program circulated virally across the Internet. When CNN cancelled *Crossfire* less than two months later, it seemed that Stewart's critique was, if not directly responsible, certainly on target (as Jonathan Klien, president of CNN, himself admitted).[26] Beyond this obvious confrontation of political insiders and outsiders, the event demonstrated how new political television was more than just a new way for audiences to relate to and understand politics. Instead, it also brought to light the failures of older, traditional means of processing politics on television—that is, news and public affairs talk programming.

Instead of just doing so through his program, here Stewart delivered the message personally.

Stewart's appearance on *Crossfire* occurred during the 2004 presidential election. The campaign itself proved somewhat surreal, where truth and fiction often seemed at odds, and the news media often seemed unable to help citizens in their efforts to distinguish between the two. With the nation's military fighting two wars and with the Department of Homeland Security's color-coded threat warnings rising and falling in response to Bush's poll numbers, "gay marriage" somehow became one of the more important wedge issues in the race (what many observers consider was an effective mobilizing force in swing states).[27] In mounting a concerted critique of the Bush administration and its dubious claims leading to the Iraq War, it took a documentary film (a format that is rarely a mainstream media draw) by Michael Moore (*Fahrenheit 9/11*) to articulate and display many of the ideas and images that seemed missing from mainstream news. Furthermore, the Orwellian-named group "Swift Boat Veterans for Truth" (a collection of Vietnam veterans with a long history of antipathy toward John Kerry) was able to attack a war hero and effectively brand him a coward and a traitor. This confrontation provided one of the more bizarre challenges to what constituted facts, truth, and lies in the campaign. The well-financed group ran a series of advertisements questioning Kerry's service record in Vietnam, and in the process, produced an avalanche of free news coverage and interviews. The group's claims were eventually debunked as inaccurate, but not before a considerable amount of political damage accrued to Kerry while the accusations were played out *as if true* in the news media and across the Internet.

In a 2004 interview with ABC's *Nightline* anchor Ted Koppel, Stewart debated the news media's handling of the Swift Boat incident and how it represents problems in journalism's ability to help society arrive at "truth."[28] Stewart critiqued the media for abdicating their duty to portray reality accurately, claiming instead that they had become little more than a conduit for the lies of political partisans. Koppel defended the press, arguing that journalists had offered the facts in this case (that these vets "were in Vietnam," that they "were on swift boats," and that "they are saying these things" now), even though he notes "the truth may not catch up for another week or two or six." Although Koppel admitted that the difference between facts and truth "is the great problem with journalism," he nevertheless contended that the truth will eventually be discovered. Stewart, on the other hand, sees a news media more committed to process, dutifully repeating what partisans say, however ridiculous or untruthful, and presenting the competing claims as "moral equivalents." This process, he argues, is the systemic vulnerability in the news media's methods for obtaining truth, even when that truth is readily available "in the public record." If facts, truth, and reality are the "god-terms" of journalism, as Barbie Zel-izer contends, then according to Stewart, the press needs to recognize that the first of these terms alone does not have a necessary relationship to the other two.[29] Furthermore, slavish devotion to certain factual reporting can create conditions where truth becomes lost in the process. In the contem-porary context of information management, the journalistic production of facts—a traditional defining feature of journalism—is simply no longer good enough, Stewart argues. That is the case because political players such as the Swift Boaters have learned to exploit the "vulnerability in the system" (as Stewart put it) of reporting the truth. "For the media to do an effective job," Stewart argues, "that vulnerability needs to be corrected. The media is getting creamed, and they need to take a more active role in safeguarding the public trust."

That trust has been lost, he argued elsewhere, because of the broader relationship that exists between news media and power politics.

> It's that the partisan mobilization [of the polity] has become part of the media process. That they realize that this real estate that you possess, television, is the most valuable real estate known to rulers. . . . The key to leadership is to have that mouthpiece to the people. And that's what this is. . . . This is the battle for the airwaves. And that's what [citizens] watch, and I think that's what's so dispiriting to those at home. . . . There's a sense here [within news organiza-tions] that you're not participating in that battle, and there's a sense at home that you're absolutely participating and complicit in that battle.[30]

Yet Stewart and *TDS* have garnered a level of credibility for "unfailingly polite but firm refusal to subscribe to anyone else's program," as *New York Times* columnist Frank Rich put it.[31] Perhaps that is why, in 2007, when a Pew Research Center poll asked respondents to name the journal-ist they most admired, Stewart was tied at number 4 with several news anchors from the broadcast networks.[32] Stewart recognizes this when, in the same interview with Koppel, he maintains that his credibility is the primary reason people watch his show. When Koppel asserts, "there are a lot of people out there who do turn to you for," but Stewart interrupts him to insist, "Not news. . . . For a comedic interpretation." But Koppel continues, "Well, they turn [to you] to be informed. They actually think that they're coming closer to the truth with your . . ." but again Stewart interrupts him to offer an alternative explanation: "That's credibility. That's a different animal."[33] Truth and the belief that what someone is telling you is the truth are two different things—something that journal-ists such as Koppel have seemingly forgotten in their insistence that the delivery of news and information is part and parcel of the establishment of "truth." Such a fallacy is questioned by John Hartley when he argues, "the fatal premise of news is this: that it simply imitates reality or nature;

it is transparent, representational and unconstructed. Therefore, so long as it avoids bias, remains impartial and sticks to plain facts in plain language, it is true, and can enforce its truth throughout the world."[34] What makes the premise "fatal" (as opposed to simply flawed) is that once society challenges the premise or stops believing it is accurate, the press increasingly finds its legitimacy as arbiter of truth in public life crumbling. Thus, it is here that Stewart must point out how contemporary political culture has changed the most—that audiences are increasingly finding old-line news media not credible, and are turning to sources like him for someone they believe is telling them the truth.

Jon Stewart and *The Daily Show* are perhaps most responsible for elevating the genre of new political television into a viable and credible source for interpretations, critiques, and "truth" about politics. While entertaining political talk shows such as *Politically Incorrect* and *Dennis Miller Live* thrust open the doors and allowed non-experts and laity into the political conversation, they never achieved the respect or critical acclaim that *TDS* has achieved. As the viewing public has increasingly cast a skeptical eye on traditional sources of political information and turned instead to alternative sources of information and truth (including blogs, websites, talk radio, and others), *TDS* has shown how entertainment television can play such a role as well. Though *TDS* uses the fake to interrogate falsities of public life, it is the resulting truths that emerge from such examinations that have made this show—and the genre itself—a valuable contribution to political culture.

Truthiness and Parodic Consequences

New political television took the questioning of the old media arbiters of truth one step further on October 17, 2005, with the debut of the faux pundit talk show, *The Colbert Report*, a *Daily Show* spin-off on Comedy Central. The show features Stephen Colbert cast in the persona of an egotistical yet ignorant right-wing talk show host, or as Colbert describes the character, "a well-intentioned, poorly informed, high-status idiot."[35] The show is constructed as a parody of cable talk shows and their hosts, such as Fox News's Bill O'Reilly (whom Colbert affectionately calls "Papa Bear"). But as Colbert explains, the persona also includes other such hosts on cable. "There's a little bit of Lou Dobbs," he notes, "where he rides the same story over and over again, the attention to sartorial detail like Anderson Cooper, absolutely bullheaded holding onto an idea, no matter how shallowly considered, like [Sean] Hannity, and almost a physical aggressiveness that O'Reilly has."[36] Colbert stays in this character for the entire show, including through his interview with guests, who good-naturedly play along with the parody. Colbert's program offers a simultaneous critique of the impassioned rhetoric and right-wing "thinking" proffered that has little relationship to facts or truth, but also the television cable news media that produce such irresponsible and spectacled political theatre in the first place.

On the program's debut episode, Colbert unveiled the word "truthiness" in "The WØRD" segment of the show (modeled on *The O'Reilly Factor*'s "Talking Points"), a made-up word that neatly summarizes many aspects of what the show parodies (what Colbert himself calls the show's "thesis statement").[37] The word refers to the elevation of feelings over facts, the tendency to act based on gut instincts instead of logic or evidence. As Colbert says in the episode, "We are [a nation] divided between those who think with their head, and those who *know* with their heart." Truth, he asserts, comes from the gut, and the people who subscribe to truthiness know what is true because it simply *feels* true. As he noted in the concluding comments of the segment, "The truthiness is: anyone can read the news to you. I promise to *feel* the news *at* you," neatly summarizing the essential motif of many cable news talk show hosts.[38] In an interview given out of character, he explains the point further. "These are all personality shows," he notes. "It doesn't matter what they're saying. Doesn't matter what the news is, it's how this person feels about the news, and how you should feel about the news. . . . I'm not playing it nearly as hard as someone like O'Reilly or Hannity does."[39] He goes on to explain that with truthiness,

> It doesn't seem to matter what facts are. It used to be, everyone was entitled to their own opinion, but not their own facts. But that's not the case anymore. Facts matter not at all. Perception is everything. It's certainty. People love [President Bush] because he's certain of his choices as a leader, even if the facts that back him up don't seem to exist.

According to Colbert, the will to truthiness lies at the heart of an essential authoritarianism present in the Bush administration and in political culture at large. After 9/11, the popular impulse was to adhere to the soothing calls emanating from the administration: "Listen to me, and just don't question, and do what I say, and everything will be fine." He continues, "So that's another part of truthiness. Truthiness is 'What I say is right, and [nothing] anyone else says could possibly be true.' It's not only that I *feel* it to be true, but that *I* feel it to be true. There's not only an emotional quality, but there's a selfish quality."[40]

A little more than six months after his program first aired, Colbert was invited to give the keynote at the White House Correspondents' Association Dinner, the annual meeting of Washington reporters and news media where the president, in attendance, is playfully teased by an invited comedian. Colbert, assuming that the event organizers understood his brand of ironic humor based in satire and parody (given his similar comedic persona for several years on *The Daily Show*), appeared in character and proceeded, in the early parts of his routine, to repeat many of the lines he had formulated in the truthiness segment of that first program. With the president and First Lady sitting a few feet away, Colbert launched into his character's egotistical ramblings, quickly identifying himself and the president as likeminded fellows, the embodiment of truthiness. "We're not so different, he and I," he states. "We get it. We're not brainiacs on the nerd patrol. We're not members of the Factinista. We go straight from the gut, right sir? That's where the truth lies, right down here in the gut."[41] Moments later, he skewered the president for his willingness to march forward undaunted by abysmal approval ratings, invoking the well-worn right-wing escape clause that if or when any fact arises that they don't like or makes them look bad, all they need to do is blame the biased "liberal media," thereby dismissing the uncomfortable fact as a partisan fabrication:

> Most of all, I believe in this president. Now, I know there are some polls out there saying this man has a 32% approval rating. But guys like us, we don't pay attention to the polls. We know that polls are just a collection of statistics that reflect what people are thinking in "reality." And reality has a well-known liberal bias.

Stephen Colbert performing at the White House Correspondents' Association Dinner in 2006 with a clearly irritated President George W. Bush looking on. With its harsh yet satirical criticisms of Bush and the Washington press corps, the performance quickly spread across the Internet by users hungry for such critical commentary and a good laugh. Mandel Ngan/AFP/Getty Images

By this point, the audience of observers realized that Colbert—a political "outsider"—was not playing by the unofficial rules that supposedly govern this light-hearted encounter of Washington insiders. Colbert was playing hardball, and the reaction shots of audience faces (including that of an irritated George W. Bush) captured on C-SPAN's broadcast of the event suggested a degree of wide-eyed disbelief, if not outright embarrassment. But Colbert marched forward in his unrelenting critique of the president, eventually wrapping up the first section of his performance by stating, "The greatest thing about this man is he's steady. You know where he stands. He believes the same thing Wednesday that he believed on Monday, no matter what happened Tuesday. Events can change; this man's beliefs never will." Colbert's portrayal of the president here is actually not too far from the truth, as the president himself has admitted his steadfast belief of sticking to your guns if you know in your heart that what you are doing is right, irrespective of other people's arguments to the contrary. But the portrayal is also the essence of Colbert's point about truthiness—that facts really don't matter, it is what you *believe* and *feel* to be true that is paramount.

Colbert then lit into the press corps seated in the audience, noting that he was "appalled to be surrounded by the liberal media that is destroying America," repeating the mantra of so many of the conservative pundits that Colbert parodies (such as Limbaugh, O'Reilly, and Hannity). As the press had recently taken a newly aggressive stance toward the Bush administration's conduct and policies (as opposed to their less than forceful prosecution in the earlier years of his term in office), Colbert didn't celebrate their achievements, but reminded them of the shoddy job they had been doing all along:

> Let's review the rules. Here's how it works: the president makes decisions. He's the Decider. The press secretary announces those decisions, and you people of the press type those decisions down. Make, announce, type. Just put 'em through a spell check and go home. Get to know your family again. Make love to your wife. Write that novel you've got kicking around in your head. You know, the one about the intrepid Washington reporter with the courage to stand up to the administration. You know—fiction!

With such biting commentary, it is no surprise that the press was not amused. The event was lightly reported in the following days, with most that didn't ignore it arguing that Colbert was simply not funny. Richard Cohen at the *Washington Post*, for instance, called Colbert "rude" and "a bully" and said the routine "wasn't funny."[42] But the liberal blogosphere erupted in celebration of the event (and attacks on the media for not covering it), widely posting transcripts and videos of it, which C-SPAN tried in vain to repress so it could sell versions of it for $24.95.[43] It became a viral video sensation, while an audio version became a top-selling hit on iTunes.[44] Colbert, perhaps like Michael Moore a few years earlier, became an immediate media folk-hero amongst critics of the Bush administration. His program saw a 37 percent increase in viewership the following week, increasing to 1.5 million viewers.[45]

As a whole, Colbert's performance was significant in several respects. Just as Jon Stewart had appeared before Washington insiders and delivered his critique personally, so too did Colbert. It was a confrontation that the insiders were neither expecting nor appreciated. But the confrontational dimension transforms the satirical critique from something potentially silly to something deadly serious. The participants were reminded that political satire is not just some trifling television amusement, sequestered from reality in the performance space of late-night cable for a self-selected audience of cynics and other societal ne'er-do-wells. Rather, satire is a hard-knuckled critique of power, a verbal attack that passes judgment on the object of that attack, enunciating a perceived breach in societal norms or values. And as the press quickly discovered, in the age of networks, their ignoring the event couldn't make it disappear. The performance went on to become a quasi-cultural "event" on the Internet, partly because of the pleasure associated with watching a grimacing Bush and a somewhat captive audience of unamused reporters receiving a communal rebuke from disaffected citizens' proxy spokesman.

The performance was also significant in that the confrontation called to the fore the dual critique that this brand of satire is making—the ways in which news media and politicians are mutually constituting and enabling. Colbert's persona (and this performance) is a critique of truthiness—how it is manifest within public rhetoric, as well as the role that media play in allowing it to happen. Given the culture of truthiness, it is impossible to criticize one set of institutional actors (politicians) without criticizing the other (reporters and television news actors). This performance was double-fisted, and it made these points very clearly. Finally, the widespread popularity and viral distribution of the performance across the Web demonstrates the ways in which new political television—its voices, critiques, personalities—are cultural phenomena that are not contained by the industrial constraints of the televisual form. As discussed in later chapters, the audience's pleasure and enjoyment of the form invites participation, including the widespread circulation and commentary associated with its spread by their hands.

It is important to note that Colbert has maintained that he is not a political person, and that he did not go there to give the president the middle finger. "I was there to do some jokes. . . . Did I expect this to be a line in the sand for people? No, absolutely not."[47] Elsewhere he has noted that "I'm not on anyone's [partisan] side, I'm on my side."[48] Yet although he may not see himself as political or intend to deliver a political message, the beauty of such a parodic and satiric performance is that it allowed for that reading. Despite perhaps his own intentions or desires, his line of work—political satire—does not permit such claims of innocent humor. That is simply not what satire as a language is about. But most importantly, innocent humor isn't what viewers who rabidly spread the video desired or read into the performance. Certainly Colbert admits as such (and clearly articulating his own commitment to politics in the process) when he notes, "It depresses me that there isn't a politician who can address that frustration that was clearly evident in the reaction to what I did [at the White House Correspondents' Association Dinner]. Where's the politician who can take advantage of that anger and that passion?"[49]

This second phase of new political television's development also includes Bill Maher's return to television in 2003, this time safely ensconced on the subscription network HBO, away from the censorious tendencies of broadcasters and advertisers and licensed to use the blue language that he typically prefers. The show, *Real Time with Bill Maher*, is essentially a reincarnated yet slightly altered version of the political entertainment talk format developed on *Politically Incorrect*. The program features three guests seated at a table facing him. The guests tend to be more prominent (A-list actors, comedians, and politicians) than those who appeared on *PI*, but the set-up means that they often talk *through* Maher rather than to each other (which was not always the case on *PI*). The program airs live, has an extended format (running 50 minutes), an opening comedy monologue, and a closing "rant" (à la Dennis Miller) called "New Rules." Here Maher crafts several brief op-ed-type comedic statements to forcefully establish a rhetorical position while still being funny. In a New Rule called "Bad Presidents Happen to Good People," Maher tried to explain to citizens in foreign countries that "we're not with stupid," and that ridiculing the president was his patriotic duty:

> If I could explain one thing about George W. Bush to the rest of the world it's this: We don't know what the hell he's saying either! Trust me, foreigners, there's nothing lost in translation, it's just as incoherent in the original English. Yes, we voted for him—twice—but that's because we're stupid, not because we're bad.[50]

Whereas Maher proclaimed himself a libertarian with Republican sympathies when *Politically Incorrect* first aired in 1993, by the time he started his HBO talk show, his politics were largely anti-Republican, while his persona had evolved into a presidential gadfly. "Politics is so off-kilter [now]," he argues. "In my lifetime, I've never seen it as bad as it has been. George Bush is such a polarizing figure. There is a hunger to see the people in power taken down because they are an arrogant bunch up there. The Republicans pretty much control everything."[51] Maher, of course, realizes that his role

Real Time with Bill Maher, *a weekly late-night talk show on HBO that blends the political and entertainment talk show genres. Maher hosts a variety of guests from the worlds of entertainment and politics, shown here with Democratic Party strategist Donna Brazile, U.S. Representative David Dreier (R-CA), and comedienne Janeane Garofalo. Chris Polk/ FilmMagic/Getty Images*

as a comedian on an uncensored public stage gives him special license and privilege to ridicule and satirize the powerful. "When people are bloated with pomposity and religiosity and arrogance and a thirst for power," he argues, "that's the perfect time for comedy."[52]

The most notable difference in Maher's return to television is the increased respect he is afforded as a political commentator. The show features a satellite hookup that allows Maher the opportunity for one-on-one interviews with politicians and other newsmakers, thereby extending the show beyond the limited political confines of Los Angeles. By interviewing via satellite, there is a level of "safety" that a politician can maintain by being interviewed solely by Maher, as opposed to being ambushed by other guests, as was sometimes the case on *Politically Incorrect*. The appearance of a bevy of high-profile politicians and public persons such as Scott McClellan, Arlen Specter, Richard Clarke, Bernie Sanders, Michael Steele, Ron Paul, Noam Chomsky, Paul Krugman, and Cornell West suggests that Maher has been afforded a level of respect as an interviewer and political commentator. But as Maher is also known for his somewhat foul and aggressive language, he certainly isn't just another entertainment talk show host in the vein of Larry King or Jay Leno. As former cabinet members, diplomats, governors, and congressional representatives regularly join in the panel discussions, their presence suggests a level of "legitimacy" that either Maher or the genre (or both) has attained. What Maher actually brings to the table as a different type of political talk show host is examined in chapter 5 through his handling of group discussions on *Politically Incorrect*.

IMITATING SUCCESS AND LOOKING
FOR AUDIENCES IN CABLE NEWS

As the joke goes, imitation is the most sincere form of television. Unsurprisingly, the success of new political television has bred imitation from within an industry desiring to cash in on the popularity of the form. What has been somewhat surprising, however, is where the imitation is occurring. The third phase of new political television's development is marked primarily by the cable news networks' attempts to introduce similar programming—sometimes directly, with programs that are imitative derivatives, and sometimes indirectly, with political talk shows that employ features more commonly associated with entertainment television than news and public affairs.

Yet it is important to note just how *unrelated* these shows are to the more critical new political television programming described above—those which have directly or indirectly challenged journalism's regime of truth. *The Daily Show*, *The Colbert Report*, and *Real Time* use satire, parody, and humor as a means of getting at deeper truths within the news-politics dialectic, including questioning the authority of the agents within that dialectic. To be somewhat reductive, those shows represent a politicization of entertainment programming. What defines the programs that have developed in the third phase of new political television's growth is the inverse—a true entertainmentization of news channel programming. That is, news channels have employed news and current events as the content for crafting low-cost entertainment programs that can "lighten" their more serious programming schedule, attract younger audiences, and attract audiences during the weekend hours of slow news. Whether these shows are humorous or entertaining is a standard that individual viewers would have to assess. But it can safely be said that there is very little that is critical in these programs in regards to interrogating power and authority. In that regard, they are similar to new political television in generic form alone.

The trend of imitation began on February 18, 2007, with the launch of what was branded a conservative knock-off of *The Daily Show* called *The ½ Hour News Hour* on the Fox News Channel. The fake news program sought to satirize "the targets that have been missed by the mainstream satirists on TV," said the show's creator, Joel Surnow, producer of the hit show *24*. Although the program was pitched to the Fox broadcast network (which passed), it was picked up by the more overtly conservative Fox News, presumably because they agreed with Surnow's contention that "You can turn on any show and see Bush being bashed. There really is nothing out there for those who want satire that tilts right."[53] The program aired in the 10 P.M. slot on Sunday evenings, but lasted only through its scheduled run of 13 episodes and two pilots, airing its last episode on September 23, 2007. The show was similar to *The Daily Show* in composition, including fake anchors offering commentary alongside video clips and fake correspondents reporting from the field. The program also included fake commercials, such as those attacking the ACLU and gun control advocates. Two recurring bits included taped skits of Rush Limbaugh cast as the president (sometimes including Ann Coulter as vice president) and a stand-up routine by Dennis Miller. The program was shot in front of an audience, but for some reason included an inane laugh track to enhance any lack of sufficient audience gaiety.

Although the program typically won its time slot in the ratings race among cable news outlets, it was widely panned by critics, with most finding it not funny or missing its satirical mark. Perhaps the reason it wasn't funny rests upon the thinking that brought the show to market in the first place—that existing political satire has a left-wing bias and agenda, that it is focused on criticizing President Bush, and that since "people are funny on both sides of the aisle" (as Surnow put it), the program could fill a market void in political humor. What the conservative producers forgot, of course, is that satire is primarily about uncovering and critiquing the arrogance and hypocrisies of those in power. In contrast, *The ½ Hour News Hour* produced one-sided ideological shots aimed solely at the political left, including the predictable targets such as environmentalists, Barack Obama (as presidential candidate), gays and lesbians, atheists, civil rights campaigners, and anti-war activist Cindy Sheehan—in other words, people *not* in power. As one journalistic critic judged the show, "an agenda is all it has. It's government-approved satire—as oxymoronic, pointless and wretched as church-sanctioned porn. But probably easier to masturbate to, assuming you get off on abject desperation."[54] Another commentator pinpointed the inverse relationship to power that was the show's primary failing: "Comedy is usually a weapon wielded by the underdog, not the establishment, and you can't get more cozy with power than Fox."[55] Truthiness ultimately underlay the thinking behind the show, with "satire" conceived as yet another rhetorical tool capable of producing intended feelings (such as outrage, hatred, or victimhood) or enunciate certain beliefs. Criticizing those with little to no power can be funny (supposedly) because it allows conservative viewers to revel in their preconceived feelings about these people or issues. But because satire is truly of a different sort, this type of thinking doomed the show to the same fate as the Republican Party in the 2006 and 2008 elections.

For its part, CNN decided to dabble in the genre as well by creating *D. L. Hughley Breaks the News*, a program designed to (as the press reported) "capitalize on an increasingly younger, increasingly diverse television audience that has been tuning in, gripped by the 2008 presidential election."[56] The show featured African American comedian D. L. Hughley discussing current events in a variety of situations. The program debuted on October 25, 2008, and it too was scheduled to fill the viewer void of late-night weekend time slots (Saturday and Sunday evenings at 10 and 11 P.M., respectively). Shot in front of a live studio audience, the show opened with Hughley sitting on an orange leather sofa with a small table in front of him, drinking coffee, discussing recent events, and trying to make them funny. He didn't engage in a typical comedic talk show monologue. Rather, as the resident comedian, he was simply expected to *be funny* about whatever he discussed. The show also included interviews with guests, both in the studio and via satellite, the occasional sketch comedy routine (as perfected by Chris Rock, Dave Chappelle, and others), and "man in the street" interviews (called "field reports").

Overall, the program was an odd amalgam of generic talk show features assembled from across the talk programming spectrum—a little bit of Bill Maher, Chris Rock, Arsenio Hall, and Chris Matthews, all thrown together into one—combined with traditional black sketch comedy. With Hughley displaying what appeared to be little more than a superficial knowledge of the day's events (much less an understanding of them), the show added almost nothing to public discourse. It wasn't satirical and was barely entertaining, and its discussions were marginally interesting or informative. If its intentions were to keep young viewers and black viewers who were politically mobilized around Barack Obama, it certainly crafted a program that essentially treated them both as idiots. Critics brutally attacked the show, with one writer for *Advertising Age* exclaiming to CNN, "What the hell were you thinking?"[57] But as with most talk shows, it was cheap to produce and therefore provided CNN with an affordable means for adding variety to its monotone line-up of interchangeable (and generally white) talking heads. The show was cancelled in March 2009.

Perhaps a more complex display of oddly assembled talk show parts appears in Fox News's weekend evening talker, *Huckabee*. Debuting on September 27, 2008, the show features former Arkansas Governor and Republican presidential candidate Mike Huckabee in a role that can best be described as a talk show version of a "Huckabee for President" campaign stop. Shot in New York in front of an adoring audience, the show opens with the former preacher, known for his charismatic and humorous personality, delivering a monologue that is little more than a politician's speech. Although the monologue is typically focused on Huckabee's thoughts about the current state of politics from a Christian conservative position (ranging from Americana and Christian values to political commentary and policy stances), its real function (for Huckabee, at least) is to sell Huckabee the brand. In one early episode, he spent much of the monologue pitching his new book (*Do the Right Thing: Inside the Movement That's Bringing Common Sense Back to America*) and its message of how to "hit the reset button on the conservative movement in this country." He then directed the audience to go to his website, MikeHuckabee.com, for the exact dates and cities of his 56-city book tour, even telling the audience to make sure their local bookstore carries his book (as he also did with his forthcoming radio commentaries on local radio stations).

The episode airing October 12, 2008, is perhaps a prime example of the amalgam of odd talk show features that truly make this show unlike anything in the history of political talk television. After his monologue, Huckabee interviews his friend Chuck Norris, the television and movie star who endorsed and supported Huckabee on the campaign trail in 2008 and who recently authored a book, *Blackbelt Patriotism*. Norris appeared on the show to discuss the crisis state of the economy, including a discussion of the possibilities of economic terrorism and the dangers of China financing U.S. debt. Huckabee then segued into an interview with two African American pastors who are part of a movement to resist Internal Revenue Service restrictions on political advocacy from the pulpit. Next the host interviewed the CEO of a Gulf Coast vacuum manufacturing company, David Oreck (appearing with two sample vacuum cleaners), who "did the right thing" after Hurricane Katrina and didn't lay off his employees. Huckabee then turns the camera on the audience to introduce three women who are the "CEOs of their families" (seriously), allowing them a brief moment to describe the difficulties of managing a family, all the while framed by Huckabee's extolling of the value and importance of such a role for women in contemporary American society. The show ends with his strapping on a bass guitar and joining his house band, "The Little Rockers"—a rotating group of Fox News employees (writers, correspondents, technicians, and others) who also happen to be musicians. On this particular show, the two African American preachers joined in as backup singers for what amounted to a wedding band rendition of "Mustang Sally."

The word "hybrid" doesn't quite capture this complex interplay of celebrity, audience participation, average citizens, musical performance by the host, political speeches, Republican Party politics, and Christian values going on here. *Huckabee* is a blend of televangelism, political talk show, entertainment talk show, home shopping program, and campaign stop all rolled into one.[58] Fox uses the show to fill the weekend evening void, as the show airs on Saturdays (repeating on Sundays) at 8:00 P.M. For his part, Huckabee is undoubtedly using the show to further his own political career and presidential ambitions, while making a living as a political commentator across media forms (television, books, and radio). The show merges politics and entertainment, but it bears little relation to the critical performances of Stewart, Colbert, and Maher in terms of the discourse they produce, critiques they levy, or entertainment they provide. It is, however, a clear example of the ways in which cable news networks and politicians now freely embrace an entertainment model of political programming.

One final imitative show not produced by the cable news networks but which claimed to be related in form to new political television was *Chocolate News*, appearing on Comedy Central. Hosted by David Alan Grier (an *In Living Color* alumnus), the show was billed as a fake newsmagazine program, but was more akin to traditional sketch comedy programming featuring race humor. Its website explained that the program "investigates inherently urban pop culture topics" and that "the point of view is decidedly from an African American perspective and everyone and everything is fair game."[59] The show somewhat picked up where *Chappelle's Show* left off, yet used a fake news motif to frame the video vignettes. The fake news motif also structured the opening monologue by Grier who, standing dressed in a suit, delivered his commentary on the events of the days in a rant comparable to those by Dennis Miller or Bill Maher. The timing of the show (which was in production for two years) couldn't have been better, as the producers attempted to link the program to Barack Obama's rise in political fortune and what that meant for race and racial politics. According to press reports, Grier also wanted to "create a show that spoofed the serious tone of the black news programs hosted by Tavis Smiley, Tony Brown, and Gil Noble."[60] But whereas the show did employ some of the conventions of the "fake news" subgenre, those conventions were ultimately in service of something other than commentary about news media or politics proper. As the show never took off with Comedy Central's most valuable audience (white males aged 18–24), it was cancelled after its original ten-episode run.

In summary, the ratings and critical success of new political television has spawned programming that uses the genre of fake news and entertaining political talk to try to imitate that success. In particular, cable news has sought to enliven their programming schedule with "lighter" fare during weekend hours. But again, it is questionable whether any of these programs use the genre to advance anything that can be considered politically meaningful. *The ½ Hour News Hour* mistook satire for ideological right-wing polemics dressed in witty garb, thus producing a show that buttressed power, not attacked it. *D. L. Hughley Breaks the News* was the opposite, producing not much of anything that can be considered political, humorous, or news. *Huckabee*, however, is saturated in politics, producing what amounts to a show that is a presidential candidate's theocratic-themed infomercial disguised as a political entertainment talk show. And *Chocolate News* foregrounded race over politics, with most of its sketches looking to African American culture, not mainstream politics, for laughs. In short, these offerings suggest a degree of legitimacy obtained by political entertainment

television, as the old-guard journalist insiders have moved toward imitation of the barbarians as the gate. With that said, it also suggests a degree
of desperation on the part of the cable news networks. Rather than produce
what they advertise (news), they further extend their willingness to rely on
programming based on cheap production costs and opinion.

CONCLUSION

Growing from its roots in the economically competitive and politically
populist era of the 1990s, new political television has matured from a
seemingly inconsequential form of humorous entertainment programming
that dabbles in politics into a more fully developed and legitimate form of
political communication and critique. What originally appeared simply as
non-experts and Washington outsiders discussing politics in an accessible
and pleasurable manner has evolved into a full-throated critique of the
political class from a variety of interrogational perspectives. This critique
includes the fundamental relationship that news media play in mediating
political life for citizens and, in the process, helps constitute political reality, even truth. The maturation of the genre is the product of the context in
which these shows were born and developed. That is to say, historical times
and circumstances have shaped the types of shows that are popular and the
types of narratives that each program can tell. Using Northrop Frye's Ari-
stotelian approach to dramatic genres, Vande Berg, Wenner, and Gronbeck
argue that dramatic narratives have an appropriate time and place. Using
Frye's metaphor of nature's seasons, they contend that:

> Comedies are summer, the season of foolishness, guile, and the bringing down
> of braggadocio bureaucrats and avaricious old men, a time even to critique so-
> cial norms and acceptable behavior; tragedies inhabit the coolness of autumn,
> in situations where individuals through pride or other dangerous motivations
> bring about their own fall from station or fall from grace; and ironic literature
> is winter, where the world is subjected to Kafkaesque tyrannies and hidden
> dictators, where the human spirit all but dies—in hopes of being reborn in
> spring.[61]

By extending Frye's conceptualization of various dramatic forms to the
humorous narratives of new political television, we see summer in the first
phase of political entertainment television crafted by Maher and Miller.
Their humor was well suited for an era of petty partisan bickering, sexual
scandal, and culture wars, when Americans were given the opportunity to
laugh at the foolishness and hypocrisy of political leaders and the ridiculousness of contested social norms played out in the political arena. But the
autumnal tragedy of 9/11 was America's fall from grace, when Americans

learned that they were no longer the shining city on the hill but were, in fact, hated as a proud and arrogant nation. At that point, neither comedy nor brash truthfulness seemed appropriate, as Bill Maher experienced his own fall from grace and Dennis Miller experienced a fall from station due to an ideological conversion experience/breakdown. In what then became a winter season, the hidden dictatorship of the Bush administration and its tyrannies became fodder for the ironic narratives told by Jon Stewart and Stephen Colbert. The wars abroad and the lies at home emboldened these two comedians to aggressively interrogate how power was manifest through public spectacle, willful ignorance, and a blatant disregard for older standards of arriving at truth. As the public responded to the winter tyrannies with a renewed political spirit and dramatically increased levels of political participation—including mobilizing around a political candidate advocating a hopeful springtime rebirth of American greatness—the path was paved for innovations in narrative programming. As with every springtime, however, such new blooms include flowers and weeds that may not survive the summer heat (as witnessed by the failed cable news imitators). In sum, the political entertainment television shows that have appeared over the last fifteen years have formulated narratives that *could* be told given the historical context of political seasons.

Most importantly, new political television has been a participant in society's more broad-based challenge to news media's (and television news media's, in particular) regime of truth. Perhaps because of its paternalistic and hierarchical establishment of what constitutes political reality (and the failings it has produced in concert with political power in that regard), the news media's authority and legitimacy as the primary arbiters of political truth is under challenge. New political television has played an important role in articulating those failings, and produced alternative narratives for what constitutes truth and political reality. One important first step, as the next chapter demonstrates, was simply allowing political outsiders the opportunity to talk and discuss politics using their own senses and conceptions of what political events ultimately mean. As a result, the insider political class's monopoly on political sense-making cannot be maintained.

5

The Competing Senses of Political Insiders and Outsiders

I have common sense. I got one week of high school. I didn't go that week. Remember that. But I'm on this show. Here's a man with no education. I'm talking to brilliant people here because I have common sense. And that's what this country don't have. We're in a nap. We're nappy. We gotta wake up and smell the roses, smell the coffee.

—Pat Cooper, comedian and guest on *Politically Incorrect*

I must say I think that letting the process work makes a lot of sense because . . . then people [in government] can lead public opinion rather than just follow it through the process.

—Cokie Roberts, cohost, *This Week with Sam Donaldson and Cokie Roberts*

From 1998–1999, President Bill Clinton's affair with White House intern Monica Lewinsky and his alleged lying about the affair in a court deposition dominated public discourse about politics, including discussions on *Politically Incorrect*. Even when other social and political topics were discussed on the program, the Clinton scandal would often find its way into the conversation. The scandal was a widely popular topic, because it not only involved America's highest elected official but also encompassed so many themes common to human behavior and cultural belief systems—sex, lying, adultery, persecution, sin, redemption, human nature. Most citizens could, in some form or fashion, understand the core issues involved in this case, as opposed to the highly complex arms-for-hostages or savings and loan scandals of the Reagan years. Moreover, this scandal provided tremendous opportunities for citizens to offer their own opinions, humor, and personal experiences. As a political scandal, it also dominated discussions of politics on other television programs, including pundit talk shows. A political scandal almost always equates to political vulnerability, and professional monitors of political power could hardly talk of anything else.

A central argument here is that laity-based television shows like *Politically Incorrect* and pundit talk shows are fundamentally different in the types of political discourse that constitute their presentations. Indeed, many scholars and political observers contend that political elites and the general populace speak different languages when discussing politics.[1] This chapter seeks to understand both how and why these differences exist and occur. Both political pundits/elites and the lay participants on *PI* offer commentary on politics, both have the job of assessing and evaluating the issues of the day, and both must offer some form of presentational stylistics to attract television viewers. But that is largely where the similarities end. Our interest here is the conversations—the political discussions that both these types of shows offer the viewing public—and what accounts for the differences in how those discussions are formulated.

Moreover, this book is interested in assessing how publics encounter politics in the everyday, and how and in what ways new political television offers cultural engagements with politics. We need to determine whether programs like *PI* contribute something new or different to the mediated public realm, and what that means for public discourse about politics. Does the show's construction and presentation as "entertainment" render the discussions nonsensical for serious public matters, as some critics maintain? Or does the show's construction based on an eclectic mix of politically non-expert guests encourage the application of more universal sense-making strategies?

This chapter examines the commonsense thinking and discourse of political outsiders by directly comparing the "sense" made or used on *PI* with the "sense" made or used on a pundit talk show. The focus here is on what these different conversations and conclusions tell us about "what made sense" to its participants and why. The issue discussed on both shows was the same—the Clinton scandal. This examination of competing discourses allows an entry point to probe factors that might account for the disjunction between elite and public opinion on the scandal. It also allows us to see how non-experts and the professional political class engage politics in dissimilar ways, and then assess what this means for public engagement with politics via television.

The analysis here centers on four weeks of programming on *PI*—January 26 through February 3, 1998, the first two weeks of revelations of the president's affair and his subsequent denial of any wrongdoing, and August 10 through August 21, 1998, the two weeks surrounding the president's admission of the affair to the American people and his testimony before a grand jury. These dates were high-water marks in the scandal, especially in regard to public interest in the matter. The first was the "gossip" period, when rumors and revelations were swirling concerning what the president did or might have done. The second date covers the period in which the president finally admitted and apologized for his transgressions.

The pundit show examined is *This Week with Sam Donaldson and Cokie Roberts*, also on ABC, which aired during the same time frame.[2] This show was selected for several reasons. First, it offers one of the more diverse mixtures of guests among the pundit talk shows. Many shows in the genre are dominated solely by journalists, or include journalists interviewing policy makers. Two senior broadcast journalists host *This Week*, and the round-table discussion includes a former top White House official and advisor to President Clinton (George Stephanopoulos), an editor of a conservative journal of political opinion (Bill Kristol), and a conservative syndicated columnist (George Will). All three guests are active in Republican and Democratic policy circles, although none is an office holder. Their presence on the show is also designed to represent both left and right ideological perspectives. *This Week* was also selected because it appears on the same network as *Politically Incorrect*. Along with *Nightline*, these three shows represent three major forms of political programming on ABC's schedule. Here we compare two of them directly.

THIS WEEK WITH SAM DONALDSON AND COKIE ROBERTS

One of the distinguishing features of the discussions on *This Week* was the high level of agreement among the participants. For an issue so discordant in American society and so contentious between political parties, there was relatively little disagreement over what the scandal "meant" at any given time on the program. Instead, these five participants arrived at their conclusions with relative ease. Their fundamental concern was for the political system, or the "constitutional order," as they referred to it. The primary issue that drove that concern was the supposed threat to the system that resulted from Clinton's lying. The singular explanation offered for this threat was the weak moral character of Bill Clinton, or "this man" as George Will often referred to him.[3] And finally, the discussants based their conclusion on an abiding faith (despite continued evidence to the contrary) that the American people would stop supporting Clinton once they realized the "truth" that these pundits knew would be made public through the institutional processes at work in the efforts of prosecutor Kenneth Starr and the U.S. Congress.

From the time the scandal broke until the president's confession some seven months later, the primary issue these pundits were interested in was whether Clinton had lied. If he had, they contended, his presidency was through.

January 25
George Stephanopoulos: Is he telling the truth, the whole truth, and nothing but the truth? If he is, he can survive. If he isn't, he can't.

Sam Donaldson: If he's not telling the truth, I think his presidency is numbered in days. This isn't going to drag out. We're not going to be here three months from now talking about this. Mr. Clinton, if he's not telling the truth and the evidence shows that, will resign, perhaps this week.

August 16
George Stephanopoulos: It all depends on what he does tomorrow. I think if he tells the truth and comes forward to the American people, he can at least go on with his presidency.

George Will: The presidency is over.

There was relatively little interest in what the president lied about or why he lied, questions that were of utmost importance on *PI*. Instead, lying itself was simply unacceptable. The act of lying was so serious that its occurrence alone meant the president would have to leave office; hence, the unanimous predictions for his early departure. Lying, their arguments suggested, is harmful in at least three primary ways. First, it damages the president's ability to lead as a politician and as a moral leader.

January 25
George Will: This man's condition is known. His moral authority is gone. He will resign when he acquires the moral sense to understand.

August 23
Cokie Roberts: There is the question of can he govern if he stays in office? Can he go up and twist an arm and get a bill?

George Stephanopoulos: He can govern, but he can't advance his agenda.

George Will: The presidency is constitutionally a weak office. There is very little he can do on his own, other than by moving the country by rhetoric that acquires its power from the hold his personality and character has on the country. This week *The New Republic* begins its editorial saying, "It's official. Bill Clinton is a lout."

Second, lying is such a gross violation of political principles that it damages the president's relationship with his own political party:

August 16
Bill Kristol: The Democratic Party needs . . . the president to say he was wrong and to apologize for it. That gets them off the hook and the party can say it was wrong. They can't appear to be covering up for the president.

August 23
Cokie Roberts: You're seeing Democratic political consultants, for instance, saying, you know, "This guy lost the House for us in 1994. He lost the House for us in 1996. . . . Now he's about to lose it for us again in 1998."

The third and most important reason they consider the president's lying unacceptable is the threat it presents to the political system:

February 1
George Will: This is a great uncontrolled experiment now under way about having vulgarians in the most conspicuous offices in the republic. And it can't be good.

August 23
Bill Kristol: To let him stay now, I think, is fundamentally corrupting.

George Will: The metastasizing corruption spread by this man is apparent now, and the corruption of the very idea of what it means to be a representative.

Bill Kristol: The president is at the center of the constitutional order. Credibility in him matters.

The explanation for why Clinton lied is simple—he has no moral character. He is a "vulgarian," a "lout." As George Will argued, "He can't tell the truth. . . . I mean, that's the reasonable assumption on the evidence informed by the context in which it occurs, which is six years of evidence of his deceit."

The pundits continued to exhibit a fundamental faith in the American public, however. With "lying" as the centerpiece of this case, the pundits maintained a hope that eventually the public would realize the wrongs that had been committed and rise up to punish the president. Ultimately, the pundits' conception of "the people" was quite paternalistic, although not condescending. For instance, George Will seemed to suggest that the public would recognize the right thing to do (what the political class already knew) once the Starr report was released. The public, he argued, "will not be able to change their mind. . . . Once that report [by Kenneth Starr] is written and published, Congress will be dragged along in the wake of the public."[4] They saw a good and virtuous public, although one that was a bit naïve and unsophisticated. As Bill Kristol stated, "I think it is that the American people are nice people. They're too nice, in fact, too trusting" (February 1). It is a public fashioned in their own image, with little connection to what people were actually saying about the scandal.

August 23

George Will: But beneath the argument there's a visceral process. And it has to do with the peculiar intimacy of the modern presidency. Because of television, the president is in our living rooms night after night after night. And once the dress comes in and once some of the details come in from the Ken Starr report, people—there's going to come a critical mass, the yuck factor—where people say, "I don't want him in my living room anymore."

This unrealistic opinion of a supposedly virtuous public and its beliefs on the matter is just one part of their overall conception of the democratic system. The pundits on *This Week* continued to exhibit faith in the ability of the system to combat the wrongs committed, to survive this crisis and restore order through processes established and codified in the constitution.

August 23

Bill Kristol: This is why democracy in elections are [sic] a good thing. . . . Right now, people can go on TV shows and say, "I'm not here to discuss that." . . . But the advantage of an election campaign, the advantage of a real debate, is one candidate will turn to the other and say, "If the president lied under oath, what do you think you should do about it? You as a member of the House of Representatives?" And I agree with George, it's the election campaign that makes this real, in a sense.

George Will: [This] is why I favor impeachment rather than resignation because I want to clear up what impeachment means in the constitution.

In summary, then, the pundits on *This Week* reduced the scandal to one fundamental question—did the president lie? If he did—which they all assumed was true because of Clinton's supposed pattern of deceit—then it would be necessary for him to depart the office, either willingly or unwillingly. The foundation of legitimacy in American democracy, they suggested, was based on the president's telling the truth, and should the president violate that cornerstone principle, then the system would remove him. It was also assumed that the public shared the same understanding of how the system works, and once the public realized the truth, they would respond in a fitting manner.

What produced these formulations, I argue, is that these pundits, as part of America's governing class, used "political sense" for assessing political matters. By political sense, I mean a learned understanding of how politics works, what actions and behaviors are admissible, correct, justifiable, and workable—an acquired sense of what matters and what doesn't. Political sense is like other intellectualized systems such as legal sense, scientific sense, artistic sense—a philosophy or an intellectual order. "Philosophy," Antonio Gramsci argues, is "official conceptions of the world" that are "elaborated, systematic and politically organized and centralized."[5] Practitioners of politics are trained (through schooling, professional experiences, upbringing, the media) to think in certain ways about how the system works.[6] To be sure, as John Dewey argues, political sense, as philosophy or science, does not exist outside of common sense: "Neither common sense nor science is regarded as an entity—as something set apart, complete and self-enclosed." Rather, without common sense science cannot exist and "philosophy is idly speculative apart from [the rudiments of common sense] because it is then deprived of footing to stand on and a field of significant application."[7] Nevertheless, the interrelationships between elements of elite and lay thinking need not obscure the broader processes of sense making that lead to such dissimilar conclusions between pundits and citizens. Instead, political sense is different from common sense in that it is a conscious creation of an abstracted mode of thinking. As Dewey notes,

> Science is the example, par excellence, of the liberative effect of abstraction. . . . The liberative outcome of the abstraction that is supremely manifested in scientific activity is the transformation of the affairs of common sense concern which has come about through the vast return wave of the methods and conclusions of scientific concern into the uses and enjoyments (and sufferings) of everyday affairs, together with an accompanying transformation of judgment and of the emotional affections, preferences, and aversions of everyday human beings.[8]

What I am arguing is that political sense used by the pundits of the "political class" (to use George Will's term) is the product of just such a transformation, an alteration of the "emotional affections, preferences, and aversions of everyday human beings" into an abstraction with its own set of rules and understandings about what is valid, right, just, and legitimate.

According to political sense, politics in a representative democracy is centered around the social contract between the polity and the trust they bestow on their elected officials to conduct the affairs of state in an open and honest fashion, and operated in the people's best interest. Political legitimacy in such a system is based on public trust. A politician caught in a lie has naturally betrayed that trust. The pundits argued that the president is at the center of the constitutional order, and to not censure his violation of that order threatens the whole system and everyone in it. The pundits recognized that the political system is fragile. Its strength, their comments suggest, is that the constitutional order is designed to purge such individuals who betray that trust.

Those who employ political sense maintain a systematic logic—a structured understanding of the workings of a complex political system that guarantees the functioning of democracy. Within that system, however, the public is only one of several factors. Executive leadership, legislative agendas, and political parties are also crucial to the system's functioning, and hence the pundits found these issues just as relevant (if not more so) as topics of discussion. But the public was also key. The political sense employed by these pundits led to a paternalistic view of the public—a public that is good and decent, but one that would need to overcome its naïveté to understand the seriousness of Clinton's violations. The pundits placed faith not in the people whom the systemic structures are ultimately designed to protect, but in the system itself. The public's role in the scandal was simply to acquiesce in what the system needed to do—to purge the breaker of trust. This type of systematic logic was so strong that the pundits' political sense was generally incapable of recognizing the overwhelming evidence to the contrary. That is, an overwhelming majority of the public was not interested in the system purging itself.[9] Indeed, the public was an abstraction for the pundits, whereas the political "players" in the scandal (whom they all knew) and the arenas in which these players operated (with which they were all thoroughly familiar) were much more real than a capricious, passive, and unthinking public—a public that is only required to react to the events produced by the political class when called upon.

What these pundits would not entertain, however, is not only that citizens might not be the mythical public they had constructed, but that citizens might employ a different means of thinking about politics altogether. The fact that many citizens considered Clinton's lying about sex a private matter, not a public concern, was the product of commonsense thinking that allowed for different versions of truth from those offered by the political class. Nor would the pundits stop to consider that new television forums might provide a site where a different "sense" of political events could now be entertained. The laity on *PI* knew quite well that the president was lying. For them, however, the issue was not whether he lied but whether lying is permissible when it is about sex and when it is the president who is engaged in such lying. The thinking that would lead from these central concerns is quite important in understanding why the public didn't respond in ways pundits had hoped.

POLITICALLY INCORRECT WITH BILL MAHER

Although the discussions on *This Week* were generally void of meaningful disagreement, the discussions on *PI* were much more contested and fractious. And despite a wide variety of guests, the arguments tended to coalesce around several issues. The concern driving the discussion was not the political system, but rather how Clinton as an individual and as a leader should be judged. The central issue in the scandal was Clinton's sexual affair and his lying about it (not any procedural or juridical concerns such as suborning perjury, obstructing justice, and so on). Because he lied about sex, the arguments split over how to assess Clinton—as a human being (which made the actions normal, comprehensible, fathomable, and ultimately benign) or as a moral leader (which made the actions unacceptable, unfathomable, and therefore a threat). Those assessments were based on whether the lying was a public or a private matter, as the following exchange demonstrates.

August 13

Carmen Pate (activist): If he would just admit it. If he would admit, "I was wrong."

Bill Maher: Why should he? It's his private life. Why should he have to admit anything to you?

Pate: It's not just his private life.

Maher: You're not his wife. Why should he have to come clean to you?

Pate: Because he represents the American people. He represents me.

Maher: Exactly. They cheat.

James Coburn (actor): Lie.

Maher: They lie. They steal office supplies. They try to get money off their income tax, and that's what I'm saying. He's just like them.

Another defense of Clinton was based on conceptions of human nature. Although Clinton may be guilty of lying, some panelists suggested, he couldn't help it because the need for sex—and lots of it—is part of the nature of men. Clinton did this, they argued, because he is a man, and it is a simple fact that men, in their efforts to fulfill these human needs, have extramarital sex and lie about it. Furthermore, that behavior is understandable, if not justified, because men need sex more than women. Behavior and agency are explained in essentialist terms, as seen in the second comment of the following exchange.

August 18

Star Parker (author): We are a land of law. And if man starts to do whatever he wants to, then so is everybody else. And when you do it from the highest office so are the lowest.

Donzaleigh Abernathy (actress): [But] they have been doing it already. They have been doing it since the beginning of time. . . . It's the nature of men. They need to cast their seed everywhere they can.

Panelists who didn't embrace essentialist gender arguments might resort to claims that all humans are fallible, and therefore deserve mercy.

August 17
Michael Moore (director): We are human beings. Have you ever made a mistake? Have you ever made a mistake?

August 19
Jo-Ellan Dimitrius (jury consultant): You know why politicians are so concerned about this issue, though, is because there is a sentiment of, "There but for the grace of God go I."

Other panelists advanced the argument that Clinton is just a regular guy, an average American who is just like everyone else. Instead of exalting Clinton as a distant leader, these panelists embraced the notion that their leader was just like them. It was not his higher moral stature that garnered respect (or the lack thereof in both instances), but rather his position as both a political leader and a regular guy that inspired them. Citizens fashioned the president in their own image (as already seen in the comments by Maher cited previously).

January 29
Coolio (rapper): What it really is, is that he's human, and that's why people like Clinton because he's showing that, "I'm human. O.K., I had an affair, whether I admit it or not, or whether I did it or not, I'm human."

Dennis Prager (talk radio host): Exactly. A guy called my show and said, "Dennis, Clinton is the sort of guy I can see drinking beers with and chasing women with."

But arguments also ensued over Clinton's position as leader and role model, and the relationship of lying to leadership.

January 29
Bill Maher: Over and over again, the polls say [the people] think he had an affair, and they don't care. So what they're saying is, let him live, we don't need him as a role model. We'll look to ourselves for our own moral guidance.

Brad Keena (political analyst): But it's important that we don't normalize this kind of behavior and that's what we're allowing to happen. . . . I think it is time to have a president, to elect a president who is a role model, someone who has good moral values.

Some panelists extended the conception of Clinton as leader a step further, invoking the metaphor of the country as a family. In the metaphor, Clinton is the "father" of the country, and by implication, the people are his "children," together constituting a "family," with the White House (the site of the indiscretions) as the family's "house."

January 26
Eartha Kitt (singer/actress): President is head of the family. He sets an example for the rest of us. If he can't live by moral standards, then what does he expect of us?

August 13
Jeffrey Tambor (actor): Any household can look within their own selves and their families and say, "There have been transgressions in my family." There are transgressions here. And the smart thing to do is separate the presidency from the man.

These arguments, in sum, form a central dialectic, a tension between the desires to separate Clinton-the-man from Clinton-the-leader. When viewed as a leader, a split occurred between those who argued that:

A. *Leaders and the people have different rules.* These discussants invoked history (all presidents have done this), explained power (men in power have affairs the world over), and made his job performance more important than his off-the-job activities (he can do whatever he wants if he's doing a good job).
B. *Leaders are not exempt from the same rules as the people.* Presidents get no special treatment when it comes to moral behavior.

When viewed as a human, a split occurred between those who argued that:

C. *Clinton should represent the people by being better than they are as a moral person.* He should be a model for how the people should be.
D. *Clinton is no different from the people he represents.* He has the same flaws and he does the same stupid things that all humans do.

It seems, then, that panelists wanted it both ways—Clinton is like the average person and unlike the average person; the president deserves special rules yet must operate by the same rules as average citizens. Despite this contradictory positioning, both liberal and conservative guests tended to adopt these dual stances. The more liberal voices tended to use arguments A and D (different rules as a leader, but Clinton the man is no different from the rest of us), while conservatives tended to use arguments B and C (leaders have the same rules as the people, yet as a man he has different rules; he should be better than we are). From the perspective of political culture in the 1990s, we might argue that these positions are grounded in the larger popularity of populism (for instance, the suspicion of political elites disconnected from the people; a desire to have politicians like the people) and the culture wars (elites who have no morals; elites as hypocritical). These positions also represent the contradictory, disjointed, and multifarious dimensions of commonsense thinking that Gramsci, Clifford Geertz, and other theorists of common sense have described.[10]

MAKING SENSE OF COMPETING SENSES

Each of these programs' structures largely determined the type of discourse that it would produce. Pundit talk shows feature individuals whose primary purpose is to establish for other insiders (and political junkies who subscribe to this way of thinking or who simply enjoy monitoring power) what the events of the week "really mean." That is, they produce an agreed-upon reality that other insiders are expected to accept (at some level). The show, therefore, is not designed to produce wide-ranging explanations or diverse viewpoints. Rather, the whole point of the show is to narrow contentious issues and events and their "meanings" so that viewers can hear the précis and then move on to new matters that will arise in the week ahead. The discursive framework for *PI*, however, is designed for entertainment and information. An eclectic array of public persons appear on the program, and as a televisual cocktail party, this mixture is intended to guarantee debate, if not acrimony and laughter. *PI* is not interested in presenting its viewers with a single conception of what "makes sense" at any given moment. Indeed, its discussions are centrifugal, not centripetal (like the pundit shows). And by including guests who have little expertise in politics, the show is intentionally structured to sound not like political insiders, but more like the viewing public who lives their lives from the private to the public.

Interestingly enough, the discussions on both shows included, at times, similar arguments. Compare, for instance, the following statements made on both programs.

> *Heavy D*: He's the father of our country. He's our dysfunctional father.
>
> *George Stephanopoulos*: In many ways, it's like this whole episode has turned the whole country into a dysfunctional family.
>
> *Victoria Jackson*: Because he lies about everything else, of course he's lying about that.
>
> *George Will*: He can't tell the truth . . . that's the reasonable assumption on the evidence informed by the context in which it occurs, which is six years of evidence of his deceit.
>
> *Michael Moore*: And they put him in office knowing exactly who he was and what he's done.
>
> *Cokie Roberts*: But is that [lying] something new? Everybody knew that when they elected him.

Similarities in the discussions across the two shows were not pervasive, but they did exist occasionally. Yet it is not surprising to see similarities in various phrases, questions, and arguments that appeared on both *PI* and *This Week*. As in the point made by Dewey, pundits must use their common sense about how the world works, while citizens on *PI* are often attuned to the general debates occurring in Washington and in the media. Citizens learn to appropriate the rudimentary terms through which political elites wage war with each other—terms like suborning perjury, obstruction of justice, quid pro quo, depositions, and so on. And pundits and citizens alike appropriate terms from other intellectual realms—terms like dysfunction—to explain the scandal. But as Hwa Yol Jung notes, "The ordinary language of political man precedes the objectified language of political science, and the second must be consistent with the first."[11]

The overriding differences in content, in focus, in overall concerns, and in the conclusions between the shows, however, were dissimilar. Whereas the "meaning" of the scandal for the pundits on *This Week* generally boiled down to how Clinton's lying presented a threat to the larger political system, the meaning of the scandal for the non-experts on *PI* was whether Clinton's lying presented a threat to certain values. Guests on *PI* often employed arguments that included claims to universality, claims based on personal or group experience, which defined the situation in universalistic terms: "Everyone does this," "All politicians lie," "Never trust a liar," "All families have problems," "All men are this way." These claims to universality render the common sense inherent in these truisms reliable, even reassuring in that this is the way of the world. Clinton is not exceptional, they argue, nor is this case exceptional. Although the scandal had Washington in gridlock, the public can understand what is going on because it rings true with their understanding of the world. Its universality is its key to being understood.

One of the most prominent themes in citizen arguments over the scandal was conflicting notions of whether this was a public or a private matter. For those who argued the latter, the liberal notions of freedom and individuality drove their arguments. For those who argued the former, republican notions of responsibility and community came to bear. Rarely were these concepts enunciated as theoretical postulates, but rather as beliefs about how the world works. As Michael Billig and his colleagues argue, "Within the ideology of liberalism is a dialectic, which contains negative counter-themes and which gives rise to debates. These debates are not confined to the level of intellectual analysis; both themes and counterthemes have arisen from, and passed into, everyday consciousness. And, of course, this everyday consciousness provides the material for further intellectual debate."[12] American liberalism battles republicanism here, yet these ideological formulations appear simply as common sense:[13] "This is none of your business," "This is between him and his wife," "If his wife is O.K. with it, what concern is this of yours?," "He did this in our house, the people's house," "What type of example does this set for people/the children?," "Lying is lying, so how can we trust a liar?"

This is the natural, thin, immethodical, practical, and accessible language of common sense as brilliantly analyzed by Clifford Geertz.[14] Through this type of language and thinking, citizens are formulating answers to questions such as, "Is this natural? Is this the way the world works? Is this the way human beings really are?" and "Do I understand this; is this something I can judge?" and "What aspects of my experience come to bear on this situation?" and "Is this right?" These aren't political questions or terms at all. Panelists did not argue from the basis of political sense—the chief law enforcement officer lying, the implications for systems of justice, the precedent this sets for future presidents, the mandate of the special prosecutor, and so on. They use accessible terms that not only make sense but also make the scandal interesting and popular to discuss. They fuse use with enjoyment. In other words, the terms and conditions of the Clinton scandal (e.g., sex, lying, adultery, cigars, dresses, semen, fellatio) favor the application of common sense, certainly in ways that the savings and loan scandal did not. People can relate to this kind of politics, for it has resonance with their own lives. As one guest on *PI* intimated, "You know, I've been following this [scandal] 'cause I haven't seen [the soap opera] *All My Children* in a long time."

That remark is telling in that it exemplifies how politics is increasingly attended to in ways quite similar to entertainment and consumer culture, and therefore, the sense used in attending to those realms will also be used in making sense of politics. With the tendency for more and more politicians to both act like and be treated like celebrities, the public then finds no reason to engage politics differently from how they make sense of and use entertainment celebrities. David Marshall argues that "the celebrity offers a discursive focus for the discussion of realms that are considered outside the bounds of public debate in the most public fashion. The celebrity system is a way in which the sphere of the irrational, emotional, personal, and affective is contained and negotiated in contemporary culture."[15] He goes on to contend that celebrities are "intense sites for determining the meaning and significance of the private sphere and its implications for the public sphere. . . . The private sphere is constructed to be revelatory, the ultimate site of truth and meaning for any representation in the public sphere. . . . Celebrities . . . are sites for the dispersal of power and meaning into the personal and therefore universal."[16] By making politics personal and universal, the invitation is made to publics that all politics be evaluated on these terms. Political sense about how politics properly functions appears as nonsense, and publics revert to the means of thinking used in the other realms of their everyday existence. Defenders of Clinton appealed to the commonsense "truth" of the private realm, including essentialist claims about a man's needs or human biology, or personal identification with Clinton because of his human frailties. For some guests, Clinton-as-celebrity was easier to judge and easier to make sense of psychologically than Clinton-as-leader and politician. Clinton's actions as a celebrity seemed all too familiar when compared with other celebrities. The foibles of Bill Clinton's and actor Hugh Grant's sexual misconduct come to be seen in similar ways when such criteria are used for judgment.

But as Joshua Gamson points out, the celebrity sign is composed of oppositional characteristics that allow for different readings, depending on the situation. "Contemporary celebrity," he notes, "is composed of a string of antinomies: public roles opposing private selves, artificial opposing natural, image opposing reality, ideal opposing typical, special opposing ordinary, hierarchy opposing equality."[17] As the previous analysis suggests, these are exactly the means through which *PI* panelists attempted to read Clinton as a political celebrity—Clinton as special or ordinary, better than the people or equal to the people, an ideal leader or a typical American. Pundit discourse based on political sense, a perspective that didn't position Clinton as a celebrity but as a politician required to play the game of politics by certain rules, was much more unified in how to make sense of the scandal.

CONCLUSION

The epigraphs that began this chapter come from participants on *This Week* and *Politically Incorrect* during this period of investigation. Both individuals embrace a particular form of sense as the means for putting the country back on a proper course. One openly acknowledges his particular brand of sense, while the other seems oblivious to the fact that hers is a brand at all. The analysis of these competing senses suggests several conclusions. The means through which talk show guests think through the political matters of the day will greatly affect the discursive realities they create. The political sense of *This Week* tended to limit debate, efficiently organizing the scandal around a particular set of meanings beyond which other explanations made no sense. This particular ordering of political reality framed Clinton as a systemic threat, and the integrity and continuity of the system necessitated his exit from the system. Alternative means of making sense of the scandal were rarely entertained.[18]

The common sense that dominated discussions of *PI*, on the other hand, provided the means for a far-reaching exploration of what the presidential scandal meant for the nation. The assorted nature of common sense necessarily means that space exists for conservative and progressive notions, Stone Age and intellectual thinking. As this analysis suggests, common sense may be conservative, advancing patriarchal notions of male leadership or entertaining essentialist formulations that excuse male behavior.

Conversely, common sense may be progressive, challenging hypocritical strictures of public morality cloaked behind legal terms and procedures. Whereas debate using political sense can amount to little more than the proper arrangement of dishes on the table, debate using common sense may result in arguments over whether the proper issue is the dishes, the table, the chairs, or the tablecloth. That is not to say that common sense is a means for liberational thinking. Common sense will not bring about a reordering of society, and it is certainly too haphazard to advance a unified or cogent substitute for that which it critiques. It does, however, provide a means for public reflection on issues in ways less commonly found in the traditional manifestations of political talk on television. Furthermore, its presence on a program like *PI* exemplifies the important shifts that are occurring in how publics are invited to make sense of politics through a cultural instead of a political lens.

The Clinton scandal also became an opportunity for citizens to explore a range of interpretations about the changing relationships between leaders and the public in contemporary America. Commonsense thinking led panelists to explore what Clinton as (fallen) archetypal hero means for America: Is this scandal just about him, an amoral and selfish baby boomer, or does this include the public in some way? Is Clinton representative of broader cultural factors, and in what ways do citizens identify with him? It also led citizens to investigate the nature of leadership and political privilege, and the normative expectations that should exist given contemporary realities. This new political television program, and the commonsense thinking it allowed for, offered a more wide-ranging exploration of the scandal than that offered by pundit television. By facilitating such an exploration, other citizen concerns become manifest in the discussions—concerns not derived solely from the immediate situation. For instance, these questions are constitutive of a populist political culture where citizens routinely ask politicians the price of a gallon of milk to check their "of-the-people" credentials. These questions arise from a political system that has seen the decline of political party affiliation, the popularity of independent candidates, and the increased role of media as the means through which we understand our leaders and their relationship to the polity. And these questions emanate from an entertainment culture in which politicians have increasingly become celebrities in their own right, trading in the currency of intimacy, gossip, image, and myth—a culture in which the lines of image and reality are hard to pin down, and in which privacy is a fleeting concept.

Geertz advocates investigations into common sense as a cultural system because those investigations should lead to "new ways of looking at some old problems, most especially those concerning how culture is jointed and put together, and to a movement . . . away from functionalist accounts of the devices on which societies rest toward interpretive ones of the kinds of lives societies support."[19] The argument I am making is that new political television offers viewers a means of discussing politics in a common vernacular. As such, the language of common sense points to means of enunciation and understanding through which societies think and argue about politics. Although such programming may come up short for advocates of a rational-critical public sphere—a functionalist account of a device on which societies should rest for many scholars—I argue that laity-centered talk shows are constitutive, representative, and contributive to the way publics commonly interact with, make meaning of, and deal with politics in their everyday lives. Common sense constitutes our cultural system, and our civic ideals should recognize its currency, its foundational presence in people's relationships with intellectualized constructions such as representative democracy. In a competitive media marketplace that exists within a political culture disdainful of politics, the language of common sense will continue to be an attractive means of addressing and incorporating audiences within television programming of politics.

It is ironic, we should note, that conservatives who led the move to impeachment had also been leading proponents in their rhetoric of a return to "common sense" government. Yet when "the people" applied their common sense to the scandal, it actually worked against the political sense that many conservatives used in their efforts to remove Clinton from office. Indeed, the political sense of politicians, journalists, and other institutional elites recognized that to remove a sitting president, certain rules would have to be followed, certain evidence obtained, and certain arguments made to the public for why those actions were justifiable. Common sense, however, suggested otherwise.

6

Changing the Conversation

The Daily Show's Interviews and Interrogations

With the electoral victories posted by Democrats in the 2006 and 2008 elections, the oft-repeated question was whether *The Daily Show* could be as funny with Bush gone and the Republicans largely out of power.[1] Wasn't its job of producing cutting-edge comedy going to be a lot harder now with the Democrats in charge? The question is telling in its misrepresentation of the show, not to mention its lack of understanding of political satire more generally. The fallacy occurs in assuming that all political speech, even satire and humor, is partisan. Satire is an equal opportunity offender, focused as it is on power and the perceived breach in social norms by the powerful. But as Stewart has pointedly noted, "The point of view of this show is we're passionately opposed to bullshit. Is that liberal or conservative?"[2] This statement highlights the primary misconception of the show: whereas it might seem that the program is a political show, or perhaps one focused on news media through its parody of television news, instead, the show is really about *honesty* in public life.[3] Stewart contends that he isn't particularly interested in politics per se.[4] Instead, it is the "bullshit" of publicity (in Habermasian terms)—the elaborate illusions offered up as truth or reality as crafted by politicians, political advocates, 24-hour cable news networks, and other actors who wield power in American society—that is the primary target of the show's satire. In turn, *TDS* has become a response to a public culture in which theatre and showmanship have all too often come to hide the machinations of power behind such spectacles. Furthermore, it is a response to the agonistic displays of vituperative verbal exchanges that all too often substitute for conversation in the public sphere that is television.

As this chapter argues, through the program's reportorial interrogations, as well as Stewart's interviews with an array of public figures, *TDS* seeks to move or change the conversation away from these misleading and spectacle-driven displays. Whether he is calling out politicians and news media through satire or earnestly discussing the findings of an author's new book through measured conversation and debate about current affairs, Stewart seeks a more genuine and less manipulative way in which media can construct public culture. The irony, of course, is that the means used to achieve this honesty is by crafting a lie; that is, his role as anchor of a (fake) news show. The conventions, techniques, and styles that typically constitute television news, however, are the means through which Stewart becomes licensed to engage in numerous on-screen behaviors. These include the anchor's ability to display and comment on news video footage, interview guests, and engage with "correspondents" who personify (and amplify) the manufactured or hyperbolic spectacles that they are supposedly reporting on. Through these actions, *TDS* works against the grain of that which it mimics and mocks in form—television news. Yet rather than creating a mockery of public life (as some critics might have it),[5] or even changing the public dynamic to one that necessitates humor, *TDS* changes the public conversation by criticizing the ways in which news media, through their daily conduct, have participated in leading society astray, and then modeling a way in which it might be done differently.

During the period in which *TDS* became a critical and popular success (roughly 2001–present), two calamitous public events occurred in the United States: the instigation and conduct of a costly war (in lives and treasure) based on a series of governmental lies and fabrications, and the near-collapse of the American (and global) economy, also based on a series of fabrications that the financial sector promulgated while government regulators turned a blind eye. In both instances, much of the news media not only abrogated its reportorial responsibilities, but can be seen as facilitators of (or participants in) the illusions upon which these catastrophes were built.[6] As Stewart claimed of the cable financial news networks that profited from such illusions, they were "not just guilty of a sin of omission but a sin of commission."[7] As such, these politically and economically cataclysmic events have shaped what *TDS* has become as it has gone about doing its own reporting on these events. That reporting is critically inclined, but it is also responsively fashioned as an alternative means through which the "truth" of public life can be achieved.

To argue that *The Daily Show* seeks to change the conversation, however, poses the question: what does the public conversation, as mediated by "real" news organizations, look like now? Television news, in its coverage of politics and public affairs, is generally constructed from two primary reportorial activities, or what are called journalistic *routines*. One is covering the public pronouncements, actions, and events surrounding the powerful (or elites)—most notably, politicians, government bureaucrats, and executives of global capital.[8] Journalists attempt to record, display, and interpret these announcements, actions, and events "objectively" through procedures that are designed to display fairness and a lack of bias in their reporting. In practice, however, the result can often seem as if journalists are little more than stenographers to power, dutifully recording and reporting what the powerful say in such situations (however true or untrue) with little in the way of critique or challenge of the orchestrated events they present. Some journalists contend that it is up to other elites, not journalists, to contest these statements if they are disputable.[9] Others argue that a journalist's first job is to report the event, and then examine it for veracity as the story continues (as we saw earlier in Ted Koppel's defense of how the news media handled the Swift Boat Veteran's campaign against John Kerry). In both instances, the press is foremost concerned with maintaining the perception of neutrality—the key ingredient in their claim to legitimacy. To actively question and contest the information management techniques of the powerful, therefore, is to run the risk of being seen as not neutral, and therefore an untrustworthy or illegitimate source of information.[10]

Television journalists' other primary activity in covering politics consists of interviews with newsmakers and other political operatives.[11] In one-on-one television interviews, reporters can maintain one of several approaches, from combative to compliant. Some have argued that reporters are engaged in a game of "gotcha" as they try to catch any misstatement or gaffe that can become newsworthy.[12] This results in a public culture in which politicians speak in a very measured way (to the point of seeming inauthentic or sterile) for fear of having their words attacked or used against them. Others have argued that the competition to get interviews with top newsmakers is so intense that television reporters bend over backwards not to ruffle the feathers of the interviewee with tough or insistent questioning for fear that they will be passed over or shut out in the future.[13] The result in this situation is that politicians can consistently lie or play loose with facts, knowing their statements won't be aggressively challenged. Finally, in what is referred to as the "talking heads" culture of cable news, much of public affairs programming features reporters or anchors who facilitate discussions among political operatives or supposed experts with differing viewpoints on public issues. The anchor mediates a back-and-forth exchange between opposing sides in hopes that the confrontation might expose different ways of considering an issue.[14] The result, far too often, is the creation of a rigid dichotomy of liberals and conservatives who engage in a partisan and impassioned shouting match that does little to create an inviting conversation or work toward a deliberative resolution in the interest of the common good.

For television news, at least, these are the primary features of the public conversation they help construct. And it is precisely at these points that Stewart inverts the conversation—being combative where news media tend toward compliance, and being constructive and respectful where reporters tend toward combativeness. As this chapter explores, Stewart uses his anchor role to question, interrogate, ridicule, and challenge the public pronouncements of the powerful as he narrates news footage. A primary means for such contestation is the editing or redaction of video footage. In using their own words against them (as assembled through edited video content), Stewart attempts to hold the powerful accountable by exposing their lies, demonstrating their propaganda techniques, and challenging their rhetoric. This interrogation of the "powerful" includes not just politicians, but news media itself. Conversely, in his interviews, Stewart seeks to hold a conversation that is honest and genuine in its exchange and debate of viewpoints and ideas, hopefully devoid of the constructed antinomies of predictable partisanship. As he sees it, the conflict of competing ideologies that dominates public talk is largely a construction by and for media's sake, and one that doesn't represent the mainstream of American society. "Liberals and conservatives," he argues, "are two gangs who have intimidated rational, normal thinking beings

Jon Stewart is able to satirize and interrogate government officials (such as the former deputy secretary of defense, Paul Wolfowitz, shown here) in his role as fake news anchor. Courtesy of Comedy Central.

into not having a voice on television or in the culture. Liberals and conservatives are paradigms that mean nothing to anyone other than the media."[15]

In short, the fake news format provides the means through which *The Daily Show* challenges the predominant ways in which the public conversation is conducted by real television news and public affairs programming. Similar to the previous chapter's focus on the effects of new political television's alternative form of political thinking and talk, *TDS* has demonstrated that the conversation here can be quite different as well. This chapter examines how that is done, starting with Stewart's interrogations of the news before moving on to his interviews with guests.

"A CLERK AND A VIDEO MACHINE": REPORTORIAL PROSECUTION THROUGH REDACTION

Jon Stewart was invited to lunch at the offices of the *New York Times* in 2006. By that point in his career, Stewart had won the respect of journalists for being much more than a late-night comedian and talk show host, but rather, for almost being one of them.[16] When he was asked to explain how *The Daily Show* had been so successful at "digging up [news] clips catching the president and other officials contradicting themselves" (as *Times* columnist Maureen Dowd recounts the story), Stewart simply replied, "A clerk and a video machine."[17] In the heart of what is perhaps the most respected news organization on the planet, a comedian had to remind the assembled reporters of the fundamentals of basic reporting—that is, research. What the *Times* reporters were marveling at were the particular techniques that Stewart employs in his reporting. In fact, much of what *TDS* does that can be considered "reporting" is based upon his use of video footage that occurs primarily in the first segment of each show. As with real news anchors, Stewart moderates a flow of clips of the day's top stories by either talking over the clip or making humorous comments between them. It is within Stewart's commentary where much of the humor of the show lies. But it is through the usage of the clips themselves that much of the show's reporting gets done.

To reiterate the point, *TDS* does actually engage in what can be considered "reporting" on the news, despite its highly manufactured quality that depends on the usage of existing news reports.[18] But to be sure, real news is "manufactured" just as well.[19] What is offered as a commercial product by media institutions and called "news" is not some self-evident or natural reflection of reality. Rather, it is a constructed product, and like other manufactured goods, is produced through specific means of assemblage or ways of doing things, be they called rituals, routines, conventions, or other terms. Therefore, news is very much the product of a set of tacitly agreed-upon values employed by the journalism profession. Those values include certain events, issues, voices, and people that are considered important, legitimate, and newsworthy, and those that are not. Thus, values lead to "choices," none of which are necessarily natural or predetermined, but instead derive from some relationship to larger economic, social, and political power.[20] Such choices are what have defined mainstream news through much of American history, as well as the forms of alternative or dissident journalism that have arisen and co-existed in response to it.[21] Likewise, *TDS* makes specific choices about what is newsworthy, whose voices matter, which issues it will cover, and so on, and then employs its own set of conventions for how these will be reported. Although there are numerous features that compose the totality of the show's "newscast" itself,[22] the specific technique of redacting existing news footage is the focus of our inquiry here.

Redaction, of course, means editing, and the selective editing of news video is central to the show's commentary and humor. But as John Hartley argues, redaction should be seen as a productive, not reductive process. Redaction is the creation of something new and meaningful from existing materials. In the age of information abundance, redaction has become a primary means through which citizens begin to "sort out order from [the] chaos," he argues.[23] Combined with the power of digital technologies, Hartley suggests that perhaps we have even become a "redactional society." He asks, "Are we in a period where it is not information, knowledge and culture as such that determine the age but how they are handled? If so, then a redactional society is one where such processes are primary, where matter is reduced, revised, prepared, published, edited, adapted, shortened, abridged to produce, in turn, the new(s)."[24] For ultimately, the significance of redaction is that it too can become a process through which news/truth/reality are constructed. "It is redaction," he contends, "not original writing (authorship) as such, that determines what is taken to be true, and what policies and beliefs should follow from that."[25] The argument here is just that: through redaction, *TDS* is engaged in a form of constructing "news," and in turn, reporting something that is "new."

Perhaps the most appropriate way of describing how *TDS* employs redaction as a form of reporting is through the metaphor of Stewart as Prosecutor. By employing four sets of redactive techniques, Stewart is able to construct evidence in ways that resemble the behaviors of a criminal prosecutor, yet also stand in contrast to that which television news does (or fails to do) in its usage of video materials at its disposal. These include: (a) *interrogating multiple witnesses*, where video segments from multiple sources are used to look across a subject, event, or programming to make the case; (b) *cross-examining a witness*, whereby video evidence from a single person is used to let them indict themselves; (c) *summarizing the evidence*, whereby the video evidence is edited to summarize a situation or event; and (d) *the closing statement*, a nonnarrated mash-up of video segments that creatively and artistically says something new in ways that are humorous yet conclusive. In each instance, it is through the use of redacted video that something new is being said. By arranging the edits in these ways, Stewart is offering a different take on what the news means. But such meaning is not necessarily arrived at through Stewart's comic asides and narration, as funny and damning as they are. Rather, I argue, what should be considered an alternative form of news reporting is located in the redacted video itself. It is here where Stewart changes the conversation from accommodation and spectacle to confrontation and accountability.

INTERROGATING MULTIPLE WITNESSES

As noted earlier, television news media have been implicated in two of the most egregious public failings of the new millennium—the fabricated reasons for conducting the Iraq War and the American banking and financial sector crisis in 2008–2009. Though *TDS* had scrutinized the press's coverage of the war for several years, the program finally turned its attention to television news media's coverage of the financial sector on March 4, 2009. The episode would be the first of a series of scathing reports and interviews that Stewart conducted over a two-week period, producing what would also become another cultural touchstone of popular critique against the news media (similar to his *Crossfire* appearance) through his interview of CNBC host Jim Cramer (discussed shortly).

While the newly empowered Obama administration continued the Bush-initiated financial bailout of failed banks, insurance giants, and automakers, its proposal to direct a portion of bailout funds to troubled mortgage holders produced an on-air tirade by one of CNBC's financial analysts, Rick Santelli. Santelli railed against the president, addressing Obama directly, telling him that hard-working people had no interest in subsidizing these "losers'" failed mortgages because they bought more house than they could afford. This "cheap populism" (as Stewart called it) that directed rage at homeowners but spared the powerful Wall Streeters who caused the crisis was all that Stewart could take. Stewart scheduled Santelli for an appearance, (which Santelli later cancelled at the last minute), but also prepared an eight-and-a-half-minute segment that would precede the interview. In Santelli's absence, Stewart nevertheless aired the segment, one that offered a blistering critique of CNBC's reporting leading up to the financial sector's collapse.

The segment begins with a clip of Santelli's rant, as well as the network's promo telling viewers that CNBC is "the only business network that has the information and experience you need." Stewart then sets up what is to follow by donning the angry persona and voice of Santelli, telling "loser" and "dumbass homeowners" why they shouldn't be rewarded after missing all the warning signs, especially those that came from the "information and experience" offered by CNBC. Of course, Stewart then proceeds to show exactly what kind of information and experience CNBC offered its viewers, airing a series of clips from CNBC programs with titles such as *Mad Money*, *Fast Money*, *Squawk on the Street*, and *Power Lunch*. Time and time again the network's assurances of financial solvency and stability within the key corporate sector that drove the financial meltdown proved disastrously wrong. Stewart airs a clip in which a network reporter makes a prediction or assurance, which is then followed by a black screen with words that narrate the end result:

> *Mad Money*, March 11, 2008, clip of host Jim Cramer saying, "Bear Sterns is fine"; [Black screen] "Bear Stearns went under six days later."

> *Power Lunch*, June 5, 2008, clip of host saying that Lehman Brothers is no Bear Stearns, and that they can't be compared; [Black screen] "Lehman Brothers went under three months later."

The clips continue to roll with examples of the network assuring viewers that Merrill Lynch, Bank of America, and A.I.G. had enough capital, were still solvent companies, and that their crises were manageable—all followed by black screens announcing the eventual (and opposite) outcome.

After a few comedic asides, Stewart then sets up the next series of redacted video by again chiding the loser homeowner viewers: "You just had to know how to listen." He then screens more clips from network reporters and program hosts, this time with their assurances that the market itself was doing fine, followed by more black screens, this time noting the value of the Dow Jones Industrial Average on the date of each broadcast:

> *Mad Money*, clip of host Jim Cramer saying, "You should be buying things and accept that they're overvalued, but accept that they're going to keep going higher. I know that that sounds irresponsible, but that's how you make the money"; [Black screen] "October 31, 2007, Dow: 13,930."

> *Mad Money*, clip of host Jim Cramer saying, "That's why the market just won't quit, no matter how poorly actual companies are doing"; cut to black screen: "February 1, 2008, Dow: 12,743."

More clips from network programs follow, each including words of assurance: "The worst of the sub-prime business is over"; "Very simply, I believe that it means it's time to buy, buy, buy"; "The fundamentals are coming back into play. I think people are starting to get their confidence back," with the final black screen announcing: "November 4, 2008, Dow: 9,625." The viewer, of course, recognizes that the day this episode of *TDS* airs, the Dow is below 7,000.

After an interlude of more comedic asides (including the line that if he'd followed CNBC's advice, he'd "have a million dollars today, provided [he] started with $100 million"), Stewart then turns his attention to the network's interviews with corporate CEOs at the heart of the financial crisis—Bear Stearns, General Motors, and Merrill Lynch. In each instance, the clips show network reporters simply sitting by as the CEOs offer up their assurances that their companies are doing just fine, with nary a challenge (including one clip of a CNBC reporter with her lips firmly planted, figuratively speaking, in a CEO's backside). Stewart concludes the segment with a clip from what he calls the "network's finest hour"—an interview conducted with Texas billionaire Sir Allen Stanford, the CEO of a bank and wealth management company that turned out to be an $8 billion Ponzi scheme. The interview includes the reporter asking how Stanford was able to avoid the subprime mortgage debacle, then ending the interview by asking him whether it "is fun being a billionaire," to which Stanford replies in the affirmative. Stewart cuts in shouting, "Fuck you!" (to wild audience applause), then ending the segment by noting, "Between the two of them, I can't decide which one of those guys I'd rather see in jail."

The segment is brutal, with Stewart using redacted video to look across the network's programs for repeated patterns over time. Some of the humor may come from Stewart's comedic interventions, but it also resides squarely in the clips themselves when we, as viewers, see how ridiculous these reports seem when removed from the typical flow of hyperbolic reporting in which they are enmeshed. Stewart's critique is not, however, that CNBC should have been able to predict where the market and these companies were headed, but to demonstrate the miserable job they did in *reporting* on Wall Street. The clips show how the spectacle/theatre produced by CNBC is as much a part of the larger bubble/mirage/game that is Wall Street than it is business journalism. Furthermore, if the network is not in bed with the powerful, their reporting at least furthers the moneyed elites' interests. In the end, Stewart shows that given the network's track record on advice, it is a bit unfair that they now turn on their viewers (the nonpowerful) for following or believing it.

CROSS-EXAMINING THE DEFENDANT

When prosecutors cross-examine a defendant on the witness stand, they often seek to create circumstances in which the defendant might say something in the courtroom that can be compared to what he or she has said elsewhere (e.g., a police report or a deposition). Any contradiction in the two statements is helpful in showing that the defendant is untrustworthy, lying, or guilty. Jon Stewart employs a similar technique through redacted video. It is when Stewart strings together several of these duplicitous moments that he makes perhaps the most powerful statement that that which government officials, pundits, and party spokespersons say are often said for expedient and self-interested political value, not to establish truth or to be intellectually honest in what they add to the public conversation. When Alaska Governor Sarah Palin, for instance, was announced rather unexpectedly as Senator John McCain's choice as the Republican vice presidential candidate, *TDS*—like other news outlets—sought to make sense of the choice by asking who is this person, is she qualified, and what about her personal experiences and circumstances is open and valid for scrutiny? But rather than employ its own set of reporters, pundits, and experts, or rather than interview its own set of spokespersons, *TDS* turned its critical eye on that which the cable news industry would offer viewers instead. To no big surprise, those who sought to defend the governor (as well as defend the choice of the selection) repeatedly showed themselves to be partisans by having said the exact opposite in previous situations involving other persons (mostly Democrats).

Stewart begins the segment by noting that Governor Palin had been earning rave reviews from pundits, including former Bush administration advisor Karl Rove.[26] Stewart shows a clip of Rove, now a commentator for Fox News, extolling Palin's credentials, including her being "the mayor, I think, of Alaska's second largest city before she ran for governor." Stewart interjects, noting that Rove is complimenting Palin for being mayor of a city with 9,000 people in it. But he then notes, "I imagine he was equally impressed last month when Tim Kaine, former mayor of Richmond, population 200,000, former Lieutenant Governor of Virginia, and now current Virginia governor was on Barack Obama's vice presidential short list." Another clip of Rove airs in which Rove dismisses Kaine's qualifications, noting that Kaine has been governor for only three years and was mayor of the 105th largest city in America. Rove argues, "Again, with all due respect to Richmond, Virginia, it's smaller than . . ." and then proceeds to list a bevy of small cities that might make the job of being mayor of Richmond seem insignificant. "It's not a big town," he continues, "so if you were to pick Governor Kaine, it would be an intensely political choice where [Obama's saying], 'You know what? I'm really not first and foremost concerned with [the question], 'Is this person capable of being president of the United States?'" Stewart summarizes the clips of Rove's doubletalk by noting, "Karl Rove appears bitterly divided on the experience issue."

Stewart then turns to the controversy surrounding Palin's pregnant, unwed teen daughter. He shows a clip from Fox News talk show host Bill

O'Reilly saying, "As long as society doesn't have to support the mother, father, or baby, it is a personal matter. People will judge Governor Palin and her family." Stewart, in agreement, exhorts, "Yes . . . teen pregnancy is an issue for which judgment is personal and must be withheld," before showing a clip of O'Reilly from a December 19, 2007, episode of *The O'Reilly Factor* taking 16-year old Jamie Lynn Spears's parents to task ("who obviously had little control over her") for letting their daughter get pregnant. O'Reilly labels them, in judgment, to be "incredible pinheads." Stewart seemingly explains O'Reilly's contradiction by noting, "You see, what happens with opinions on teen pregnancy is that they gestate over a period of months . . . you pinheads."

Stewart then announces the next set of clips by proclaiming, "Clearly, though, we should not even be talking about this, because it is sexist." He first airs a clip (from September 2, 2008) with Fox News's Sean Hannity interviewing commentator Dick Morris at the 2008 Republican National Convention:

Hannity: There have been tougher and harder questions that have been asked relentlessly by a biased news media about her daughter than about Barack Obama, who's been running for 19 months.

Morris: A man would never have had to go through this. [Edit cut.] It's a deep sexism that runs through our society.

Stewart: The sexism is so deep. It is the very same sexism that Hillary Clinton faced—right, Dick Morris?

(From November 5, 2007) *Morris*: When a woman wants to be president, she shouldn't complain based on gender. [Edit cut.] 'I'm going to take my toys and go home because the big boys are picking on me.' What happens when the boys in the Middle East, or the boys who run Russia, or the boys who run China start picking on you? Are we going to have the president of the United States saying the boys are picking on me? [Edit cut.] This is what Hillary always does. Whenever she gets under fire, she retreats behind the apron strings.

Stewart: (in response to loud audience groans) Now, now, now. In Dick Morris's defense, he is a lying sack of shit (to audience cheers and applause). Dick Morris certainly isn't the only one who thought that Hillary was playing the gender card.

(From November 5, 2007) *Nancy Pfotenhaur, McCain Senior Policy Advisor*: "The people who think they are helping [Clinton] by playing this gender card are hurting her. [Edit cut.] It would be a terrible mistake for her to play this victimology or this victimization card, because it is just not what we want in a president.

Stewart: Absolutely. That's Nancy P-fotenhaur. I think you know what's coming [next] (as he signals the upcoming clip on his monitor).

(From September 3, 2008) *Pfotenhaur*: I think the nature of these attacks [on Sarah Palin], because they involve family members, and because they are just so disrespectful to her as a woman [sic]. [Edit cut.] I also would have hoped that they'd have learned by now not to be so quick as to belittle the accomplishments of women. [Edit cut.] There were questions about, she has young children. From a female's perspective, I found that to be one of the most outrageous double standards I'd ever seen.

Stewart: Really? One of the most outrageous double standards you'd ever seen? I think I've got some clips you should see (to audience laughter and applause).

Indeed, it is this call-and-response of video evidence showing duplicitous and hypocritical commentary that best makes the case for how the voices that often dominate the public conversation are repeatedly engaged in outrageous double standards based on their or their party's vested interests. Stewart would have us recognize such duplicity, while also being aware of the role that cable news plays in structuring such conversations. This cross-examination technique is also useful in introducing a critical awareness, or what is often called media literacy, to *TDS* viewers. And the awareness we should take from this example is that many of the voices found on cable news networks are less interested in establishing truth or providing honest information or expert opinions than in advancing partisan agendas.

SUMMARIZING THE EVIDENCE

With the daily product that is called "news," facts, events, and stories are offered daily and then, staying true to its name, are replaced by "new" sets of facts, events, and stories the following day. Although some become continuing stories, this constant appearance of new information makes it difficult for viewers or readers to account for their larger meaning over time. Reporters may focus on the specific event or storyline, but miss the repeated patterns that are occurring across the broad swath of public occurrences. Similarly, in the flow of a complicated or complex set of occurrences that happen in a single event or setting, reporters may not summarize the broader patterns that can help citizens make sense of what is occurring. It is in both instances that Stewart offers redactive techniques that are seldom employed by real news media. With presidential rhetoric, for instance, Stewart will show a politicians' talking points, or repeated words and phrases that political actors employ over and over again to shape how people talk and think about something. With a single event, such as a congressional hearing, reporters may summarize the mood and tone of the proceedings or offer a few sound bites of the more confrontational encounters, but they rarely use video to show the repeated language games that people play in such situations. Redacted video can illustrate the repetition, bringing the patterns to light and providing a different perspective on what viewers may not see through typical news reporting.

The August 25, 2005, episode exemplifies Stewart's use of redaction to illuminate presidential talking points. Throughout the segment, Stewart moderates and explains the strategy or techniques that the Bush administration was using to shape public thinking about the Iraq War, highlighting the specific words and phrases repeated over and over to accomplish that. Stewart begins by explaining that as Bush "travels the country speaking about the war, it is clear that he has developed a sophisticated exit strategy . . . (pause) for getting out of questions about the war. It is a strategy called repetition or . . . (pause) repetition. It is one he has used with great success many times before." He continues by explaining,

> *Stewart*: First step is to let people know you are aware of their questions. Then the president can reduce these nuanced concerns into a simplistic, misguided concern that he can easily refute.
>
> [Plays three different clips of Bush recognizing people for "wondering about troop withdrawals."]
>
> *Stewart*: See. He hears the concerns that make you look like a pussy. So staying the course in Iraq is the plan. But what about all the violence and chaos we see? Pah! It's no match for a simple eight-letter word. See if you can pick out the one he uses.
>
> [Plays seven different clips of Bush talking about making "progress" in Iraq.]
>
> *Stewart*: So we're doing the right thing and we're making good progress. I guess that means, if I hear you correctly . . . that soon we'll be able to talk about concrete troop withdrawals?
>
> [Plays six different clips of Bush saying there are not going to be any "artificial timetables" for troop withdrawals.]
>
> *Stewart*: Now here is why staying on message with your talking points is difficult. Back when the war began, the talking points for the president centered on weapons of mass destruction. Really drilled that into our heads, actually, quite a lot of talk. That doesn't seem to come up so much anymore. But you just know some nosey reporter's always going to ask. So the key for your new war rationale talking point is delivering them as if the person who asked is retarded.
>
> [Plays seven different clips of Bush saying, patronizingly, that the U.S. will "defeat them there so we don't have face them here."]
>
> *Stewart*: Of course, sometimes, no matter how good your talking points, no matter how many times you repeat them, there are still some dissenters and some nonbelievers. If only there was a way you could shut these remaining people up with some kind of emotional bludgeon.
>
> [Plays five different clips of Bush connecting 9/11 to the war in Iraq.]
>
> *Stewart*: And there you go. Talking points. Simple. Catchy.

Similar to the cross-examination redaction mentioned previously, Stewart is offering a lesson in how to pay critical attention to rhetorical language that politicians use for repetition and amplification across media outlets. But by looking across events, he is also offering a level of scrutiny that journalists all too often ignore in their daily production of news. The news value of these speaking engagements, Stewart demonstrates, is not the particular events themselves but Bush's overall salesmanship of his policies over time, such as this language that would have us continue the war in Iraq or Bush's linking that conflict to 9/11. As Stewart notes in his moderating comments, it was just such a pattern (which news media dutifully reported) that led to the effective sales effort for going to war based on the phrase "weapons of mass destruction." What is the new catch phrase, Stewart asks, and how might it too lead citizens to think in ways the president would prefer? The redaction illuminates the president's rhetorical tactics clearly, while removing other aspects of the speeches that might obscure these essential points.

Stewart and *TDS* have also mastered the ability to report on a complex event or occurrence and use redacted video to summarize essential points or exchanges from an event. For instance, when Attorney General Alberto Gonzalez appeared before the Senate Judiciary Committee on April 19, 2007, to account for his role in the firings of eight U.S. attorneys (perhaps for politically motivated reasons), Stewart offered background information from two previous media appearances in which Gonzalez addressed his role in the scandal. Stewart then reported evidence (from a *Washington Post* report) that in preparing for his senate testimony, the attorney general had spent several days, for up to five hours a day, rehearsing for the hearing through mock testimony. Stewart then began rolling video clips of the senate appearance, including nine straight in which Gonzalez replies to senators' questions with "I don't recall," followed by a clip of him saying, "I firmly believe that nothing improper occurred." Stewart then explains what this all means: "After weeks of mock testimony, there you have it. Alberto Gonzalez doesn't know what happened, but he assures you what he doesn't remember was handled properly." He goes on to note, "By the way, there were no duplicates there. Alberto Gonzalez used the phrase 'I don't recall' forty-five times before lunch. I should point out at this point, that's a lot." By not just reporting Gonzalez's obfuscation but actually demonstrating it repeatedly, the viewer experiences for his or herself one of the more essential points of the proceedings. There is a particular power in seeing for yourself something being done over and over again, and in this instance, knowing it occurred another thirty-six times.

Through these two sets of redacted video, then, Stewart has attempted to summarize the most important aspects of these public performances. Political actors take to the stage, and part of what they expect is that news media will dutifully circulate their pronouncements. Although Gonzalez would certainly have preferred not to be involved in this performance, he would surely be comforted in knowing that news media typically frame such performances as encounters between opposing sides (Democrats versus Republicans, the legislative versus the executive branch, or two strong-willed personalities). Similarly, when Bush tours the country selling his ideas about how the war should proceed, he can expect that news media will carry his words repeatedly and often. And as Stewart notes, when things are said repeatedly enough, they tend to *become* true simply by virtue of being said over and over (or at least by shaping the terms of debate).[27] What Stewart has done through redacted video, however, is frame these public performances differently. By isolating Gonzalez's attempts at obfuscation (as also shown by additional clips within the segment), it is Gonzalez alone that is under scrutiny, not the opposing side that the viewer is also invited to interrogate (and side with or against) in the journalists' frame.

With the president, the redaction serves to illustrate what talking points are and how they work. Journalists typically broadcast the talking points or highlight what it is the president is selling, but it is the event itself that matters most as a "news" event (which dictates how it should be reported). Journalists will rarely show the viewer what such performances look like over time. This, of course, is exactly why Bush was touring the country in the first place—to drive home his point again and again over time. Thus, Stewart focuses in on precisely this—the points that really matter only as related to the president's rhetorical intentions. And as was the case with previous Bush talking points such as the nonexistent "weapons of mass destruction," everything else is ultimately irrelevant if we come to believe in the larger initiative being sold. Again, redaction that succinctly summarizes these intentions helps us see the point more clearly.

CLOSING STATEMENTS

If a prosecutor's closing argument consists largely of a summary of evidence designed to appeal to the jury's desire for rational closure amidst the sea of information that has been presented to them, the prosecutor's closing statement might best appeal to the jury's emotions. The closing statement is the poetry that follows and concludes the prose, offering a more poignant and emotionally loaded point from which the jury should begin its deliberations. *The Daily Show* employs this technique as well, using redacted video as an aesthetic treatment of that which has been handled previously in a more methodical and rational manner (as per the previous discussion). This version of redaction, however, alters the public conversation by adding a degree of playful commentary unlike almost anything found on American television. *TDS* employs what is commonly referred to as a "mash-up" video, where snippets of speech performances are linked together to create a verbal and visual montage, while often including music for playful and humorous effect. In this way, the show offers up what is more commonly associated with alternative media expressions known as "culture jamming."[28] Indeed, in explaining the impetus behind some forms of culture jamming, Michael Strangelove explains how "commercial media inhibits [sic] audiences' ability to see interconnections, cumulate information, organize it into patterns, and draw conclusions about actions and consequences within the social system."[29] Montage produced through redaction, however, does just this. And although *TDS* is certainly "commercial media," it nevertheless has adapted these techniques to make its own political statements in new and creative ways.[30] In these mash-ups, Stewart no longer narrates the video, but instead lets the artistry of creative and critical redaction do the talking for him.

Following the segment on Bush's talking points described earlier, for instance, *TDS* produced a 1:07-minute mash-up called "MC Dubya," in which the talking point words were then mashed together in a cartoonish and poetic fashion aided by a hip-hop dance beat. The message here is driven less by imagery and more by the cutting and splicing of Bush's words to create a new statement. Each word derives either from a separate speech or a single speech, with the words then repeated several times. The video begins by crafting a syncopated rhythm of Bush's words, with him saying, "Progress, pro-pro-progress," immediately followed by "September 11, 2001." Bush's words continue to roll forward rapidly with a thumping rhythm that provides a foundation for the words' own syncopation:

> Terrorists, terrorism
> attacked, attacked, attacked
> Iraq
> defeating them where they live
> Iraq, Iraq, Iraq
> before they can attack us here at home
> Iraq, Iraq, Iraq
> Aaafghaaaaaniiiistaaaaan (with the enunciation of the word greatly retarded)
> Any weapons of mass destru— (interrupted by the sound of squealing car tires)
> Freedom

The mash-up continues in the same vein. The newly assembled message seems fairly obvious, including the point that we should slow down and recognize that Afghanistan is where the terrorists live, as well as the Bush administration's rhetorical ploy/excuse of "weapons of mass destruction" has been interrupted and replaced with new mobilizing language (e.g., "freedom").

On the last day of the Bush presidency (January 19, 2009), *TDS* offered another mash-up as its "Moment of Zen" segment which closes the show. Stewart began by noting,

> I'd like to take a minute to acknowledge the end of an era. These last eight years have been, gosh, just, well, great for this show. So we wanted to recognize some of the people without whom we couldn't have done our program. So please, pay attention to the credits. It's all the people who made this possible for the past eight years.

The mash-up then runs through a series of redacted clips of prominent Bush administration officials making some of their more famous or embarrassing pronouncements. Somewhat cast as a typical blooper reel that accompanies the credits of a Hollywood comedy film, the right side of the screen offers the "credits" to which Stewart referred, while the clips roll on the left. The credits include, "Written and Directed By Karl Rove; Cast in Order of Appearance: Decider, George W. Bush; Actual President, Richard Cheney." Barbara Streisand's rendition of "Memories" accompanies the video. The clips that make-up the segment include:

> *Deputy Secretary of Defense Paul Wolfowitz*: "We're dealing with a country that can really finance its own reconstruction relatively soon."

> *Attorney General Alberto Gonzalez*: "I don't recall remembering."

> *Press Secretary Scott McClelland*: "I was a part of this propaganda campaign, absolutely."

> *Secretary of the Treasury Henry Paulsen*: "Our markets are the envy of the world."

> *White House Advisor Karl Rove*: [rapping in his infamous performance as MC Rove . . . in a tuxedo]

> *Secretary of State Condoleezza Rice*: "I believe the report was titled 'Bin Laden Determined to Attack Inside the United States.'"

> *Defense Secretary Donald Rumsfeld*: "It is not knowable how long that conflict would last. It could last, you know, six days, six weeks, I doubt six months."

> *Vice President Dick Cheney*: "There is no doubt that Saddam Hussein has weapons of mass destruction."

> *President George W. Bush*: "I couldn't imagine somebody like Osama Bin Laden understanding the joys of Hanukkah."

In one minute and thirty-one seconds, the program had served up a damning yet humorous indictment of the Bush administration that hit many of the high/low points of their eight-year tenure. The indictment is delivered in the words by those who actually spoke them, with each offering a nice summary of that individual's primary role in the administration. The segment concludes with the final credit roll, "Special thanks to 537 confused elderly voters in Florida," referring to the voters who helped put Bush in office through their inability to handle paper ballots properly (at least as constructed by liberal mythology). What a mash-up like this provides that the other redacted videos discussed previously do not is a poetic statement that needs little in the way of additional commentary to make it humorous or meaningful. It succinctly summarizes, while offering a potent flavor of political commentary. There is no mistaking what the intentions are here. *TDS* is not "reporting" on the Bush administration in these instances. It is passing judgment, and it is asking the jury—the viewers at home—to do the same.

In sum, *TDS* is very much involved in the business of reporting. Although it does not "gather" materials anew (as does real television news media), it does process the extant materials into new forms, offering a different means through which such materials should be viewed and processed. While one might be tempted to argue that what *TDS* offers is simply a clever form of political commentary as opposed to reporting, two points militate against that reading. First, although humor punctuates the evidence, it is the evidence itself—as presented through redacted video—that is ultimately most important in conveying the point of these exposes. Like a criminal prosecutor, Stewart is assembling and presenting evidence here, not opinions. Second, what Stewart is using is the same materials as does "real" news. He is simply arranging it differently, showing different parts, and leading the viewers to examine it critically. Stewart is violating the tacitly agreed-upon news values—and the choices that follow from them—that largely determine how most news organizations present information. Whether this should be labeled an "alternative" form of journalism is less important than recognizing that Stewart is, in fact, changing the public conversation by interrogating these materials of public life in newly critical ways.

WHAT ARE INTERVIEWS FOR, ANYWAY?

In the early years of Stewart's tenure at *TDS*, the guest interview segment of the program most often featured a celebrity pitching his or her latest project (as is typical on most other late night talk shows). In 2002, Stewart explained the use of celebrity interviews as a time-filler: "Honestly, one of the reasons that it's there is we just can't write that much. . . . It's not part of the show that any of us necessarily go, 'I can't wait to get hold of that interview segment and make it happen.'"[31] By 2005, the show's approach to the interview segment began to change. When the program moved to a new studio and constructed a new set, the producers removed the traditional late-night talk show couch and simply placed the guests across the desk from Stewart in a less comfortable, more business-like chair. More than simply an aesthetic change, however, the move actually reflected the more serious and concerted approach the show was taking in its guest interview segment. Although the show still includes a smattering of celebrities, the segment has now become a forum through which Stewart primarily interviews at least two sets of guests—politicians and government officials, and an array of book authors, journalists, and writers who might be able to offer some insight into contemporary public affairs. For the first week on the show's new set (July 11–14, 2005), for instance, the program hosted three book authors and one magazine reporter. The authors included a constitutional law scholar discussing her book on church-state relations, a magazine reporter who covered the 2004 presidential campaign, and a former reporter who wrote a book that could be seen as part of the culture wars. By February 2007, the show's tendency to host authors of nonfiction books had become so frequent that the *New York Times* reported the trend in an article titled, "Serious Book to Peddle? Don't Laugh, Try a Comedy Show."[32] In it, the *Times* reported how book publishers praised *TDS*, along with *The Colbert Report*, for being the premier location on television (with *Oprah*) for driving book sales. Furthermore, the show's hosts are also credited with helping elucidate the book's primary points and arguments. As one author noted in praising his experience on *TDS*, "It's not just that serious books get a hearing on comedy shows . . . but serious books get a serious hearing, as well as a funny one, on comedy shows."[33]

It is the "serious hearing" that has attracted the attention of scholars. Geoffrey Baym, for instance, has examined the interview segment of *TDS* and argues that Stewart "reworks the rules of news and celebrity interviewing," in the process blending postmodern aesthetics with "a modernist ethos of rational-critical dialogue."[34] Elsewhere Baym has noted the important change of tone that has resulted from Stewart's interview style, in particular Stewart's desire to achieve "civility of exchange, complexity of argument, and the goal of mutual understanding. Lying just beneath or perhaps imbricated within the laughter is a quite serious demand for fact, accountability, and reason in political discourse."[35] In his interviews, Stewart is resolutely polite, and like other great media interviewers (such as public radio and public television's Terry Gross and Charlie Rose, respectively), seems particularly focused on holding a *conversation*, not just conducting an interview. Gross and Rose have up to an hour with their guests, but Stewart must hold that conversation typically in about five to seven minutes (although some interviews can run upward of fifteen minutes). But in so doing, Stewart demonstrates how it is possible to change the type of public conversation that is typically constructed through news and public affairs interviews, even under the constraints of limited time.

The interviews examined here all feature guests with whom Stewart, at some level, disagrees. These include Stewart's polite challenge to conservative author Bernard Goldberg, his desire to debate political talking points with former Arkansas Governor Mike Huckabee, and his full-throated demand for accountability and responsibility from CNBC television host Jim Cramer. With all three, Stewart models how interviews can be conducted differently, while also demonstrating the importance of disagreement as a means of producing conversations which advance the public good. That is to say that he shows how using the deliberative ideal of respectful disagreement can bring us closer to mutual understanding and acceptance—even when both sides agree to disagree in the end.

The week that *TDS* initiated its set redesign, Stewart hosted author and former CBS journalist Bernard Goldberg to talk about Goldberg's book, *100 People Who Are Screwing Up America (and Al Franken is #37)*.[36] In his retirement from journalism, Goldberg has entered the realm of ideological book publishing, churning out tomes that stoke the flames of readers who are suspicious of controlling elites with titles such as *Arrogance: Rescuing America from the Media Elite* and *Bias: A CBS Insider Exposes How the Media Distort the News*. His *100 People* book's cover, which Stewart displays for the audience, includes photographs of some of the supposed screwer-uppers, including Michael Moore, Al Sharpton, Eminem, Michael Jackson, Ted Kennedy, and Barbara Streisand. This is one of those occasions in which Stewart is truly interested in debating the merits of an author's thesis. Yet he also desires told hold a conversation that focuses squarely on that disagreement, not partisan bickering that can quickly consume many cable news interviews.

The interview begins with Goldberg enunciating the book's central argument, which is that the cultural environment has become angrier, nastier, and more vulgar in recent years, and those who have made it that way are largely a set of liberal cultural elites. Stewart spends much of the interview politely advancing the point that Goldberg has the wrong cast of characters in his scope. As a case in point, Stewart highlights Goldberg's inclusion of Barbara Streisand as enemy number 91, an insignificant voice that Stewart jokes "hasn't ruined the culture since *Yentl*." Rather than the unimportant though clearly visible celebrities Goldberg has targeted, real power, Stewart argues, is located in politics:

> *Stewart*: So much focus is on culture, and so little is on government and the real seats of power.
>
> *Goldberg*: And you don't think culture is a powerful force out there?
>
> *Stewart*: Not nearly as much as government.
>
> *Goldberg*: When the Hollywood blowhards out there throw the word "Nazi" around, I don't like that anymore than I would like it if some bigot in the old days would throw the word "nigger" around, and that's the culture. That's not government; that's culture.

Stewart: I've been to L.A. and I've been to Washington. They're the same city. The only difference between L.A. and Washington is they think they have power in L.A. They don't. It's the same insular assholes you find in both areas.

Goldberg: Yeah, I agree.

Stewart: But in Washington, they actually do have power. And that I think is the concern. So much is focused on this elitist culture of Hollywood, but [then] they, you know, [say] "Damn you," and then, "I'm gonna go out and write a song" (audience laughter). But in Washington, they are really controlling and changing people's lives. The focus should be on them.

Goldberg: If you wanna make believe it doesn't matter what kind of songs people write, then when they write that women are nothing but bitches and hos, let's just sit there and say, "Hey, it's no big deal. It's only culture." It's either a big deal or it isn't.

Stewart: Nah, I disagree with that. I think it is the general detritus and static that exists in a world that is complex. But in Washington, transparency is the real issue. I wish smart guys like you spent more time not worrying about Barbara Streisand, but worrying about, you know, Richard Perle, Karl Rove, or whoever the Democrats would have had in that position during the Clinton years. That's all I'm suggesting.

Later, to prove his point of cultural vulgarity, Goldberg notes that comedian and actor Chevy Chase went to a Washington gala at the Kennedy Center, and felt emboldened enough by the culture to call the president of the United States a "dumb fuck." Stewart replies,

Stewart: Once upon a time Thomas Jefferson fucked slaves. Like, I guess what I'm saying is nostalgia for the culture is . . . (interrupted by audience laughter)

Goldberg: I'm supposed to take the other side of that?

Stewart: No, but what I'm suggesting is, yes, Chevy Chase used a bad word on TV at the Kennedy Center, but segregation no longer exists, slavery is gone.

Goldberg: Ahh.

Stewart: That's real culture and real vulgarity. This is just words.

Goldberg: Just words. Well, Ok. Ok. Let's say we have a bigot channel.

Stewart: We do.

They then engage in some back and forth, with Stewart never saying that Fox News is the bigot channel he was thinking of, although the audience seemingly knows that Fox is the object of his joke. Goldberg proceeds, trying to make the point that words do matter, and if there *were* a bigot channel, liberals would be up in arms to regulate it. Noting its hypothetical cultural significance Goldberg continues:

> *Goldberg*: It's still out there. It's still nasty. It's still mean-spirited. It's still wrong. I don't want a law, even against the bigot channel. But I wanna talk about it.
>
> *Stewart*: I understand that.
>
> *Goldberg*: I wanna say it's cheapening the culture.
>
> *Stewart*: I definitely understand that. You know, listen. I don't disagree that there are certain broadcast limits that have been, for better or worse, lessened or weakened over the years. I guess my point is that there is a larger issue of, most everybody I see in your book is powerless, and I think there is a much larger issue of people in power creating problems, not Barbara Streisand on her blog.

It is rare for interviewers to assert their opinions and point of view so directly. But given that the guest is promoting a book built around that thesis, to openly disagree is to challenge its merits and perhaps even repress sales. Not only does Stewart disagree, but he also offers an alternative argument or hypothesis. His point is not to make Goldberg look bad or to say that his book is crap, but to address that which he finds as a spurious but common ideological argument that misses the far more important and pressing point about power. He is politely insisting that the entire argument is contrived and fails to adequately conceptualize the central ingredients of the discussion within the larger flow of history—what is "culture," what is "vulgarity," who really has "power," and what truly constitutes a "threat"? In so doing, he has changed the terms of debate instead of accepting the argument at face value, as television journalists are apt to do.

Not only is he changing the conversation by playing outside the bounds of the typical back-and-forth between left and right and their talking points. He is also changing the assigned role that the interviewer is supposed to play in crafting those conversations, moving from what often amounts to being a publicity agent for the media product being hawked (the unwritten rule of such appearances) to one in which the interviewer should engage, debate, challenge, and refuse to accept the argument if he or she disagrees. This dimension of Stewart's interview style is best demonstrated when Chris Matthews, the cable talk show host, appeared on October 2, 2007, to promote his book *Life's a Campaign*. The book's thesis, as Stewart explains, is that "people can use what politicians do in political campaigns to help their lives." Stewart quickly noted that he found that thesis "fundamentally wrong," and that the book seemed a "recipe for sadness." After a brief debate, Matthews objected, accusing Stewart of "trashing my book," to which Stewart replied, "I'm trashing your philosophy of life." Completely frustrated that Stewart was challenging him, Matthews then exclaimed, "You are unbelievable. This is a book interview from hell. This is the worst interview I have ever had in my life." In other words, how dare Stewart not play by the rules of publicity culture? The typical television interview is one in which the interviewer helps promote the book by asking "questions," or really just prompts, that allow the interviewee to sell it, not be challenged on the book's actual argument or merits. Stewart has violated those rules here, and Matthews bluntly points it out in return.

Yet given this propensity to debate his guests when he finds their argument weak or wrong, we also see from the Goldberg interview how Stewart's manner and demeanor invites a discussion built around non-adversarial exchange. Both sides admit or concede good points and arguments, while also politely disagreeing on their central point. Neither Stewart nor Goldberg is attempting to win by belittling, shouting down, ridiculing, or making the other person into an enemy. They seem to be genuinely involved in a discussion about ideas, not a verbal confrontation for theatre's (or ego's) sake. As Baym would have us see, the discussion truly is a model of rational-critical discourse.[37] And for that reason, it seems amazingly different from much of what constitutes political discourse on television.

When former Arkansas governor and Republican presidential contender Mike Huckabee appeared on the show (December 9, 2008), it was also under the auspices of promoting his book, *Do the Right Thing: Inside the Movement That's Bringing Common Sense Back to America*. But as Stewart quickly pointed out, the book is essentially Huckabee's platform statement for another presidential run in 2012. As such, the debate that followed was less about the book and more about Huckabee's conservative stance on issues. What is distinctive about the interview—and how it highlights the ways in which Stewart is changing the public conversation—is that it really isn't an "interview"—it is a conversational debate. And what is also distinctive is that there really are few other places on television with this type of debate format, one that affords a citizen (because Stewart isn't a journalist) the opportunity to directly challenge and debate the merits of a politician's reasoning and positions over the course of 15 minutes, one-on-one. Most television interactions with major party politicians are in the form of a news or public affairs show interview, or perhaps even the broadcast of politicians debating each other in formal debates during election season. Yet here the two sides aren't "moderated," thereby letting the debate take its own form, and the exchange isn't structured around a question and answer format. As Stewart is not seeking office or trying to maintain the news media's perception of "neutrality," the format allows for a spirited give-and-take unlike most any other public affairs programming on television.[38]

The second part of Stewart's two segments with Huckabee focuses specifically on the issue of gay marriage. Stewart begins by asking Huckabee to explain why conservatives are against it:

Stewart: Respectfully speaking, I guess the one thing I don't understand about social conservatives—I get pro-life . . . it's very easy for me to understand it. . . . The gay marriage issue, and why conservatives are against it. You write that marriage is the bedrock of our society. Why would you not want more couples to buy into the stability of marriage? Why would you want that precluded for an entire group of people?

The two then debate Huckabee's position for the remainder of the segment. What stands out about the exchange is the differing uses of moral and logical reasoning and argumentation employed by Huckabee and Stewart over the course of the interview. Huckabee essentially serves up a litany of well-honed conservative talking points on why gay marriage is unacceptable. Yet every single one of the "reasons" put forth is what students of rhetoric and argumentation call rhetorical fallacies, or errors in reasoning. In making an argument, one commits a rhetorical fallacy when the truth of the argumentative claim does not follow from the reasoning put forth to support it.[39] Listed here is each of Huckabee's arguments (in order) about gay marriage, followed in parentheses by the fallacy:

- "Marriage still means one man, one woman." (Appeal to Common Practice)
- "Even anatomically . . . the only way we can create the next generation is through a male-female relationship." (Appeal to Consequences of a Belief, in addition to being factually incorrect)
- "For 5,000 years of recorded human history, that is what marriage has meant." (Appeal to Tradition)
- "Thirty states have had it on the ballot, and in all thirty states, [Defense of Marriage Acts have] passed." (Appeal to Popularity)
- "If we change the definition, then we really do have to change it to accommodate all lifestyles." (Slippery Slope)
- "Marriage still means a male and a female relationship. Until the law is overturned, it still means that." (Appeal to Authority)
- ". . . a person practicing a lifestyle." (Red Herring)
- "They're asking to redefine the word." (Appeal to Belief)
- "We are not banning; we are affirming what has always been." (Appeal to Tradition)
- "But if the American people are not convinced that we should overturn the definition of marriage, then I would say those who support the idea of same-sex marriage have a lot of work to do to convince the rest of us." (Burden of Proof; Appeal to the People)

- "I think we have to be very thoughtful and careful before we say that we're going to undo an entire social structure." (Slippery Slope)

For an ordained Southern Baptist minister, it seems odd that Huckabee never relies on religion or even moral language and thinking to make his case, perhaps reflecting his current political instincts for mass (secular) appeal. Instead, he is dependent on a litany of spurious claims that cannot be supported logically. Yet Stewart doesn't challenge Huckabee based on this fallacious reasoning. Instead, it is Stewart who uses morality, in addition to history, to form the backbone of his counterarguments and critiques. From an historical perspective, Stewart repeatedly reminds Huckabee that definitions and standards have changed over time: in the Bible, polygamy was the norm; marriage has evolved over time, including its function as a property arrangement; at one time, different races couldn't marry; marriage was not a sacrament until the thirteenth century; segregation was once the "law of the land" until the courts intervened; and so on. But morality—equality, fairness, rights and privileges—becomes the center of Stewart's challenge to Huckabee's claims:

"I don't know why polygamy is the issue here. It seems like a *fundamental human right*. You write in your book that all people are *created equal*, and yet for gay people, you believe it is corrosive to society to allow them to have the *privileges* that all humans enjoy."

"But it does beg the question, why? You keep talking about it would be redefining a word. It feels like semantics is cold comfort when it comes to *humanity*, and especially [from] someone such as yourself."

"You talk about the pro-life movement [sic] being one of the great shames of our nation. I think if you want number two . . . it is an absolute *travesty* that people have forced someone who is gay to have to make their case that they deserve the same *basic rights* as someone else."

Thus, Stewart attempts to move the conversation away from political talking points (however fallacious) toward a central question of societal decency and justice. Stewart seems focused on reminding the good reverend of what "doing the right thing" looks like when based on the "common sense" of moral reasoning. As the conversation ends, Huckabee admits that he and Stewart are "probably not going to come to terms" in the exchange, and that he "respects" their disagreement.

It is a remarkable display of political debate for television. Huckabee and Stewart are not shouting at one another via a satellite link. There are no intermediaries to steer the conversation, ask distracting questions, or change the subject. Nor is there concern for offending the politician by simply challenging his thinking. Instead, sitting across from one another, Huckabee is asked to make his case, and then to defend it point by point. The audience then witnesses two lines of reasoning in an unfettered seven-minute debate. And all of this occurs within the structure of an entertainment show (although Stewart attempts little in the way of comedy). Again, there is little else on television that compares to this type of citizen-politician exchange, and in that regard alone, Stewart and *TDS* have offered a refreshingly genuine contribution to the larger public conversation.

One final, if not also extraordinary example of the way in which Stewart uses the interview segment of his program to change the public conversation occurred on March 12, 2009, when Stewart interviewed Jim Cramer, host of the CNBC program *Mad Money*. As discussed previously, the financial news network became the object of criticism when Stewart ran a segment of redacted video ridiculing the network for its shoddy reporting. As Cramer was notably featured in several of those redactions, he quickly took to the airwaves (across NBC Universal's various media properties, including MSNBC and NBC's *Today* show) in the days following the criticism to defend himself and dismiss *TDS* as little more than a "variety show." Stewart then responded with two more segments aimed at CNBC and Cramer on March 9 and 10, 2009. As Cramer thus became the public face of the critique, he agreed to appear on the program.

Although the interview itself was deadly serious, with Stewart uncharacteristically becoming downright angry at times, the show nevertheless opened with a satirical flourish. In a manner similar to its typical mocking of the way in which cable news creates hyperbolic and spectacle promos for their shows and specials, *TDS* began with the following video clip:

Announcer: March 12, 2009. You've watched snippets of them for days, or meant to after your friends sent you the link. You twit blogged it on the interscape. People on TV have talked about how much people have talked about it.

Clip of CNN Reporter: "The ongoing grudge match between *Daily Show* host Jon Stewart and CNBC host Jim Cramer."

Announcer: "People staying in hotels are wondering why it's on the cover of their free paper [image of *USA Today*]. Tonight, the weeklong feud of the century comes to a head. Cramer. Stewart. In a 12-minute faceoff that could marginally increase the very rate Comedy Central charges for 30-seconds of advertising time. [Image of fake logo] Welcome to "Brawl Street." Get ready to "Buy Low and Sell Die."

Stewart then airs a clip of himself "preparing" all day for the confrontation by being coached in the arcane language of markets and finance. He then shows clips of what Cramer had been up to that day—appearing on Martha Stewart's show. Stewart wryly notes, "How weird is our world when Jim Cramer's on TV baking pie and Martha Stewart's the one that went to jail for securities fraud?" Stewart then introduces Cramer, and immediately asks, "How the hell did we end up here, Mr. Cramer? What happened?" After some small talk, he points out that *TDS*'s criticisms were not directed at Cramer per se, and that it was unfortunate he had become the public face of the controversy. Cramer immediately launched into his own apologies for "getting it wrong" (offering bad advice), noting that "everyone got it wrong." But Stewart tries to clarify why CNBC had come under attack from his program:

> *Stewart*: So let me tell you why I think this has caught some attention. It's the gap between what CNBC advertises itself as, and what it is, and the help that people need to discern this. Let me show you. . . . This is the promo for your show.
>
> [Video clip voiceover]: An economy in free-fall. Investments on the brink. When you don't know what to do, don't panic. Cramer's got your back. *Mad Money with Jim Cramer*.
>
> *Stewart*: Look, we are both snake oil salesmen to a certain extent, but we do label the show as snake oil here. Isn't there a problem with selling snake oil and labeling it as vitamin tonic and saying that it cures impetigo etc., etc., etc. Isn't that the difficulty here?

Cramer responds by seeming particularly focused on his making some "bad calls." Stewart notes that he's missing the point; that the issue isn't good and bad calls, but the role that CNBC plays in creating the mirage of what the market really is, or what Stewart calls the "the real market and unreal market":

> *Stewart*: Now why when you talk about the regulators, why not the financial news network? That is the whole point of this. CNBC could be an incredibly powerful tool of illumination for people that believe that there are two markets: One that has been sold to us as long-term. Put your money in 401Ks. Put your money in pensions and just leave it there. Don't worry about it. It's all doing fine. Then, there's this other market; this real market that is occurring in the back room. Where giant piles of money are going in and out and people are trading them and it's transactional and it's fast. But it's dangerous, it's ethically dubious and it hurts that long-term market. So what it feels like to us—and I'm talking purely as a layman—it feels like we are capitalizing your adventure by our pension and our hard-earned money. And that it is a game that you know. That you know is going on. But that you go on television as a financial network and pretend isn't happening. (Applause)
>
> *Cramer*: Okay. First, my first reaction is absolutely we could do better. Absolutely. . . .

CNBC program host and analyst Jim Cramer appearing on The Daily Show *on March 12, 2009, to account for why his network did such a poor job of financial news reporting prior to the meltdown of the American economy. AP/Wide World Photos*

Stewart then shows several webcast video interviews of Cramer on TheStreet.com, where Cramer essentially brags about various ethically dubious trading practices:

> *Stewart*: I gotta tell you. I understand that you want to make finance entertaining, but it's not a fucking game. (Applause) When I watch that I get, I can't tell you how angry it makes me because it says to me, "You all know." You all know what's going on. You can draw a straight line from those shenanigans to the stuff that was being pulled at Bear and at AIG and all this derivative market stuff that is this weird Wall Street side bet.
>
> *Cramer*: But Jon, don't you want guys like me that have been in it to show the shenanigans? What else can I do? I mean, last night's show—
>
> *Stewart*: No, no, no, no, no. I want desperately for that, but I feel like that's not what we're getting. What we're getting is . . . Listen, you knew what the banks were doing and yet were touting it for months and months. The entire network was and so now to pretend that this was some sort of crazy, once-in-a-lifetime tsunami that nobody could have seen coming is disingenuous at best and criminal at worst. (Applause)

The conversation continues, eventually turning again to the shoddy reporting that CNBC has done in reporting the lies of CEOs of the failed financial institutions:

Cramer: But Dick Fuld who ran Lehman Brothers . . . He brings me in, lies to me, lies to me, lies to me. I've known him for twenty years.

Stewart: The CEO of a company lied to you.

Cramer: Shocker.

Stewart: But isn't that financial reporting? What do you think is the role of CNBC?

Cramer: Look, I have called for star chambers—I want kangaroo courts for these guys—

Stewart: It's very easy to get on this after the fact . . . CNBC could act as—No one is asking them to be a regulatory agency, but . . . whose side are they on? It feels like they have to reconcile, is their audience the Wall Street traders that are doing this for constant profit on a day-to-day for short-term? These guys at these companies were on a Sherman's March through their companies, financed by our 401Ks, and all the incentives of their companies were for short-term profit. And they burned the fucking house down with our money and walked away rich as hell, and you guys knew that that was going on. (Applause)

Cramer continues to be contrite and apologetic, as he has been throughout the interview. Stewart again reiterates his regret that Cramer has become the face of the controversy over CNBC's reporting. But then he ends the conversation with one last chiding:

Stewart: So maybe we could remove the "financial expert" and the "In Cramer We Trust" and start getting back to fundamentals on reporting as well, and I can go back to making fart noises and funny faces.

Cramer: I think we make that deal right here (as the two shake hands).

The confrontation was nothing less than extraordinary. Stewart noted as such when introducing the show's "Moment of Zen" by saying, "I hope that was as uncomfortable to watch as it was to do." Tom Brokaw once called Jon Stewart a "citizen's surrogate," and that is perhaps never more true than in this interview.[40] Stewart unabashedly expresses frustration and outrage of his own, but also seemingly for all who have seen their retirement savings diminished by at least one-third while the top executives who drove the market into the toilet walked away with enormous bonuses. He repeatedly invokes an "us"—"our pensions and our hard earned money," "our 401Ks." But it is the journalist watchdog, the cable channel that labels itself a "news" organization, that is the primary target of Stewart's ire. What he repeatedly demonstrates—through his clips of Cramer, but also through his explanations—is that the dogs watching the hen house are actually running with the foxes.

It might be tempting to argue that Stewart is not changing the conversation through confrontations such as this, but is instead simply joining the ranks of other cable news shouters and foot-stompers, from Bill O'Reilly and Glenn Beck to Keith Olbermann and Chris Matthews. Yet there is something fundamentally different going on here, I suggest. First, Stewart almost never treats his guests this way, so the departure from the genial, likeable comedian who rarely raises his voice is all the more jarring (and attention getting) as a result. *TDS* had aired three previous satirical segments on CNBC and the crisis, and had one of the network's reporters cancel an appearance. By the time a guest from the network appeared, Stewart wasn't in a joking mood. But more importantly, he uses the occasion to serve up his own provocative explanation for the complexity of the situation that had transpired. He offers more than vituperation and disgust, but also a theory for what is going on and why the network should feel bad about it while giving Cramer the opportunity to explain why such theories are incorrect or naïve (which Cramer never does). Finally, he also does something that cannot be found elsewhere on television—he advances a critique for how a news organization is yet again a participant in abrogating the public trust they profess to maintain and defend ("Cramer's got your back"). If public affairs programming on television is largely conducted by news organizations, it is a rare day when the news media cast a critical spotlight on themselves. It is therefore left up to a comedian with an entertainment show to lose his sense of humor for such a critique to get the media's attention.

But the agent's of the old regime of truth were having none of it. Tucker Carlson, the former *Crossfire* cohost who is still smarting from the public spanking he received from Stewart five years earlier, took to the airwaves to proclaim Stewart a "partisan hack."[41] Jim Cramer skipped a scheduled appearance on MSNBC the morning after this *TDS* appearance, but finally emerged to proclaim that Stewart's critiques were "misleading" and "naïve."[42] Even the president of NBC Universal, Jeff Zucker, rose to defend the integrity of his company's media properties, chiding Stewart for being "absurd" and "unfair" and complaining that Stewart was "completely out of line."[43] Such defenses are not surprising, given the potential damage to the network inherent in Stewart's critique. As one news analyst put it, "The entire neo-liberal economic orthodoxy is at risk of being discredited. If that goes, CNBC's foundational identity goes with it."[44] Also unsurprisingly, new media outlets on the political left embraced Stewart's critique. Arianna Huffington, founder of *Huffington Post*, saw Stewart's dogged interrogation of Cramer as a proper model for television journalists to follow, penning a blog post titled "What If Jon Stewart, Instead of John King, Interviewed Dick Cheney."[45] Meanwhile, an Alternet blogger saw in Stewart the spark for political action: "Fix CNBC: Jon Stewart Made the Case, Now We're Demanding Action."[46] And blogger Andrew Sullivan also saw a clarion call for an overthrow of the old regime of truth. On his blog the next day, he addressed old media practitioners such as CNBC directly: "It's not enough anymore, guys, to make fantastic errors and then to carry on authoritatively as if nothing just happened. *You will be called on it.* In some ways, the blogosphere is to [mainstream media] punditry what Stewart is to Cramer: an insistent and vulgar demand for some responsibility, some moral and ethical accountability for previous decisions and pronouncements."[47] For his part (as might be expected), the next edition of *TDS* saw Stewart going back to doing what he always does, with nary a word about the previous show's confrontation.

CONCLUSION

As seen in previous chapters, new political television is challenging how news media construct and present political reality. Part of that challenge is demonstrated by the ways in which Jon Stewart and *The Daily Show* go about their own brand of reporting the news and interviewing public figures. As we have seen, Stewart changes the public conversation crafted by news from one of spectacle and accommodation to indictment and prosecution through creative redactive reporting, all punctuated by satirical yet earnest ribbing. And he changes the conversation achieved through interviews by conducting them in a manner in which the discussion and debate about ideas are paramount, while the promotional aspect of a guest's media appearance becomes secondary. In both instances, any concern over the show's donning a fake and humorous motif misses just how serious Stewart and the show are in their prosecution of public life. The program contributes to public discourse by simply doing it differently than most real news organizations.

Geoffrey Baym has argued that *The Daily Show* is "reinventing" political journalism.[48] Stewart is certainly practicing a form of reporting, although there doesn't seem to be much evidence that he is "reinventing" television news. As explored in chapter 4, all attempts to copy the program have failed. And although he has demonstrated to journalists how better to do their job, few have shown a willingness to replicate his practices (with Keith Olbermann's redactions being a notable exception). Although print journalism will certainly be reinvented as its economic model collapses and a new form of digital journalism rises from its ashes, the economic model for cable television news remains strong. As discussed in chapter 3, television

journalism was actually "reinvented" in the 1990s with the rise of competitive cable news channels and their reliance on cheap hyperbolic talk and
spectacle aesthetics to fill their 24-hour schedules and attract audiences.
That model is still quite profitable, and won't be going away as long as
citizens believe they are being informed or feel that their emotional needs
are being met by the performances. And that, of course, is what Stewart
spends so much of his time attacking—the ways in which cable news has
been transformed into tasty junk, albeit packaged as healthy treats for the
informed citizen. It has required Stewart to become dead serious at times
to get the media and public's attention, most notably in 2004 on *Crossfire*
after the Iraq War and a surreal presidential campaign, and again in 2009
on *TDS* amidst the meltdown of the economy and global recession.

What Stewart and *TDS have* done is educate audiences on how the public
conversation can be held differently. Through its reporting and interviews,
the show challenges the relationship of accommodation between news
media and politics, demonstrating how the powerful should be scrutinized
and why that is important. In the process, the show challenges the spec-
tacle-centered displays that stand for television news "reporting" and the
provision of public information, calling into question the role that media
play in creating and sustaining public artifice that enables power and, at
times, malfeasance. Stewart also demonstrates how to hold the types of
conversations where the interviewer is allowed to explain, politely disagree,
challenge talking points, and be serious, playful, or downright angry. What
Stewart and *TDS* do less well is point out the political economy of it all.
That is to say, the show rarely explains *why* these relationships between
news media and politics exist, or what can explain the spectacle and accommodation that drives news media to act in the ways that it does. One
of the exceptions was in the opening segment before the Cramer interview,
when its faux promo/intro noted that the upcoming "12-minute faceoff
that could marginally increase the very rate Comedy Central charges for
30-seconds of advertising time." Similar critical awareness of the economics
that is central to it all could certainly occur more often.

To his credit, though, Stewart has introduced, through his redactions and
interviews, critical literacy to political speech and news media broadcasts.
He has made holding media and politicians accountable both fun and
satisfying for audiences through the show's seriousness and laughter. But
Stewart also sees what he does as cathartic, a way of therapeutically dealing
with disturbing issues. His program, in many ways, is a means for addressing his and his staff's frustrations with the surreal quality to contemporary
politics. "The absurdity of what you imagine to be the dark heart of con-
spiracy theorists' wet dreams," he argues, "far too frequently turns out to
be true." Satire, then, becomes one means of addressing the absurdities.
"It's a wonderful feeling," he notes, "to have this toxin in your body in the

morning, that little cup of sadness, and feel by 7 or 7:30 that night, you've released it in sweat equity and can move on to the next day."[49]

Theorists of satire suggest that laughter is one of the four primary attributes of the form (with aggression, judgment, and play being the others).[50] It is a form of attacking power and passing judgment on public wrong-doing, all in a playful and entertaining way. The satirist demands communal evaluation and rebuke. In turning to the next section, we can see that satire's coupling of aggression and judgment with play and laughter becomes perfectly manifest in the genre of fake news, reporting, and talk. And one of the earliest American progenitors of fake news reporting with a strongly satirical bite was Michael Moore.

III

FAKING IT (FOR REAL) IN
NEWS AND TALK

7

Muckraking Through Fake Newsmagazines

Michael Moore's Satire TV

> What they have to deal with, with us, is not language or nudity or violence, it's ideas—and that's really dangerous.
>
> —Michael Moore, on network censorship of *TV Nation*

In the second-season premier (July 28, 1995) of Michael Moore's satirical newsmagazine show *TV Nation*, Moore introduced viewers to Crackers, the Corporate Crime-Fighting Chicken. If certain social problems had mascots such as Smokey the Bear (forest fires), Woodsy the Owl (pollution), and McGruff the Crime Dog (street crime), Moore and his producers believed America should also have a mascot to bring attention to the relatively underreported problem of corporate crime. With one of the show's writers dressed in a seven-foot chicken costume, Crackers sought an explanation for how it was possible for First Boston Corporation to get a $50 million dollar tax break from New York City by promising not to eliminate any jobs, and then lay off more than 100 employees 30 days later. Crackers began his investigation by going to the corporate headquarters of First Boston, only to be escorted from the building by a security officer who tells Moore that Crackers is "persona non grata," to which Moore retorts, "He'd be more like chicken non grata, wouldn't he?"

Crackers then heads to City Hall to get an explanation from New York Mayor Rudolph Giuliani. Unable to get an audience with the mayor, Crackers attempts to attend the mayor's weekly press conference. Though Crackers is barred entry, Moore attends and seeks an answer from the mayor in Crackers's stead. In an honest and serious tone, Moore asks the mayor, "When you gave them this tax break in January, and then a few weeks later, they turn around and lay off two hundred people, didn't you feel a little used? I mean, they must have been planning these job layoffs for some time." Giuliani dismisses Moore's inquiry by stating, "It's a very silly description of a very complex thing that is very important to this city." After that brush-off, Moore then asks the mayor, "Why won't you meet our Corporate Crime Chicken, Crackers, and discuss this?" Giuliani angrily snaps, "Because this isn't a joke, and you're presenting it that way." "Well," Moore responds, "this *isn't* a joke. That's our point."

Moore's critics have consistently pointed to such staged instances to demonstrate why he is contemptuous, cruel, and a grandstander, or that his efforts result in little more than lame pranks, humiliation, or harassment.[1] Yet like the Yippies who shaped Moore's approach to political engagement and social satire, Moore appreciates the difference between the sophomoric and the subversive.[2] When corporations refuse to speak and when politicians speak only on their own terms, using a man in a chicken suit to call attention to important issues while also highlighting the means of obfuscation used by the powerful turns out to be an effective—if socially "illegitimate"—means for advancing a political critique of the players involved and the system itself. By Moore's working-class thinking, a guy in a chicken suit seeking legitimate answers to corporate and government malfeasance is no more ludicrous than a guy in a business suit offering lame excuses for wasting tax dollars to benefit the rich. Plus, it's funny. As Moore explains, "If you try to have a straight argument or discussion with [the big corporations], they'll have all their standard one-liners. So you kind of disarm them with their weakness—their inability to laugh or have a sense of humor. It's like the difference between judo and karate—there's no way you're going to win with a karate chop to the neck of corporate America."[3]

What such tactics highlight as well is Moore's unruly approach to political discourse. Through his television programs and films, Moore consistently attacks the controlled (and controlling) nature of power in American life. Central to both political and corporate power is the control of political language and discourse—whether it is the scripted language of politicians and corporate spokespersons, the structured engagements between journalists and these elites (with unwritten rules governing who gets to talk about what subjects, in what ways, when, and in which places), or the accepted silences on matters of great social importance (such as class, gender, racial, corporate and political privileges). Moore wants to disrupt them all, bringing the silences to life and turning the controlled speech that dominates public life upside down. By making the silent speak, he reveals the areas of democratic discourse that are typically off-limits, as well as the lengths the powerful go to keep them that way. By turning scripted engagements on their head, Moore has disturbed the familiar and the predictable. For many viewers, such encounters can produce uncomfortable levels of social friction, because the norms of social interaction have been violated. Yet

Moore has brought us, as viewers and citizens, exactly to the place where democratic discussion and deliberation should exist: a debate, however messy, over ideas, not in the controlled "publicity" that has taken its place in the public sphere.[4]

Unruly political discourse, however, is not the currency of news media, the primary arbiters of political life for many. As argued in chapter 4, news is a manufactured commercial product derived from a series of accepted norms, routines, and conventions that are central to the construction of what is considered "news."[5] And although the journalists who participate in constructing this social reality can be watchdogs of power, they are just as capable of being conduits for the messages and meanings preferred and proffered by societal elites.[6] The public information officers, public relations experts, press agents, and company "spokespersons" typically at the center of Moore's filmic encounters are, by their title and functions, representative examples of the relationship between the press (a corporate enterprise also concerned with the bottom line) and the powerful. It is a controlled relationship, and one that rarely produces disorderly, undirected, or free and unfettered exchanges.[7]

In the summer of 1994, Michael Moore began offering television viewers his own brand of news reporting that would operate outside the parameters of such controlled political discourse. First under the title *TV Nation* (on NBC, then Fox), and a few years later, *The Awful Truth* (on Bravo), Moore produced a television newsmagazine in the tradition of *60 Minutes, Dateline, 20/20*, and *Primetime*. When *TV Nation* first aired, NBC labeled the show an "investigative, comedic newsmagazine," while Moore preferred to describe it as "*60 Minutes* if it had a sense of humor and a subversive edge."[8] The show mimicked the generic conventions of the newsmagazine format, using investigative segments filed by correspondents, introductions of each by the host, and a repertoire of narrative approaches for framing each report. One difference between Moore's brand of newsmagazine and those produced by network news departments is the types of stories pursued. Moore covered topics that most news operations won't, or if they do cover such topics, typically it is done from a dominant or mainstream ideological perspective.[9] Moore's favorite topics (as repeated across all seasons of his shows) include corporate malfeasance, the corruption of the political system, racism, environmental pollution, gun violence, the prison industry, worker rights, the health care system, and global conflict.

In covering these issues, the series was not content simply to highlight specific problems, but usually aimed its sights higher. "Even the better news magazine shows like *60 Minutes*," Moore notes, "they go after the one doctor who is defrauding the medical health system, but it's really rare that they'll go after the bigger fish and even rarer that they go after what is wrong systemically. The profit, the greed, they'll never approach that. We're unique on that level."[10] Moore's goals are to lead the viewer to see the assumptions of the system differently; to make these assumptions strange; to hold them up for scrutiny and criticism (or at least raise awareness); and if successful, to lead people to get involved in advocating for change.[11]

The other primary difference between Moore's brand of newsmagazine and that of the networks is the use of humor to make his point. Like all newsmagazines, Moore employs a set of narrative techniques and reportorial conventions for presenting the story. For Moore, however, the fact that humor can be used as a weapon wielded by the weak against the powerful was central to each report. He argues, "Comedy and humor is a great way to discuss politics, not just because you can reach people who would otherwise be bored by it, but I also think it's a very effective tool and sometimes a weapon which people can use, especially when they don't have the money to fight the powers that be with the politicians in their back pocket."[12] Humor changes both the terms and the means of debate. The technique most often employed in his strategic use of humor is his on-screen persona as the hapless, everyday guy who simply seeks direct answers to his questions from politicians or heads of corporations. Yet his stories also exhibit several other narrative techniques quite unusual for traditional newsmagazines. These include staged encounters featuring costumed characters (such as Crackers), game shows or sporting contests, street theatre, traveling road shows, and diplomatic conclaves (bringing enemies together, often to sing a children's song).

All of these playful means serve to highlight the changed terms of debate, namely Moore's populist perspective on the differences between "us" (the common working people, including the assumed viewer) and "them" (the elite wrongdoers).[13] The ludicrousness of his scenarios often forces those he seeks to criticize into uncomfortable circumstances—at times, so comfortable they incriminate themselves. As the "villains" seek to reestablish the appropriate terms of debate, they are highlighted as either ridiculous or agents of obfuscation. Perhaps this is an unfair tactic, as critics suggest, but what relevance does "fair" have when one chooses to play outside the rules of the game? Moore admits his tactics are unfair, but in his conception of unruly political discourse, the ends (true democratic discourse) justify the means. "Yes, we are unfair," Moore says. "We have feelings and opinions and a point of view, and we're going to be shameless about what we believe in. I think that's healthy again in a democracy. I think that's why people have tuned out to what's going on in the world these days. It is because it's all presented in such a bland way. Or people are always trying to sit on the fence. Or not make waves."[14] Moore can rationalize this by claiming his objects of investigation/ridicule are also not "playing fair," however he defines that term.

In short, Moore's approach to political discourse is a messy one, but one that nevertheless plays off the conventions of form (both journalistic and televisual) to achieve its ends. This chapter first describes the structure and format of *TV Nation* and *The Awful Truth*, exploring the production aspects associated with offering such groundbreaking political humor on advertiser-supported television (network and cable). The analysis then turns to the various patterns of "reporting" that comprised the show, including the intertextual features that gave the programming its entertaining yet powerful critical perspective. The chapter concludes by examining Moore's legacy to political entertainment programming. In particular, it examines how programs such as *The Daily Show* and *The Colbert Report*, but also *The Chris Rock Show* and *Da Ali G Show*, owe a particular debt to the techniques developed or deployed here first. The newsmagazine format allowed for a critique not only of political and corporate power, but also the news media that have become ineffective agents of monitoring and criticizing that power, or as Moore says, "doing what the media should be doing."[15]

The fake news form also becomes a perfect vehicle for critiquing the reality presented by news media. As Jonathan Gray has argued in discussing the relationship between "fakeness" and "reality" in such programming, "we all have a basic working knowledge that there is a gap between the media's presentation of the real and that which is in fact real. . . . One of the most valuable types of media product we need, then, are those that draw attention to the gap, and that honestly observe its existence. It is these shows that . . . many viewers will regard as realistic."[16] Moore's play on form highlights the unrealistic nature of much news content. His programs, then, criticize—both implicitly and explicitly—the role of television news and entertainment in supporting the inequality endemic to America's corporate capitalist democracy, yet which is rarely highlighted in American media.

TV NATION

TV Nation, the satirical newsmagazine produced by Michael Moore and his wife, Kathleen Glynn, debuted on NBC on July 19, 1994. Executives from the network had approached Moore two years earlier after having seen Moore's breakout documentary film, *Roger & Me*, inquiring whether Moore had any ideas for a television series. Moore reports that he believed his pitch to the executives would be the end of the idea, assuming that the famously cautious television producers would find him either crazy or dangerous. Moore proposed that the newsmagazine program include a segment in which he would attend twenty different Catholic churches, confess the same sin, and see which would give him the harshest penance in a bit he called "The Consumer's Guide to Confessionals." Instead of kicking him out of the room, Warren Littlefield, the president of NBC Entertainment, told Moore, "That's the funniest idea I've ever heard."[17] The project was then green-lighted for Moore to shoot the pilot, and though successful with focus groups, it would eventually take cofinancing from BBC television (40 percent) for the initial series to be shot and aired.[18] NBC decided to use the program as a summer replacement series, placing the program on the Tuesday night schedule at 8:00 P.M. (EST).

Each program was an hour in length, composed of five eight-minute segments. As host, Moore would introduce each piece from Times Square. Although Moore would be featured in one or two of each week's segments, the show also employed numerous "correspondents" who would file reports as intrepid investigative journalists. These correspondents, almost all of whom had roots in comedy, included Janeane Garofalo (*The Larry Sanders Show*), Rusty Cundieff (*Fear of a Black Hat*), Merrill Markoe (*The Late Show with David Letterman*), Karen Duffy (*Dumb and Dumber*), Ben Hamper (author of *Rivethead*), Louis Theroux, Roy Sekoff, Jeff Stilson, and John Derevlany (as Crackers).

Each episode also included a "TV Nation Poll" that would air in the segment leading into the commercial break. Like other news organizations that *create* "news" by commissioning polls, Moore and crew decided to contract with its own polling agency in Flint, Michigan—Widgery & Associates—to conduct a more parodic take on the genre. Polls aired during that first episode, for instance, included the results such as "10% of the American public would pay $5 to see Senator Orrin Hatch (R-Utah) fight a big mean dog on Pay TV. 86% of all viewers would root for the dog. 100% of women viewers would root for the dog." A poll that aired during the second episode showed that "65% of American women believe there is 'a lot of difference' between a campaign contribution and a bribe. Only 35% of men see a difference."

Although Moore never explained the choice for the title, the opening montage and music suggest possible answers. As he did with *Roger & Me*, Moore deftly uses imagery and music from 1950s and 1960s television programming and advertising to reference the dreamland of consumer leisure and pleasure that the new medium offered Americans, as well as ironically invoking a sense of nostalgia. The American Dream has always loomed large for Moore, particularly the myth as portrayed on television—a narcotic that corporations and politicians have used to promise the working class the commodity-based utopia to which their hard work would supposedly help them arrive.[19] The program opens with a montage of older news and advertising imagery, cutting back and forth between momentous historical news events and this consumer paradise. The pulsating music, written by the group tomandandy, sounds like *Leave It to Beaver* meets Metallica. The impression is a blending of consumption and nationhood. For Moore, America is a nation of television watchers. We love entertainment, and as John Hartley has put it, we are as much "citizens of media" as we are citizens of a nation-state.[20] Moore realizes that for the working class—to whom and for whom he believes he speaks[21]—to care enough about politics to watch it during prime time, it is almost necessary to blend entertainment and politics.

Yet this is not to say that Moore finds his audience stupid, or believes that they are only capable of consuming "information-lite." To the contrary, Moore contends that the audience is actually smart enough to get the cheekiness and irony that is his intent. "I end up trusting the intelligence of the audience," he says, "that they'll get it and they'll know where we're coming from. Too much of TV talks down to people and has very low expectations of the audience and I think that all contributes to the dumbing down of our society. I would rather expect something greater from the audience, and so we stick to our guns in terms of the kind of humor and the way that we want to present this material."[22] What it does show, however, is Moore's belief in the power of humor to attract and enlighten. Humor is used to "bring people into these issues, (and) make it funny so it won't be like PBS."[23] The viewers he is addressing, therefore, constitute a TV nation, and a newsmagazine show that presents politics in appealing and entertaining ways, he announces with the title, is what is being offered.

Segments in the first episode included Moore's decision to (supposedly) move the show's production to Mexico, taking advantage of the low wages guaranteed by the North American Free Trade Agreement (NAFTA). Other reports included a test to see whether it was harder for a famous black actor (Yaphet Kotto) to catch a cab in New York than a convicted white felon; a visit to a prison built to improve the local economy, yet which housed no prisoners;[24] a corporate CEO challenge in which the heads of various corporations were confronted to see whether they knew how to perform routine tasks associated with their company's product; correspondents hunting for houses in the contaminated Love Canal; and Moore's visit to Moscow to find the missiles that were pointed at his home town during the Cold War. Although the series covered such topics as relocating manufacturing operations to Mexico, corporate downsizing consultants, sabotage in the workplace, and corporate corruption in governmental contracts, the network owned by General Electric remarkably did not censor a single segment during the show's summer run. As Moore later noted, "We actually had a pretty good relationship with NBC. I'm surprised we got away with some of the things we did."[25]

Although the series posted respectable ratings, it didn't prove to be the surprise hit that the network presumably hoped for (it was, after all, a summer replacement series). The premiere scored a 6.9 rating/13 share, and ranked 54 in the Nielsen ratings.[26] Although the numbers decreased slightly as the summer progressed, industry trade magazines report that the show consistently won its time slot with the important 18–49 demographic that

In the "CEO Challenge" segment from TV Nation's *first season, Michael Moore attempts to enter the headquarters of Philip Morris to see if the corporation's CEO knows how to roll a cigarette. Moore's staged confrontations attempt to highlight the disconnect between America's ruling elite and its citizens. Catherine McGann/Hulton Archive/Getty Images*

advertisers covet. Nevertheless, the show was not picked up as a midseason replacement by the network. Moore and company did produce a year-end special (airing December 28, 1994) that parodied network news's tendency to summarize the year's big stories or make predictions of stories to watch in the coming year. For instance, because American troops were increasingly deployed around the world (Somalia, Haiti, Kuwait), the show surveyed people to see which country the United States should invade in 1995. Perhaps the most outrageous segment was called Corporate Aid, in which the show attempted to "help out" corporations that had received large fines from the government during 1994. Moore attempted to give a giant-sized $10,000 check to Pfizer (lying to the FDA) and the same amount in gold to United Parcel Service (OSHA violations). With the spirit of using concerts to raise money for worthwhile causes (such as Live Aid and Farm Aid), *TV Nation* put on a "Corp-Aid" concert staged on flatbed truck outside the New York Stock Exchange, with live music provided by the band the Meat Puppets. The money raised was to help Exxon pay for fines related to the Exxon *Valdez* accident. The concert raised $275.64, which Moore then attempted to present to the chairman of Exxon at the company's headquarters in Dallas.[27]

With NBC not picking up the option for another season, *TV Nation* moved to Fox, presumably with the promise of more money and greater creative freedom. Although the network is owned by conservative Rupert Murdoch, Fox had previously shown a willingness to air programming rich in social satire such as *The Simpsons, In Living Color,* and *Married with Children.* With the move, the series kept its name and general format. The second season on Fox also turned out to be a summer replacement series only, airing a total of seven episodes. Besides the Crackers segment discussed earlier, the season premier included *TV Nation* running its own candidate for president—Louie Bruno, a convicted felon; black correspondent Rusty Cundieff going to Mississippi to own six white slaves for a week (because the state had yet to ratify the Thirteenth Amendment to the U.S. Constitution outlawing slavery); "invading" a taxpayer-supported private beach in Greenwich, Connecticut; and accompanying a couple who own a business cleaning up violent crime scenes.

As it turned out, Fox showed that it was much more willing to censor certain programming ideas than NBC. As Moore reported at the time, "This show makes Fox executives extremely nervous. There's a daily phone call from them, and we're constantly fighting for what should be on the show. That means we're doing our job. If they didn't call, I'd think something was wrong, because it meant they felt safe and comfortable."[28] Although often meeting initial resistance, most of the show's controversial programming ideas were eventually approved, including "Love Night," where *TV Nation* visited various hate groups (featuring multiracial dancers outside an Nazi/Aryan/Klan encampment in Idaho singing, "Stop! In the Name of Love," and a gay men's chorus at the home of Senator Jesse Helms singing "What the World Needs Now Is Love"), and "Cobb County," in which Moore visited Newt Gingrich's Georgia congressional district to see why this suburban county received the third-highest level of federal funds when its congressman was the leading campaigner against "big government." Stories that were shot but never allowed on the air, however, include "Whatever Happened to Those S&L Crooks?" (following the fate of those responsible for the savings and loan scandal, including attending their "therapy sessions"); "Harassing Gays for Extra Credit" (where students earned extra credit in a Topeka, Kansas, school for participating in Reverend Fred Phelps's "God Hates Fags" campaigns); "Re-enacting the L.A. Uprising" (where Civil War re-enactors simulated the Rodney King beating and riots); a report on those who advocate killing abortion doctors; and a segment on the search for small condoms (as Moore and Glynn note in explaining this segment, if condom sizes are only offered in regular and "EXTRA LARGE. MAGNUM. MAX," then "what about that other all-important size—*small*?")[29] All were deemed too controversial for the "family hour" of television, with the exception of the savings and loan piece, where no explanation was given for refusing to air it beyond it was "old news."[30]

In retrospect, what is remarkable about this short-lived series—with a total of 105 segments aired on 17 episodes over a 15-month period of time—is that it made it onto network television at all. Moore believes the reason the networks would allow a show that often explicitly critiqued the fundamental assumptions of the capitalist system is simple—money. Invoking Marx, he notes, "One of the beauties of capitalism is that they'll sell you the rope to hang themselves if they believe that they can make money [doing so]."[31] He recognizes that if *TV Nation* had garnered strong ratings, the networks would most likely have continued to air his subversive programming. But with its airing during two summer schedules and in such an early evening time-slot, the show was never really given much of a chance to succeed. The show's ratings fell during its run on Fox, with viewership generating Nielsen ratings between a 3.8 to a 2.9.[32] Nevertheless, it was nominated twice for a primetime Emmy Award, and actually won the award for "Outstanding Informational Series" for its 1994 season. The award was presented, ironically, on the night following the series' last episode on Fox.

THE AWFUL TRUTH

Moore returned to U.S. television in April, 1999, this time on the arts and culture cable channel Bravo. The program was produced by Canadian company Salter Street Films and financed by Channel 4 in Britain. The reformatted version of the newsmagazine was named *The Awful Truth*, and was reduced to thirty minutes in length (allowing for only two filmed segments in each show). During the first season, the show began with a new introduction that recast both Moore and the show as a socialist/communist savior of democratic thinking from domination and control by large media conglomerates. Talking over an animated graphic showing a cartoonish rendering of five CEOs of media corporations (Ted Turner, Rupert Murdoch, Bill Gates, Sumner Redstone, and Michael Eisner), the announcer intones, "In the beginning, there was a free press. Well, not really, but it sounded good. By the end of the millennium, five men controlled the world's media. Yet there was one man who operated outside their control (showing a shot of Michael Moore). He and his motley crew were known as the People's Democratic Republic of Television. Their mission—to bring the people the Awful Truth." Here again, Moore links citizenship to television, and the video montage which follows—showing a series of political and entertaining events—drives home the point further.

Unlike *TV Nation*, the first season of the show on Bravo was shot in front of a live audience at the Illinois Institute of Technology in Chicago—presumably a "middle America" location where Moore's populist, working-class politics would be received warmly. Moore sets up each piece by engaging with the audience assembled in the auditorium, including cracking a few jokes. What results is part stand-up routine, part town hall meeting. Though highly edited, this town hall effect fits nicely with Moore's unruly approach to the type of political discourse he prefers. "I wanted the people at home," he explains, "to see that it's not just me and a couple of crazy people in Times Square that believe in these things. It's like a big town meeting—1,000 people in the room and they're all hooting and hollering and mixing it up. I like that."[33] Yet despite the populist "we the people" approach, the combination stand-up routine/town hall meeting somehow sapped the filmed segments of their full humorous effect. The elements simply didn't go well together (not to mention being more expensive to produce), so the producers returned to Moore introducing each video segment from New York's Times Square for what became the show's final season in 2000.

The series retained correspondents Karen Duffy and Ben Hamper, while adding Jay Martel, Jerry Minor, Katie Roberts, and Gideon Evans (as the new "Crackers"). The opinion polls from *TV Nation* days were retained in season one, and introduced simply as "tonight's Awful Truth." During season two, however, the producers changed the formulation a bit by introducing "Lenny, the Awful Truth Bookie" (a real-life bookie who refused to give his last name, but admitted that he had been arrested three times) who would give odds for various predictions that the show's producers came up with. For instance, Lenny's "Odds that the winner of this year's election will lead the U.S. into a New Golden Age of Prosperity" were 20 to 1, while the odds that the winner would lead the United States "straight to hell in a hand basket" was 40 to 1.

Also during the second season, each episode followed a particular theme between the segments. The theme for the second season premier, for instance, was "Advertiser Appreciation Night," in which the show ridiculed celebrity endorsements by having convicted felons endorse products such as American Express, Budweiser, and Microsoft Windows. The felons first identified themselves, including the crime they committed and time served, and then made their advertising pitch. Each segment (also filmed on the streets of New York) was used, ironically, as the show paused for commercial breaks. The episode "Compassionate Conservatism Night" used a games motif (of the county fair variety) to pit rich Wall Street traders against each other in a sporting competition, using poor homeless people as the objects in each competitive event. The traders formed two teams—Team Dow versus Team Nasdaq—and then engaged in contests such as "Dunk the Homeless," "Pie the Poor," and "Working Poor Chicken Fight" (where we see whether it really is possible to "balance our economy on the backs of the poor"). Although somewhat over-the-top in its polemics, the segments proved quite humorous nonetheless.

Over the course of the run on Bravo, *The Awful Truth* produced twenty-four episodes and landed an Emmy nomination in 1999 as "Outstanding Non-fiction Series." Yet with the series appearing on a cable channel with limited carriage by cable companies, *The Awful Truth* did not have access to the potential eyeballs it did when its predecessor aired on network television.[34] Nevertheless, the series helped cement Moore's appeal as an irreverent, left-wing icon who was willing to take the fight to the "enemy." His stature and fan base were allowed to grow further, of course, when the entire two seasons on Bravo were later released as a DVD box-set.

SATIRICAL REPORTER FORMULAS

Journalists are, of course, storytellers. Their job is to transform human experience into manageable, understandable, and memorable narratives that fit within the audience's cognitive and ideological frameworks. In television newsmagazines, this is no less the case. Richard Campbell's analysis of *60 Minutes*, for instance, demonstrates how the landmark television newsmagazine consistently employs a set of formulaic narratives built around three central metaphoric roles for its reporters: that of the "detective," "analyst," and "tourist":

> The detective, for instance, taps into our desires for truth, honesty, and intrigue. The analyst helps us come to terms with our inner self, with order, and with knowledge about experience. The tourist cherishes tradition, nature, and authenticity. These metaphorical transformations of the reporter offer us figures of and for modernity, carriers of ways of knowing and interpreting complexity.[35]

All of these roles create a mythic construction of Middle America, Campbell argues, a middle-class mythology that affirms "that individuals through adherence to Middle American values can triumph over institutions that deviate from central social norms."[36]

Michael Moore also employs a set of storytelling techniques designed to make sense of the world and impart meaning to Middle America. Yet Moore's Middle America is a different conception, one centered not on individualism and capitalist values, but the community of "have nots" who are done in by the "haves" of capitalist society. Moore's vision is a populist one, a belief and rhetoric that date back to the founding of the United States.[37] The language of populism is one in which goodness is located in the common working people who are hurt by exploitative, "self-serving and undemocratic" elites.[38] Indeed, Moore's stated intentions in his television programming are to show "complete and utter disrespect for people with money who hurt those that don't have money."[39] Therefore, when Moore examines corporate crime, corrupt politicians, wealthy elites, worker rights, and substandard health care for the working poor, he is operating from this populist perspective.

But Moore is more than simply a populist throwback to the late nineteenth century.[40] He is also a twenty-first-century progressive who opposes the death penalty and racism and believes in gay rights, gun control, campaign finance reform, and environmental protection. He is an unrepentant leftist, but as with his populist leanings, he knows how to wrap such progressive ideas in the language of common sense. His comic partisanship is obvious, but as Charles Schutz argues, humor can be used to mollify the separating tendencies of that partisanship, bringing the audience together over common things and common values:

> The comic partisan is once-removed from the immediate fray in that his claim is presented in the guise of humor. Thus, its overt aggressiveness is sublimated into a peaceful mode that pacifies the opponent while it covertly appeals to the audience on the grounds of commonly shared interests and values. The very nature of political humor as a communicative act requires its transcending of special interest in an issue and embracing a general interest of its audience. In the very act of challenging his opponent, then, the comic partisan by his humor declares for peace with him, calls upon the community of feeling, and reminds the audience of their moral commonality.[41]

Though today Moore is often seen as a politically divisive or polarizing figure, the humor of his newsmagazine segments, paradoxically, almost always has this appeal to shared values and moral commonality. A display of racism by New York taxicab drivers, for instance, becomes an appeal for equality. Questioning the tactics of the gun lobby appeals to a desire for child safety. Criticism of Special Prosecutor Kenneth Starr and Congressional Republicans appeals to a sense of propriety. The humiliation of a Health Maintenance Organization and its representatives becomes an appeal for fairness for a dying man. And ridiculing the hatred displayed by citizens of warring nations comes across as an appeal for peace. Such appeals to common values ultimately rely on the common sense thinking of viewing audiences—the way such endpoints are not seen as "political" or partisan, but rather, as worthwhile "truths" because they are simple, self-evident, accessible, and practical.[42] Again, for some viewers, Moore's tactics or persona might distract from the larger rhetorical project that leads to common values. But for others, these results are certainly more important than the means he uses to get there.

Part of the appeal for commonality is also located in the intertextual nature of Moore's televisual rhetoric. The narrative devices he uses are all too familiar to a nation of television watchers. A segment on corporate crime resembles a Cop Show by employing the appropriate music, voice-over, intonation, and dress of the genre. A piece on the death penalty adopts the style of NFL Films, pitting the states of Texas and Florida (and their governor brothers) against each other while employing the *mise en scène* of cheerleaders, a pro-death penalty pep rally, marching band music, a scoreboard, chalkboard, and color commentator. A report on the lack of gun control legislation in the wake of school shootings references a kid's show by employing children to embrace and sing a song with a costumed character—a big purple handgun named Pistol Pete. And an attempt to highlight class differences in America becomes a quiz show ("Beat the Rich") when Moore interrogates the residents of working-class Pittsburgh and upper-crust Manhattan on the cost of common consumer products, using on-screen graphics and bells and buzzers to keep score for the viewers at home. A TV Nation indeed!

As noted previously, *60 Minutes* places the reporter at the center of each story by constructing the reporter as hero—the Detective, Analyst, or Tourist who leads the viewer to the middle-class values that Campbell argues is central to the meaning of the program. Moore's storytelling formulas, however, are rarely centered on the reporters themselves (the prime exception, of course, being Moore, the show's only true star). More often than not, though, he and his writers and producers frame each story by using one of several types of performative scenarios. Across the seventeen episodes of *TV Nation* and twenty-four episodes of *The Awful Truth*, a few repeated framing patterns emerge.

Beyond the technique of using other popular television genres to frame the story, the producers also relied heavily on the spectacle provided by street theater.[43] In "A Cheaper Way to Conduct a Witch Hunt," correspondent Jay Martel and a troop of hysterical women, all dressed in Puritan costumes straight out of *The Crucible*, enact a puritanical "witch hunt" on the streets of Washington, D.C., including outside the White House and on Capitol Hill to mock the Republican proceedings against President Bill Clinton. Moore accosts some Republican congressmen about their own sinful ways, while Martel paces the sidewalk reading aloud some of the more sexually graphic sections from the "Book of Starr" (*The Starr Report*). In "Funeral at an HMO," a sketch that previewed Moore's focus on America's failing healthcare system in the film *Sicko*, Moore conducts a funeral—with bagpipes, a casket, preacher, and hearse—outside the headquarters of health-insurance provider Humana for a man who is likely to die (yet still alive) because he was denied a pancreas transplant due to a loophole in his insurance coverage.

In "Presidential Mosh Pit," Moore promises Republican and Democratic presidential candidates that they will receive the endorsement of the show if they jump in a mobile mosh pit of rampaging youth. As Moore tells Senator Orrin Hatch, "This is the easiest endorsement you'll ever get. It doesn't require any favors, no backer meals, no dirty money; just ten seconds in the pit with these kids."[44] And after an unarmed black man was shot nineteen times by New York City police while pulling out his wallet, Moore goes to Harlem and sets up an "African American Wallet Exchange" stand on the sidewalk. Reminding the pedestrians (with a bullhorn) about the dangers of being black and using a black wallet at night, he distributes day-glow orange wallets to people willing to exchange their black and brown ones—all while the police watch nervously nearby. In each of these scenes, it isn't the outcome (African Americans becoming safer) or even spectacle (presidential candidates debasing themselves by jumping in a mosh pit) that Moore is interested in. Rather, it is the ability that such public scenarios afford him to enunciate a political critique—in his own language and on his own terms—to the powers that be. The interest is in polemic and protest, not dialogue, for the public square is rarely a place for deliberation and compromise.

A third formula involves the usage of costumed characters such as Crackers the Corporate Crime Fighting Chicken, who became a recurring character on the show. Beyond taking on First Boston Corporation in New York, Crackers also visited Detroit (newspaper strike), St. Louis (lead pollution), Philadelphia (banking overcharges), and Disney World (employment practices). The show also featured an unemployed Joe Camel looking for work; Thomas Jefferson heckling U.S. Representative Lindsey Graham during an impeachment press conference; and Pistol Pete, a gun advocate. After noticing that the National Rifle Association had created a mascot named Eddie Eagle to teach kids what to do if they came across an unattended gun, *The Awful Truth* decided to create its own costumed character to appeal to children. After teaching children a pro-gun song, Pete goes to a gun show convention in Las Vegas (where he is warmly received), pays a visit to the NRA headquarters to ask their PR man to remove a gun slug from a piece of bloody meat, and goes to Congressman John Dingell's office in Washington to thank him for thwarting gun control legislation. When Pistol Pete and correspondent Jay Martel are removed from the Capitol by police, Martel concludes his report by noting, "Thanks to Pete, at least they can agree to one form of gun control. Sure, it only applies to big purple guns, but it's a start." The segment then ends with the following statistics flashed on the screen: "In the ten weeks since 6-year-old Kayla Rolland was killed: Approximately 936 American children have been killed by guns. Nearly a million guns have been sold. Congress has not passed any gun control laws."

A fourth popular formula for framing stories involved bringing enemies together. This usually took on one of two forms: invasion or détente. Invasion-framed stories typically involved Moore transporting one group of people (such as gays or blacks) into the space of other groups of people known for their hatred of the former. For instance, Moore constructs a "sodomobile" (a pink Winnebago) to take a group of gays and lesbian "Freedom Riders" on a tour of the twenty states with sodomy laws. The segment concludes in a square-off with the infamous "God Hates Fags" preacher from Topeka, Kansas—Reverend Fred Phelps—and his followers.[45] When Moore attempts détente, he brings together Pakistani and Indian citizens, for example, to demonstrate the ridiculousness of nuclear proliferation and dispel the conception that humans can actually survive a nuclear attack. To drive the point home, Moore teaches them a children's song ("Duck and Cover") from a Cold War–era cartoon used in America to teach kids preparedness for nuclear warfare.[46] In another episode, he brings together diplomatic representatives from Bosnia and Croatia to share a pizza (which they squabble over as if it were territory), ending the segment with them singing the song from Barney the Purple Dinosaur ("I love you. You love me. We're a happy family").

Finally, both *TV Nation* and *The Awful Truth* often hired a "specialist"—especially in the realm of politics—to assist in demonstrating some larger truth. In an attempt to show that politicians can be easily manipulated by lobbyists, the producers hired their own lobbyist to get a bill passed in Congress (which he achieves by obtaining a congressional proclamation for "TV Nation Day"). To further Moore's contention that politicians are "whores" for accepting special interest money, he hires a bona-fide pimp. To show the lack of alternative choices citizens have in selecting political candidates, the producers hired a convicted felon, Louie Bruno, to run for president. And simply to be funny, the show hired Yuri Svets, a former KGB agent, as their very own *TV Nation* spy to investigate such issues as "who is actually buried in Nixon's grave" and finding the "heart and soul of the Democratic Party."

In sum, Moore realized that his programs would have to be composed of much more than scenes of him chasing after corporate executives or politicians (his *Roger & Me* shtick) if he wished to keep an audience week after week. And whereas he was criticized for violating the unwritten rules of the documentary tradition through his work in film, by working in television, he recognized that the medium provided numerous avenues for creative freedom. First, he was provided a generous budget with which to interrogate a broad array of issues and topics, several of which would later be developed into feature films, including gun control (*Bowling for Columbine*) and health care (*Sicko*). But with television's short form, he could visit topics more quickly and easily than the years needed for a feature film on a single topic.[47] Second, by working in television, Moore could make fun of the medium itself while simultaneously utilizing its strengths to make his points. Costumed characters already inhabit the world of television. Click the channel and the viewer will find other sporting contests and quiz shows nearby. News carries the story of warring nations and peoples everyday. Moore, therefore, uses the codes and conventions of television because they are familiar, but in the process, also highlights the manipulative nature of the codes themselves (such as the way ominous music is used to introduce certain criminals/"bad" people, but not others).

Third, a technique such as street theater combines the spectacle that is the currency of television with the openness of the street. Not only do such antics push the issue or point to an extreme, but they bring the burden of "publicness" to bear on those who might be targeted by the spectacle. When Moore enters a corporate office, the audience knows in advance that his questions won't be entertained or debated (signifying the larger social silences on the matter). The audience even anticipates the fact that those with power will drag him off the stage to shut him up. But with street theater, the process is inverted. Moore is on a public stage, and the silences of the businesses or politicians are no longer their power but their weakness. The laughter of the pedestrians participating in the witch hunt over "fornicators," for instance, thunders down Pennsylvania Avenue. The horror on the faces of Humana's employees as they leave work, not knowing whether they should walk through a funeral or stop and pay their respects, speaks volumes. And the look of disdain on the policemen's faces as Moore and the black citizens of New York express their own disgust and dismay is palpable.

Finally, the creative formulas that Moore and his writers pursued showed the limits of the traditional investigative model employed by newsmagazines. "Truth" is not always revealed by simply reporting "facts." As Moore noted, programs like *60 Minutes* will go after individual wrong-doers, but rarely examine the larger picture. But when *TV Nation* hosts a Corporate-Aid concert on Wall Street, the program calls attention to the fact that numerous major corporations are constantly violating the law in a given year. The program adds it all up for viewers, not hoping that citizens will have read all the individual stories of corporate malfeasance buried in the business section of the newspaper and then be able to construct the larger meaning or "truth" of the matter. Moreover, traditional newsmagazines depend on the myth of objectivity to convince viewers that the stories they create are true. The use of humor to reveal alternative truths punctures that myth, and for some, that is the appeal of Moore's work. As one fan wrote about *TV Nation*, "[Networks] usually follow a very well-established set of codes to maintain a false sense of objectivity. '*TV Nation*' works by acknowledging that any statement made in a public forum implicitly carries a political position."[48]

MOORE'S LEGACY TO
POLITICAL ENTERTAINMENT TELEVISION

When *TV Nation* first aired, Moore seemed to recognize not only that his show was groundbreaking, but that there would be imitators to follow. In interviews at that time, one reporter noted that "Moore says it could be the first show of an as-yet-unnamed comedic genre; it's not a news-division show [for NBC], and even the entertainment division doesn't know whether to put it under drama or comedy."[49] Moore's prediction would, in many ways, prove correct. The genre of political entertainment television was just being born, with *Politically Incorrect* and *Dennis Miller Live* appearing at roughly the same time. But *TV Nation* and *The Awful Truth* weren't talk shows. Instead, these satirical yet serious takes on the newsmagazine genre directly employed the techniques of news reporting while simultaneously holding the industrial product known as "news" up for scrutiny. As one television critic put it at the time, "At last! News to amuse. If *TV Nation* exposes anything, it's the excesses and clichéd devices of those ubiquitous newsmags that take themselves so seriously."[50]

Since that time, programs such as *The Daily Show* and *The Colbert Report* have appropriated aspects of Moore's comedic style, as well as taken his critique of news and politics a step further. When *TDS*'s correspondents file taped reports from the field or when Stephen Colbert interviews politicians in his "Better Know a District" segment, they deftly use Moore's straight-faced style of asking simple yet ridiculous questions in interviews, letting the bizarre people or politicians with bizarre ideas incriminate themselves. By using the strategy of serious reporting in the right places (such as *TDS* correspondent Jason Jones interviewing delegates at the Republican National Convention on small-town values), the humorous or satirical often presents itself without much need for further comedic treatment.[51] Similarly, like Moore's, these shows also realize that there are many stories of political life that need telling, and are always on the lookout for stories that display deeper truths about the political world that structures public life (as seen in chapter 6 with *TDS*'s coverage of the shoddy reporting done by CNBC that perhaps contributed to the effects of the economic meltdown, making this entertainment show one of the first to make the critique).

Another program indebted to Moore is *Da Ali G Show*. British comedian Sacha Baron Cohen embodies three character-personas—a dim-witted British-Jamaican hip-hop poser, a smarmy gay Austrian fashionista, and an anti-semitic Kazakhstani reporter—all of whom pose as television personalities from these countries interviewing Americans. The humor most often arises because the interview subjects don't recognize that their interviewer is putting them on. The result is a damning critique of dominant culture (and the bigotry and ignorance that supports it) through the lens of race, class, sexuality, and ethnicity. Like Moore's newsmagazines, the premise of an interview allows the subjects to incriminate themselves. And by also having an interviewer who is unafraid to violate the unwritten rules of political and social discourse that usually structures such mediated engagements, the humor results from watching these people (with almost every episode featuring a politician, bureaucrat, or political pundit) try to regain their footing within the mediated encounter.

CONCLUSION

Moore's newsmagazines were more critical successes than ratings hits or revenue earners. Yet his foray into entertainment television proved that aggressive and subversive political critique can get aired on television (including network television) if it is packaged as entertainment. Audiences, in other words, will watch the programming *because* it is amusing and different, and social and political issues typically not covered by news agencies can therefore be brought to wider audiences via entertainment television. Nevertheless, with one network requiring funding from the BBC to get the show on the air and the other network more actively censoring the material, Moore demonstrated that certain ideas in a capitalist society are, as he notes in the epigraph, indeed "dangerous." Moore's programs offered a different means of thinking about such issues at a time when Republicans were complaining that a Democratic president was stealing their ideas. By utilizing hegemonic thinking and turning it on its head, he showed how the powerful can be forced to justify their actions and, by emulating Moore and his correspondents, why citizens should refuse to accept the standard lines as adequate answers. The controlled nature of political and corporate speech and spin is challenged, and in its place, an unruly form of democratic discourse emerges.

Furthermore, Moore's satire doesn't just deconstruct, but also offers the potential for alternative politics. By focusing his video vignettes on a series of political issues that typically receive scant attention by most mainstream television news organizations, Moore advances a progressive political agenda. Yet this agenda is established in ways beyond simply focusing attention on issues rarely debated on television. Moore's critiques mobilize affective political feelings through the symbolic displays of inattention, obfuscation, disregard, lack of concern, and outright arrogance by the agents of corporate and government power that appear in his programs. The "work" of the critique often comes through the construction of binary opposites (either present or absent in the text), and hence viewers are offered a position or alternative stance to that possessed by those targeted in the critique. Humor, then, does more than simply ridicule or question power (and is therefore more than just a negative art). It constructs the potential for productive political alternatives to the assumptions maintained by the logic of power elites and their management of the public agenda. For some, the means of getting to this place might seem unfair. But in an age of spin and information management, such forms of political thought and discussion in a democracy is something Moore suggests that television could use more of.

8

Fake News vs. Real News

The Case of *The Daily Show* and CNN

> What distinguishes one [news] service from another, one newspaper from another, is not so much what gets said but how it gets said—and the fact that it gets said when it is supposed to get said.
>
> —Theodore Glasser[1]

A recurrent claim about young Americans is that they increasingly get more of their news about politics and current events from late-night television comedians than they do from the news media. This claim began with a statistic that appeared in a 2000 survey of the electorate conducted by the Pew Research Center for the People & the Press which reported that 47 percent of people under thirty years old were "informed at least occasionally" about the presidential campaign by late-night talk shows.[2] Though there are numerous methodological and interpretive problems raised by this simple yet ultimately flawed statistic, journalists and other critics have nevertheless transformed it into a myth about young people and their news consumption habits. Regardless of its accuracy, it seemingly explains why young people have increasingly turned away from traditional outlets of political communication, namely newspapers and television news. It also addresses journalistic concerns that audiences are attracted more to entertainment than serious public affairs reporting, and what's worse, that they may not even be able to distinguish between the two. It also seemingly verifies fears of public ignorance of the political process, youth disengagement from politics, a declining reading culture, couch potato kids, the entertainmentization of politics, and the cynicism that supposedly grips our society.[3]

This chapter begins by examining and questioning this myth. But as with many myths that circulate in society, the critic's ability to refute the accuracy of the myth is not likely to diminish its popularity or widespread circulation. Instead, it may be more effective to show why the basic premise of the myth itself is incorrect. That is, in this instance, the idea that late night comedic television does not (or cannot) impart important news or information about public affairs and thus, by definition, only traffics in the trivial, inane, or absurd. In this chapter, I turn the myth on its head by asking: What if the myth is true and young people *are* "getting their news" from popular late-night comedy programs such as *The Daily Show with Jon Stewart*? What is it they might learn about politics or current events from this show, and how does that compare with what they might learn about politics were they to watch more respected sources of news such as CNN instead? To begin answering this question, I compare a news item as reported by *The Daily Show* with the same story as covered on CNN. I follow the Pew Center's lead by examining news reports of the 2004 presidential election, yet from broadcasts much later in the campaign when the viewing public is typically more raptly attuned. I analyze the type of information that is offered in the two reports, and how the resulting meanings or "truths" compare.

I argue that even though *The Daily Show* is a fake news show, its faux journalistic style allows the show's writers and host to question, dispel, and critique the manipulative language and symbolizations coming from the presidential campaign while simultaneously opening up deeper truths about politics than that offered by the "objective" reporting of mainstream journalism. By actually showing the high levels of spin and rhetoric produced by the candidates and their campaigns, then offering humorous retorts that cut to the heart of the matter, *The Daily Show* offers its viewers particular (and perhaps more useful) information about the campaign that is often missing from "real" journalist reports on the news networks, and hence, informs its viewers in ways that mainstream journalism rarely does. Given the extraordinary level of outright distortions, lies, and spin that dominated both the Republican and Democratic campaigns in this election, this paper concludes that perhaps the postmodern notion that the "fake" is more real than the "real" is not such an unsettling notion when it comes to citizens looking for truth in contemporary political communication on television. And, in turn, perhaps young citizens—if they do indeed get their information from political comedians on television—may not be as misinformed as the current myth suggests.

THE MYTH OF YOUNG PEOPLE
AND KNOWLEDGE OF PUBLIC AFFAIRS

In February 2000, the Pew Research Center for the People & the Press reported that 47 percent of people under thirty years old were "informed at least occasionally" about the campaign or candidates by late night talk shows (13 percent regularly and 34 percent sometimes). The poll was conducted January 4–11, 2000, before any party primaries had taken place. In January 2004, the Pew center repeated this survey (conducted December 19, 2003, through January 4, 2004), this time asking respondents if they "learned something" from comedy shows. Twenty-one percent of people under the age of thirty reported learning something from programs such as *Saturday Night Live* and *The Daily Show* (roughly the same number who learned something from the Internet). As the Pew study notes, "For Americans under 30, these comedy shows are now mentioned almost as frequently as newspapers and evening network news programs as regular sources for election news." Furthermore, the report exclaims, "one out of every two young people (50%) say they at least sometimes learn about the campaign from comedy shows, nearly twice the rate among people age 30–49 (27%) and four times the rate among people 50 and older."[4]

Before taking these statistics at face value, however, we should examine both the questions and the resulting statistics more closely. Certainly political insiders, heavy news readers/watchers, and political junkies are attuned to news so early in the campaign, for no other reason than to be able to handicap the upcoming horse race. As for the rest of the polity, however, the electoral contests in the small yet important states of Iowa and New Hampshire certainly receive much less of their attention, because the party nominee is generally a forgone conclusion by the time most Americans have the opportunity to vote in their state primary election. Hence, for a poll to attempt to measure political knowledge and information about an election so early in the campaign is specious.

What is worse, though, is the wording of the question itself: "informed at least occasionally." What does it mean to be "informed" about the campaign—knowledge of who is running for office, what their positions are on issues, who is ahead in the race, who has the biggest war chest, what gaffes have occurred to this point, the names of their wives, what type of underwear they prefer? At what level can most any type of non-fiction program—news reports, talk shows, documentaries, stand-up comedy, advertisements—provide *some* of this information? The question doesn't help us understand the underlying normative assumption of whether the respondent should know the differences in Al Gore's and Bill Bradley's positions on social security reform, or whether the respondent is simply expected to know their names and that they are running for office. Furthermore, the question asks "at least occasionally." Does that mean every day, once a week, or once a month, or does it suggest a regular and consistent pattern of consumption? Finally, what assumptions of intentionality are included here? Does the question seek to identify whether citizens brush up against news, or whether they intentionally turn to certain forms of programming for "information"? The survey results provide no answers to these questions. In short, the response to this question really only tells us two things—that comedians mine current affairs for humorous content, and that different programming types differ in their popularity among different demographic groups. It certainly does *not* measure whether the only or primary source of information about current affairs is obtained by watching late-night comedians on television.

Nevertheless, that hasn't prevented journalists from using the statistic to develop a full-blown myth about young people and their news consumption habits. For instance, CNN anchor Judy Woodruff began a question to *The Daily Show* host Jon Stewart by stating, "We hear more and more that your show and shows like your show are the places that young people *are getting their news.*"[5] Ted Koppel, the anchor for ABC's late-night news show, *Nightline* (a program that directly competes with these entertainment shows), similarly assailed Stewart by noting to his viewers, "A lot of television viewers, more, quite frankly, than I'm comfortable with, *get their news* from the comedy channel on a program called *The Daily Show.*"[6] And perhaps most egregiously, *Newsday* reporter Verne Gay wrote, "A recent study from the Pew Center found that 8 percent of respondents *learned most everything they knew* about a candidate from shows like *The Daily Show* and *Saturday Night Live.*"[7]

As these quotes suggest, reporters have taken great liberty in revising and expanding what the statistic actually reveals. Yet the results of a campaign knowledge test conducted on more than 19,000 citizens in the summer and fall of 2004 by the University of Pennsylvania's National Annenburg Election Survey did little to temper the myth. The survey reported that "viewers of late-night comedy programs, especially *The Daily Show with Jon Stewart* on Comedy Central, are more likely to know the issue positions and backgrounds of presidential candidates than people who do not watch late-night comedy," noting that *Daily Show* viewers "have higher campaign knowledge than national news viewers and newspaper readers."[8] The survey concludes, "traditional journalists have been voicing increasing concern that if young people are receiving political information from late-night comedy shows like *The Daily Show*, they may not be adequately informed on the issues of the day. This data suggests that these fears may be unsubstantiated." The survey also points out, however, "these findings do not show that *The Daily Show* is itself responsible for the higher knowledge among its viewers."

In summary, journalists and other critics of entertainment television have propagated a myth based on dubious evidence that late-night comedy television programming is a central location for the delivery of news (and, by inference, misinformation and ignorance about politics) for young people, a myth that competing quantitative evidence suggests is incorrect. What neither of these surveys reveal, however, is an assessment of the *content* of these shows—whether they offer viewers anything of value or are relatively meaningless, whether the information provided is accurate and truthful or biased and incorrect, or even how this material compares with other sources of information on public affairs. There is no qualitative assessment, only the assumption that what appears in these formats is not equivalent to that which could be obtained from traditional sources of political information. What follows, then, is an attempt to examine these questions directly, looking at how *The Daily Show* "reports" news and information, and its comparative value in light of reporting available on a more culturally acceptable and respected news source, CNN.

NEWS REPORTS BY *THE DAILY SHOW* AND CNN

I examined one week of *The Daily Show* during the late stages of the 2004 presidential campaign—October 4–7—one week after the first presidential debate. I selected one program during this period as a representative text (Thursday, October 7) for a close textual analysis. This limited selection allows for an in-depth analysis of the information and commentary provided, as well as a direct comparison with news reports from CNN on the same day. Most studies of *TDS* look across episodes for patterns in reporting (as I have done in earlier chapters). Here, though, the intention is to make a direct comparison of two entire news reports on the same event. The intentional circumscribing allows for the close reading of a text that cultural studies has proven to be of value. The episode selected illustrates the type of information provided in typical news reports by both *The Daily Show* and CNN, allowing us to compare not just the variety, but also quality of the reports and conclusions that can be drawn from them. The CNN reports come from three programs, all of which appeared on the same day as *The Daily Show* broadcast: *American Morning* (7:00 A.M.), *CNN Live Today* (10:00 A.M.), and *News From CNN* (12:00 P.M.).[9]

CNN began its 7:00 A.M. broadcast by reporting on Bush's campaign appearances the previous day, as well as the release of the CIA's Iraq Survey Group report investigating the existence of weapons of mass destruction in Iraq. In reporting Bush's campaign stop in Pennsylvania, CNN White House Correspondent Elaine Quijano pointed out:

> The president made no mention of a new report by the Iraq Survey Group, which found no evidence of stockpiles of weapons of mass destruction in Iraq when the U.S. invaded last year. Still, Mr. Bush is standing by his decision, insisting that after September 11, the country had to assess every potential threat in a new light.
> [Video clip of President Bush speaking in Wilkes-Barre, Pennsylvania]: Our nation awakened to an even greater danger, the prospect that terrorists who killed thousands with hijacked airplanes would kill many more with weapons

of mass murder. We had to take a hard look at every place where terrorists
might get those weapons. One regime stood out, the dictatorship of Saddam
Hussein.

During the 10:00 A.M. report, CNN decided not to continue airing the clip
of Bush's speech, instead letting Quijano summarize the president's central
point in the statement, as well as note the official White House "reading"
of the report, attributed here to "administration officials":

> But the president did not mention that new CIA report, which found no
> weapons of mass destruction in Iraq when the U.S. invaded last year. Instead
> Mr. Bush repeated his argument that taking Saddam Hussein out of power
> has made the world safer. Administration officials say they believe the report
> shows Saddam Hussein was a threat that the U.S. needed to take seriously.
> They also say they believe it shows that he had the intent and capability to
> develop weapons of mass destruction.

By 12:00 P.M., CNN was simply reporting the release of the report as this:
"Bush also defended the war in Iraq, just as the CIA prepares to report that
Saddam Hussein did not have weapons of mass destruction or the means
to produce them before U.S. troops invaded Iraq."

Jon Stewart also began his broadcast by announcing the release of the
CIA report and noting its conclusions:

> Everything we've been waiting for happened today. The official CIA report,
> the Dulfer Report, has come out, the one they've been working on for the past
> two years. It will be the definitive answer on the weapons of mass destruction
> programs in Iraq, and as it turns out, not so much. Apparently, there were no
> weapons of mass destruction in Iraq, and their capabilities have been degraded
> and they had pretty much stopped trying anything in '98. And both the presi-
> dent and vice president have come out today in response to the findings and
> said that they clearly justified the invasion of Iraq. Some people look at a glass
> as half full, while other people look at a glass and say that it's a dragon.

In this segment, Stewart provides roughly the same amount and type of information provided by CNN, but then goes out of his way to establish that
despite clear and convincing evidence to the contrary, Bush and Cheney
continue their act as either liars or highly delusional people; they see what
they want to see. Here Stewart offers not just the facts, but also draws conclusions from those facts. Journalistic adherence to norms of objectivity
generally prevents many reporters and anchors from looking across specific
events to explicitly point out repeated patterns of deception or misjudg-
ment by politicians and government officials (unless the reporting occurs
in investigative or opinion-editorial pieces). *The Daily Show*, of course, is
not limited by such professional constraints. Viewers are thus invited to

focus on the most important aspect of this news event—that this is not just another investigation that proves the official reason for invading Iraq was misguided and wrong. Rather, the import is that the Bush administration repeatedly refuses to admit its mistake.

CNN, on the other hand, simply repeats the administration's position, as is standard journalistic convention. Yet because numerous investigations have produced the same findings (which in the world of science and social science would amount to the establishment of "truth"), why should news media continue to repeat a position that has no basis in fact—just because the government continues to assert the position? Is that "newsworthy," and if not, what news value is being fulfilled? Daniel Boorstin contends that assertions such as this amount to "pseudo-events," a story created by politicians and journalists that has no intrinsic value as a news event per se, but is only deemed as such by journalists in the era of "objectivity."[10] Stewart refuses to play along, and again, ignores the administration's "reading" or justifications because they have no basis in reality (as determined by the numerous other officials, institutions, and nations that have concluded the same thing).

Stewart then turns his attention to a Bush campaign stop the day before. "Let's begin tonight on the campaign trail," he says, while talking over a video clip of President Bush in Wilkes-Barre, Pennsylvania. Bush is standing in front of a backdrop/banner with the words "A Safer America, A Stronger Economy" over both of his shoulders. "Yesterday, President Bush's advisors alerted the networks he would be making a major policy speech in Wilkes-Barre, Pennsylvania. The subject . . . *[the graphic highlights the slogan "A Safer America"]*—no, not that. *[The graphic highlights "A Stronger Economy"]* Uh, wrong again. *[The graphic then shows a crossed-out slogan, superimposing the hand-scrawled message, "Recover from unbelievably poor debate performance"]* That's it! That was the subject. Yes, in the week of his, let's call it 'weak' showing against Senator John Kerry on Thursday, the president and his handlers snookered the cable news networks into giving him one hour of free full-on campaign stop pablum."

CNN also covered this campaign stop in all three of its morning broadcasts. For both the 7:00 A.M. and 10:00 A.M. reports, Quijano simply referred to two campaign stops (one of which was in Pennsylvania), noting that Bush had "stepped up his attacks" and had come "out swinging hard" against his opponent, "blasting" Kerry and delivering a "blistering assault on Kerry's record." The reporter seeks to summarize the tone and substance of the president's speeches, while characterizing him as on the offensive—exactly what the campaign hopes will be reported. Only the 12:00 P.M. broadcast noted the campaign's intentions in changing the focus of the speech. Wolf Blitzer introduced the subject by referring to Bush's "attempt to try to re-establish some political momentum," while the correspondent reporting the event pointed out the change in plans: "Well, Wolf, as you know, initially this was a speech that was supposed to focus on medical liability reform. But after President Bush's widely viewed disappointing performance in the first presidential debate, there was a difference in strategy, a change in strategy from the campaign. They changed this to sharp attacks against Senator Kerry and his record on the war on terror, as well as the economy."

CNN's reporting of this event is characterized by three tendencies that political scientists argue is typical of news media's reporting in elections— (1) framing the campaign as a sports contest (horse racing, or in this instance, boxing), (2) the focus on campaign strategies more than the issues themselves, and (3) parroting the messages that political campaigns want reported, including the circulation of campaign rhetoric and slogans without intensive scrutiny or criticism.[11] Stewart also points out the campaign's strategy of deflecting attention from Bush's weak showing in the presidential debates by going on the offensive, but he also insists on calling attention to the manipulative aspects of the event itself—both the campaign's misleading the press about making a major policy statement (when the presence of the banner itself clearly shows the forethought and planning for this attack speech) and the oral and visual rhetoric that the campaign wants the news media to report and show its viewers. Stewart doesn't accept the contention that the speech is about national security or the economy, and focuses instead on the artifice of the event. It is an artifice that the news media help create and facilitate by uncritically continuing to air the Bush speech live, even though the speech does not include the policy material they initially agreed merited free air time as a newsworthy *presidential* statement (as opposed to that of a candidate for office). As Stewart has noted about his show in an earlier interview, "What we try to do is point out the artifice of things, that there's a guy behind the curtain pulling levers."[12] Here he does just that.

Stewart then shows several clips from the Bush speech that CNN chose not to air in any of its three reports.

Stewart: [Bush] began by throwing out the first pander.

Bush: It's great to be in Wilkes-Barre, Pennsylvania. It's such an honor to be back here. It's great to be in a part of the world where people work hard, they love their families . . .

Stewart: (*said out of the side of his mouth*) Yeah, not like New York—family-hating jackasses; lazy family haters.

CNN does not show this clip because, given the news values of mainstream journalism, such statements by politicians are not newsworthy; they are typical of political speeches. For reporters assigned to follow the candidate's campaign, in fact, they have heard such statements countless times by this point in the campaign, said to different crowds in different places. For Stewart, however, the clip merits the viewers' attention, because it shows not only that the statement itself is ridiculous, but that it is not beneath the president to pander to audiences. This is part of the overall point that Stewart attempts to make throughout the entire news segment—he continually asks the viewer to step outside the staged event to assess what information is available that might shed light on both presidential candidates' fundamental character as people and leaders.

Stewart continues covering the event by again showing another clip that CNN chose not to air:

Stewart: But then it was rival bashing time. Bush warmed up with a few insults aimed at the Democrats' number-two man and his performance in Tuesday night's debate.

Bush: America saw two very different visions of our country and two different hairdos. I didn't pick my vice president for his hairdo. I picked him for his judgment, his experience.

Stewart: *(showing a picture of a balding Dick Cheney)* Which, sadly, is as good as his hairdo.

If pandering isn't enough, Stewart shows that it is not beneath Bush to engage in ad hominem attacks. Again, CNN chose not to report this part of the president's speech, recognizing that attacks on one's opponents are simply part of electoral politics. Stewart, however, shows the clip not just to provide evidence of Bush's character and campaign style, but also to question the actual point that Bush is attempting to make so unproblematically—the quality of his administration's "judgment and experience" in the conduct of governmental affairs. Both CNN and *The Daily Show* have already provided evidence earlier in their broadcasts that the administration's "experience" of deciding to wage war, based on their "judgment" that there was trustworthy information to do so, was faulty. *The Daily Show*, however, is the only one to make the connection and point it out to viewers.

Like CNN, Stewart then focuses on the major policy statements within Bush's speech:

Stewart: Bush then moved onto his economic policy regarding Kerry.

Bush: Now the Senator's proposing higher taxes on more than 900,000 small business owners. He says the tax increase is only for the rich. You've heard that kind of rhetoric before. The rich hire lawyers and accountants for a reason—to stick you with the tab.

Stewart: Let me get this straight. Don't tax the rich because they'll get out of it? So your policy is, tax the hard-working people because they're dumbasses and they'll never figure it out? So vote for me, goodnight?

Only during its 12:00 P.M. broadcast did CNN report this aspect of the president's speech, noting that Bush "also twisted Kerry's plan to roll back the cut taxes for those making more than $200,000, describing it as a tax increase for more than 900,000 small businesses." The CNN report is critical at this juncture by pointing out the Bush campaign's distortion of Kerry's proposal (that is, rolling back Bush's tax cuts does not amount to a proposed tax increase). CNN's focus is on the rhetorical slight of hand. But that is the extent of their report. Stewart, however, returns the focus to the president's rhetoric by carrying the point to its logical conclusion. He illuminates the contradictory nature of the populist statement by questioning what it is exactly that Bush is trying to articulate, while also reminding viewers of where Bush really stands on taxes and how his policies actually belie the rhetoric employed here. It merits noting that news programs rarely offer direct and damning evidence of contradictory statements or duplicitous comments. The convention they typically rely upon is to quote someone else who will point this out.[13] CNN did not even air the actual clip, relying instead on its reporter to summarize Bush's statement. One might argue that CNN has done Bush a favor by *not* airing a statement that is logically somewhat ridiculous, and instead, doing the hard work of actually deciphering for the viewing audience what the president means, thereby making him look more presidential in the process.[14]

The only clip of the president's speech that CNN showed in all three of its broadcasts occurred in the 7:00 A.M. report—his statement concerning the supposed threat posed by "the dictatorship of Saddam Hussein" (quoted earlier). *The Daily Show* also reported this part of the speech, but with much more scrutiny to what Bush actually said. Stewart here engages in a rhetorical back-and-forth with the video clip of Bush's statement, attempting to come up with the right answer for which nation it is *exactly* that threatens America with weapons of mass destruction:

Stewart: Finally, the president brought the mood down a little, as only he can.

Bush: After September 11, America had to assess every potential threat in a new light. We had to take a hard look at every place where terrorists might get those weapons and one regime stood out.

Stewart: Well, that's true. It would be Saudi Arabia. Fifteen of the nineteen terrorists were actually from there.

Bush: . . . the dictatorship of Saddam Hussein.

Stewart: No, no. I don't think that's it. Um. Oh. It was Iran—proven Al-Qaeda ties, building up the nukes program. I think it was them.

[repeating the tape of Bush]: . . . the dictatorship of Saddam Hussein.

Stewart: No, no. I'm sure . . . Pakistan. Top scientists sold nuclear secrets to—

[repeating the tape of Bush]: . . . the dictatorship of Saddam Hussein.

Stewart: Could be Yemen. *[A graphic of a clock face with spinning hands is superimposed over a slightly faded image of Stewart, suggesting his thinking for quite some time of the possible countries, all the while Stewart thinks out loud.]* Oh . . . Kazakhstan is actually a very dangerous . . . Uzbekistan has always created problems in that region . . . Turkey—very dangerous. Lebanon has some . . . Qatar *[The graphic removes the clock face, and the camera focus on Stewart again becomes clear.]* Oh, oh, oh. North Korea. They have the bomb. Their leader is crazy. North Korea.

[repeating the tape of Bush]: . . . the dictatorship of Saddam Hussein.

Stewart: *[Holding out his arms in front of him and speaking in a slow monotone voice with a staccato cadence, imitating a robot.]* "The-dic-ta-tor-ship-of-Sad-dam-Hus-sein. Too-tired-to-fight-it. Must-learn. Re-pe-ti-tion."

Stewart scrutinizes the president's statement on its own terms—"in *every* place where terrorists might get those weapons": Saudi Arabia, Iran, Pakistan, North Korea, and so on. Then, through video repetition, Stewart highlights how the administration continues to repeat assertions over and over until the viewer is turned into an unthinking (or worn-out) robot. In the speech itself, of course, Bush does not repeat the line. Yet Stewart recognizes that single speech events such as this do not constitute the reality that news media report and, in turn, help create. Instead, his usage of manipulated video emphasizes the repeated pattern of administration efforts to establish something that is untrue, yet which citizens must work to resist because of its repeated assertion. As Stewart has been quoted as saying, "We're out to stop that political trend of repeating things again and again until people are forced to believe them."[15]

Stewart finishes the show's coverage of the Bush speech by returning one last time to a Bush pronouncement that was simply too good to pass up for its comedic value, yet also affirms the point about Bush's character that he has attempted to make throughout the segment:

Stewart: But for all that, perhaps the most telling line of the speech came during Bush's seemingly innocuous segue into a story about his wife.

Bush: You're not going to believe this. It's a true story, or kind of true.

Stewart: *[With sheepish grin]* George W. Bush—I can tell a lie.

Again, CNN doesn't air this clip because there is no news value here—from their perspective, it is a meaningless aside unrelated to either campaign strategy or policy stances. For Stewart, however, it not only ties in nicely with the previous statement about Saddam Hussein and 9/11, but it also neatly demonstrates *exactly* what is at stake in the election of the president. Bush's proclivity to lie, in fact, was something the news media generally ignored in the election campaign, yet was an important criticism of Bush often addressed in numerous venues of popular culture during the campaign—most famously in Michael Moore's documentary film, *Fahrenheit 9/11.*

Stewart concludes the news segment of the show by turning to an event not widely covered by the news media—both John Kerry and Bush soliciting votes by appearing on *Dr. Phil,* an afternoon therapy and relationship talk show. Here he attempts to highlight the deeper truths at work, this time with the Democratic nominee:

> *Stewart*: But like Bush's speech, Kerry's *Dr. Phil* appearance had one moment that most clearly captured the essence of the candidate.
>
> *[Video clip of the* Dr. Phil Show, *an interview with Senator Kerry, conducted with the assistance of Dr. Phil's wife.] Dr. Phil's wife*: Is one of your daughters more like you than the other?
>
> *Kerry*: Yes. No. That's . . . gosh . . . I'd like to . . . yes. But I guess . . . yes, the answer is yes.
>
> *Dr. Phil's Wife*: Which one do you think is more like you?
>
> *Kerry*: Well . . . um . . . I . . . that's why I hesitated, because I think in some ways my daughter Alexandra is more like me, but in other ways my daughter Vanessa is more like me.
>
> *Stewart*: *[Burying his face into his hands, then moving his hands over his bowed head, gripping his hair, then the back of his neck. Stewart makes no comment, but simply looks at the camera with exasperation and dismay. The audience erupts in laughter.]*

When presidential candidates first began appearing on such talk shows with regularity in 1992, the news media covered these appearances as newsworthy events. They did so, in particular, because of the unusual nature of the appearances, but also because the news media disliked the "softball" questions offered up by these "illegitimate" nonreporters.[16] Because such appearances rarely feature the candidate's saying much about their position on issues (focusing more instead on personal matters), the news media now generally turn a blind eye to these "campaign stops," treating them as *de rigueur* in the hustle to reach disparate voter groups. *The Daily Show,* however, calls attention to the spectacle performance, not just for its groveling and humiliating aspects, but rather also to highlight how such performances might actually tell us something important about the candidates. In this instance, Kerry confirmed everything the Bush campaign had said about him: that Kerry is unwilling to be pinned down on anything (despite how insignificant the matter), yet paradoxically, will say anything to get elected if he believes that is what the audience wants to hear. That truth comes to light very clearly for viewers when the matter is something as trivial as reflecting upon the relationship with one's daughters. Viewers may not be able to discern whether Kerry is a flip-flopper on foreign policy issues (say, for instance, his various votes on the Iraq War), but they can certainly recognize mealy-mouthed remarks when it comes to interpersonal relationships.

The Daily Show, therefore, has constructed a narrative, weaving together campaign events to give the viewer insight into the candidates and who they might really be. This narrative is formulated from information derived from planned campaign events, yet woven together to tell a story that allows for evaluation of the candidates. Perhaps this is simply an entertainmentized version of a "news analysis" or "op-ed" journalism. But it is a particular brand of "reporting" that might illuminate for viewers the larger issues at stake beyond the isolated events that typically dominate news reporting.

In summary, then, *The Daily Show* has provided viewers information on several major political events that occurred the day before: the CIA report on weapons of mass destruction, Bush's campaign speech, and Kerry's appearance on a popular television program. The audience learns what the CIA report says, learns two of the main points in Bush's speech also reported by news outlets, and learns about Kerry's personal life. *The Daily Show* has not, therefore, short-changed the viewer on information they would have seen by watching a "real" newscast.

Yet *The Daily Show's* audience also sees more material on these events than that provided by CNN, learning things that CNN didn't report. First, *The Daily Show* highlights political rhetoric itself, showing the false statements, ad hominem attacks, pandering, and populist appeals of candidate Bush, not seeing such language as a "given" in politics, but instead, as a disturbing quality that exemplifies the character of the politician. Second, and perhaps more importantly, the program offers viewers information they have previously heard, yet are reminded of here as a means of making sense of the events covered in the daily news report: there were no weapons of mass destruction; the administration's actions exemplify its use of bad judgment because they went after the wrong regime; their economic policies are the opposite of what they say they are. Continually, Stewart will not let the viewer lose sight of the greater truths at stake here. He is constantly keeping score, adding it all up, reminding the viewer of what this says about the candidates and the larger terms upon which they should be evaluated. In a single news report, the television news reporters rarely put things together in such a manner. Yet what the news media ignore may actually provide citizens with the type of meaningful information upon which they can base their electoral decisions. By Stewart's doing so in a typical news reporting

Jon Stewart, host of The Daily Show, *anchors a fake newscast, but his reporting may at times prove more useful to citizens than what is offered in "real" television newscasts. Courtesy of Comedy Central © 2009. All rights reserved.*

format, he demonstrates the failings of news media in informing viewers, drawing attention to how media serve as a conduits for false information and image management, and how it would be easy for citizens to become the unthinking drones and robots that such unquestioned lies and manipulative imagery could lead them to become.

One might be tempted to criticize *The Daily Show* for its redaction techniques—selecting damning video clips that are taken out of context and then used to ridicule or embarrass politicians, all for a laugh. As we have seen, however, the clips used by Stewart are no more out of context than the single clip shown by CNN. Both Stewart and CNN actually highlight the context of the speech—the poor debate performance, as well as the release of the CIA report—yet it is *The Daily Show* that provides even more depth to the speech by showing viewers more of it (six clips compared to one by CNN). Just because CNN and other news organizations make claims of neutrality and objectivity doesn't mean they aren't being selective in what they report and how they report it. Furthermore, Stewart reports the same events and highlights the same "newsworthy" items as CNN, including reaching many of their same conclusions. As journalism critics have pointed out, not only have the length of sound bites drastically decreased over the last twenty years, but they are increasingly disappearing altogether from television news reports (despite a very large news hole with 24-hour cable channels). Instead, reporters are simply summarizing what candidates and government officials say, then interpreting those comments in a conversation with the news anchor. Yet as we have also seen, those interpretations offer the viewer little in the way of substantive critical assessments because of the norms and conventions of the profession.

In short, *The Daily Show* has matched CNN's coverage of this particular campaign event, even surpassing it by providing viewers additional information about the candidates beyond policy positions and campaign strategies and maneuvers. Of course, CNN provides a wealth of information about national and world affairs that a comedy program like *The Daily Show* can never cover. Nor would I suggest that citizens could be fully informed by watching a comedy show that provides little more than ten minutes of "reporting." Nevertheless, if we are to assess the quality of information about the presidential campaign provided by a fake news show versus a real one (as the Pew study normatively asserts), then the analysis here suggests that *The Daily Show* can provide quality information that citizens can use in making informed choices about electoral politics.

FAKENESS, REALITY,
AND THE POSTMODERN VIEWING PUBLIC

By most accounts, the institution of journalism is in a state of crisis in America.[17] As discussed above, the myth that young people get their news from late-night comedians is partly a desire to explain why young people, in particular, are turning away from broadcast news or print journalism as primary sources of news and information.[18] With declining readership and viewership, the institution is economically challenged by dwindling advertising revenues as well as increased costs of production.[19] Recent scandals related to professional norms and ethics (from story fabrication by Jason Blair at the *New York Times* and Stephen Glass at *The New Republic* to poor fact checking on President Bush's Air National Guard records by Dan Rather at *CBS News*) have contributed to a decline in trust with news media consumers.[20] Concurrently, with new media technologies such as blogs and search engine portals, citizens are questioning the top-down, gatekeeper role of news media, and instead, increasingly desire a more active role in the determination and construction of what constitutes news and who gets to make it.[21] Furthermore, the press's timidity in questioning and thwarting overt propaganda efforts by the Bush administration (as both the *New York Times* and *Washington Post* offered a *mea culpa* for their lack of serious reporting on assertions and evidence by the Bush administration in the run-up to the Iraq War) also weakens the news media's claim to serving as effective and trustworthy watchdogs to power.[22] Indeed, government propaganda combined with competition between news outlets that offer not just "competing views of the world, but different realities" (such as Fox News, the *New York Times*, and Al-Jazeera) leads to what Kristina Riegert calls the "struggle for credibility" with viewing audiences and voting publics.[23]

Hence, what is also in crisis is the belief that news media provide a *realistic* picture of the world (as discussed in chapter 4). The public is well aware that both television and politics are spectacle performances, and indeed, that the press and government are two mutually reinforcing and constituting institutions.[24] News media are *part of* the political spectacle,[25] including journalists cum talk show pundits who act more like lapdogs to power than watchdogs of it, cheerleading embedded reporters, and patriotic news anchors who wear their hearts on their sleeve. An increasingly media-savvy public realizes that news programs such as CNN are no more "real" than *The Daily Show* is "fake." Yet mainstream news media continue to believe their claims to truth—and the authenticity of those claims—because of their *authority* to make them in the first place. It is an authority they have asserted (and the public has granted) through their title, special status, institutional-based legitimacy, access to power, and the means of production and distribution. But as Foucault also reminds us, "'truth' is a type of discourse that societies accept and *make function as true*."[26] And as postmodernists would have it, the "authentic" exists only in "the imaginings of those who yearn for it."[27] Were that to change, or should citizens come to believe that news is inauthentic, untrue, or just another form of constructed spectacle (that is, the credibility gap becomes a chasm), then they might yearn for other means of establishing truth and reality.

The institutional practice of journalism is a modernist means of constructing knowledge of public life that for many years has been widely accepted. Increasingly, though, this means of taking account of the world is being questioned, if not discredited.[28] In a useful summary of postmodernist thinking, Frank Webster argues that "the modernist enthusiasm for genres and styles [of which news is one] is rejected and mocked for its pretensions [by postmodernists]. From this it is but a short step to the postmodern penchant for parody, for tongue-in-cheek reactions to established styles, for a pastiche mode which delights in irony and happily mixes and matches in a 'bricolage' manner."[29] And in steps *The Daily Show*, with just such a tendency for postmodern playfulness.

But *The Daily Show* is fake only in that it refuses to make claims to authenticity. But being fake does not mean that the information it imparts is untrue. Indeed, as with most social and political satire, its humor offers a means of reestablishing common sense truths to counter the spectacle, ritual, pageantry, artifice, and verbosity that often cloak the powerful. The rationality of political satire is that it "reminds of common values," and "in its negative response to political excess, it serves to restore equilibrium to politics."[30] Citizens know that public artifice exists, which is ultimately why the satire that points it out is funny—they just need someone skillful enough to articulate the critique. Though this fake yet real reporting has led Baym to argue that *The Daily Show* is "reinventing political journalism," I contend that it is the postmodern audience that comprises its viewership and has made it popular, more accurately, who is reformulating what it is they want from political communication, including journalism.[31]

Though scholars often attack the press for its supposed cynicism (for example, the way in which reporters point out the man behind the curtain), I contend that the press may not do this enough. Shelving journalistic conventions to get at important truths is less cynical than turning a blind eye to the manipulation by either contending that politics will always be this way or assuming that viewers *should* be informed enough or smart enough to connect all the dots themselves. A program like *The Daily Show* refuses to sit idly by while political lies and manipulative rhetoric go unchallenged (or as Stewart says, "until it becomes true"). Unhindered by the self-imposed constraints placed on reporters by the profession (as well as the codependent relationship that exists between government and the press), *The Daily Show* uses a fake news platform to offer discussions of news events that are informative *and* critical, factual *and* interpretive, thorough *yet* succinct. Does that make it biased, unfair, or unbalanced? Not when the program aims its sites on the powerful. As Bryan Keefer, editor of Spinsanity.com, has argued, "the media need to understand that pointing out the truth isn't the same as taking sides."[32] This, of course, is what a fake news show is licensed to do, and why I contend that it provides such an important voice of political critique on the American political landscape.

In an opinion piece in the *Washington Post*, Keefer dares to speak for his generation, justifying their changing relationship to traditional news media and their search for better alternatives. He contends that:

> We live in an era when PR pros have figured out how to bend the news cycle to their whims, and much of what's broadcast on the networks bears a striking resemblance to the commercials airing between segments. Like other twenty-somethings, I've been raised in an era when advertising invades every aspect of pop culture, and to me the information provided by mainstream news outlets too often feels like one more product, produced by politicians and publicists.[33]

If the myth of young citizens turning to comedians for news and information about politics ends up proving true, then as this analysis suggests, the fate of the republic doesn't seem in jeopardy if a comedy program like

The Daily Show is a source for their knowledge of public affairs. As Keefer's comments suggest, at least when people watch a program that blatantly embraces its fakeness, they don't feel like they are being sold a bill of goods (or as Stewart himself said in critiquing CNBC host Jim Cramer, "we are both snake oil salesmen to a certain extent, but we do label the show as snake oil here").[34] Hence, the postmodern claim that the "fake" is more real than the "real" is perhaps not such an unsettling notion after all.

9

Faux Real and Faux Play

The Parody of Punditry in *The Colbert Report*

Stephen Colbert is a big fat idiot.[1] Not really, but he plays one on TV. He isn't fat either, at least in the traditional sense of the word. But he does portray an idiot with a big fat ego and sense of self-importance in his parody of right-wing television talk show hosts. And it is a parody he plays mercilessly. Watching Colbert leads one to wonder why it took so long for such a figure to appear with the ability to show viewers the way, the truth, and the light out of the cloud of idiocy that so often substitutes for rational and deliberative thought on prime-time cable television. Colbert has transformed a character that was once a correspondent on *The Daily Show* (*TDS*) into a megalomaniacal host of *The Colbert Report* (*TCR*), which appears Monday through Thursday immediately following *TDS* on Comedy Central. If *TDS* is a show that satirizes the news, *TCR* satirizes those who cover the news, who talk about what it means, and how viewers should process it. And how viewers should process the news, according to talk show hosts, is exactly how they tell them to think about it. When Colbert was offered this point in an interview, his response was, "Don't worry your pretty little head. Open wide, baby bird, because Papa's got a fat nightcrawler of truth for you."[2]

But, as we saw in previous chapters, "truth" is not exactly what prime-time cable talk shows are really about (hence, Colbert's concept of "truthiness"). As Colbert notes, these hosts are "not a huge fan of facts. It's really more about what [they] feel in [their] gut." They take "little snatches of information and then make broad generalizations based on that."[3] What Colbert highlights, then, is the faux realities constructed here within this personality-centered emotional rhetoric, with parody as the vehicle for bringing these observations to light. But the play of parody is also faux play, which is to say that this isn't *just* play, but play with a serious intent. There is a very serious critique of the politics at work directly in these pundit shows, as well as a challenge to the broader social and ideological grounding upon which these show's stand. As Jonathan Gray notes, "parody's act of stepping onto another text's or genre's space thus threatens to destabilize that space and, with it, that text's or genre's power."[4] Furthermore, Colbert is not simply targeting a single talk show host such as Bill O'Reilly, as is often assumed (and indeed, who Colbert calls "Papa Bear"). Rather, he is engaged in what Gary Saul Morson calls an "anti-genre" critique, where parody attempts to discredit "not a single work in the target genre, but the genre as a whole."[5] Colbert has crafted a character built as an amalgam of hosts (such as O'Reilly, Sean Hannity, and Lou Dobbs, among others), so the parody therefore is a broad-based critique and comment on the devolution of public affairs talk into the irresponsible and incomprehensible nonsense that is paraded as "truth."

This chapter sets out to explore the complex interactions and levels of critique that occur in this tension between the fake and the real in Colbert's parodic performance. We begin by examining the formal characteristics of the show, including further exploration of what it is that Colbert is parodying and why. The chapter then analyzes the parodic techniques at work in several features of the program, including Colbert's reflections on the news, "The WØRD" segment, and interviews with guests. The chapter concludes with a reflection of just what makes this an important and much needed form of political critique on television today, including the role of fakeness in achieving realistic understandings of political rhetoric.

CHAMPION, CONQUEROR, VICTIM

In earlier chapters, we explored the reinvention of journalism during the Vox Pop phase of news-talk television's history. What replaced news in prime time is talk shows with opinionated hosts whose role it is to reflect upon and interpret the day's news. *The Colbert Report* directly parodies this transformation of the genre, as Colbert himself explains: "What the character [he plays] expresses in specific reference to American television is the post evening-news, personality-driven, single-camera shout-fest interviews."[6] To be sure, the interviews are not the primary function of such shows, though that too serves as an outlet for the host's political affect. Instead, the central focus is the hosts, and the role they craft as personalities to be watched, adored, followed nightly, and whose other commercial products one should consume. Again, Colbert argues, "These are all personality shows. It doesn't matter what they're saying. Doesn't matter what the news is, it's how this person feels about the news, and how you should feel about the news."[7]

To achieve this, the talk show host must create a special relationship to his audience, binding them together in agreement and shared feelings, garnering their trust by flattering and seducing them, and then joining together to attack their common enemies or perceived opposition (real or imaginary).[8] Colbert explains how this seduction works by reference to Bill O'Reilly's techniques: "He prefaces his arguments by saying, 'You're not gonna hear this from anyone else,' 'I'm not gonna make any friends by saying this,' 'They don't want you to hear this, but this is what I'm gonna tell you,' and 'I'm looking out for you,' as if everything he is doing is completely altruistic and only for the good of the audience. And that's a wonderful attitude to have because it establishes trust between you and your [audience]."[9] From there, the next steps are easy. The host simply makes a hullabaloo out of the public attacks he endures as proxy for the audience and what they together believe in and support, and then rails about that persecution repeatedly. "The sense of victimization is just wonderful for the character," Colbert notes, "because it allows you to be both a champion and a conqueror and a victim at the same time. . . . You've got all your bases covered."[10] From there, it isn't difficult to see the messianic quality to the relationship. The host is the source of truth, and because the host shares that truth with the viewers, he must suffer and endure attacks (as messenger of the truth) from those who don't want to hear it and for the sake of the audience who believes in it and him.

Colbert and his production crew were very intentional in designing the show's set and its iconography to reflect this aspect of the character and this special "religious" relationship to his audience. As Colbert describes it,

> Everything on the show has my name on it, every bit of the set. One of the things I said to the set designer . . . was, "One of your inspirations should be [DaVinci's painting] *"The Last Supper."* All the architecture of that room points at Jesus' head, the entire room is a halo, and he doesn't have a halo." And I said, "On the set, I'd like the lines of the set to converge on my head." And so if you look at the design, it all does, it all points at my head. And even radial lines on the floor, and on my podium, and watermarks in the images behind me, and all the vertices, are right behind my head. So there's a sort of sun-god burst quality about the set around me. . . . I said, "I don't want anything behind me [like television sets behind news anchors' heads], because I am the sun. It all comes from me. I'm not channeling anything. I *am* the source."[11]

The added dimension that makes this messianic reading all the more powerful is the way in which many Americans have traditionally blended God and country, or what sociologist Robert Bellah described as the "public religious dimension expressed in a set of beliefs, symbols, and rituals" that is perhaps best conceived as America's "civil religion."[12] Roderick Hart describes this as "civic piety," and notes the ease with which God and country are fused in a form of religious patriotism: "Religion gives us faith in faith. And when religion shares the motivational cosmos with government, it becomes only a short emotional step from faith to patriotism and from God to country."[13] The religious right in America has perfected this short step for the last thirty years, which is very much a component part of much right-wing talk show rhetoric. Colbert's character, then, is partly an enunciation and critique of this tendency, as he explains in one interview: "At the heart of this is America as the chosen country of God. It's a conflation of the Statue of Liberty and the crucifix: American religiosity and American destiny are one and the same. That's why George Bush was chosen by God to lead the world. Manifest destiny is an old idea, but now it's just expressed in different ways."[14]

But to be clear, Colbert is not just commenting on this quite old reflex in American political culture, but instead critiquing the way in which cable talk show hosts have taken it one step further by crafting *themselves* as stand-in saviors—a cult of personality built on this blend of victimization, patriotic worship of country, ideological and religious certainty, political fervency, and the desperate desire for truth amidst confusing times. The show's set design represents this worship of self, country, and God through its own creative blend of narcissistic iconography. The halo effect described is merged with a red-white-and-blue background composed of pictures

The Colbert Report's *set design blends together the iconography of God and Country with the host illuminated as a star-striped messianic figure. Courtesy of Comedy Central* © 2009. All rights reserved.

of the Statue of Liberty, a bald eagle, a bald eagle crest, a single star, Mt. Rushmore, and two giant letter Cs. Colbert's desk is also a giant C, and the windows that sit behind his interview table are church-styled ogee-arched stained-glass windows that also blend the worship of Colbert and country. One of the more humorous manifestations of this self-worship is Colbert's portrait of himself in front of a portrait of himself that sits over his fireplace. On the fireplace mantle sits his Emmys and his Peabody Award, which he constantly refers to as public celebration of his greatness.

The final component of this elaborate parodic construct, of course, is the adoring audience—those who would follow and obey. What has resulted since the show's debut is that Colbert's audiences have played along with gusto, assuming their role as an essential character on the show, becoming the worshipful followers that such a parody calls for. As Colbert notes, they too are a *necessary* character for the parody to be complete.[15] What has also occurred, somewhat unexpectedly, is that the program has developed a particularly ardent fan following itself. The next chapter discusses Colbert's fans and what their actions and relationship to the show means as a form of political engagement.

As noted in earlier chapters, *The Colbert Report* appeared at a time in which cable talk show hosts not only crafted this personality-centered, emotion-driven discursive style of television talk, but shared a symbiotic relationship with the thinking and feeling of George W. Bush—an administration that also based its popular appeal on a mix of personality, politics, and piety.[16] What Colbert has done through crafting this anti-genre parody, then, is link the televisual form to the broader political context in which it resides, for, as Morson notes, "parody works by etiology. The parodist uncovers for each target an 'irony of origins,' which is to say, he or she reveals the relation of the text to the compromising and conditionalizing context of its utterance."[17] Though critics have charged such shows with being an echo chamber for Republican Party talking points, what we can clearly see is the similarities these shows share with an administration focused on affect, disregard for facts, impatience with disagreement, and an unerring belief in their possession of "truth." Morson argues further that "a text or genre will be vulnerable to parody . . . to the extent that it ignores or claims to transcend its own originating context: parody is most readily invited by an utterance that claims transhistorical authority or implies that its source does not lie in any interest or circumstances of its speaker.[18] Colbert's parody is that much richer simply because talk show hosts such as Lou Dobbs or Bill O'Reilly consider (and proclaim) themselves "journalists" and appear on news channels that lay claim to norms of journalistic objectivity with slogans such as "Fair and Balanced." Though they are political commentators, they attempt to hide behind the legitimating authority of news media and deny their own interests as entertainers. They also deny

The narcissism of right-wing cable talk show hosts is captured here by Colbert's portrait of himself in front of his portrait. Courtesy of Comedy Central © 2009. All rights reserved.

their place in the broader political and ideological context of the times in which they appear. *The Colbert Report* is an uncomfortable reminder and uncovering of just these things.

PARODYING PUNDITRY

The Colbert Report is formally composed of numerous segments and recurring features, including many that play upon the oversized ego of the host and his role as champion, conqueror, and victim as already described. These include intermittently appearing segments such as "Better Know a District," where Colbert interviews members of Congress;[19] "Formidable Opponent," where Colbert engages in a debate with the only person who is truly capable of matching his intelligence and cunning —himself (using two cameras and different background visuals to create a mock debate); "On Notice," in which Colbert puts various enemies "on notice" by placing their name on a giant blue "On Notice" board; "Who's Not Honoring Me Now," examining people or organizations who are not acting deferential to Colbert's greatness; and the obvious "Who's Attacking Me Now." The three primary segments that occur most often include Colbert's general run-down of the news (broadly defined), a verbal essay that is based upon a single word (called "The WØRD"), and his in-studio interview with a guest. Each provides a different vantage point from which to investigate Colbert's parody of the genre as a whole.

The News

The news segments can assume a similar parodic style as that found on *The Daily Show*, in that Colbert introduces a topic in the news and makes satiric comments on it. The satiric twist here, though, comes through the parody of how the *host* handles or interprets the news, not the news events themselves. For instance, when Sonia Sotomayor was nominated to become a justice of the United States Supreme Court, Colbert introduced the dilemma not as a news anchor, but as an offended commentator:

> I'm a member of a persecuted minority—white males. Last week, my people were marginalized even more when President Obama nominated Sonia Sotomayor for the Supreme Court. There wasn't a single white male on his short list. That sends a terrible message to all the little white boys out there who dream of one day having their judicial reputation destroyed by the media. But Sotomayor isn't just a Latina. She's also a racist. Just ask any old white man who supports a border fence.

Colbert then shows three news clips of older white men (Tom Tancredo, Pat Buchanan, and Rush Limbaugh) decrying Sotomayor as a racist. The clip ends with Limbaugh calling Sotomayor a "reverse racist." Colbert angrily jumps in, "Exactly! A reverse racist! We call it that because it's the opposite of the way you're supposed to be a racist."[20]

As theorists of parody have explained, parody includes a "double-voiced word" or "utterance that [is] designed to be interpreted as the expression of two speakers."[21] In this instance, those speakers are Colbert the fellow right-wing talk show host and Colbert the comedian who is making fun of them. As Mikhail Bakhtin pointed out, "in parody, two languages are crossed with each other, as well as two styles, two linguistic points of view, and in the final analysis two speaking subjects. It is true that only one of these languages (the one that is parodied) is present in its own right; the other is present invisibly, as an actualizing background for creating and perceiving."[22] The two languages here are that which is present—the words and rhetoric of persecution and victimization by right-wing talk show hosts—and the underlying perception that the comedian's intent and meaning are the opposite of what his character is saying. For, as Morson explains,

> A parodic utterance is one of open disagreement. The second utterance represents the first in order to discredit it, and so introduces a "semantic direction" which subverts that of the original. In this way the parodied utterance "becomes the arena of conflict between two voices . . . the voices here are not only detached and distanced, they are hostilely counterposed."[23]

That new semantic direction comes from the inaccurate descriptions (white males as persecuted and a minority), incongruous statements (media circus and dashed dreams of opportunity), ironic juxtaposition (anti-immigration advocates calling a Latina a racist), and literalist pun (correct and incorrect ways to be racist) that Colbert laces with the serious and somewhat familiar protests of right-wing commentators. Morson also points out, "The parodist recognizes language as dialect or idiolect, as *characteristic* of some group or speaker. Taking speech as an index of its speaker or listener, he or she selects and draws attention to whatever most clearly uncovers their affectation or folly."[24] Thus, Colbert clearly calls attention to the central characteristic of right-wing hosts—their race and sex, and how that then plays out in the ludicrousness (or "folly") of their rhetoric of reverse racism.

In what might be seen as a double parody, Colbert not only embodies the parody of a right-wing talk show host, but also occasionally focuses his news segments directly on these real-life hosts and their shows. Twice in one month, for instance, Colbert turned his attention to Fox News host Glenn Beck and Beck's increasingly scary, apocalyptic ranting about the Obama administration and the upcoming downfall of American society.[25] Though *The Daily Show* is famed for turning its satirical eye to media programming, it must always do so in a third-person voice, critiquing from a "he-she-they" descriptive position. By Colbert embodying that which he critiques, though, he can adopt the first-person "I-me-we" vantage point that parody provides. On the March 4, 2009 show, for instance, Colbert congratulates Beck for the outstanding job he was doing, and then turns to a second camera to address Beck directly: "Dude, you are rocking it. I know some people say you're an unstable individual and to give you a public forum is grossly irresponsible, but remember—they crucified Jesus. Crank up the crazy and rip off the knob." Colbert doesn't stand outside the scenario here; parody positions him on the inside looking out. He identifies with the like-minded Beck, cheers him on, and admits their mutuality and commonality. As such, Colbert the parodist says that *others* may call Beck "unstable" and that *others* may think that Beck's having such a forum is "grossly irresponsible," but not him (for they are alike). The parody allows for an attack without it *being* an attack. Colbert's own messianic persona and craziness gets yoked with Beck's, all of which sets up the continuation of the parody that follows.

Colbert informs his audience that Beck has introduced a new segment called "The War Room," in which Beck assembles two guests to entertain possible doomsday scenarios that America may find itself in, supposedly as a result of the Obama administration's "socialist" policies. We then see clips from Beck's "War Room" segment, including his introducing scenarios such as: "The year is 2014. All the U.S. banks have been nationalized; unemployment is between 12 and 20%; the Dow [Jones Industrial Average] is trading around 2800; the commercial real estate market has collapsed." Beck and his guests then play out wild scenarios of "ghost malls" and decimated cities occupied by "ignorant" and "illiterate" people "whacked out on drugs such as hillbilly heroin" with "nothing to lose." Beck then says in his closing comments, "We're not predicting these things are going to happen," but then later, "You not only have a right to prepare yourselves mentally and physically, you also have a responsibility." Colbert then brings the two points together to add mockingly, "A responsibility to prepare yourself for things that are not going to happen."

In talk show host solidarity, Colbert attempts to support Beck's efforts by creating his own "Doom Bunker" and assembling a panel of guests to play out Colbert's fantastical scenarios—a retired Army colonel and MSNBC military analyst, and an editorial writer for *The Wall Street Journal* (who just happened to be one of Beck's experts on the "War Room" segment). Using the same lighting as Beck but introducing a fog machine for added doomsday effect, Colbert then plays out four scenarios with his expert guests, each more ridiculous than the next. Each scenario, however, also contains at least one nugget of real-life contemporary right-wing rhetoric (highlighted in italic here), therefore making the scenario not *completely* outlandish:

Scenario 1: The year is 2012, the Dow is below 1000, unemployment is 40%, and there is an armed insurrection in El Kañsas [where *everything west of the Mississippi is now Mexico*].

Scenario 2: The year is 2014, the Dow is below 250, the Koala Pox *epidemic* has wiped out all the livestock, soybeans are our currency, and there is a werewolf in Congress.

Scenario 3: The year is 2019, the *U.S. auto industry is destroyed*, and every car in the U.S. turns out to be Decepticons [from *Transformers* toys and media products].

Scenario 4: The year is 2012, Obama's policies work, leaving Iraq was the right call, the stimulus plan helps the Dow rebound to 12,000, and faith in government is restored.

Colbert is obviously engaging in exaggeration here, a technique that informs "readers that the text is a parody . . . [and indicates] what is objectionable in the original."[26] As Colbert's preface to the Doom Bunker suggested, what is objectionable is the creation of outlandish doomsday scenarios that have no basis in reality, all in an effort to whip the audience into a state of panic and hysteria while increasing ratings. The next parodic step then is simply to extend the scenarios to their logically ridiculous endpoints, especially since they have no basis in reality (Decepticons, werewolves, and so on). But Colbert's fourth scenario is the one in which the most pointed political critique is made, a scenario that does have some basis in reality and the one that should truly be debated. As Morson notes,

Parody aims to discredit an act of speech by redirecting attention from its text to a compromising context. That is, while the parodist's ironic quotation marks frame the linguistic form of the original utterance, they also direct attention to the occasion . . . of its uttering. The parodist thereby aims to reveal the otherwise covert aspects of that occasion, including the unstated motives and assumptions of both the speaker and the assumed and presumably sympathetic audience.[27]

What scenario four demonstrates, then, are the covert aspects of this occasion to rehearse doomsday fantasies, including the unstated motives and assumptions of the speaker (Beck) and his "presumably sympathetic audience" (those who can sit through such fantasies). That is, what this is all about, Colbert argues, is the desire by Beck (and others) to see President Obama's policies fail. For Beck's career and the profits at Fox News, that truly would be the worst outcome of all. For Beck's viewers, Obama's success would suggest that this contrived notion of "socialism" they are being fed had triumphed, something they have been ideologically prepared their whole life to believe is impossible. In short, for these heavily invested parties, scenario four truly is the most realistic (and horrible) of all.

The WØRD

One of Colbert's most popular segments is called The WØRD, an opportunity for Colbert to present an essay-rant in the style of Bill O'Reilly. Instead of using bullet points on the right side of the screen to summarize his claims (as does O'Reilly), here they are used more subversively. As Colbert explains, the "bullet points end up being their own character. Sometimes they're reinforcing my arguments, sometimes they're sort of countermanding my argument, but its sort of a textual addition of jokes or satire to the verbal essay I'm doing at the moment."[28]

On May 5, 2009, Colbert performed a WØRD segment based on the release of Bush justice department memos that supposedly gave legal "approval" of interrogation tactics, actions that many people believe constitute torture and therefore a violation of the Geneva Conventions on the treatment of prisoners. Colbert introduces the segment by proclaiming that "the president's recent decision to release the torture memos was a huge mistake." After a few jokes, Colbert quickly gets to the heart of the parodic inversion:

Colbert: Of course, the big question is how will we treat prisoners in the future? And not the guys at Gitmo. I'm talking about the prisoners of public opinion, like Dick Cheney, Condi Rice, John Yoo, Stephen Bradbury, and Judge Jay Bybee [the architects of the policy and the lawyers who crafted the administration's "legal" justifications for it]. These people can't go out in public without facing relentless interrogation [cutting to a clip of Rice defending the president's actions after being asked about it by students at Stanford University].

Condoleezza Rice: "By definition, if it was authorized by the president, it did not violate our obligations under the convention against torture."

Colbert: She, of course, was quoting the landmark position of Frost v. Nixon [cut to videotape of Richard Nixon's famous interviews with British journalist David Frost].

Richard Nixon: "When the president does it that means that it is *not* illegal."

Colbert: Which raises the philosophical question, if a president passed a law requiring him to break that law, could he do it? Or did I just blow your mind?

Nation, if we don't resolve these issues, these patriots' reputations could be damaged forever, which brings us tonight's WØRD: "Captain Kangaroo Court."

There's only one way to clear the names of these individuals [Bullet point: New names?]: A torture trial. Now a lot of my colleagues in punditry think torture trials could never be fair [cuts to clip of pundits on Fox News].

Brit Hume: I predict, Mara, based on what you're saying is that any prosecutions that would come out of this will be a total farce [Edit cut] . . . a series of Grand Inquisitions.

Colbert: And Grand Inquisitions should only be used for rooting out communists (displaying a picture of Senator Joseph McCarthy) and consensual hummers (displaying a picture of former White House intern Monica Lewinsky).

Colbert: But still employed Bill Kristol sees this crisis as an opportunity [cutting to a clip from the same Fox News discussion].

Bill Kristol: Now that the door is open, I say bring it on. Let's have a big national debate on this. Let's have Steve Bradbury confront his accusers who are one-tenth the lawyer he is.

Colbert: Yes! We must finally get the answer to the most troubling question of the entire torture scandal: Who's the best lawyer. [Bullet: And why is Bill Kristol still employed?]

As a parody of right-wing thinking, Colbert inverts the concern for the rights of prisoners not to endure torture to the rights of those who crafted the policies and legal justifications for violating prisoner rights. Colbert casts them as prisoners of public opinion with the potential for damaged reputations and the threat of a criminal trial. By titling the WØRD "Captain Kangaroo Court," Colbert is making two plays—*Captain Kangaroo*, the famous children's program, and kangaroo court, dictionary definitions of which include descriptions such as "self-appointed," "disregards existing principles of law or human rights," "violates established legal procedures," and "characterized by dishonesty."[29] Yet the "court of public opinion" that Colbert is mocking is the one crafted by the self-appointed conservative punditry that is intellectually dishonest in its disregard for law and human rights. Instead, the conservative pundits are concerned with Grand Inquisitions (except when they supported one against a presidential blowjob) and lawyering battles. That is, they are concerned with the processes associated with maintaining the reputations of "these patriots" (as Colbert calls them) more than the legitimacy of established legal procedures. Though some people might be tempted to suggest that Colbert's creative redaction of these video clips to highlight these pundits' hidden interests takes these discussions out of context, Morson suggests the parodist is doing just the opposite:

By pointing to the unexamined presuppositions and unstated interests that conditioned the original exchange, the parodist accomplishes what Fielding calls "the discovery of affectation"—the divergence between professed and unacknowledged intentions—or the discovery of naïveté, the difference between belief and disconfirming evidence. He or she does not, therefore, quote "out of context," as the targets often respond, but rather in "too much" context—in a context the targets would rather have overlooked.[30]

Colbert focuses on this broader context, demonstrating these pundits' loyalty to ideology over truth by their refusing to debate torture on the legality of the issue. Instead, the discussion they wish to have is centered on other issues.

What Colbert also highlights is that college students and children, not pundits, seem to be asking the right questions. The parody continues:

Colbert: And so, I'm all for a trial, but it's got to be the right kind of trial. [Bullet point: I heard military tribunals are fair.]

I heard some news this past weekend that gave me an idea. On Sunday, Condi Rice visited an elementary school where she was asked about enhanced interrogation policies by a fourth-grade boy. [Bullet point: Could have been [George Stephanopoulos]. Of course, Secretary Rice responded [cut to video of Rice].

Rice: President Bush was very clear that he wanted to do everything he could to protect the country, but he was also very clear that we would do nothing, nothing that was against the law.

Colbert: And, by the law of double negatives, nothing-nothing means everything. [Bullet point: "Two wrongs make no rights."]

This little kid gave me a great idea: our torture trials should be conducted by children. [Bullet point: PRECEDENT: Rubber v. Glue.]

You see, kids have no political agenda, and they ask great questions like, "Do dogs go to heaven?" and "When is it appropriate to abandon the values of our country in order to save our country?" [Bullet point: "When you move out of this house, young lady."]

Plus, kids will accept "Because I told you so" as a legitimate answer. So let's have Rice, Cheney, and everyone else explain the nuances of their rationale to a jury of children. For example, [as Colbert turns to face another camera, the visual frame changes to that of a children's picture frame, with a music-box version of "Rock-A-Bye Baby" playing in the background]:

Kids, Mr. Bunny was a bad, bad bunny. And he had information that President Raccoon needed. So the president got his lawyer squirrels to write a magic letter, which made everything he did perfectly legal. Then Mr. Bunny was strapped to an incline bench with a blankey over his nose and mouth and Willy the Whale squirted water into his face so that Mr. Bunny thought he was drowning. But remember, President Raccoon had a *magic* letter so it was not a violation of Common Article Three of the Geneva Conventions. Then, he married a princess. The End.

[Moving out of the children's picture frame visual, back to The WØRD.] So I say, let the children decide whether these men and women should finally be free from a life sentence of relentless accusations about their character and actions. [Bullet point: President Raccoon should have pardoned them.]

After all, remember, children are the future. And if we explain torture to them right, it will be a future where torture isn't wrong.

And that's The WØRD.[31]

Morson again provides an important theoretical perspective on parodic techniques and their function as tools for interrogating truth. "An especially common technique [in parody]," he notes, "is the introduction of an element—an incident in the plot, let us say, or an unexpected choice of words—that is incongruous with the tone or generic conventions of the original. In this case, readers are implicitly invited to discover the new point of view from which the incursion was made, and a new structure that would resolve the incongruity."[32] Colbert has cunningly introduced just such an element by adopting the metaphor of children (and the ways in which parents treat them and talk to them) as a way to see this issue more clearly.

The critique quickly highlights the paternalistic approach the administration took in its relationship to the American public (using any means necessary "to protect us"), and in the process, treating citizens like children. The "two wrongs" pun exemplifies the way we teach children in aphorisms (two wrongs don't make a right) and language rules (double negatives), but then plays with these to demonstrate that the two "wrongs" of torture + creative lawyering = no rights for detainees. Colbert points out how kids ask naïve questions, but sometimes those questions are also naïvely honest and direct ("When is it appropriate . . ."), questions that adults often don't want to answer or respond to with authoritarian pronouncements ("When you move out . . ."). Again, adult justifications of their actions to children ("Because I told you so") harkens back to Rice and Nixon's assertion that the president's *word* is equal to law, as well as the concept of kangaroo court justice—no need for law or procedure; the president's words and administrative "memos" suffice. The children's story of Mr. Bunny and President Raccoon reduces the issue to its most basic and easily understood components, including the "magic letter." The new point of view of the story is not whether what the president did was legal, but that by somehow crafting a letter, such documents magically become more important than conventions or law. The last lines of the segment ("children are the future") clearly get to the heart of the conservative defense of torture that is on trial here: torture itself is neither right nor wrong; there are only right and wrong ways of explaining it.

As a parody, Colbert doesn't have to use counterarguments and polemics to attack the reasoning of Rice (Bush) and the conservative punditry that would have us think of anything but torture itself. Instead, by aligning *with* them as fellow conservative, he destabilizes their rationales by crafting a narrative that recontextualizes their thinking. By using jokes with that narrative, he is able to challenge the rationalizations they offer. As anthropologist Mary Douglas argues,

> A joke is a play upon form. It brings into relation disparate elements in such a way that one accepted pattern is challenged by the appearance of another which in some way was hidden in the first. . . . The joke . . . affords the opportunity for realizing that an accepted pattern has no necessity. Its excitement lies in the suggestion that any particular ordering of experience may be arbitrary and subjective.[33]

Using ironic incongruity (interrogation of lawyers/interrogation of prisoners; children's court/kangaroo courts; magic letters/administrative memos; and so on), Colbert relates elements of this story in a way that demonstrates how the "ordering pattern" offered by the Bush administration and its defenders is arbitrary and subjective, not natural or necessary. In many ways, this calling into question of the ordering pattern of political elites is similar to the questioning of elite common sense by entertaining talk show guests seen in chapter 5. Here, though, that questioning occurs through humor and by the hands of someone who is seemingly one of their own.[34]

Guest Interviews

Turning finally to the interview segment of the show, Colbert hosts a parade of guests, many of who are authors of nonfiction books promoting their work, but also journalists, actors, politicians, and others. With each interview, Colbert remains in character, but tells his guests backstage that they should simply be themselves. What makes the interviews fascinating, though, is not how the guests handle being thrust into the parodic skit as noncomedians, but how Colbert must largely improvise his unscripted encounter from an ideological standpoint. What often results is a complicated shell game in which the audience is constantly trying to discern Colbert's real point from his put-on. The audience must track the voice he is imitating and the voice that is his own. Furthermore, as a parody of a right-winger, he must also make his character look bad, which is generally achieved by making the positions he takes (and the way he does so) look ridiculous. When sparring with liberals, then, he typically creates a conversation in which it is relatively easy for them to make him look foolish. Either through prompts or outright declarations of their opinions, liberals respond in ways that allow Colbert to position himself accordingly.

Such can be seen with Colbert's April 21, 2008, interview with Senator Bernie Sanders, a Democratic Socialist from Vermont. When Sanders suggests there is something wrong with giving tax breaks to billionaires when the United States has the highest rate of childhood poverty of any major country, Colbert jumps on him with the conservative counterargument of punitive sanctions:

> *Colbert*: So we should punish the billionaires for being successful. You're gonna increase their taxes.
>
> *Sanders*: Damn right I am!
>
> *Colbert*: That's a punishment.
>
> *Sanders*: No, no, no. [Sanders then goes on to explain the hundreds of billions of dollars in tax breaks billionaires received under the Bush administration.]
>
> *Sanders*: We now have a situation where the upper one-tenth of one percent earn more income than the bottom 50 percent.
>
> *Colbert*: Have you ever heard of the dribble-down theory [of economics]? We give everything to the super rich. They gobble everything up, and then some of it trickles down into their beard, and then the poor get to climb up their chest and suck the nutrition of what's leftover in the rich guy's beard. Is that too complicated for you?

Again, Colbert not only looks ridiculous, but serves up the opportunity for liberals to make their case while Colbert simultaneously ridicules a caricature of a real-life Republican-favored economic theory.

The encounters with conservatives are much trickier. Because there is typically nothing very humorous in two people agreeing, Colbert can't count on the clash of values or conflicting points of view for the comedy. What is worse, two conservatives agreeing also runs the risk of making the parody disappear altogether—that is, making the parodist *not* look so ridiculous after all. Therefore, Colbert must use conservative thinking to undermine himself *and* his guest in the process, as ultimately his conservative guest is often guilty of the same fallacious reasoning that Colbert the comedian is attacking. A June 2, 2008 interview with conservative television punditry's most prominent old-guard member, George Will, demonstrates this nicely. Colbert begins by drawing a distinction between Will's form of punditry and the brand of opinionated talk that Colbert parodies (while also paying Will a compliment):

> *Colbert*: You've been in television punditry a long time. Why don't you guys over there shout [on *This Week with George Stephanopoulos*, where Will appears every Sunday morning]?
>
> *Will*: We've outsourced that job.
>
> *Colbert*: I mean, it just makes more work for guys like me, I'll admit, but how can you tell, you know, between you, and Cokie, and George, and Sam, who's right if you don't measure it by who's loudest?

The conversation eventually turns to the book Will is promoting (*One Man's America*), with Colbert using the book's thesis as an opportunity to interrogate Will's interpretations of ideological distinctions in American democracy.

> *Colbert*: What do you think the difference is between conservatives and liberals?
>
> *Will*: It's the difference between truth and confusion, basically [as the audience laughs, Colbert leans over to shake Will's hand]. A slightly longer answer is that the competing values are freedom and equality at all times. Conservatives tend to favor freedom, and are willing to accept inequalities of outcome from a free market. Liberals tend to favor equality of outcomes, and are willing to sacrifice and circumscribe freedom in order to get it.
>
> *Colbert*: So conservatives are for freedom, and liberals are for equality of outcome, meaning the government should take action to level the playing field, and conservatives are more like, uh, let's just create a freedom terrarium, where we basically put a dome over this free area, keep outside influences from coming in, and then you put like a turtle and a fiddler crab in there and like, a fern to create some oxygen, you know, maybe a cricket or something like that, and then these things all just feed each other, and then it's okay if the turtle eats the fiddler crab. You know, to hell with the fiddler crab. What's he doing in there with the turtle in the first place?
>
> *Will*: Exactly. It was his choice [leaving a smiling Colbert speechless].

To challenge such conservative beliefs, Colbert uses an example to get at what "freedom" means in real life (not theory), yet does so through the analogy of a different ecosystem. Freedom, he demonstrates, is creating an environment in which people can do what they want, including eat each other (metaphorically) in the fight for survival. Colbert then plays up his own conservative thinking by noting that if the crab didn't want to be eaten, he shouldn't have been there in the first place. Yet Will confirms what Colbert meant as a critique of conservative thinking by falling back on the traditional conservative justification for such outcomes—the crab had free will; he chose to stay. Will willfully ignores, however, that the glass encasement (again a metaphor for real life) won't actually allow for such "freedom" of choice, thereby confirming the illogic of the position (and leaving Colbert speechless).

Colbert continues this same line of questioning:

> *Colbert*: So let me make this clear. . . . So some people call the liberals more idealistic—we should all be equal. Do conservatives say that if we just have freedom, everything will be OK, or do they say, if we just have freedom some people will get screwed but hey, that's life?
>
> *Will*: Pretty much that. What conservatives say is we will protect you against idealism. We will protect you against the liberal faith that they can make something straight from the crooked timber of humanity. We understand that the government's job is to deliver the mail, defend the shores, and get out of the way.

Rather than directly attack this simple formulation (and because Will has essentially confirmed that conservatives, by his definition, believe life is about survival of the fittest), Colbert continues by using an example that, in effect, demonstrates what is lacking or unfulfilled in conservatives' own "faith" in the "frees"—freedom, free will, free market:

> *Colbert*: So like universal health care, this is what I love. Democrats have this illusion, this delusion, that they can deliver universal health care, when conservatives know that the free market left to its own device will just provide it for everybody, you know . . . eventually. It hasn't happened yet, but it's coming. Just be patient. You know what I think about a free market? Free market to me is, like, uh, Christian Science, except switch out God and throw in money. Everything is going to be fine if you just have faith in it.

Will tries to make a joke off Colbert's Christian Science analogy, but it falls flat. Rather than interrogate the issue further, Colbert turns to questioning Will on his faith in God, to which Will says he is agnostic. Unintentionally so, then, this exchange demonstrates that Will's greatest faith (and perhaps even that of the brand of conservative thinking he espouses) is in Mammon, not God.

The interview concludes with a discussion of political labels, such as those applied to the two major political parties in America. Will quotes

Henry Adams's famous formulation that "politics is the systematic organization of hatreds," to which Colbert responds, "That sounds like freedom to me!" Will concurs simply with, "Exactly." Again, perhaps unintentionally, the exchange reveals the core of what this member of the conservative old guard considers central to political life—organized hatred or organized animosities. Throughout the exchange, Colbert's conservative parody has facilitated Will's enunciation of this dark view of political life—from the freedom to hurt to the freedom to hate, but freedom at all costs. Colbert has had to work harder in this situation to enunciate his critique than he does with liberals, but even in an exchange of two "like minds," the critique is nevertheless present.

THE POLITICS OF PARODY

So what makes this form of playful entertainment political? As we will see in the following chapter, some viewers and fans may choose not to see the political in what Colbert is doing, focusing instead on the play and enjoyment, while others enthusiastically embrace the political critique (as is easily witnessed in the raucous cheers for liberals such as Bernie Sanders). Obviously, given the topics covered in this chapter, Colbert's program is filled with politics and political critique, especially as the target of his parodic attacks is right-wing thinking and behaviors. Colbert argues that he is not a political person, and that he is no warrior in anybody's army. Yet by simply conducting such an attack, it is hard not to see his show as political.

Yet—to complicate matters further—some researchers have claimed that not all audiences may be in on the political joke against right-wingers. Rather, some conservative viewers may hear Colbert's conservative argument as making good political points or even affirmations of their own thinking (what social scientists call "confirmation bias" or the desire to see what a person wants to see).[35] Such research is preliminary and tentative, at best, or specious at worst. Nevertheless, the ambiguity introduced by the double-voiced utterances of parodic performance virtually guarantees enormous leeway in audience interpretations of the political critiques being made.

What this chapter has hopefully demonstrated is that the politics here is in the ways in which parody serves as a playful means for interrogating the faux realities constructed within the realm of political discourse—whether through conservative and right-wing pundits or presidential administrations. Parody becomes a means to ridicule and question those who would employ such discourses to lay claim to authority and truth through emotional appeals or logical obfuscation. Parody uncovers the compromising contexts through which such claims are made. For sure, parody's methods are playful, but the intent is faux play, a deep seriousness only masked by the fun. The fake, therefore, becomes a vehicle for getting at the real through means *other* than more of the same—that is, without imitating the red-faced screeds from the other ideological side (à la Keith Olbermann).

The previous chapter concluded that the postmodern claim that the fake may be more real than the real is perhaps not such an unsettling notion after all. Here it may be more productive to speak of "realistic" or "realism" than "real." As Jonathan Gray explains,

> Either the [two] terms are completely meaningless, since all media is unreal. Or we need to parse out what we really care about when we talk of "realism." And I'd pose that what we really care about is a show's ability to create room for us *to reflect upon the real*. To defamiliarize. To present difference. To make us think about the real and to analyze how it is and how it works.[36]

And it is in that regard that the faux play serves the political function of leading viewers to reflect upon, think about, and analyze that which would be so easy to consume uncritically, or perhaps just as dangerously, willfully ignore outright. Parody becomes the perfect means through which to defamiliarize that which has become so familiar on television's political landscape. As an anti-genre critique, Colbert asks the viewer to step back and examine what such programming is and how it does its political and ideological work. By parodying right-wing talkers, he *becomes* one of them, and in many ways, becomes *more* realistic than his targets because his exaggerations highlight their essence stripped bare.

As Gray also argues, when audiences claim that certain programming is *more real* or *more realistic* than other television depictions (say family life on *The Simpsons* is more real than on *Full House*), such claims reflect the essential point that "realism is about relativism—it's not about the individual text's relationship to the world. Rather, it's about the individual text's relationship to the entire media system, and in turn, the world" (or how the world is constituted through media).[37] The reality of that world may be constituted in familiar and comfortable ways (such as with the ontological security provided by news or talk shows), or in unfamiliar and uncomfortable ways (such as the cringe-inducing inversions produced through satire and parody). The reality or realism of *The Colbert Report* is a relative question, for it only exists as a reflection and comment upon the fakeness of the all too real programming it critiques and ridicules. In that regard, it truly is faux real and faux play.

IV

AUDIENCES/FANS/CITIZENS

10

Viewer Engagement Beyond Information Acquisition

Celebrity, Talk, and Play

> In the context of citizenship, the first issue is not what entertaining politics does to citizens, but what citizens do with entertaining politics, for citizenship is not something that pertains if it is not expressed in everyday talk and actions, both in the public and private domain. Citizenship . . . is something that one has to do, something that requires performance.
>
> —Liesbet van Zoonen[1]

Through most of the twentieth century, democratic theory's dominant normative conception of media has been the need for quality information so that citizens may fulfill their obligations as members of a polity.[2] As regards citizenship and communication, the result has been a valuation of information as a key ingredient for rational thinking over other forms of communication that do not serve those ends, such as entertainment and its supposedly dominant affective qualities. This "entertainment" versus "information" dichotomy continues to this day, and has been the primary heuristic employed in conceptualizing just what the genre of political entertainment television does or doesn't offer citizens. But as is somewhat obvious, the duality structures entertainment in contradistinction to information—therefore *a priori* frivolous—and audiences for entertainment as not attending to their citizenship duties. The binary is also an extraordinarily limited conception of the relationship that exists between audiences and political communication, undervaluing what a variety of political narratives can provide, as well as what audiences need from such narratives, extract from them, and do with them.

This chapter complicates such simplistic notions by examining audience engagement with the entertaining political talk on *Politically Incorrect with*

Bill Maher and the faux pundit talk on *The Colbert Report*, programs from the first and second phases of new political television, respectively. The analysis focuses on the ways in which these two types of political entertainment programs provide entry points to political engagement and allow for the performance of citizenship. The analysis of *Politically Incorrect* examines the articulation between the private and public spheres as enabled by the program, encouraging a performance of talk and discursive engagement when politics becomes linked with the pleasures of popular culture. Furthermore, the analysis reveals a crisis of representation that arises from the rejection of expert political talk and embrace of celebrity as a realm with meaningful affective attractions. The analysis of *The Colbert Report* demonstrates a positive relationship between fandom and citizenship, including the commonality of performance, community, and emotional investment to both. The program's parodic engagement with politics further invites the audience to play with politics, thereby offering not only pleasure and inclusion, but a degree of interpretive agency in constructing political meaning and understanding through such participation. But first, we turn our attention to several theoretical models and areas of research that might prove helpful in moving beyond the binaries that limit our understanding of this form of programming, as well as our understanding of the audiences that use it as tools for civic engagement.

BEYOND THE AUDIENCE-CITIZEN DIALECTIC

As noted, the "entertainment versus information" heuristic clouds our understanding of audiences for new political television. As seen in chapter 8, for instance, if young people are getting their "news" (read: information) from late-night comedy shows (read: entertainment), then we are led to believe that democracy is endangered. The purpose of the binary, though, has less to do with properly labeling this content than in highlighting and critiquing the audiences who consume it. As noted earlier, such strict segregation of entertainment and political content in television was partly the product of broadcast programmers' usage of news as a means for fulfilling licensure obligations. But the dichotomy also arose from the normative ideals of social critics and policy makers who saw much of television as a "vast wasteland," a medium that did a better job of producing consumers in a capitalist society than in shaping citizens in a democracy.[3] Programming news/public affairs as something separate from entertainment thus supposedly produced an antidote. Yet the heuristic is also related to some early scholarly models for explaining not just content, but also audience behavior outside of strict "effects" studies, in what is known as "uses and gratifications" research.[4] Here "information" has important instrumental use value in a democracy, while "entertainment" excels in addressing audience's needs for and pleasures in gratification.

Viewed differently, the entertainment-information dichotomy is subsumed under the broader conception and segregation of viewers into the categories of "audiences" (entertainment) *versus* "publics" or "citizens" (information). Both terms are loaded with assumptions of value and legitimacy, with audiences often on the losing end of the binary.[5] As Sonia Livingstone has pointed out, the audience versus public formulation is actually built upon an array of competing value assumptions of viewer behaviors, practices, and status, including consumers versus citizens, private versus public, affective versus rational, passive versus active, withdrawn versus participatory, tastes versus ideals, apathy versus attention, ignorance versus informed, indiscriminate versus discerning, and so on.[6] Although cultural studies research has complicated these simplistic binaries by exploring the behaviors of "active audiences" over the last thirty years, what are largely normative *assumptions* of audiences (based on content value) are still resident in much writing that occurs outside the borders of cultural studies.

Though some scholars speak of a "blurring of boundaries" between entertainment and information—within news as well as popular entertainment programming—explaining the changes in television as a move toward hybridization doesn't solve the primary dilemma that still exists by not rejecting the terms outright. That is to say, by focusing primarily on the content itself, "hybridization" and "blurred boundaries" doesn't address the complexity of the *audience's* relationship to media content. "Entertainment" and "information" are overly broad terms that have little explanatory power in understanding the specific narrative appeals or the complex relationships that audiences maintain with such programming. Furthermore, as both audiences *and* citizens, these simplistic binaries do little to further our understanding of viewers' cognitive, affective, and behavioral relationship to this programming.

In seeking an alternative, let us look at one model that accounts for the variety of narratives resident in television news reporting—a model that I suggest might prove useful in reconceptualizing the audience's relationship to political programming. The Entertainment-Information binary is comparable to the "expressive" (affective-aesthetic) and "analytic" (propositional-argumentative) dimensions of television news that Simon Cottle and Mugdha Rai have labeled in their study of television news in six countries. Yet, as they contend, "When seeking to understand how television journalism serves to summon publics in respect of events and issues, and does so in culturally expressive and affective ways as well as through informational and propositional means, less dichotomized thinking is clearly called for."[7] Instead, Cottle and Rai propose a model comprised of numerous "communicative frames" that, taken together, form a broader "communicative architecture" of television news. Their data reveal that news stories employ narrative frames that can be categorized in the following ways: Information, Propositional/Argumentative, Deliberation/Dialogue, Conflictual, Understanding, Aesthetic/Expressive, Display, and Consensual.[8] As the title of their article suggests, they are interested in how television news narratives function "between display and deliberation," or what occurs beyond the traditional dichotomy of informational/dialogic narratives and their aesthetic/affective counterparts.

As this book has explored, the programming that constitutes new political television cannot be limited to an entertainment/aesthetic/affective category alone. But neither should we be content in simply saying that these shows are high in information/deliberative content as well. Indeed, the analysis so far has demonstrated how programs such as *The Daily Show*, *The Colbert Report*, and *Real Time/Politically Incorrect* also employ many of these narrative frames. The various presentational/narrative styles of "fake" television news offered by *The Daily Show*, for instance, can provide new information, engage in reportage about a campaign, offer deliberative exchanges with guests, produce exposés using redacted videos, craft aesthetic/expressive displays in mash-up videos, and work to achieve consensus through communal laughter at satirical rebukes. Likewise, a program such as *The Colbert Report* may offer narratives that are simultaneously playful *and* conflictual, offering opportunities for pleasure and anger. In short, new political television doesn't offer just entertainment *and* information (much less entertainment *or* information), but an array of appealing narratives that can engage citizens beyond the limits inherent in the uses and gratifications model. Though the Cottle and Rai model is focused on content, it should, by extension, also direct our attention to how these different narratives offer distinctive and differing appeals to the audience's identity as citizens (or conception of their own citizenship)—or, as Cottle and Rai put it, how these narratives "serve to summon publics."

Citizenship is more than membership in a society, or the rights and obligations associated with such membership. It is also a component of our identity, and like other aspects of personal and communal identities, is a cultural phenomenon that is conceived, negotiated, assembled, fought over, and so forth, through our everyday interactions within that society.[9] The integrated public *and* private spheres resident in such contemporary notions of citizenship is enhanced by the changing media environment that offers a "set of resources through which everyday meanings and practices are constituted" which in turn "shape identity and difference, participation and culture."[10] The segregation of citizenship from consumption, public from private, rationality from emotion, and so on, is no longer tenable. As John Hartley rightly notes, television has moved to center stage in society as the primary place for the constitution of personal identity, including identification as a citizen. In turn, citizenship is increasingly a "do-it-yourself" enterprise of "semiotic self-determination." Citizenship, he argues, is "no longer simply a matter of social contract between state and subject, no longer even a matter of acculturation to the heritage of a given community; DIY citizenship is a choice people make for themselves."[11] Therefore, the constant and habitual scanning of mediated political culture for persons, issues, values, styles, rhetoric, and even commodities (such as Ann Coulter books, for instance) is the means through which civic identity is increasingly established, constituted, and maintained. Thus, the argument here is that through engagement with the world of politics, television viewers approach that world with needs, desires, interests, feelings, and cognitive expectations *as citizens*, all of which television can and does work to fulfill through its various political narratives. Political identities (at the micro level) and political culture (at the macro level) are the product of interactions with the array of mediated political narratives that citizens encounter, including the cognitive and emotional experiences that result.

Though the cognitive demands of a rational and informed decision-making public have dominated political science scholarship for decades, the more nascent field of political psychology has offered alternatives for understanding the affective dimensions of citizenship.[12] Emotions, these scholars argue, don't exist outside of or in opposition to the reasoning process, but are "required to invoke reason and to enable reason's conclusions to be enacted."[13] Emotions and feelings such as anxiety, enthusiasm, loathing, and revulsion, in particular, have been examined for the role they play in structuring political behavior and sense making. Moving such research to a broader communicative and cultural level, however, might demonstrate how television forums such as Fox News (for the political right) or *The Daily Show/The Colbert Report* (for the political left) provide programming that addresses numerous other emotional needs, feelings and desires in citizen-viewers, including pride, anger, retribution, superiority, joy, celebration, playfulness, belonging, and others that might not be subsumed under existing analytic variables.[14] So here as well, we should move beyond the highly rational model of information acquisition to fulfill cognitive needs to one in which we are also aware of how political programming engages citizens' emotional needs as well.

In sum, this discussion seeks to move beyond the easy binaries that construe entertainment and information as opposites, as well as audiences and publics as normatively different. We want to highlight instead how audience engagement with popular media is intimately involved in processes of citizenship, including how popular media provides emotional and cognitive resources for civic identity. We see in the variety of narratives outlined by Cottle and Rai numerous position points through which audiences may employ the rational and emotional, consume the deliberative and aesthetic, and embrace the individualistic and communal. In short, audiences can engage political narratives in quite complex ways, and have multiple reasons for doing so.

AUDIENCE ENGAGEMENT
WITH ENTERTAINING POLITICAL TALK

Chapter 2 advanced the argument that much of a citizen's daily interactions with the political world is, for better or worse, textual in nature—that is, through engagement with political content in media. As such, it was asked how we might rethink the conception of "civic engagement," given what existing qualitative and cultural studies of citizen interactions with television tell us about the current state of mediated citizenship. The studies reviewed there showed how the political world crafted by journalists and pundits seems distant from citizens' daily lives. Conversely, popular television brought politics to life, allowing people to engage with the characters and narratives they found there, even providing characters (both fictional and nonfictional) that citizens employ when making sense of politics. Furthermore, citizens believe that the central political practice available to them is discursive, while the studies also demonstrated that political views are often discovered and developed through discursive engagements. Citizens routinely examine television content for its plausibility and authenticity, and feel an obligation to respond when television doesn't correspond to their beliefs, values, and realities. Finally, they don't see the artificial boundaries between politics and popular culture that journalists and others erect, and instead, are accustomed to "brushing up against" politics in an array of media as they lead their daily lives.

Do these finding hold true for viewers of new political television? Almost without exception, the answer is yes. What follows are the results of an investigation of audiences for the program *Politically Incorrect with Bill Maher.* Audiences were studied from three vantage points—viewer mail to the program, personal interviews, and through an on-line discussion forum (see the appendix for the methodological details). These avenues of inquiry allowed for access to viewers' unprompted remarks (mail), prompted remarks (interviews), and both prompted/unprompted remarks in the on-line forum (although prompted only by other discussants' comments and questions). Though many of the respondents were fans of the show, each of the three forums included people who were not. In each instance, these viewers had chosen to engage the program in some way—by writing a letter to the program, auditioning to be a participant on the show, being a studio audience member, or talking on-line with other viewers about the show. It would be customary here to say that because these viewers are somewhat "self-selected," these findings are therefore not necessarily that of the "typical" viewer. Yet there really is no such thing as a "typical viewer," one who is "representative" of the viewing population (even networks and advertisers don't construct this category). The interest here is in what this show does for citizens who intentionally engage it (even if through loathing and contempt), not for those who would rather watch David Letterman instead.

As per the findings in chapter 2, viewers live their lives from the personal to the political/public, where the values, language, and issues that structure and consume everyday life are the ones that matter in the political realm as well. What is often the case, however, is that traditional public affairs programming (especially pundit talk shows) constructs politics as a world apart, one with little relation to what common people think, how they talk, or what they value. The world of Washington is inauthentic, and therefore is a world many citizens don't wish to inhabit. About half of the interviewees I spoke with said they watched the traditional pundit talk shows on television at least some of the time. Typically they felt ambivalence about them (though tending to emphasize the role the shows play in imparting information) but not expressing any fondness for them. The other half, however, communicated strong disdain for shows such as *Crossfire, Meet the Press,* and *The McLaughlin Group* (all named specifically). Some viewers stated their disconnect with insider talk very bluntly, as one woman did when she remarked, "The thing that Washington forgets is that things that are serious inside the Beltway, the rest of the country doesn't give a rat's ass about." Other viewers found pundit talk too scripted. "I think the people that go on the news shows," one woman noted, "so much of what they say is packaged, and so much of it is formatted that there is no spontaneity, there's no reality, and they're all worried about their careers."

Other viewers framed their enjoyment of *Politically Incorrect (PI)* by overtly or implicitly contrasting it with the distant world that pundit shows create, a world that seems foreign to their real life concerns. Hence, the interviewees asserted that both the issues and the type of language used on *PI* were more accessible and "real" for average citizens. One viewer argued that *PI* "deals with real issues that are on people's minds, the questions that are out there," while another contended that the show "touches on more, I guess you'd say, the topics that your 'regular' people have more concerns about." Other respondents focused on the accessibility of *PI* versus the distance they felt from insider political talk. For instance, "The issues [on *PI*] are simple as they are presented without a lot of the doublespeak. The variety of the panel is guaranteed to draw in a diverse market versus watching the shows where the stiff political pundits are there. [That] turns me off a lot of times." Another viewer argued that *PI* is "more like real life discourse. Like, you know, five people in a bar sitting around talking about something," while another compared the talk to "the same tenor of conversation around the water cooler." One person was perhaps more blunt when he argued that the guests on *PI* were "not afraid to say the dumb things that everybody's already thinking." Some viewers also found the program more indeterminate than the pundit shows. One female viewer asserted, "The whole world isn't black and white, and that is one thing I like about [*PI*]. It's the biggest gray area on television, and nobody's preaching to you how you should feel."

Viewer mail demonstrated similar feelings of disconnect from traditional political talk programming while celebrating a more "real" and honest conversation in *PI*. The following quote is instructive in the ways the writer juxtaposes *PI* and Maher with other programming on television that she finds timid, fake, and manipulative, and as a result, both deceitful and monotonous:

> What I find most riveting about your show is your frankness about your own opinions concerning issues that no one else on television attempts to broach. It seems to me that you have no hidden agenda in voicing your views, and I guess that's why I find your show . . . non-tiresome. You come across as a real person, someone I might work with or socialize with, an unusual thing when it comes to the media of television. Your integrity is refreshing and should be an example to all other types of shows.

Here too the writer is living life from the personal to the political, using her judgment of persons she works and socializes with as the measure of trust in people she finds discussing politics on television. Authenticity is also of central importance in her evaluations, her judgments based upon what reflects reality here as she knows it.

Many viewers said that the show was a distinctive and compelling addition to television discourse because it offered a forum for conversation, for diverse and competing viewpoints and opinions. "Thanks to you and your guests' discussion of important issues from diverse political views," wrote one woman from Oregon. The forum itself was key for many letter writers. "Your show . . . does present a forum like virtually no other," notes one viewer, while several others said "thanks for giving the little people something *real* to watch," and thanks for "giving the viewing public the most refreshing and thoroughly enjoyable program to ever hit the air waves." For them, television was finally offering something that was politically meaningful because of the type of forum it was creating. As one viewer noted, "I had damned-near stopped watching television at all . . . but the resulting lonely cynicism was getting to be a bit much."

A second point that ran through all three data points and aligned with the findings in chapter 2 were the ways in which the program encouraged a response. Viewer mail demonstrated a burning desire by citizens, transformed from simply being viewers, to engage in political conversation with Maher. That is, it didn't matter if viewers agreed or vehemently disagreed with him or the comments by guests on the show—either way, they wanted to talk politics, sometimes at great length and sometimes with much vituperation. In fact, a vast majority of the mail I reviewed contained a politically discursive focus. Here are a few examples:

> "Thank you for expressing some of my views. . . . We concur on women, population explosion, personal responsibility, and reprehensible Republicans."

> "Here are a few comments on subjects discussed on PI in recent days. The subjects are the free classical music CD's and the protesters at abortion clinics."

> "I am very excited finally to have the opportunity to contribute something to the lively discussions which have kept me fascinated and entertained these past few years."

Some letter writers pointed to the fact that the show creates political conversation in their homes—between husband and wife, or parent and child. One writer noted, "I encourage my 14-year-old daughter to watch [the show] . . . so that she can learn debating skills and develop her own ideas about issues. We talk about the various topics, and the guests responses, during commercials and I think she's learning a great deal." Another letter signed by husband and wife notes, "Although I don't always agree with you, the topics never fail to bring about great conversation around the house. I believe that conversation (real talk, mind you) is what is missing in many homes. . . . Your show won't save the world, but it has expanded at least a couple of minds."

Many interviewees, as with letter writers, appreciated the show for the significant role that argumentation plays within the program, and how that then structures their relationship to the show. Numerous viewers I talked to said they generally enjoy watching people argue and hearing other people's opinions. One interviewee maintained that the show "encourages" a particularly agonistic environment. Furthermore, she noted, "People will say things that may sound completely off the wall and bizarre, but when they stand up and fight for it, that's what makes it worthwhile and one of the things you really enjoy seeing on the show: someone who's willing to take a stand and work it and fight it." This same viewer also maintains that the show won't allow the viewer to remain neutral when watching it, but instead it "kind of forces people to take a side, one way or the other."

This description accurately portrays the program's effect on some viewers due to the fact that they tend to become involved in joining the conversation in one way or another. That is, several people reported that the program "spark[ed] lively debates" between themselves and their spouses, including providing rhetorical ammunition in long-running arguments. As one woman revealed, "See, my husband is a real conservative and I'm fairly liberal. We both watch it and it's like, 'Hey, did ya hear that? Did ya hear that? Hey, I told you so!'" Others noted how the program drew them into the debate. "I project myself on[to the program] hoping that somebody would ask the question that I would want to ask," noted one male respondent. Another person stated, "I just love the issues, even if somebody is completely off the wall, because I sit there and think, 'What would I say or what would I think about that issue?'" And leading the viewer to consider the issues the program presented was a common attraction for many of my interviewees. One viewer put it succinctly when she said, "Overall, it does stir the mind and causes you to pause and think about what the issues are."[15] Finally, one woman simply said, "Anything that will stimulate thought is good. Anytime you can exchange ideas is great."

The point here that audiences understand yet critics of these types of shows seemingly don't is that what is discursively produced on television is not a product to be chosen (e.g., the most intelligent thought or rationally correct idea). Instead, what they desire is simply the *process* of being able to speak and hear others like themselves speak, of bringing about public thinking in a language they understand and that is heartfelt and sincere, despite the possibility that such thinking might be misguided. The audience implicitly asserts that it is within *them* that truth and meaning will be made, not selected from choices developed by "experts." The facilitation of thinking public thoughts is the benefit of televised political discourse for these viewers. The irony here is that critics of this form of television are the ones advocating a citizen-consumer model, whereas the viewers who attend to the programming are interested in a more thoughtful and deliberative process for understanding politics.

With the on-line discussion forum (alt.tv.pol-incorrect, or ATPI), here too an entertainment television program became the jumping-off point from which quite extensive and substantive discussions of politics regularly occurred. Like the letter writers and interview subjects, participants in ATPI really wanted to talk about political issues across a range of topics: welfare, gun control, immigration, environmental regulations, taxation, animal rights, free speech, education, race, violence, health care, law enforcement, and so on. The discussants bring with them their own personal characteristics and experiences from different parts of the nation (and Canada). For instance, one reader complained that Maher unfairly characterizes her age-group (Gen Y) as unwilling to work in grunt or entry-level jobs. A discussion then ensued in which people offered their perspectives based on personal experiences with twenty-somethings in the workplace (March 26, 2002). Similarly, a show that included Arsenio Hall discussing his family's time on public aid blossomed into a conversation about food stamp cards, with posters contributing information about the success or failure of these electronic cards in their home states of Texas, Illinois, and Minnesota (February 21, 1998).

Furthermore, comments on one topic might spark discussion across an array of subjects. For instance, when Maher was belligerent toward guest David Duke, a Duke supporter appeared with numerous links to websites supporting Duke's arguments. Although the actual program may not have been the best forum for the wide exchange of ideas in certain instances, ATPI allowed viewers to hold a much more extensive, dispassionate, and reasoned argument than that hosted on the program. In a different vein, a comment by Maher that society should "stop punishing the smokers" (February 17, 1998) started a conversation where posters, in a single thread, discussed taxation policies, Freon, smog, the framers of the constitution, Thomas Paine, various books to read, libertarianism, and other issues. One might wonder, however, whether these viewers could go to another forum to talk politics—say, for instance, alt.talk.politics. What is significant, however, is that they don't (or if they do, they still come to ATPI). They link their pleasure in watching a television program that features wide-ranging discussions of politics to then activate their interests in participating in their own wide-ranging discussions of politics. They desire to share information (news articles, hyperlinks, experiences) and engage in knowledge formation. As one user wrote to the group, "Thanks [for the postings], I often lol [laugh out loud] and the level of discussion has stopped me in my tracks more than once." And as with the other two sets of *PI* audiences discussed above, the participants here desire to assert their own views, however profound or trivial. In short, the show activates a certain set of desires for political engagement that *PI* often initiates and that ATPI hosts. Television may seemingly be a one-way communication technology, but the Internet certainly is not.

As with David Thelen's findings of how viewers responded to the Iran-Contra hearings (as reviewed in chapter 2), viewers here also sought some form of "representation" within the programming.[16] That is to say, when it came to political talk programming, it was very important that viewers be able to identify with speakers or issues, or perhaps even see themselves in the proceedings in some way. For instance, according to the show's producers, one of the most highly requested changes to the show's format was the desire to see an average citizen appear alongside the other guests (which came to be known as the "Citizen Panelist" when the show finally did institute this feature for a brief period). While they enjoyed watching celebrities discuss politics, the show also seemingly needed "someone from the 'real world,'" as one letter writer put it, someone who "might be able to give more insight into a particular problem or situation." Many of these writers, as one might imagine, also volunteered themselves for that role.[17] Again, why watch and listen when you really desire to contribute, or perhaps even become a "celebrity" yourself?

A second set of suggestions popular with letter writers was requests for specific guests to appear on the show. One writer from Canada assembled a list of thirty-six different panels she would like to see on the show, complete with names linked to particular subject matters. To discuss the issue of "The Monarchy, the Paparazzi, and the 'Tabloidization' of America (re: Diana's death)," she proposes "Arianna Huffington, Karen Finley, Jerry Springer, and Ann? (political Irish singer with Chumbawamba)." Viewer desire in helping produce this television show is not necessarily based on what specific guests have to offer intellectually to a subject as much as on the viewer's identification with and pleasure in seeing these particular celebrities or public persons engage the issues of the day.

What these unsolicited contributions and recommendations amount to is the recognition by viewers that television can and should represent them in some way—either their bodily representation through the surrogate citizen panelist (or guests known for a particular point of view), vocally through the issues they wish to have aired publicly, or mentally through the "dream team" they would like assembled for discursive battle. For them, television is a participatory realm. To see one's self, one's desires, and one's concerns shared and experienced publicly is what makes popular culture such a powerful attachment in modern society. For a program to articulate these ritualistic ways of attending to television and popular culture with the political realm offers a whole new avenue for viewer pleasure. Viewer activity around *PI*, then, demonstrates an articulation between lifestyle pleasures and concern for civic life.

Pushing this point further in my interviews with viewers, I was interested in how they viewed the celebrity guests. The show's inclusion of celebrities discussing politics was one of the central criticisms of the show.[18] To my surprise, the interviewees universally embraced the role of celebrities. These viewers were honest about the role that fascination with celebrity plays in many people's lives. They also recognized the fact that celebrities (including celebrity politicians) are the primary figures in public life that people care about. As one man simply put it, "Well, people listen to celebrities." There was also, of course, the enjoyment many people expressed in seeing how celebrities they "knew" from other pop culture venues felt about political issues. Somewhat recognizing his own confusion between fiction and reality, one viewer noted, "So many times you see somebody play a character and you think that's how [the actor] think[s], and then you get to see what the actual person thinks." Other viewers expressed their interest in witnessing whether the celebrity was actually smarter or dumber than they had previously imagined—"that person's such a bimbo, that person's such a dork, or very intelligent," one person noted. But again, these viewers were very forthcoming in stating the place that celebrities occupy in their lives. "I like to see what people that I watch and care about, even in a small regard, what they have to say about things," one woman intoned.

When these viewers were asked if we should be concerned that these celebrities may not be very informed on the issues they were discussing, numerous people responded with remarks such as, "Most people are not particularly informed; it's representative," and, "I think a lot of us are kind of ignorant in the political arena. They're no worse than anybody else." Another respondent stated the point more eloquently when he said,

> To a certain extent, *Politically Incorrect* is more where you see political discourse on a raw level, whereas if you watch, like, *Meet the Press*, it's been refined. But if you take the person who is . . . a singer or an actor, they're not reading position papers. They're essentially forming their opinions not much differently than a person sitting at home watching the program. I'm not certain one is more valid than the other.

As with this person, the populist leanings are also evident when a woman dismissed the notion of expertise entirely in favor of other, more important criteria: "It's great to have someone that is not a professional politician to speak from their heart or to speak on the issues, whether they are misguided or not."

This identification with celebrity as a "representative" figure for the viewing audience should come as no surprise, according to David Marshall. He contends that "the celebrity is both a proxy for someone else and an actor in the public sphere. . . . From this proxy, the celebrity's agency is the humanization of institutions, the simplification of complex meaning structures, and principal site of a public voice of power and influence."[19] As traditional institutions (e.g., political parties and the news media) are increasingly seen as less legitimate representatives of public concerns, the celebrity as representative sign has stepped in to fill the public void. The "simplistic" political analyses that celebrities might offer that so frustrates critics yet pleases these viewers is the natural outcome of the celebrity's role as public proxy. Celebrity lack of knowledge, therefore, represents the same lack possessed by the viewing public, and hence suggests that this talk is just as valid as pundit talk.

Marshall argues further that "celebrity is the site of intense work on the meaning of both individuality and collective identity in contemporary culture. It is the capacity of these public figures to embody the collective in the individual, which identifies their cultural signs as powerful."[20] Because celebrities do not maintain the partisan or ideological baggage that other political representatives do, their ability to be new and enticing voices in the realm of politics as unexpected representatives of multiple collectivities is enhanced. As the viewing public attempts to make sense of political life, a television program that offers such representative public personalities with whom audiences maintain an affective relationship (from other cultural sources) is embraced for the feelings it ignites, more so than any reasoned logic these celebrities might offer. As Marshall argues, "What is privileged in the construction of public personalities is the realm of affect. Affect moves the political debate from the realm of reason to the realm of feeling and sentiment."[21] In short, then, audiences have embraced a program that intensifies broader processes that are at work within public life as citizen-viewers maintain intense commitments to popular culture while politics is often kept at arm's length.

Celebrity political talk emanates from the same sources as the audience, and it is stated in the same raw and unrefined ways as one would find in a bar or at work, as a result enhancing its validity. Therefore, the audience appreciates the means and manner in which the program and its celebrity guests have articulated the public with the private. Marshall argues that because the celebrity "text" retains such affective power, it can move easily between the public and private spheres. He notes,

> Fundamentally, celebrities represent the disintegration of the distinction between the private and the public. This disintegration, as represented by celebrities, has taken on a particular form. The private sphere is constructed to be revelatory, the ultimate site of truth and meaning for any representation in the public sphere.[22]

As with the discussion that occurred on *PI* about President Clinton (examined in chapter 5), the private sphere becomes the site for establishing truth and meaning as both celebrity discussants and the viewing audience attempt to make the public sphere more closely resemble the private.[23] Critics have increasingly argued that it is television or politicians that are responsible for this blending or merging of the public and private as politics and pop culture, celebrity and politician are supposedly becoming one and the same. The data offered here suggest that perhaps it is a public that is disillusioned or disaffected from previous models of political representation and discourse. The public itself is therefore driving this change as a means of achieving something more politically real and relevant to their lives.

Finally, when examining audience opinions about the blending of entertainment and information, viewers suggested it wasn't a big deal. Viewer mail displayed expressions of pleasure and enjoyment with the program based on its mix of entertainment and intelligent conversation. Contrary to the belief by critics that entertainment and information belong in separate realms, many viewers wrote to express just the opposite: their sheer joy at finding both intelligent *and* entertaining programming. "There's just nothing like *Politically Incorrect* for its intelligent, fascinating, and entertaining combination of news, humour, and opinion," wrote one viewer, while another contends that the show "offers humor, thought and criticism and absolute pure enjoyment with the many 'crazy' current events of our time." One viewer was even more specific in locating why she likes the program:

"Your show makes me think and laugh and sometimes get a little riled up and I really enjoy it."

In the on-line discussion forum, there was little in the way of direct discussion of the blending of information and entertainment. Rather, a demonstration of how such boundaries are truly artificial was in the way that posters themselves freely bounced back and forth between cultural and political talk. As a political talk show, the program does not stand apart from the wider array of popular culture or the meanings resident there for television viewers. Indeed, the program's format—its inclusion of all sorts of public persons, including mass media stars, authors, musicians, politicians, athletes, and so on—is designed to link all of these popular people and their opinions to the issues of the day. Although the program was criticized by political elites and cultural arbiters because it constructed this supposedly unholy union between sacrosanct politics and profane popular culture, such a linkage already exists in the minds of viewers. The same viewers who hold smart, rational, informed, and thoughtful discussions of political issues in ATPI are the same viewers who carry in their heads a whole array of politically irrelevant but culturally attuned information. A discussion thread on presidential candidates, for instance, stood next to another on where one can download full episodes of Seinfeld on the Internet. Or better yet, a discussion of presidential candidates would include references to music and parental advisory lyrics that candidates' wives have inserted into popular culture (February 23, 2000). As seen in the research by Michael Delli Carpini and Bruce Williams reviewed in chapter 2, governors and senators stand in the viewer's mind next to public personalities such as inane comedians (Carrot Top), religious and secular pundits (Jerry Falwell and Pat Buchanan), and characters found on fantasy television shows (*Star Trek*), or obnoxious advertisements (Miss Cleo).[24] These are all essentially players on the same public stage.

The show also serves as a linking mechanism between politics and other viewer interests, and between various domestic media practices and activities in which viewers regularly participate. Those who post messages argue political issues, but also discuss hair style or weight gain of panelists, second-guess the show's producers, applaud the wit of guests, address Maher directly, debate the validity of arguments, introduce evidence from other media sources as rebuttal, attack each other personally, speculate on panelists' sex lives, or denounce them as moronic, and so on. Viewers tend to engage the program as both politics *and* television. That is, they read *PI* on its own terms—part real, part constructed, part important, part frivolous, part serious, part playful, part engaged, part distant, part ironic, part outraged, part sanctimonious, and part satisfied.

Furthermore, on-line viewer activity parallels the assumptions of new political television: that politics is not something that is attended to separately, cordoned off from the rest of one's identity, activities, or existence in the world. Politics is one of many facets of a person's life, and it too includes drama and humor, seriousness and entertainment, importance and triviality. Both *PI* and the on-line audience activity surrounding the show reflect that understanding. In short, the evidence here suggests that new political television is important as a spark for drawing viewers toward greater discursive participation in politics—one that includes their ritualized habits and lives as cultural beings *and* citizens.

Looking across these data points, we see that audiences for *Politically Incorrect* are an engaged and discerning viewing public who are intensely focused on the authenticity and plausibility of what constitutes political talk on television. Traditional pundit talk shows are seen as scripted, agenda-driven, or distant from life's realities, but *PI* offered something more authentic and real. Those conclusions were based, in particular, on the show providing something that viewers could identify with or feel some connection to. Viewers needed to feel represented in some way, even if by celebrities with whom they maintained some affective relationship (as "constructed" or "fake" as celebrities may or may not be). Through such celebrity representatives, viewers found something that activated and connected with their own political and cultural interests. *PI*, then, spoke to viewers on their own terms (even if we qualify that by noting the terms to be those of entertainment culture and consumerism), not terms dictated by Washington insiders. Furthermore, the program not only demonstrated discursive politics on the screen, but helped produce it among viewers themselves in the viewing culture. In each instance (viewer mail, interviews, and on-line observation), audiences reported or displayed how they were mobilized for discursive engagement with others by involvement with the program. And perhaps most importantly, audiences announced how political truth would be established—not from the opinions of political experts appearing on television, but through their own discursive and cognitive engagements. Finally, the program moved away from the seemingly monotonic politics of pundit talk television, instead producing many points of entry and sustained interest for viewers desirous of a more expansive political relationship—news, humor, opinion, and criticisms that ignited thinking, laughter, anger, joy, and numerous other cognitive and emotional needs of viewers.

Returning to the discussions that began this chapter, this audience data provides evidence to support the theoretical points made by Livingstone, Hartley, and Cottle and Rai. As per Livingstone's observation of the normative segregation and positioning of audiences *versus* publics, we see that the private is also involved in audience's attention to and engagement with the public; the affective is intimately connected to the rational; the consumer is simultaneously a citizen; that audience tastes coexist with democratic ideals;

and so forth. Hartley's DIY citizens also seem evident here in their construction of a meaningful relationship to politics on their own terms, cobbled together through an assemblage of cognitive and affective demands built upon persons, issues, styles, feelings, and interests that they find appealing. Finally, as per Cottle and Rai, viewers maintained numerous points of connection to the show between (and including) display (affective/aesthetic) and deliberation (information/dialogue). This was seen nowhere better than in the on-line discussion forum.

Nancy Baym's study of on-line soap opera discussions reports four primary fan practices, ones that also occurred in the alt.tv.pol-incorrect discussion forum: *informing* others of what occurred in missed episodes; *speculating* about where the show's content will or should go; *criticizing* the show, its narratives, its actors, or other postings; and *reworking* the show's text in various ways.[25] For example, discussants in ATPI shared information about a specific program that others may have missed. Under the posting title "What happened on the 5 year celebration Show?" (February 23, 2002), for instance, a person asked, "What did Ann Coulter say. [sic] What were the three topics? Thanks for the info," followed by numerous replies that harshly criticized Coulter, discussed the guests that appeared that evening, reviewed things viewers thought were funny and comments that they found either right or wrong. ATPIers also speculate about Maher or guests on the show, debating, for instance, whether John McCain is a racist for anti-Vietnamese remarks (February 22, 2000) or whether the comedian Carrot Top is Jewish (March 11, 1998). The act of criticizing—Maher, the program, and the guests that appear—is one of the most frequent activities that occur in the forum. Indeed, Maher and his guests are more frequently criticized than celebrated. Finally, the participants in ATPI rework the program in various ways. As with letter writers, one popular form of reworking is the (re)construction of favorite past panelist lineups or assemblages the audience should see. Other reworkings might include clarifying Maher's statements or his particular thinking on issues, requesting changes in set design, inserting pop culture references, or integrating outside information to "fill out" the text in some way. This reworking is central to the pleasure that the show provides, thereby allowing viewers to participate in the construction of what the show then means to these viewers.

In short, the array of communicative frames that Cottle and Rai found in television news is on display here as well, as these posters created narratives that ranged from the informative, argumentative, and deliberative to those with the purpose of aesthetic or display, even those seeking community/consensus. *PI* is much more, then, than just an "entertainment" show or even one that provides important political "information." Rather, its most important function, perhaps, is how it served as an instigator for a whole range of discursive practices about politics and culture as citizen-viewers constructed their own relationships to and truths about current events and political life.

The connection, though, between these on-line practices and those of other "fan" communities, as well as the relationship to celebrity demonstrated earlier, presents this question: Does political entertainment programming also have some relationship and connection to viewers *as citizens* that other talk programming does not? Can the case be made that celebrity and fan culture provide *different avenues* for an active DIY citizenship via television? The following analysis offers potential answers, as we turn now to an examination of the special relationship that exists between performer Stephen Colbert, his television persona on *The Colbert Report* as conservative talk show host, and his devoted audience and fans known as the Colbert Nation.

FANS AND POLITICAL PLAY

Stephen Colbert has created one of the most complex characters of politically satiric comedy in American television history. But what makes the character all the more powerful as a parody of contemporary television political commentary is the invitation it extends to audiences for participation with the show. Audiences in the studio and at home, as well as fans on-line, all have a role to play in "making" the show. But it is a unique form of audience participation, unlike the deliberative forums of talk television that are typically viewed as providing the means of political engagement via television.[26]

Colbert claims that his program "is a sketch comedy show. So far, it's a 2½-year sketch. I think of the entire show as a single scene."[27] The long running sketch, as we have seen, is of an egotistical, idiotic talk show pundit. But central to this continual narrative is the host's role as stand-in or proxy for the audience, a person who is both a defender of the audience's interests but also their surrogate victim.[28] As Colbert describes his embodiment of this role, "The emotion of the moment is assumed and amplified by a single voice and regurgitated back to the country at the lowest common denominator. It can be swathed in idea, but it's essentially an emotional event. I'm regurgitating back to you how you feel about it—I am you. I am you!"[29] The audience, therefore, is central to who the character is and what he does to us (the audience), for us, *as* us. Colbert points this out when he notes, "The studio audience and the audience at home are a character in a scene that I am playing. I want them to think the way I think—and to like me, because my character's insecure. And I'm so happy that my audience has accepted that role. And through the Internet, thousands of people get to be in the show as the collective beast, the Colbert Nation."[30]

The specific role the audience is asked to play is twofold. First are the particular demands of the studio audience. They must play their role in supporting the faux pundit by cheering him when he is rude, applauding him when he is nonsensical, adoring him when he needs flattering, and reaching out to him when he needs their touch—as when he triumphantly embraces the audience with high-fives before many of his interviews (for the interview, of course, is ultimately about him, not the guest). Furthermore, this worshipful role is played to ridiculous links when the audience at home engages in numerous directives, dictated by the host, through online activities (discussed below). Yet in its second role, the audience laughs not just *with* Colbert (as he attacks his liberal villains), but also *at* him. That is, audiences are more than just actors in this parody. For the comedic portrayal of the right-wing blow-hard to be complete, they also must celebrate the playfulness, ingenuity, and creativity of the comedian's performance, while simultaneously ridiculing and vilifying the inanity of his distorted logic.

One fan explained this dual role particularly well in the program's online discussion forum: "During the WØRD [segment], when Stephen says something completely bogus, we applaud and cheer, playing up our character as His Followers, but when the WØRD's Bullet [point] makes a witty remark and rips Stephen's logic to shreds, we choose to cheer it on as well, returning to (some twisted form) of reality and [acknowledging] the absolute ridiculousness of what Stephen is saying." One of Colbert's on-line fan sites extends the observation: "A similar dynamic occurs in Stephen's interviews with guests, when the audience typically cheers both Stephen's ridiculous points and the guest's well-expressed counterargument."[31]

This reaction is, of course, the essential effect or function of parody. Mikhail Bakhtin maintained that parody includes a "double-voiced word," or "utterance that [is] designed to be interpreted as the expression of two speakers."[32]

> The author of a double-voiced word appropriates the utterance of another as the utterance of another and uses it "for his own purposes by inserting a new semantic orientation into a word which already has—and retains—its own orientation." The audience of a double-voiced word is therefore meant to hear both a version of the original utterance as the embodiment of its speaker's point of view (or "semantic position") and the second speaker's evaluation of that utterance from a different point of view.[33]

Therefore, the audience hears both Bill O'Reilly (for instance) and Stephen Colbert's critique of O'Reilly (and people like him). But again, the audience isn't just hearing the parody and laughing. They are being asked to play along and make the parody complete by verbally affirming its content *and* "effect," that is, by being worshipful subjects.

This is a peculiar and unusual position for audiences of televised political talk, even of the humorous and entertaining variety (although this same quality is at work with the audience's relationship to the correspondents on *The Daily Show*). Most political talk is agonistic, with clearly drawn lines of partisanship and ideological identification. Viewers are offered an "either-or" option from which they are expected to pick sides and react accordingly. Here, though, the parodic duality asks audiences to embrace both sides, though in different ways—by being emotional and rational, playful and serious. And even *within* these thoughts and feelings, there may be a duality at play. Emotions may vacillate between the joyfulness of the play and indignation at the logical stupidity of ultra-conservatives. Likewise, rational engagement might allow the viewer to see the lack of logic in Colbert's position while also entertaining the broader "logic" of how conservatives could put two plus two together and think it equals five. How much and in what ways specific audiences shuttle between these emotional, rational, and behavioral positions is an empirical question that seems particularly difficult, if not impossible to answer (although some "effects" researchers have tried).[34] Let it suffice to say here that *The Colbert Report* offers a textual "openness" that invites an indeterminate audience engagement with political issues and ideology unlike anything seen on American television, but one that is ultimately both critical and playful at its core.

What is also particularly unusual for political talk is that Colbert and his show have developed a devoted legion of "followers" or fans. As with other right-wing talk show personalities (such as Rush Limbaugh's "Dittoheads"), Colbert's fans hold him up worshipfully through their myriad activities of interactive engagement with his show via the Internet. As Colbert reflects on the phenomenon, "The funny thing is, I knew when we were developing this show, we were doing a show that parodies the cult of personality. And yet, if the show was successful, it would generate a cult of personality. It had to. That means it's working."[35] And indeed, the audience has embraced their role in this regard. Through their collective actions in his name, they have created a community of fans, which in the language of democracy we might consider a "nation" (as Colbert's fans and the show's website is playfully known—"Colbert Nation"). Liesbet van Zoonen notes just this analogous relationship between fan communities and political constituencies in what she brands the "fan democracy"—how both "come into being as a result of performance"; both "resemble each other when it comes to the endeavors that make one part of a community; and . . . both rest on emotional investments that are intrinsically linked to rationality and lead to 'affective intelligence.'"[36]

Performance, community, and emotional investment are just what Colbert's fans have created and display in their on-line activities. As fan studies have ably demonstrated, performance is not a "necessary" component of a fan's relationship to a text, but often does comprise a central dimension of many fan behaviors.[37] Fans performatively "act upon" their object of affection (such as writing fan fiction, creating fan Web pages, dressing and acting like the star, and so on), and in the process, imbue it with additional (personal and, at times, public) meaning. Colbert's fans too are actively engaged with their object/sign, from blogging and fan pages on the Internet, purchasing and consuming Colbert's various media commodities, and using the Internet to act out his on-screen commands. Again, Colbert's egotistical character is insecure, so he regularly prompts his viewers to do things that will celebrate him and his greatness. This has included imploring his fans through direct televisual address to enter various "naming" contests or polls in real life, where some object is named and Colbert fans vote for "Stephen Colbert." This was most famously done with a bridge in Hungary, when Colbert's fans registered 17 million votes (using computer bots) for Colbert in a nation with only 10 million people. Since then, Colbert and fans have also sought to use his name in the NASA space station, as the mascot for a hockey team in Michigan, and as winner of VH1's "Big Breakthrough" award.

This audience-centered playfulness also occurred early in Colbert's show in a WØRD segment called "Wikiality." In making fun of the ease with which people can effectively construct "reality" through the creation or edition of encyclopedia entries in Wikipedia (which is created and maintained through mass collaboration), Colbert encouraged his viewers to go to Wikipedia and "create an entry that says the number of elephants [in Africa] has tripled in the last six months. . . . Together we can create a reality that we can all agree on—the reality we just agreed on."[38] His fans, of course, did just that. As one of Colbert's Internet fan sites reports it, "the onslaught from fans was so instantaneous and persistent that Wikipedia eventually locked some 20 elephant-related entries, barring editing altogether. . . . Irritated by what they considered Wikipedia's overreaction, Colbert fans created the parody site Wikiality.com, which continues merrily to this day."[39]

Is this citizen engagement with politics or simply consumerist diversion and entertainment? By my reading, it is actually both. Certainly fans are enjoying themselves, engaging in what to many people might be considered an insider's joke or amateurish prank on mass society. They are also playing out their assigned "role" as members of the Colbert nation. But let's not miss the politics here amidst the seeming frivolousness and fun. Like "truthiness," "Wikiality" is one of Colbert's primary readings and critiques of contemporary political culture. If "truthiness" is a term designating the way that contemporary right-wingers—George W. Bush and Bill O'Reilly chief among them—employ emotions as reason, or feelings as logic, then "Wikiality" is its *agency*, the way such feelings become manifest in action. Colbert brings that point home within the original program segment by referencing Bush's own wikiality when it comes to the *belief* (and the ability to propagate that belief in others through shear repetition of the lie as fact) that Saddam Hussein possessed weapons of mass destruction:

> As usual, the Bush administration is on the cutting edge of information management. While they've admitted that Saddam did not possess weapons of mass destruction, they've also insinuated he *did* possess weapons of mass destruction . . . insinuations that have been repeated over and over again on cable news for the past three and a half years. And now the result is, 18 months ago only 36% of Americans believed it but 50% of Americans believe it now.

Again, while Wikiality is a humorous and entertaining concept, it does relate to real world politics. Take, for example, Conservapedia, the on-line encyclopedia inaugurated by the son of arch-conservative Phyllis Schlafly as a "much-needed alternative to Wikipedia, which is increasingly anti-Christian and anti-American."[40] Conservapedia seeks to offer conservative definitions of contested words and terms, from evolution and global warming to dinosaurs and kangaroos. Though such an endeavor is, on its face, patently absurd, the notion behind the site is quite powerful. These are the *real* truths, the site proclaims, and the ability now exists for conservatives and Christians to create their own public space where they need not endure the falsities propagated by the anti-Christian and liberal establishment that have dominated public thought through their ability to define the world. Such a site is the culmination of years of effort to challenge the supposed hegemony of liberal media, government, and academics, and it does so by the establishment and control of language upon which reality is built. Whether effective or not, simply by its existence, the site actively contests the legitimacy of other such locations for the establishment of definitional truth, be it Wikipedia, *Encyclopedia Britannica*, *Webster's*, or some other. It challenges its users to question *all* such informational resources for their ideological biases before using them. Thus, the truthiness of Conservapedia is not in its ideas or "definitions," as much as its epistemology. Colbert, of course, is pointing this out as part of the broader mandate (and his critique of it) that is radical conservatism.

But Colbert's fans don't just watch an amusing program and then go to bed. Many of them jump into action, such as those who took Colbert's point a step further by creating an actual site called "Wikiality: The Truthiness Encyclopedia"[41] (a link to which is featured on Comedy Central's Colbert Nation website). Here users can purposefully and playfully engage in such truthiness behaviors that Colbert describes and that Conservapedia actually employs. Consider, for instance, the politics inherent in the Wikiality entry for the word "Conservapedia:"

Conservapedia (including *Encyclopedia Conservativia*) is a Stalinist Republic [with Stalinist Republic intentionally crossed through for humorous effect] patriotic, faithful collection of truth, and the latest player in the free market of realities. Conservapedia was founded by Ronald Reagan's Ghost's gut, in contrast to this wiki, which was founded by Stephen Colbert's gut. It is a place where wikicons can gather and post the truth about subjects such as evolution, safe from the tyranny of the liberal wikinazis on Wikipedia (and later, the RationalWiki Cabal). It has received acclaim from the Founding Fathers and Jesus.[42]

The politics here is not just in the language or content of the posting, or even in the meanings of Colbert's critique. Rather, the politics is also in the actions themselves, in what can best be described as serious play.

In an insightful application of Hans-Georg Gadamer's theorization of "play" in relation to journalism, Theodore Glasser argues that play "does not reject the world around it but rather suspends that world and substitutes for it a world of meaning and order—a world that now finally makes sense and makes sense in a way quite satisfying to the individual who created it."[43] Whether you are Stephen Colbert or one of his fans, engaging with the anti-intellectualism, willed ignorance, and arrogant forthrightness of those whom Colbert parodies is not easy and not easily made sense of. Yet by *becoming* that world—by entering into it through playful means— one may have some chance of coming to terms with it (as with the quote by Jon Stewart earlier in the book in which he explained his work as a means of releasing "toxins" of frustration from his body, a way of staying sane through such daily purges). Though hyperrationalists may object to these arbitrary, perhaps even ridiculing means of engagement that seemingly eschew dialogue and deliberation, Glasser (and Gadamer) suggest that play is a more complex ontological and epistemological enterprise than such binary thinking accounts for:

> Play's creativity . . . highlights nothing less than the nature of meaning and understanding. Viewed as a mode of being, play reveals the "subtle dialectical and dialogical relation" . . . that exists between interpreters and what they seek to interpret; it offers an alternative to the dualistic thinking that holds that meaning and understanding can be reduced to a mere measure of "subjective attitudes toward what is presumably objective." For Gadamer, in short, play illustrates how individuals *participate* in the meaning of what they encounter.[44]

The politics of play is inherent, then, in the way viewers/fans "work through" (as John Ellis puts it) the meaning of Colbert's persona and what he parodies, but also their role in the formulation as the adoring fans of such megalomaniacs.[45] For again, "the concrete dealing with a text yields understanding only when what is said in the text begins to find expression in the interpreter's own language."[46] The activities described here are not the discursive or deliberative engagement of audiences for *Politically Incorrect*, or the affective attachment audiences felt with celebrities who provided an important articulation of the private and public spheres. This is political expression and engagement through the fans' own language of play, one in which they too are creators and interpreters of meaning.

It is important to note, however, that not all Colbert fans may be attracted to the show for its politics. In their study of Colbert fans, Catherine Burwell and Megan Boler suggest the possibility for an anti-political stance within the fan cultures of both Stephen Colbert and Jon Stewart. They observed one Stewart fan website that clearly offered the label, "if you want politics, go away." Likewise, the creator of a prominent Colbert fan site on the Web, DB Ferguson of the No Fact Zone, also argues that her fandom comes first. She notes in an interview with the authors, "You'd be amazed at how unpolitical the Colbert fan community is."[47] Both instances are anecdotal and could perhaps be countered with evidence obtained by measuring the sheer volume and analyzing the content of the political discussions that appears within the program's Colbert Nation website discussion forums. With that said, it is important to note that this is exactly the type of relationship that scholars of fandom highlight as central to fan behaviors—that the text they appropriate and have an emotional relationship to is open to (m)any meanings of the fans' choosing, including in this instance the general refusal of politics, however seemingly unavoidable it is within the text itself.[48] The refusal of politics is invited further by the structured openness of the parodic performance. Parody is almost by definition inconclusive and open to many interpretations, including the reading that Colbert might be *celebrating* conservative thinking or the reading of Colbert as a comedian who is simply entertaining.[49]

In short, we would be mistaken to overdetermine the politics at work in *The Colbert Report*, especially given the central relationship that exists between audience/fans and the performance/construction of the program. Nevertheless, as hopefully demonstrated, play should not necessarily be associated with frivolity. Play is one of many subjective positions from which political engagement can occur, and if Colbert's program is in some way political, then the play it encourages contains the possibility for politics as well. Furthermore, the playfulness encouraged by the (political) text stands in contrast to the dominant forms of news-centered public affairs programming that have historically dominated television's presentation of politics. As Glasser notes, "news today appears as a 'closed' text, one that invites readers to consider only what reporters and their sources say. But play thrives on an 'open' text, one that invites readers to consider what writers *mean*. The difference is important if the goal of journalism is to encourage understanding and not merely promote the acquisition of knowledge."[50] This is one of the central points made throughout this chapter: new political television becomes a site for moving beyond information or knowledge acquisition of politics as news, instead encouraging and allowing for multiple points from which citizens can engage with and construct for themselves the meaning of politics, including through the openness allowed for by this special form of politically parodic performance. For as Jonathan Gray argues, the news "must matter to the individual and must be consumed emotionally to some degree if it is to become meaningful to its viewers."[51]

Colbert describes how he and his writers take the news and transform it into play, but that such a process must itself be open to discovering where the play should lead next in conjunction with the audience. "What we're doing is difficult," he notes in explaining the show's creative process. "We deconstruct the news into a joke, and then we falsely reconstruct the news into how my character would see it. The writers and I talk about how it's like driving an 18-wheeler backward down a highway. It's possible, but you have to constantly readjust the steering."[52] As with driving a trailer backward, those readjustments are hard to predict and must be open to "making it up" as going along. Elsewhere Colbert explained the thinking behind the production process: "But we don't plan. It's all been discovery, and that's something that we're working very hard to maintain. . . . We want to keep the show . . . [a] discovery. You tend for one thing, but you discover along the way something better. I never intended to do half the things we did this year. We discovered that we can, as a show."[53]

A perfect example of this was Colbert's "Green Screen Challenge" in the 2008 presidential election. When Barack Obama finally secured the Democratic Party's nomination in June, John McCain made an appearance before a small crowd that evening to offset Obama's big news night on television. The contrast between the two speeches, though, could not have been starker, with McCain making a lackluster appearance in front of an even more unappealing green backdrop. Because a "green screen" is what television and film producers use for shooting a character in a scene that can then be enhanced with a computer-generated fake background (as is done, for instance, when *Daily Show* correspondents report "live" from, say, Baghdad), Colbert decided the following night to issue a green screen challenge by posting a video of McCain's own green screen appearance on its website, and then invited viewers to download it and make computer modifications to it in order to "Make McCain Exciting." Viewers did just that, and three months later, Colbert played the results during his broadcast, featuring three of the viewer submitted mash-ups, and then a montage sequence of twenty-nine additional entries (with visual backgrounds including *Citizen Kane, Saturday Night Fever*, Elvis, and even Colbert's own show) run together with McCain's speech connecting them all—a mash-up of mash-ups by the show's writers, if you will.[54]

Here we have the essence of Colbert's quest for comedic "discovery" that resides between the daily news, his writing staff, and where his interactions with a playful audience might take the show. In the process, viewers are invited to make their own meanings of politics and the news by playfully reinterpreting McCain—McCain's vision of grandeur and self-importance as Charles Foster (Citizen) Kane, McCain as a dinosaur, McCain as corporate newspaper management in *The Wire*, and so on. These viewers' video statements were political, sophomoric, or plenty of things in-between. Regardless, viewers were offered the opportunity to engage with politics, to perform it, and to enjoy it in the process. The components of fan culture *and* citizenship—performance, community, and emotional investment— are all present here in the actions of this "Colbert Nation." This is simply one example of how this form of new political television contributes to citizenship. For as van Zoonen notes, "popular culture . . . needs to be acknowledged as a relevant resource for political citizenship: a resource that produces comprehension and respect for popular political voices and that allows for more people to perform as citizens; a resource that can make citizenship more pleasurable, more engaging, and more inclusive."[55]

RETHINKING TELEVISION'S RELATIONSHIP TO CIVIC ENGAGEMENT, PART II

Looking across this study of audiences, what we see is a crisis of representation. *PI* audiences described a fundamental disconnect from the political world created by insider pundit talk television, seeking instead the "realness" seemingly provided by the forum, the talk, the issues, and the people who inhabited Maher's show. Paradoxically, what seemed more real to them was celebrity, a fabrication (or mutually agreed upon delusion) if nothing else. Nevertheless, celebrities, including Maher, were representational figures with whom they felt some affective attachment, a bond more powerful in connecting them to public life than the logical arguments presented by political experts with whom they felt no such connection. The argument here is that what audiences are ultimately seeking is the ability to see *themselves* portrayed on screen, even if in ideal form. Whether realistic or not, popular culture is a place where that happens, where people shape their identities based on what they find there, including their identity as citizens. In that regard, celebrity does provide some level of representation, which is perhaps easier to understand if one thinks of other representational celebrities such as Sarah Palin, Barack Obama, or Rush Limbaugh. Even the right-wing talk show hosts that Colbert parodies are involved in promoting this crisis of representation. They suggest that the liberal media, liberal politicians, liberal encyclopedias, and so on, don't understand citizens or are leading citizens astray. But audiences can trust (in the representation of) the talk show host as citizen surrogate and surrogate victim, the person who will go into battle for them and who suffers for them as well. While the real life manifestations of Colbert's parody are no joke, Colbert's parody certainly is, and his audiences gleefully participate in the representational ploy. They playfully embrace the cult of personality and do the host's bidding, demonstrating their (faux) need for such guidance all the while using Colbert as their own (celebrity) critique of the phenomenon and the politics behind it.

Representation therefore also involves the possibilities for (and invitation to) action in the form of talk and play. As audiences for *PI* made clear, the program provided an accessible forum through which they could hear others speak in a language they understood. *PI* was a rejection of the sealed and inaccessible world of insider political talk, primarily because such shows never invited them to the table. As van Zoonen argues, "politics has to be connected to the everyday culture of its citizens; otherwise it becomes an alien sphere, occupied by strangers no one cares and bothers about."[56] *PI*, however, not only offered accessible and meaningful political discussion, it provoked discourse and argumentation within viewers themselves, instigating a range of discursive practices within viewers' private realm. Political meaning, then, occurs through opportunities to speak, to hear others speak, to project oneself into the conversation, and to merge these with one's life, thoughts, feelings, and attachments. In the case of Colbert, political meaning can also be arrived at through opportunities for political play and the performance of politics. Play becomes a means of extending one's relationship to the (political) text, and as Glasser puts it, provides an "opportunity for individuals to engage in a very public world in a very private and personally satisfying way."[57]

Both programs have made politics pleasurable, but not just through laughter. Rather, those pleasures also occur through the deeper levels of identification and activity they provide for viewers as citizens. For as van Zoonen also notes in the epigraph that starts this chapter, what is important is "what citizens *do* with entertaining politics, for citizenship is not something that pertains if it is not expressed in everyday talk and actions, both in the public and private domain. Citizenship . . . is something that one has to do, something that requires performance."[58]

Returning to Cottle and Rai's model, we see how viewer engagement with both shows afforded opportunities for argumentation and expression, deliberation and display, information and understanding, conflict and consensus. This model, I suggest, provides a much richer explanation for what narratives such as *PI* and *TCR* actually offer viewers than the more simplistic notions of entertainment and/or information, as the analysis here seems to support. New political television allows for a range of cognitive and emotional interactions with what is found on the screen, while also providing behavioral invitations to talk and play in ways that encompass many of these opportunities. Far from the assumption that television saps the participatory souls of citizens, the evidence here suggests that new political television offers a much needed and welcome invigoration of citizenship—at times serious, at times playful, but always enlivened by these new opportunities that seem politically meaningful, if not downright enjoyable.

11

The Expanding and Contested Boundaries of New Political Television

As political entertainment television has matured as a genre, it has received both critical acclaim and popular success.[1] Through that process of maturation, it has also expanded the existing boundaries of television's relationship to politics. In the competitive economy of post-network television, for instance, Michael Moore first demonstrated broadcast networks' newfound willingness to program strong-armed political satire as entertainment programming, even if the critiques were destined to ruffle powerful feathers. Bill Maher, with his move to a broadcast network in the mid to late 1990s, led the way in successfully desegregating and retailoring the talk show genre by creating a cacophonous and pluralist talk forum minus the fawning pretensions of celebrity talk or the boy's club insularity of political talk. But it was Jon Stewart's deft deployment of the fake news format in the years following 9/11 that perhaps did the most to convince people that this genre could serve an important role as a form of *political* (not just entertaining) television.

Playing with the codes and conventions of television news, Stewart challenged the boundaries of journalism by engaging in his own brand of satirical reporting to mount persistent, penetrating, and much-needed critiques of the constantly shocking policies and people of the Bush administration at a time when the "real" TV news media had largely abandoned that role. What did and continues to make Stewart's show so powerful (partly by simply doing a good job at getting at truth as a "fake" news program) is its critical assessment of what constitutes television news and how poorly it serves the public good. Night after night and month after month, the audience is led to question just who is guarding the henhouse, and what role television news media play in

235

distracting the public's attention from sources of power that can do real harm, both political and economic. Finally, Stephen Colbert has taken these critiques one step further by directly challenging the integrity and veracity of political talk on cable news more broadly, including its most successful talk program (*The O'Reilly Factor*), among others. More importantly, though, Colbert has mounted the first sustained critique of a *political culture*, connecting the underlying "thinking"/feeling of political commentators on television to the rhetoric and operationalization of a presidential administration's ideology, even including an indictment of the citizen-audiences that support and sustain such fabrications and affronts to truth.

In each of these instances, new political television has challenged the boundaries of what does or should serve as the relationship of television to politics. Satire, parody, and humor constitute the primary instruments for challenging who gets to talk about politics, in what ways, and with what authority and legitimacy. What these challenges have proved is that any claims that entertainment and information belong in separate spheres are simply no longer credible. Furthermore, these shows have challenged the privileged position that news media (as reporters but also arbiters of political talk) play as society's regime of truth, our primary institution for establishing truth in public life. That challenge has been exacerbated by new political television's extension into and convergence with new media and social media (as discussed shortly). Extending the boundaries of push media (television) into pull mediums (the Internet and social media) creates spaces, Henry Jenkins argues, where "news [becomes] something to be discovered through active hashing through of competing accounts rather than something to be digested from authoritative sources."[2]

The maturation and success of the genre has also been accompanied by a set of recurring questions and claims about the genre, including its supposed effects on young citizens. Given the all-white male make-up of new political television's hosts, including the perception that they are all liberals, questions of representation abound. Why are there no conservatives doing political entertainment television and why are none of the hosts women or minorities? Even though this genre has challenged the previously existing boundaries that defined political news and talk on television, are there not still other boundaries these shows wittingly or unwittingly maintain? One response, that conservatives and minorities have had programming in the genre but failed, still doesn't answer the larger question about why they haven't been successful. More importantly, the question itself is worth entertaining for what it tells us about Americans' conception of political "representation" through television.

One final question concerns the boundaries of acceptable engagement with this programming form: does entertaining politics create misinformed or cynical citizens? Chapter 8 addressed the supposed deleterious effects on viewer knowledge about politics, current events, or "the news," and chapter 10 addressed the ways in which viewers have employed this programming as a means of engagement with politics. This chapter addresses the repeated claim that satire and political humor (and its hosts) are cynical or creates cynical attitudes toward politics as an effect. Though much of the analysis so far has hopefully provided sufficient data to make the opposite claim—that new political television consistently engages in political critique because it believes that politics and power actually *do matter*, and that both should be taken very seriously, even if through scornful ridicule and a mischievous smile—we should nevertheless address the assumption that criticism plus laughter equals cynical nihilism.

ISSUES OF REPRESENTATION

A persistent question that typically accompanies a discussion of political entertainment television concerns ideology and/or partisanship. Jon Stewart, Stephen Colbert, Bill Maher, and Michael Moore are all considered liberals in this formulation, and their shows are seen as leaning to the left. The question then becomes why aren't there any conservatives doing political satire, humor, or even entertaining political talk on television?[3] I suggest that there are several possible answers to the question. First, there have been a few attempts at using conservative hosts or programming geared toward conservative audiences, but most have failed. From 2004–2005, Dennis Miller hosted a talk show on CNBC simply called *Dennis Miller* that included roundtable talk in the vein of *Politically Incorrect*.[4] On the first show, Miller admitted his more conservative turn of thinking and opinion since 9/11, all the while allowing for Ellie the chimpanzee to sit and bounce on his lap. Similarly, as discussed in chapter 4, Fox News attempted *The ½ Hour News Hour*, a *Daily Show*–style fake news program, but it too fell flat from poorly written material and humor aimed at the right's standard liberal bogeymen (typically the powerless). What might prove more viable for conservatives is the *Huckabee* brand of talk show that offers a wider range of discursive appeals, such as one critic described conservative talk show host Glenn Beck's stand-up comedy tour—"an odd and unwieldy combination of stand-up, revival meeting, motivational seminar and stump speech."[5]

The second answer is to question the assumption that the comedy of Stewart, Colbert, and Maher is actually liberal (although for Moore that is certainly the case).[6] Theories of political humor and satire give numerous reasons to question this premise. Writing on political humor in American politics more broadly, Charles Schutz contends that:

> American political humor is basically negative. It is anti-political and anti-partisan; it ridicules and derides government and officialdom; and, last, political humor even completes the circle by attacking the people themselves. Yet, true to the genius of comedy, the negative serves the positive. Negative political humor supports politics and democracy, and the existence of the former is a sure sign of the health of the latter.[7]

Though Schutz locates government and "officialdom" as typical targets of political humor, a more expansive reading would construe those agents as "the powerful," whether we are talking about political or economic elites. As the analyses of Stewart, Colbert, Maher, and Moore in this book have demonstrated, the object of their critiques has been the powerful, political as well as the economically powerful.[8] But Schutz also makes another important point: "political play and its comedy have another function; they counteract the ideological fanaticism of contemporary politics."[9] Whether we are describing the Republican witch hunt against President Clinton's sexual indiscretions, the right-wing orthodoxy that dominated the presidency of George W. Bush, or the ratings dominance of right-wing pundits on cable television such as Bill O'Reilly and Sean Hannity, what is clear is that these comedians have all located such ideological fanaticism as the targets of their humorous attacks.

Theories of satire, in particular, provide an even more focused portrait of political humor's focus on power. Satire is verbal aggression that exposes some aspect of reality to ridicule in the form of an aesthetic expression. Furthermore, it "involves at least implied norms against which a target can be exposed as ridiculous, and demands the pre-existence or creation of shared comprehension and evaluation between satirist and audience."[10] Satire, then, becomes an artistic means of pointing out and holding up for scrutiny and criticism that ridiculousness by, ironically enough, being somewhat ridiculous. Satire is also, as George Test notes, "mainly about a time and a place and people."[11] Therefore, the "implied norms" or breech in social standards as well as the "shared comprehension and evaluation" that exists are dependent on the times in which they are enunciated as speech acts. When Bill Maher's program *Politically Incorrect* debuted, for instance, he might have been read as a conservative, because his show was intentionally designed to attack the new norms of "political correctness" as ridiculous and a violation of the more long-standing norms of common sense.[12] Looking back through American history, it is difficult to say whether the great American satirists such as Mark Twain, Will Rogers, Art Buchwald, and Mort Sahl, for instance, were conservative or liberal, but they all responded to the historical context/times in which they lived. One might want to suggest that by their pleas for common sense, they were generally moderates. As Schutz argues further, "The creative impulse of humor constantly generates alternative logics of political rule and ceaselessly challenges the conventional wisdom of even the sovereign people. . . . Thus, the critical realism of political humor balances the political regime toward the mean and away from excesses of right and left."[13] In that regard, perhaps it is most appropriate to see new political television humorists as those seeking moderation from the extremes. Jon Stewart certainly has argued as such when he contends, "My comedy is not the comedy of the neurotic. It comes from the center. But it comes from feeling displaced from society because you're in the center. We're the group of fairness, common sense, and moderation."[14]

Yet it is the question itself—"Where are the conservatives to balance these (supposed) liberals?"—that is perhaps the more interesting one. What it actually reflects is contemporary conceptions of partisan politics and ideology and the audience's desire to see television providing a "representative" balancing within or amongst them. As with the crisis of representation discussed in the last chapter, here too we have a question of television's role in the process of political representation. Americans seemingly have a need to see two opposing sides in political debate, if not politics more generally. Perhaps this is the product of an American political system that essentially structures a two-party system (not allowing for the many parties that populate a proportional representation system of governance), or perhaps it is the result of Americans seeing the bifurcation of ideological reasoning in cable and network political talk shows. Either way, it demonstrates this desire to see more than one side represented, irrespective of the quality that goes with it. As long as we see two sides represented, our adversarial system should guarantee a proper outcome, we hope.[15] This has certainly been the case with many pundit talk shows, such as *Crossfire* or even *Hannity and Colmes*—never mind that person occupying the "liberal" seat on the show isn't a person with whom liberals or progressive agree, or never mind that the designated person may be a moron.

But what this question ultimately ignores or obscures is the "hole" in American political communication that new political television is currently filling. Instead of focusing on the ideology or supposed partisanship of these hosts, perhaps the appropriate focus should be the critical voice being supplied by them and why it is even necessary. As I have argued throughout this book, new political television redresses some of the deficiencies that have arisen due to the crisis in news media, and in particular, journalism's crumbling "regime of truth." When news media largely failed in their role as watchdogs of power in three of America's worst crises of the last generation—presidential impeachment, the War on Terror, and the near collapse of the financial sector—it was new political television that most consistently and persuasively offered needed critiques.

Given the power and success of these critiques, a second and related question then is why these shows haven't been sufficiently emulated or copied—not so much in commercial form, but in how they go about their business. Why have journalists not emulated Stewart's usage of video redaction to uncover truth or to contradict elites who serve up outright lies? Why have interviewers not copied Stewart's style of discursive exchange with his interview subjects to change the conversation from publicity to deliberative dialogue toward the common good? Why does *Editor & Publisher*, the newspaper industry's central trade publication, still need to write an article arguing that Stephen Colbert did a better job than the *New York Times* in addressing the dangerous speech emanating from right-wing television talk show host Glenn Beck in the spring of 2009?[16] In short, questions of ideological representation seem to miss the broader point that is imperative in a democratic system: what television needs to supply is not competing partisan positions, but voices that will interrogate power and hold it accountable to the people. If news media no longer sufficiently perform that task, then we should be thankful that entertainment television has found it economically profitable to do so in journalism's stead.

A related question of representation that is also repeatedly asked concerns questions over race and sex. Why are there no people of color or no women as hosts of these shows? Why the parade of white men? The question is an important one, but here too the particular formulation of what constitutes "representation" may be missing the more significant issue of social and political criticism that currently exists (outside the obvious benefits of having such hosts). As discussed in chapter 4, with Comedy Central's *Chocolate News* and CNN's *D. L. Hughley Breaks the News*, two networks have experimented with African American hosts. But the failure of these shows has as much to do with the (economic) failure that typically accompanies new shows on television (from writing, to network schedule and placement, to poor execution, and so on) as they do with a broader public rejection of African Americans as hosts of this type of entertaining political television.[17]

What has happened instead is that as *The Daily Show* became more popular and its cast of largely white men correspondents began leaving the show (including Mo Rocca, Steve Carrell, Ed Helms, Rob Corrdry, and Stephen Colbert), the program replaced them with a more diversified cast (though largely still male). The "news team" correspondents and contributors in 2009 are (among other white males) Samantha Bee (joining in 2003), Larry Wilmore (2006), Aasif Mandvi (2006), Wyatt Cenac (2008), and Kristen Schaal (2008). The importance here, of course, is not filling some diversity quota, but in how *TDS* has allowed these comedians to bring the critical voices that diversity often represents to the news through their "reporting" and commentary. Mandvi, an Indian-born Muslim immigrant raised in the United Kingdom and the United States, argues that it is "an important time to say something as a Muslim-American, as a brown person, as an immigrant. I feel like a lot of my work is about [exploring] that gap between cultures." Furthermore, by being these things, he notes, "I can say stuff on the air that resonates in a way that if a Caucasian guy said it, it wouldn't resonate the same."[18]

Mandvi's point is demonstrated quite well through the example of "Senior Female and Women's Issues Correspondent" Samantha Bee. When Republican Presidential Candidate John McCain made the surprise pick of Alaska Governor Sarah Palin as his choice of running mate in the 2008—following the enormous success of Hillary Clinton and the fervency of her supporters in the Democratic contest—*TDS* questioned whether the McCain camp chose this questionably qualified person simply because they thought she would, as a woman, tap into the supposed desire of women voters to have *any* woman in office, irrespective of her ideological stance on issues. Bee was in place to assume the parodic role of inversion—saying the opposite of what the critique actually means—that *TDS* correspondents usually assume in their commentary (with Stewart playing the straight man). In the segment, Bee notes that as a "proud vagina American" she was going to vote for McCain. When Jon Stewart objected, arguing that in many ways "Governor Palin is the ideological opposite of Senator Clinton," Bee retorted, "Oh yes, but she's her gynecological twin." After Stewart persisted with a list of objections, Bee interrupts, "Can you just stop overloading my lady-brain? John McCain chose a woman who is almost completely unprepared for the job, and who disagrees with me on every core value I believe in, but I will be voting McCain in November because he understands women don't vote with the big head, they vote with the little hood."[19] Bee's being a woman essentially allows this critique to happen, as the segment would lack power coming from a man, perhaps even seeming misogynist.

Wilmore, the show's "Senior Black Correspondent" makes this point as well when he argues that "part of [his] niche on the show is covering some of the topics 'The Daily Show' has never had a chance to cover because sometimes you can take it better when it comes from somebody who's your own kind."[20] So, for instance, Wilmore is asked by Stewart whether Black History Month served a useful purpose, to which he replied, "Yes, the purpose of making up for centuries of oppression with twenty-eight days of trivia. I'd rather we got casinos" (referring to legislation that allows another historically oppressed people, Native Americans, to run gambling operations on their lands). It is hard to imagine a white male making such a critique or joke.

In short, while these improvements to *TDS* don't overcome the pluralistic potential that diversification of the host role in political entertainment television could add, the changes in the show's composition has allowed for the inclusion of diverse critical voices and commentary that would largely be absent without their presence in the genre. The overall point I am making, then, is that the issue of representation is important, but we should also recognize what is present and absent in the actual *critical assessments of politics* occurring within the genre, not basing our judgments solely in its overly broad labels of "liberals," "conservatives," "women," or "Muslims."[21]

BEYOND THE TV SCREEN

There is little doubt that the programs that constitute new political television are successes within the medium. What is also important to note, however, is the ways in which this programming is extended outward beyond the boundaries of the television screen, network schedules, and viewers' ritual habits with television.[22] When YouTube first appeared in 2006, users repeatedly posted clips of *The Daily Show* on the social networking site, prompting Viacom (the owner of Comedy Central) to struggle constantly to have them removed or banned from the site (eventually suing Google, YouTube's owner, as a strong-armed effort in that regard).[23] In October 2007, the network saw the handwriting on the digital wall (so to speak), and changed its policies toward one of promiscuity. They created separate websites (distinct from Comedy Central) for *The Daily Show* and *The Colbert Report*, and included all episodes of these programs (for *TDS* dating back to 1999), broken down into segmented clips for viewers to watch within the site. Users can search and retrieve by date, tags, segment, and other means. The clips are also available for download via mobile media (providing the network with another revenue stream), with *TDS* being the most popular and downloaded show for mobile media customers in 2007.[24] The network even facilitates and encourages the reposting and sharing of these clips on websites, blogs, and social networking sites such as Facebook by providing users with links to these sites and the codes needed to embed the clips. Although the network can capitalize on this by showing advertising for the clips housed on its site, few additional revenue streams are available when the clips are posted elsewhere on the Web. So beyond just making money, the network realizes the additional value that is gained by allowing for the wider circulation and disbursement of the programs. Perhaps that value comes in the wider cultural cache these programs (and the network brand) maintain by being "water cooler" moments the following day(s), even if the water cooler is now a virtual one.[25]

A political value also accrues through the wider circulation of these materials due to their availability and retrievability. By putting the entire library of *TDS* and *TCR* on-line for anyone to freely access, share, and reference, the programming becomes an enormous resource for the broader circulation of the critiques, public statements, and reporting that occurs there.[26] Geoffrey Baym charts the ways in which both shows now participate in the larger social and political conversation, as numerous activists, websites, and special interest groups pick up the arguments or comments from guest appearances and use them in their own politically discursive efforts. Maintaining that these shows become important "discursive resources to be used, not simply consumed, by increasingly active audiences," he argues that they also tend to "stimulate engagement, reaction, and response."[27] Christian Christensen makes a similar point when arguing that the "immediate and extended afterlife" of events such as Jon Stewart challenging Jim Cramer's and CNBC's financial news reporting are a significant factor in assessing the way that nonjournalists can uses such events to fill informational holes not supplied by mainstream journalists. The availability and circulation of these materials via social media such as YouTube, Google Video, iFilm, and others, he argues, serve as "relay and replay mechanisms," ones with the potential to "recalibrate informational balances of power" and "challenge the professional news status quo."[28]

In the previous chapter, we explored the extensions of *TCR* occurring through the Web as Colbert's fans interact with and perform their assigned role as adoring followers in Colbert's faux cult of personality. We should also realize that in addition to Baym's expanded "town square" and Christensen's "new journalism" approaches, the Web also serves as a performative space, one in which these shows are extended outward across platforms but also across nonpolitical venues for the performance of politics. The Web as political performance space can also be seen quite clearly through the veritable explosion of political satire and humor on-line that occurred during the 2008 presidential election. From for-profit websites to advocacy groups and anonymous user-generated mash-ups, satire served numerous ends as a language through which people and groups communicated political favor or disfavor with the candidates (and even critiques of voters themselves). Commercial websites such as Barely Political, Funny or Die, College Humor, 23/6, Headzup, JibJab, and the Onion News Network all constructed numerous satirical performances in short clips that were easily posted and circulated across the Web. For instance, when John McCain released a television ad attacking Barack Obama as little more than a political version of celebrities such as Paris Hilton and Britney Spears, Funny or Die crafted a satirical response that mocked McCain's charge by featuring Paris Hilton posing lustily in a bathing suit, announcing she was running for president, and citing her smartly written policy proposals on energy independence.

The political interest group MoveOn.org offered a parody of the infamous "Talk to Your Kids about Alcohol and Drugs" public service announcement, transforming it into "Talk to Your Parents about McCain," featuring a chorus of youthful celebrities as spokespersons. Another video, this one funded by the Jewish Council for Education and Research, featured comedienne Sarah Silverman in a video called "The Great Schlep" (attracting 7 million views within the first two weeks of the video's release). Though crossing all boundaries of taste while flouting any religious, racial, or ethnic sensitivity, Silverman offered an outrageously funny plea that young Jews need to convince older Jews not to be fearful of Obama, and that doing nothing in this campaign is not really an option. And finally, user-generated mash-ups of candidates appeared, including several of Hillary Clinton that offered a highly unflattering yet humorous mocking of her ambition. One video merged Clinton with the character Veruca Salt in *Willy Wonka and the Chocolate Factory* (singing "I Want It Now"), while another fused campaign trail footage with similar clips from the movie *Election* (and its hero/villain Tracy Flick). In short, satire and parody became a political language that could be easily crafted and distributed via the Web, yet with generally low cost of entry for such speech (as opposed to expensive television advertising campaigns).

It is too much to suggest that this sudden plentitude or popularity of on-line satire is the direct result of new political television's success. With that said, it is perhaps worth exploring what this form of political expression shares with the satirical and parodic forms of political entertainment television such as *TDS* and *TCR*, and why both television and on-line versions may be similarly attractive to certain audiences. First is satire's distinctive voice, one that enunciates political critiques without relying on the well-worn sermonic, polemical, and partisan talk that has dominated public discourse for the last generation. It offers a fresh means for expressing outrage, disappointment, and so forth without being hortatory. As George Test argues, satire takes natural human emotions—"anger, shame, indignation, disgust, contempt"—and channels or domesticates them, transforming "a potentially divisive and chaotic impulse . . . into a useful and artistic expression," one made socially acceptable by its playful nature, yet one also with enormous political power.[29]

Second, satire offers not just a way of talking about politics, but a means for creating appeal and tapping the audience's attention. The parodic utterance, for instance, is based on taking something recognizable—say a preachy PSA or a bloviated talk show host—and turning it on its head. The outline, style, and contours of the form are familiar yet become strange; they are known yet are waiting to be (re)discovered. Parody taps into existing cognitive frames rather than asking viewers to start anew. Furthermore, the parodic utterance isn't a lecture. It grants the viewer interpretive authority to make his or her own reading. As we saw in the previous chapter, it is the *facilitation* of thinking public thoughts that is appealing, a process in which truth and meaning will be arrived at through the audience's own thinking, not selected from choices developed by "experts." Satire and parody open up spaces in which that can occur by affording the viewer a level of respect.

Given both of these points, then, it is perhaps worth entertaining whether humor and satire, *as forms of political speech*, comprise a generational language. Certainly a person of any age will be attracted to satire, as evidenced by the fact that there are twice as many viewers of *TDS* who constitute an older demographic (25–49) than the stereotypical younger viewer (18–24) of this show.[30] But what is distinctive about so many of the on-line satiric videos in the 2008 election is their generational appeal—from using young stars, to directly addressing their audience as youthful, to their use and parodying of youthful popular music and music videos that few older people might recognize (not to mention a propensity toward crassness and blue language that can dominate such programming). These included the Paris Hilton, Sarah Silverman, and MoveOn videos mentioned above, as well as Funny or Die's "Vote for John McCain" (featuring Hayden Panettiere) and College Humor's "Head of Skate" (ridiculing Sarah Palin). Satirical music videos and music mash-ups included Barely Political's "I've Got a Crush on Obama," Soulja Boy's Presidential Debate Remix ("Yahh"), "Barack Gets That Dirt Off His Shoulders" (ripped from Jay-Z's song "Dirt Off Your Shoulder"), and "Hillary's Baggage" (or "junk in her trunk," based on the Black Eyed Peas' "My Humps"). Though the "comic sages" that dominated political humor earlier in American history were typically older (Mark Twain, Will Rogers, Art Buchwald), one could argue that from the late 1950s to the present, political and social satire has had much stronger youth appeal, from Lenny Bruce, *Mad Magazine*, and *National Lampoon* through *Saturday Night Live*, *The Simpsons*, and *South Park*.[31]

This concept of satire as a generational language will be explored further shortly, but to bring this discussion of new political television's extension beyond television to a close, it is perhaps instructive to return to the role of entertaining politics as circulated through social media networks described by Baym and Christensen. The morning after Jon Stewart's cringe-inducing discussion with CNBC host Jim Cramer, political blogger Andrew Sullivan saw similarities between Stewart's holding the old guard of mainstream news media accountable for their lack of responsibility to the public trust, and the tasks that bloggers routinely perform. He noted, "In some ways, the blogosphere is to [mainstream media] punditry what Stewart is to Cramer: an insistent and vulgar demand for some responsibility, some moral and ethical accountability for previous decisions and pronouncements. Braver, please. And louder."[32]

This discussion of new political television's centrifugal push beyond the confines (and economics) of television attempts to highlight the way this material gets used on-line as discursive resources in dialogic politics, as well as performance in venues such as on-line satirical play. The argument here harkens back to the theoretical discussions of audiences and narratives in the previous chapter. That is, we see the cognitive, emotional, and behavioral appeal of new political television's narratives in providing opportunities for argumentation and expression, deliberation and display, information and understanding, and conflict and consensus beyond the television viewing context. Given the possibilities of user-centered, "prosumer" interactivity (producers and consumers) through digital media, the language of entertaining politics becomes a more broadly dispersed means of political discourse and critique. New political television, therefore, challenges the boundaries of public engagement with politics and how those are constituted via mass and social media.

SATIRE AND THE ASSUMPTION OF CYNICISM

Given the crisis in journalism described throughout this book—including audience fatigue and disaffection from the public affairs talk shows that have been the dominant form of political discussion in the age of television— the satire and parody of entertaining politics may be a preferred means of political communication for those raised in the digital era. As the youthful editor of Spinsanity.com, Bryan Keefer, quoted at the end of chapter 8, put it, "Like other twenty-somethings, I've been raised in an era when advertising invades every aspect of pop culture, and to me the information provided by mainstream news outlets too often feels like one more product, produced by politicians and publicists."[33] Despite (or perhaps because of) its ironic tone, the language of satire therefore may seemingly maintain a degree of *authenticity* to younger citizens simply because it doesn't seem so closely aligned with the "manufactured" realities that politicians, advertisers, and news media construct and would have them believe. The question, of course, is whether it is the ironic stance itself that seems authentic (because it is cool, edgy, ridiculing, anti-authority, or whatever) or simply that this more joyous, entertaining, critical, and seemingly less agenda-driven language offers a respite from so much of the manipulative political language that surrounds it.

Amber Day notes that despite the ironic language, appeal, and stylistics of many of the on-line satiric videos in the 2008 election, they nevertheless contained a high level of earnestness in their imploring youth to take a stand, engage in certain political behaviors, or simply care. Comparing this earnestness with criticisms that maintain that irony is the handmaiden of a supposed "lack of conviction, smugness, detachment, and cynicism" in young people,[34] she concludes that these videos provide one source of evidence that "gives lie to the argument that irony is analogous with disengagement and cynicism. If anything, irony is becoming a new marker of sincerity."[35]

This discussion leads us to the larger and more prevalent claim that satire is somehow fundamentally linked to political cynicism, perhaps precisely *because* young people are attracted to it—the same demographic that largely fails many "good citizen" tests in terms of a lack of knowledge of public affairs, low readership and viewership of news, low voter turnout, low trust in government, and so forth. Although there is not room here to engage in a full-blown discussion of why many of these measures are misplaced when it comes to youth and civic participation (such as statistics showing increases in volunteerism, increases in voting and voter registration in the last two election cycles, the forms of media young people employ, how they go about getting their "news," and so on), we should nevertheless engage this presumed linkage between satire and cynicism directly.

A 2006 scholarly study drew big headlines and wide circulation in the popular press by supposedly proving a *"Daily Show* Effect" (as it was titled). The authors conducted an experiment on college students by subjecting them to clips of *The Daily Show* that dealt with the 2004 presidential election. The study concluded that their subjects were likely to rate the candidates for office more negatively as a result of watching *TDS*, and that the students exhibited "more cynicism toward the electoral system and the news media at large" as a result. The authors drew conclusions from their numbers by arguing that *"The Daily Show* may have more detrimental effects, driving down support for political institutions and leaders among those already inclined toward nonparticipation."[36] Another study by Dannagal Young, however, claims to have demonstrated just the opposite through similar measurements—not only is exposure to *TDS "not* exerting a *negative* impact on healthy democratic behaviors and characteristics, but that audiences of these programs are often *more* participatory, efficacious, and engaged in politics than people who don't watch [the show]."[37]

Looking beyond effects studies to rhetorical criticism, Roderick Hart and Johanna Hartelius made a splash in scholarly circles in 2007 by proclaiming Jon Stewart a "heretic" of democracy for his "unbridled political cynicism." Stewart was found guilty of "leading the Children of Democracy astray" by planting in them "a false knowledge [and] a trendy awareness that turns them into bawdy villains and wastrels."[38] The authors argue, "cynicism is a language, not a feeling state," and that "like any language, cynicism is taught, practiced, and perfected." They note further, "cynicism involves an athletic depiction of human frailty and institutional corruption and an artful delineation of mass unhappiness"[39] (Shakespeare anyone?). Stewart then, as youthful and hip progenitor of such a language and nightly creator of such depictions, is seen as the master cynic. To support their

charges, they claim to uncover the "essential nature of cynicism" by returning to the Greeks. From there they highlight two rhetorical tropes found in
classical Cyncism (diatribe and *chreia*) that Stewart seemingly employs, and
voilà! Stewart is a cynic, and consequently dangerous. It's difficult to know
where to begin with such a hysterical screed, especially since the authors
don't examine actual *Daily Show* audiences to prove their point of cynical
effects (leading children astray) and hardly examine Stewart's television
broadcasts to demonstrate that he and his rhetoric are cynical, depending
instead on Stewart's *book* as evidence most of the time.[40]

Perhaps it is best to refer to others who have also studied the ancient
Greek and arrived at opposite conclusions. Philosopher Simon Crichtley
examines the Cynic Diogenes, but argues instead that:

> [Cynicism is] actually not at all cynical in the modern sense of the word. It
> bears no real resemblance to that attitude of negativity and jaded scornfulness
> that sees the worst of intentions behind the apparent good motives of others.
> True cynicism is not a debasement of others but a debasement of oneself—and
> in that purposeful self-debasement, a protest against corruption, luxury and
> insincerity.[41]

He maintains that cynicism has a place in contemporary attitudes toward
politics, primarily because of what it is an objection to—the "boundless
self-interest, corruption, lazy cronyism and greed" from which we are trying
to rid ourselves as a polity. The reason why cynicism is merited is because
it is "basically a moral protest against hypocrisy and cant in politics and
excess and thoughtless self-indulgence in the conduct of life."[42]

Peter Sloterdijk's voluminous history of cynicism leaves him also with
the conclusion that we live in cynical times. But he more helpfully contrasts a proactive or offensive cynicism ("morose, resigned, apathetic")
with a "kynicism" that "invokes the power of laughing and parodic/
satiric ridicule" as a defense mechanism."[43] Sloterdijk maintains that
cognitive kynicism is a *"form of dealing with knowledge,* a form of relativ-
ization, ironic treatment, application, and sublation"[44] that, as Jonathan
Gray argues,

> represents an "urge of individuals to maintain themselves as fully rational
> living beings against the distortions and semirationalities of their societies."
> . . . Where cynics have lost faith in the existence of truth, and where their
> cynicism serves as a reaction to this loss of faith, kynics hold on to a notion
> of truth, but since they see it being perverted all around them, their kyni-
> cism and laughing ridicule serves as a defense and an offense to this state
> of affairs."[45]

Certainly any honest assessment of the political and economic events and
context of the 2000s reveals the distortions and semirationalities that per-

vaded both the Bush administration and Wall Street, while an American society desperately sought truth amongst such fabrications from a news media that was of little help. Furthermore, truth was easily perverted by political and media agents engaged in what our satirists have playfully identified as "truthiness." In response to these conditions, Jon Stewart has repeatedly said that his show is simply a means through which he and his writers use satiric and parodic ridicule as a therapeutic endeavor, a means of staying sane.[46]

Gray employs Sloterdijk's conclusions to address again the context from which the satiric response emerges:

> We could paraphrase Sloterdijk's criticism of the modern age as being concerned with complicity. Almost all forms of knowledge are bound up with undesirable discourses of power that are themselves in need of criticism, a situation that inspires the widespread cynicism that we see today. However, Sloterdijk sees kynicism as a viable response precisely because its laughing nature and eagerness not to take itself so seriously succeeds in partially sidestepping the dangers of complicity."[47]

The Daily Show is nothing if not a nightly criticism of discourses of power and an attack on the complicity of news media in constructing and circulating such discourses. Given this context, it is wholly rational that individuals might hold cynical attitudes and emotions, or even engage in cynical behaviors as a response to how the political world is constituted. Yet Barack Obama was able to win the presidency in 2008 partly on a message of *hope*, while Stewart placed fourth in a 2007 Pew Research Center poll asking Americans to name the *journalist* they most admired and trusted.[48] What Stewart's satire and humorous criticisms offer, then, is not cynicism, but just the opposite—a firm insistence that politics and the conduct of public life need not be this way.

What this discussion demonstrates is how Hart and Hartelius have largely divorced their analysis from contemporary politics. Instead, what these authors are ultimately interested in is a critique of popular culture, and television in particular—a rehashed and warmed-over version of Hart's polemic against television from a decade earlier.[49] The following hyperventilated paragraph demonstrates this line of attack perfectly:

> Stewart is also very, very popular. That is part of our charge against him. Jon Stewart makes cynicism attractive; indeed, he makes it profitable. Each night, he saps his audience's sense of political possibility even as he helps AT&T sell its wares. Stewart urges them to steer clear of conventional politics and to do so while steering a Nissan. Mr. Stewart is *especially attractive to young people*, so his website offers them portable cynicism in the form of CDs, DVDs, clothes,

books, and collectibles. Stewart knows there's money to be made in cynicism.[50]

It would be hard to imagine a more *cynical* set of conjectures than this, although Lance Bennett rightly claims that "there are few purveyors of public knowledge today more cynical than the press."[51] But let us turn to Stewart himself (and even Obama) for one example of why studying contemporary politics provides a better means for assessing and understanding contemporary cynicism than a focus on the popularity of a television comedian and his youthful audience.

I can't think of a better example than *The Daily Show*'s March 18, 2008 broadcast, the day that Barack Obama, speaking still as a contender for the Democratic Party's nomination, gave his famous speech on "Race in America" in Philadelphia. After weeks of being linked to his inflammatory former pastor and the charges of racism and anti-Americanism that circled around the Reverend Jeremiah Wright, Obama sought not only to distance himself from Wright, but frankly and honestly address why African Americans *and* Caucasians had legitimate reasons for their conflicted and conflicting feelings about race. As the day's top story, Stewart began with a five-and-a-half-minute segment on the speech, filled with his typical mix of news and humorous observations. But in closing the segment, he showed one last extended clip from the speech. The future president noted America's choices in the starkest of terms: "We can tackle race only as spectacle, as we did in the O. J. [Simpson] trial; or in the wake of tragedy, as we did in the aftermath of [Hurricane] Katrina; or as fodder for the nightly news. We can play Reverend Wright's sermons on every channel every day and talk about them from now until the election. We can pounce on some gaffe by a Hillary [Clinton] supporter as evidence that she's playing the race card. Or, at this moment, in this election, we can come together and say, 'not this time.'" Stewart, looking straight into the camera, says seriously and simply, "And so, at 11:00 A.M. on a Tuesday, a prominent politician spoke to Americans about race as though they were adults."

Both Stewart's observation and Obama's speech clearly capture the darker nature of contemporary political life. Obama calls out the societal agents that can so easily dispirit the citizenry through their cynically treating such important issues as race (and the feelings that surround them) as weapons for political gain, spectacle for continued divisiveness, and fodder for television ratings. Stewart takes it one step further, distilling the observation to its core—adults are capable of having an honest conversation on such matters, if only others (such as politicians, pundits, and news media) would stop treating citizens as dupes and simpletons in their own cynical games. This earnest and honest observation is perhaps one important reason young people seem so attracted to Obama and Stewart—here are two individuals who refuse such cynical ploys and insist that we not only act like adults, but treat each other (including young people) as such in the process.

Which returns us to the question of whether satire is a form of generational language. What we have seen throughout this book, but also encompassing the discussions here about satire as a kynical defense mechanism, is that satire and political humor have become the means for "relief in hard times," especially given the political context of two successive baby-boomer presidencies (Clinton and Bush) and their questionable relationships to truth.[52] Yet, as Sloterdijk notes, "despite all apparent lack of respect, the kynic assumes a basically serious and upright attitude toward truth and maintains a thoroughly solemn relation, satirically disguised, to it."[53] Satiric language, then, is perhaps just that: a clever disguise of the earnestness, sincerity, and hope young people may feel that truth and the common good have not been completely obliterated by the cynical machinations of those who wield power, including the discourses of power that construct such Kafkaesque realities. Satire is a biting attack, and as such, automatically thwarts any charges that young people are overly idealistic and naïve (as opposed to their baby-boomer parents, who actually embraced such idealism in its rawest and most nondistilled forms; idealism was their language). Satire may indeed be a new generational language simply by its existence and usage in opposition to that. But then again, perhaps its ultimate power, as Sloterdijk notes, is that "respectable thinking does not know how to deal with" it.[54]

CONCLUSIONS

The discussion here of new political television's expanding and contested boundaries suggests why this television genre is important. As opposed to the seemingly sealed world of news and public affairs programming, new political television is a location of political engagement where people want to see themselves and their fellow citizens represented, including the varied viewpoints such representation would inevitably bring. New political television has also become a resource for alternative forms of discourse about politics that is increasingly used and deployed in ever expanding ways across the Internet. Finally, it has become a way of talking about politics in a language that sits outside discourses of power, perhaps even inspiring a language through which younger generations can express their own civic hopes for a democratic future more inspiring than the one they've recently endured but not quite grown accustomed to.

In earlier chapters, we explored the expanding boundaries of the genre as an alternative form of reporting and reflecting on news. From Michael Moore to Jon Stewart and Stephen Colbert, fake news is often "real" and "news," just with a different label. Furthermore, it provides a way of talking about politics and issues in ways rarely found on television. New political television programming has also expanded the targets of popular critique from politics and media to the interrelationship between the two. It has explored the gaps in knowledge and truth that appear as a result of those relationships, as well as the willed truthiness that can come from such symbiosis. Michael Moore's programs, in particular, demonstrate the productive potential of satire to highlight political issues not raised within mainstream television, while offering options for an alternative politics. Finally, new political television has expanded the boundaries of critical media literacy by casting a spotlight on the news media and its techniques for constructing truth and reality, again something rarely found elsewhere on television.

The evidence presented here on this genre's relationship to public knowledge, civic engagement, and anti-cynicism may not placate the critics of political entertainment television who often seem to conjure myths of the genre into being, seemingly for their own interests and purposes, and often irrespective of data. But as long as new political television continues to do what it is doing, it will ultimately prove such naysaying wrong simply by being the resource for citizenship that it has already become.

Appendix

Methodology for Audience Research

VIEWER MAIL

The staff of *Politically Incorrect* granted me access to all letters sent to the program since its move to ABC. Hence, I examined letters dating from February 1997 through March 2000 (the month I visited their studios). I scanned through almost all of the letters, selecting and photocopying ones that I felt were representative of the various types of viewer response the show received. I photocopied approximately 95 pieces of mail for in-depth analysis.

INTERVIEWS

Interviews with viewers were conducted on these dates at these locations: KTRK, Houston (6/18/99); WMAR, Baltimore (10/15/99); WSB, Atlanta (11/20/99); and CBS Television City (studios for *Politically Incorrect*), Los Angeles (3/21–22/00). In Houston, Baltimore, and Atlanta, the interview subjects were auditioning to be a "citizen panelist" on *PI*. In Los Angeles, interviewees were queued outside *PI*'s studio to watch a taping of the program.

Interview subjects were asked some or all of the following questions:

1. Do you watch the program? If so, how often?
2. [If program is on too late in the evening] Do you tape the program to watch the following day?
3. Do you enjoy the program? Why?
4. Who in your family watches the show besides yourself?

5. Does the show lead to political discussions or arguments with others who watch in your family?
6. Do you discuss the show with friends or coworkers?
7. Is this an entertaining show? How so?
8. Is this an informative show? How so?
9. What do you think about the guests that appear on the program?
10. Do you watch based on who is appearing that evening?
11. Are there particular guests who frequently appear that you really like/dislike? Why?
12. Does it bother you that few of the guests are political "experts"? What do you think about celebrities discussing politics?
13. What is your opinion of Bill Maher as a host?
14. Do you talk back to the television set during the program?
15. Do you ever get mad or frustrated enough with the show to turn it off? Why?
16. Do you think this program is good or bad for American democracy?
17. Do you listen to talk radio?
18. Do you read a daily newspaper? Do you read letters to the editor?
19. Do you watch pundit/Sunday morning talk shows? Why? How do they compare with *PI*?
20. Do you participate in political discussion sites or groups on the Internet?
21. How would you characterize your current attitudes toward politics (in general)?
22. Do you identify with a single political party? Which one?

ONLINE DISCUSSIONS

Postings to the Usenet News site (now managed by Google Groups) dedicated to *PI*, alt.tv.pol-incorrect, were examined for the following months. Listed are the number of postings that occurred during that period, as well as the major event (if any) that corresponded with that period:

February 1–March 1, 1997: Newsgroup is formed; Program moves to ABC network.
20 postings.

February 1–March 1, 1998: News of the Clinton-Lewinsky affair surfaces in the media.
329 postings.

August 1–September 1, 1998: Clinton admits affair and testifies before a grand jury.
337 postings.

February 1–March 1, 1999: [No major events of note]
2,870 postings.

February 1–March 1, 2000: Presidential primaries.
1,510 postings.

February 1–March 1, 2001: Bush inauguration two weeks earlier; contested election results.
2,900 postings.

September 11–October 11, 2001: Terrorist attacks; Maher makes "controversial" comments.
7,840 postings.

February 1–March 30, 2002: Announcement made of show's imminent cancellation.
3,900 postings.

February 1–March 1, 2003: *Real Time with Bill Maher* premiers on HBO.
1,030 postings.

Between February 1, 1997, and February 1, 2004, the newsgroup received approximately 98,000 postings. ABC began hosting a similar discussion forum on its website dedicated to *PI* in 2000, but no data was collected from that forum (which has since been removed).

Notes

CHAPTER 1

1. Steve Linstead, "'Jokers Wild': Humor in Organisational Culture," in *Humor in Society: Resistance and Control*, eds. Chris Powell and George E. C. Paton (New York: St. Martin's Press, 1988).
2. Although it is difficult to measure the effect of the Fey parodies on voter perception of the candidate (segregating them, as one must, from other negative news coverage), there certainly existed a correlation between the satirical impressions and Palin's declining favorable poll numbers. One survey did make claims on effects, reporting that two thirds of voters saw the *SNL* parodies and that "10 percent said the program had an influence on their vote." See Josh Kurtz, J. "Voters Mad but Hopeful in Roll Call Survey," *Roll Call*, 10 November 2008, http://www.rollcall.com/issues/54_55/politics/30001-1.html.
3. Vlada Gelman, "'The View' Finishes Ahead of Daytime Pack," *TV Week* (November 13, 2008); Robert Seidman, "Sarah Palin Delivers Highest 'Saturday Night Live' Ratings Since 1994," *TVbyTheNumbers.com*, 19 October 2008, http://tvbythenumbers.com/2008/10/19/sarah-palin-delivers-highest-saturday-night-live-ratings-since-1994/6500.
4. For studies of the role that popular culture has played in recent presidential elections, see Jeffrey P. Jones, "Pop Goes the Campaign: The Repopularization of Politics in Election 2008," in *The 2008 Presidential Campaign: A Communication Perspective*, ed. Robert E. Denton, Jr. (Lanham, MD: Rowman and Littlefield Publishers, 2009), 170–90; Jeffrey P. Jones, "The Shadow Campaign in Popular Culture," in *The 2004 Presidential Campaign: A Communication Perspective*, ed. Robert E. Denton, Jr. (Lanham, MD: Rowman and Littlefield, 2005), 195–216.

5. See Jeffrey P. Jones, "Believable Fictions: Redactional Culture and the Will to Truthiness," in *The Changing Faces of Journalism: Tabloidization, Technology and Truthiness*, ed. Barbie Zelizer (New York: Routledge, 2009), 127–43.

6. For a historical recounting and analysis of the relationship of entertainment television and politics, see Jonathan Gray, Jeffrey P. Jones, and Ethan Thompson, "The State of Satire, the Satire of State," in *Satire TV: Politics and Comedy in the Post-Network Era*, eds. Jonathan Gray, Jeffrey P. Jones, and Ethan Thompson (New York: NYU Press, 2009), 3–36. For a discussion of post-network television, see Amanda Lotz, *The Television Will Be Revolutionized* (New York: NYU Press, 2008).

7. Leslie Phillips, "BCP-TV: Bush, Clinton, Perot," *USA Today*, 5 June 1992, 7A; Ed Siegel, "Playing the Softball Alternative," *Boston Globe*, 7 October 1992, 17.

8. When queried why he wouldn't talk to reporters during the campaign, candidate Bill Clinton responded, "You know why I can stiff you on the press conferences? Because Larry King liberated me by giving me to the American people directly." Quoted in John Thornton Caldwell, *Televisuality: Style, Crisis, and Authority in American Television* (New Brunswick, NJ: Rutgers University Press, 1995), 256. King's subsequent book on the election lists candidate appearances not only for his program, but also for others within the genre during the 1992 election. See Larry King, with Mark Stencel, *On the Line: The New Road to the White House* (New York: Harcourt Brace and Company, 1993).

9. For MTV, see Geoffrey Baym, "Emerging Models of Journalistic Authority in MTV's Coverage of the 2004 U.S. Presidential Election" *Journalism Studies*, 8 no. 3 (2007): 382–96. For Court TV, see Marjorie Cohn and David Dow, *Cameras in the Courtroom: Television and the Pursuit of Justice* (Lanham, MD: Rowman and Littlefield, 2002), 124–35. For HBO, see Jeffrey P. Jones, "Comedy Talk Shows," in *The Essential HBO Reader*, eds. Gary R. Edgerton and Jeffrey P. Jones (Lexington: University Press of Kentucky, 2008), 172–82. For Bravo, see chapter 7 of this book.

10. *Politically Incorrect* was a twist within the genre of talk television in general. It differed from the traditional political talk show by offering a comedian as host/star of the show, by offering a comedic monologue composed primarily of political jokes, and by featuring guests who are not "experts" or insiders to talk about politics. It altered the late-night variety/interview show by focusing on serious political issues—something the other shows largely avoid—in a discursively conflictual but also entertaining manner. And it altered the daytime talk show format by dealing with social issues in specifically political ways, in offering guests the opportunity to talk to each other without having to talk through the host or to invited "experts," but reducing the role of the studio audience to observers.

11. See the first edition of this book for a detailed history and analysis of *Politically Incorrect*. Jeffrey P. Jones, *Entertaining Politics: New Political Television and Civic Culture* (Lanham, MD: Rowman and Littlefield, 2005).

12. Ethan Thompson, "Good Demo, Bad Taste: South Park as Carnivalesque Satire," in *Satire TV: Politics and Comedy in the Post-Network Era*, eds. Jonathan Gray, Jeffrey P. Jones, and Ethan Thompson (New York: NYU Press, 2009),

213–32. See also Brian C. Anderson, *South Park Conservatives: The Revolt Against Liberal Media Bias* (Washington: Regnery, 2005).

13. For both Bush programs, see Jeffrey P. Jones, "With All Due Respect: Satirizing Presidents from *Saturday Night Live* to *Lil' Bush,*" in *Satire TV: Politics and Comedy in the Post-Network Era*, eds. Jonathan Gray, Jeffrey P. Jones, and Ethan Thompson (New York: NYU Press, 2009), 37–63.

14. For a discussion of each of these shows, see Jones, "Comedy Talk Shows."

15. Jill Abramson, "Hyperreality TV: Political Fact Meets HBO Fiction," *New York Times*, 24 August 2003, AL1, 8.

16. Marc Andrejevic, "Faking Democracy: Reality Television Politics on *American Candidate*," in *Politicotainment: Television's Take on the Real*, ed. Kristina Riegert (New York: Peter Lang, 2007), 83–107.

17. Carina Chocano, "Turn on, Tune in . . . Then Go Vote," *Los Angeles Times*, 23 May 2004, E1.

18. The programs, respectively, are *24, Alias, The Agency, The X-Files, The West Wing, First Monday, The Court, Spin City, JAG, AFP: American Fighter Pilot*, and *The American Embassy*. Institutional branches of government, it seems, have finally become a programming subgenre similar to police, legal, and hospital dramas. See James Poniewozik, "The New Capitol Gang," *Time Magazine*, 1 April 2002, 64.

19. Peter C. Rollins and John E. O'Conner (eds.), *The West Wing: The American Presidency as Television Drama* (Syracuse, NY: Syracuse University Press, 2003); Trevor Parry-Giles and Shawn J. Parry-Giles, *The Prime-Time Presidency: The West Wing and U.S. Nationalism* (Urbana-Champagne: University of Illinois Press, 2006).

20. Brian Stelter, "Following the Script: Obama, McCain and 'The West Wing,'" *New York Times*, 30 October 2008.

21. Timothy Dunn, "Torture, Terrorism, and *24*: What Would Jack Bauer Do?" in *Homer Simpson Goes to Washington: American Politics through Popular Culture*, ed. Joseph J. Foy (Lexington: The University Press of Kentucky, 2008), 171–84.

22. Jones, "With All Due Respect."

23. Chris Smith and Ben Voth, "The Role of Humor in Political Argument: How 'Strategery' and 'Lockboxes' Changed a Political Campaign," *Argumentation and Advocacy* 39, 2002. We should note, however, that as with the 2008 election, the 2000 race included no incumbent candidate and two competitive party contests. The ability for satire to help "write" the candidate, therefore, is much greater under such circumstances.

24. http://www.cmpa.com/media_room_comedy_12_29_08.htm.

25. Jay Carson, spokesperson for Senator Hillary Clinton, summarized why he encouraged such appearances on entertainment talk shows: "The interviews are usually very issue-oriented and not process-focused, and it's an important way to reach a lot of voters who may not be watching the Sunday shows every Sunday." Julie Bosman, "Sex? Yawn. Politics? That's Hot!" *New York Times*, 8 May 2008, G1.

26. For a full recounting of the Letterman-McCain brouhaha, see Jones, "Pop Goes the Campaign," 178–79.

27. Mark Jurkowitz, "Manhunt Gets Prime-Time Priority on Crime Program," *Boston Globe*, 13 October 2001, A11.

28. Katherine Q. Seelye, "TV Drama, Pentagon-style: A Fictional Terror Tribunal," *New York Times*, 31 March 2002, A12.

29. Barbara Slavin, "Sex, Politics, but No Rock 'N' Roll: Powell Talks Openly with World Youth," *USA Today*, 15 February 2001, 10B.

30. Darel Jevens, "Dave Goes Digital by Accident," *Chicago Sun Times*, 4 March 2007, D1.

31. Henry Jenkins, *Convergence Culture: Where Old and New Media Collide* (New York: NYU Press, 2007).

32. Robert Putnam, *Bowling Alone: The Collapse and Revival of American Community* (New York: Simon and Schuster, 2000).

33. Neil Postman, *Amusing Ourselves to Death: Public Discourse in the Age of Show Business* (New York: Penguin Books, 1984).

34. Roderick P. Hart, *Seducing America: How Television Charms the Modern Voter* (New York: Oxford University Press, 1994); for a more recent version with similar overtones, see Roderick P. Hart and E. Johanna Hartelius, "The Political Sins of Jon Stewart," *Critical Studies in Media Communication* 24, no. 3 (2007): 263–72.

35. Neil Postman treats the phenomena as relatively new and the direct product of television. He uses the Lincoln-Douglas debates to argue that citizens had attention spans that allowed them to attentively listen to the minutiae of politics for hours and days on end (as compared to today's culture shaped by television). See Postman, *Amusing Ourselves to Death*, 44–49. Michael Schudson, however, correctly points to the civic culture of mid-nineteenth-century America that treated such debates as entertainment. See Michael Schudson, *The Good Citizen: A History of American Civic Life* (New York: The Free Press, 1998), 136–37. See also Charles Schutz, *Political Humor: From Aristophanes to Sam Ervin* (Rutherford, NJ: Fairleigh Dickinson University Press, 1977), who argues that politics is drama, and hence is part of show business.

36. John Street, *Politics and Popular Culture* (Philadelphia: Temple University Press, 1997).

37. Or when they do, it is survey data such as number of viewing hours, number of television screens per household, channel surfing habits, viewing habits, and so on. In short, they don't speak with viewers to see what the medium actually means to them.

38. Thomas E. Patterson, *Out of Order* (New York: Alfred Knopf, 1993).

39. A possible exception being the critical praise and scholarly attention to *The West Wing*.

40. Hart and Hartelius, "The Political Sins"; Jody Baumgartner and Jonathan S. Morris, "*The Daily Show* Effect: Candidate Evaluations, Efficacy, and American Youth," *American Politics Research* 34, no. 3 (2006): 341–67; Michael Kalin, "Why Jon Stewart Isn't Funny," *Boston Globe*, 3 March 2006.

41. Geoffrey Baym, "*The Daily Show*: Discursive Integration and the Reinvention of Political Journalism," *Political Communication* 22, no. 3 (2005): 259–76.

42. Jonathan Gray, "Real (and) Funny: Animated TV Comedy's Political Voice" (paper presented at the annual meeting of the International Communication Association, Montreal, Canada, 22–26 May 2008).

43. Gray, Jones, and Thompson (eds.), *Satire TV*, 18.

CHAPTER 2

1. Roderick P. Hart, *Seducing America: How Television Charms the Modern Voter* (New York: Oxford University Press, 1994); Matthew Robert Kerbel, *Remote and Controlled: Media Politics in a Cynical Age*, 2d ed. (Boulder, CO: Westview Press, 1999); Jeffrey Scheuer, *The Sound Bite Society: Television and the American Mind* (New York: Four Walls Eight Windows, 1999); Neil Postman, *Amusing Ourselves to Death: Public Discourse in the Age of Show Business* (New York: Penguin Books, 1984), 44–9; Neil Gabler, *Life: The Movie: How Entertainment Conquered Reality* (New York: Knopf, 1998).

2. Robert D. Putnam, "Tuning In, Tuning Out: The Strange Disappearance of Social Capital in America," *PS: Political Science & Politics* (December 1995): 677; Robert D. Putnam, *Bowling Alone: The Collapse and Revival of American Community* (New York: Simon and Schuster, 2000).

3. Putnam, *Bowling Alone*, 246. Emphasis added.

4. His use of the analogy to a crime is even more stark in the 1995 journal article: "I have discovered only one prominent suspect against whom circumstantial evidence can be mounted. . . . This is not the occasion to lay out the full case for the prosecution, nor to review rebuttal evidence for the defense. However, I want to illustrate the sort of evidence that justifies indictment. The culprit is television" (Putnam, "Tuning In, Tuning Out," 677).

5. Pippa Norris, *The Virtuous Circle: Political Communications in Post-industrial Societies* (Cambridge: Cambridge University Press, 2000). See also Norris, "The Impact of Television on Civic Malaise," in *Disaffected Democracies: What's Troubling the Trilateral Countries*, ed. Susan J. Pharr and Robert D. Putnam (Princeton, NJ: Princeton University Press, 2000), 231–51. Here Norris contends that it matters what you watch and how much you watch.

6. Doris A. Graber, *Processing Politics: Learning from Television in the Internet Age* (Chicago: University of Chicago Press, 2001).

7. Michael Schudson, *The Good Citizen: A History of American Civic Life* (New York: The Free Press, 1998), 136–37.

8. Henry Jenkins, "'Geeking Out' for Democracy (Part One)," Confessions of an Aca-Fan Blog, posted May 1, 2009, http://henryjenkins.org (accessed May 1, 2009).

9. Jay G. Blumler and Michael Gurevitch, "Rethinking the Study of Political Communication," in *Mass Media and Society*, 3d ed., ed. James Curran and Michael Gurevitch (New York: Oxford University Press, 2000), 166; Lawrence Grossberg, *We Gotta Get Out of This Place: Popular Conservatism and Postmodern Culture* (New York: Routledge, 1992), 15.

10. Hermann Bausinger, "Media, Technology and Daily Life," *Media, Culture and Society* 6 (1984): 343–51.

11. James W. Carey, *Communication as Culture: Essays on Media and Society* (Boston: Unwin Hyman, 1989).

12. Peter Dahlgren, "The Transformation of Democracy?" in *New Media and Politics*, ed. Barrie Axford and Richard Huggins (London: Sage, 2001), 85.

13. Dahlgren, "The Transformation of Democracy?" 85.

14. John Street, *Politics & Popular Culture* (Philadelphia: Temple University Press, 1997), 60.

15. Street, *Politics & Popular Culture*, 21.

16. Street, *Politics & Popular Culture*, 57–58.

17. Kevin Barnhurst, "Politics in the Fine Meshes: Young Citizens, Power and Media," *Media Culture & Society* 20 (1998): 212.

18. Schudson, *Good Citizen*, 197.

19. Schudson, *Good Citizen*, 9.

20. Schudson, *Good Citizen*, 310–11.

21. Bausinger, "Media, Technology, and Daily Life"; James Lull, ed., *World Families Watch Television* (Newbury Park, CA: Sage, 1988); Roger Silverstone and Eric Hirsch, eds., *Consuming Technologies: Media and Information in Domestic Spaces* (New York: Routledge, 1992); Roger Silverstone, *Television and Everyday Life* (New York: Routledge, 1994); Shaun Moores, *Satellite Television and Everyday Life: Articulating Technology* (London: University of Luton Press, 1996).

22. This summary is provided by Ian Ang, "The Nature of the Audience," in *Questioning the Media: A Critical Introduction*, ed. John Downing, Ali Mohammadi, and Annabelle Sreberny-Mohammadi (Thousand Oaks, CA: Sage, 1995), 217.

23. The term "lifestyle politics" has also been used but is often a part of the larger conception of postmodern political practice. See Peter Dahlgren, "Media, Citizenship and Civic Culture," in *Mass Media and Society*, ed. Curran and Gurevitch, 310–28; John Gibbons and Bo Reimer, *The Politics of Postmodernity* (London: Sage, 1999); Barrie Axford, "The Transformation of Politics or Anti-Politics," in *New Media and Politics*, ed. Axford and Huggins, 22–25.

24. Dahlgren, "Media, Citizenship," 312.

25. Dahlgren, "Media, Citizenship," 318.

26. Margaret Scammell, "Citizen Consumers: Towards a New Marketing of Politics?" in *Media and the Restyling of Politics*, ed. John Corner and Dick Pels (London: Sage, 2003), 117–36.

27. Dahlgren, "Media, Citizenship," 312.

28. Gibbins and Reimer, *Politics of Postmodernity*, 113. Original emphasis.

29. Blumler and Gurevitch, "Rethinking," 163–4.

30. Blumler and Gurevitch, "Rethinking," 162.

31. Blumler and Gurevitch, "Rethinking," 167.

32. Barnhurst, "Fine Meshes," 201–18.

33. Barnhurst, "Fine Meshes," 216.

34. Barnhurst, "Fine Meshes," 216.

35. Barnhurst, "Fine Meshes," 216.

36. Barnhurst, "Fine Meshes," 209.

37. Michael X. Delli Carpini and Bruce A. Williams, "Constructing Public Opinion: The Uses of Fictional and Nonfictional Television in Conversations about the Environment," in *The Psychology of Political Communication*, ed. Ann N. Crigler (Ann Arbor: University of Michigan Press, 1996), 160.

38. Delli Carpini and Williams, "Constructing Public Opinion," 161–62.

39. Delli Carpini and Williams, "Constructing Public Opinion," 153.

40. Delli Carpini and Williams, "Constructing Public Opinion," 173.

41. Ron Lembo, *Thinking through Television* (Cambridge, UK: Cambridge University Press, 2000), 113.

42. Lembo, *Thinking through Television*, 111–12.

43. Lembo, *Thinking through Television*, 170.

44. Lembo, *Thinking through Television*, 190–91.

45. Lembo, *Thinking through Television*, 169.

46. Lembo, *Thinking through Television*, 234.

47. David Thelen, *Becoming Citizens in the Age of Television* (Chicago: University of Chicago Press, 1996).

48. Thelen, *Becoming Citizens*, 5.

49. Thelen reports that more than one-quarter of all letters sent to Congressman Lee Hamilton were signed by both a husband and a wife. Thelen, *Becoming Citizens*, 102.

50. Thelen, *Becoming Citizens*, 47.

51. Thelen, *Becoming Citizens*, 105.

52. Thelen, *Becoming Citizens*, 23.

53. Thelen, *Becoming Citizens*, 67.

54. Thelen, *Becoming Citizens*, 75–77.

55. Thelen, *Becoming Citizens*, 9.

56. Sonia Livingstone and Peter Lunt, *Talk on Television: Audience Participation and Public Debate* (London: Routledge, 1994), 29.

57. Thelen, *Becoming Citizens*, 2.

58. The military metaphor is Thelen's as he describes how citizens moved from "the dismissive role of monitor to the activist role of citizen-soldier." Thelen, *Becoming Citizens*, 46.

59. Jerome Bruner, *Acts of Meaning* (Cambridge, MA: Harvard University Press, 1990), 34. Emphasis added.

60. Bruner, *Acts of Meaning*, 95.

61. Bruner uses the term "folk psychology," although he allows for the more common term "common sense." Bruner, *Acts of Meaning*, 34–35. See also Antonio Gramsci, *An Antonio Gramsci Reader*, ed. David Forgacs (New York: Schocken Books, 1988); Clifford Geertz, "Common Sense as a Cultural System," *Antioch Review* 33 (Spring): 5–26; Michael Billig and Jose M. Sabucedo, "The Rhetorical and Ideological Dimensions of Common Sense," in *The Status of Common Sense in Psychology*, ed. Jurg Siegfried (Norwood, NJ: Ablex Publishing, 1994); Serge Moscovici, "The Phenomenon of Social Representations," in *Social Representations*, ed. R. M. Farr and Serge Moscovici (Cambridge: Cambridge University Press, 1984); Jeffrey P. Jones, "Rethinking Hegemonic Common Sense in Media Studies," in *Creating Sense: Texts and*

Realities, ed. Desmond Allison (Singapore: National University of Singapore, 1999), 61–82.

62. Horace Newcomb and Paul M. Hirsch, "Television as a Cultural Forum," in *Television: The Critical View*, 4th ed., ed. Horace Newcomb (New York: Oxford University Press, 1987).

63. Geertz, "Common Sense," 8.

64. Bruner, *Acts of Meaning*, 35.

65. Bruner, *Acts of Meaning*, 42. Geertz, too, argues that common sense cannot be found "by cataloguing its content, which is widely heterogeneous. . . . One cannot do so, either, by sketching out some logical structure it always takes, for there is none. And one cannot do so by summing up the substantive conclusions it always draws, for there are, too, none of those" (Geertz, "Common Sense," 25). Instead, he suggests we look to the "tone," "temper," and "style" of common sense if we wish to uncover it.

66. Bruner, *Acts of Meaning*, 35.

67. For instance, audiences who were shown both a news report and a docudrama about the effects of toxic pollution on children were equally moved and convinced enough to foreground concerns about children in their discussions, despite the potentially fictional aspects of the docudrama. Delli Carpini and Williams, "Constructing Public Opinion," 166.

68. Hegemony theory recognizes the spaces for contestation and opposition, of course. But again, the point here is not capitalist dominance but the ways that pluralist thinking occurs within the limitations of liberal capitalist societies.

69. Bruner, *Acts of Meaning*, 95.

70. John Ellis, "Television as Working Through," in *Television and Common Knowledge*, ed. Jostein Gripsrud (London: Routledge, 1999), 55.

71. Ellis, "Working Through," 55.

72. Newcomb and Hirsch, "Television as a Cultural Forum," 459.

73. Newcomb and Hirsch go on to say, in an important caveat, that television "is an effective pluralistic forum only insofar as American political pluralism is or can be." Newcomb and Hirsch, "Television as a Cultural Forum," 461.

74. Michael Billig, Susan Condor, Derek Edwards, Mike Gane, David Middleton, and Alan Radley, *Ideological Dilemmas: A Social Psychology of Everyday Thinking* (London: Sage, 1988); Michael Billig, *Ideology and Opinions: Studies in Rhetorical Psychology* (London: Sage, 1991); Billig and Sabucedo, "Rhetorical and Ideological Dimensions."

75. Billig, *Ideology and Opinions*, 71.

76. Ellis, "Working Through," 57–58.

77. Livingstone and Lunt, *Talk on Television*; Paolo Carpignano, Robin Anderson, Stanley Aronowitz, and William DiFazio, "Chatter in the Age of Electronic Reproduction: Talk Television and the 'Public Mind,'" in *The Phantom Public Sphere*, ed. Bruce Robbins (Minneapolis: University of Minnesota Press, 1993).

78. Carpignano et al., "Chatter," 96.

79. Thelen, *Becoming Citizens*, 13–14. Thelen reports that "between 1934 and 1981 the number of communications to Congress rose from an estimated 6 to 9 million pieces in the first Roosevelt Congress to an estimated 92.5 million pieces in the first Reagan Congress. Congress received, on average, a com-

munication from 5 percent of all Americans in 1934 and from 25 percent of Americans in 1981." Thelen, *Becoming Citizens*, 23. See also Roderick P. Hart, "Citizen Discourse and Political Participation: A Survey," in *Mediated Politics: Communication in the Future of Democracy*, ed. W. Lance Bennett and Robert M. Entman (Cambridge: Cambridge University Press, 2001), 407–32.

80. Carpignano et al., "Chatter," 119. For me, this is a declaration that is quite similar to arguments made by Carey and Dewey. See Carey, *Communication as Culture*, and John Dewey, *The Public and Its Problems* (Athens: Ohio University Press, 1954).

81. Street, *Politics & Popular Culture*, 9. See also Grossberg, *We Gotta Get Out of This Place*; Simon Frith, *Music for Pleasure* (Cambridge, MA: Polity Press, 1988), 123.

82. Bruner, *Acts of Meaning*, 52.

83. Dahlgren, "Media, Citizenship," 323.

CHAPTER 3

1. See Michael Schudson's argument about periods of civic culture in American history, including the Informed Citizen model that grew out of the Progressive Era reforms of the early twentieth century and that, in many ways, we still operate under today. Michael Schudson, *The Good Citizen: A History of American Civic Life* (New York: The Free Press, 1998).

2. Eric Alterman, *Sound and Fury: The Making of the Punditocracy* (Ithaca, NY: Cornell University Press, 1999); Alan Hirsch, *Talking Heads: Political Talk Shows and Their Star Pundits* (New York: St. Martin's Press, 1991). Alterman provides an interesting discussion of the history of punditry on television dating back to Walter Lippmann's writings in newspapers. See also Bernard Timberg, *Television Talk: A History of the TV Talk Show* (Austin: University of Texas Press, 2002).

3. Indeed, Nielsen ratings for the Sunday morning talk shows suggest that more than eight million audience members still tune in to these programs. For instance, average audience ratings for the Sunday morning pundit talk shows for the 2006–2007 television season are: *Meet the Press* (3.0 million); *Face the Nation* (2.3 million); *This Week* (2.0 million); Fox News Sunday (1.0 million) (Nielsen Media Research).

4. Included in this discussion is political talk programming that appeared with the first generation of cable programming, that is, on CNN during the 1980s. Although appearing on cable, this approach to political talk was very similar to that found on public television and the networks, with only slight modifications that led to an increase in spectacle performances. It was not until the 1990s when numerous new cable channels began appearing (what I call the second generation of cable programming) that pundit political talk would be both challenged by other forms of talk and expanded upon using similar generic features.

5. Rick Ball, *Meet the Press: Fifty Years of History in the Making* (New York: McGraw-Hill, 1998).

6. Dan Nimmo and James E. Combs, *The Political Pundits* (New York: Praeger, 1992), 6.

7. Nimmo and Combs, *Political Pundits*, 8.

8. William F. Buckley Jr., *On the Firing Line* (New York: Random House, 1989).

9. Hirsch, *Talking Heads*, 13.

10. Hirsch, *Talking Heads*; Alterman, *Sound and Fury*; Nimmo and Combs, *Political Pundits*.

11. Pat Buchanan was Richard Nixon's speechwriter and also worked in the Reagan administration; John McLaughlin was personal friends with Reagan, and his wife was appointed secretary of labor by Reagan; Chris Matthews worked for Jimmy Carter; George Will was close personal friends with Ronald and Nancy Reagan, and his wife worked in the Reagan White House and was also a manager in Bob Dole's 1996 presidential bid.

12. The case of television pundit and columnist Robert Novak's "outing" of an undercover CIA agent at the behest of "unnamed" Bush administration officials in 2003 is perhaps the most glaring recent example of this.

13. Alicia Mundy, "Showtime in the Capitol," *MediaWeek* 6 (15 January 1996): 20–22.

14. Hirsch, *Talking Heads*, 181.

15. Nimmo and Combs, *Political Pundits*, 43–44.

16. As Alan Hirsch warns, because success breeds imitation, most commentators "now travel the celebrity path" and probably will not heed the warning of celebrity pundit Jack Germond: "Celebrity impinging on your ability to do your job well is a genuinely serious concern and it requires people to be damned careful." Hirsch, *Talking Heads*, 182–83.

17. As Wayne Munson asks, "Is it 'talk' or 'show'? Conversation or spectacle? Both? Neither?" in *All Talk: The Talkshow in Media Culture* (Philadelphia: Temple University Press, 1993), 15.

18. Or as Robert Dallek puts it, Reagan's "pronouncements on everything from abortion to welfare proved to be more symbolic than substantive," proving his "extraordinary mastery of public symbols that resonated so effectively with millions of Americans." His "public goals satisf(ied) psychological needs as much as material ends." Robert Dallek, *Ronald Reagan: The Politics of Symbolism* (Cambridge, MA: Harvard University Press, 1999), viii, xiv, xxiv.

19. See Allen D. Hertzke, *Echoes of Discontent: Jesse Jackson, Pat Robertson, and the Resurgence of Populism* (Washington, DC: Congressional Quarterly Press, 1993).

20. Michael Oreskes, "As Problems Fester, Voters Send Pink Slips," *New York Times*, 23 September 1990, 4:5; John Dillin, "American Voters Disgusted, Angry with Politicians," *Christian Science Monitor*, 17 October 1990, 1.

21. For analyses of Perot as a "populist," see Dennis Westlind, *The Politics of Popular Identity* (Lund, Sweden: Lund University Press, 1996); Linda Schulte-Sasse, "Meet Ross Perot: The Lasting Legacy of Capraesque Populism," *Cultural Critique* (Fall 1993): 91–119.

22. See Larry King, with Mark Stencel, *On the Line: The New Road to the White House* (New York: Harcourt Brace and Company, 1993).

23. Maureen Dowd, "Populist Media Forums and the Campaign of '92," *New York Times*, 3 November 1992, A14.
24. Harvey Mansfield, "Newt, Take Note: Populism Poses Its Own Dangers," *Wall Street Journal*, 1 November 1994, A1. For a more general assessment of the 1990s as a "populist" political era, see Sean Wilentz, "Populism Redux," *Dissent* 42 (Spring 1995): 149–53; Paul Piccone and Gary Ulmen, "Populism and the New Politics," *Telos* 103 (Spring 1995): 3–8. For commentary on how the populist overtones of the decade don't live up to the "true" definition of "populism," see Molly Ivins, "Just What Is a Populist, Anyway?" *Austin-American Statesman*, 6 February 1996, A9.
25. See E. J. Dionne Jr., *Why Americans Hate Politics* (New York: Simon and Schuster, 1991); Seymour Lipset and William Schneider, *The Confidence Gap*, 2d ed. (Baltimore: Johns Hopkins University Press, 1987); Susan Pharr and Robert Putnam, eds., *Disaffected Democracies: What's Troubling the Trilateral Countries?* (Princeton: Princeton University Press, 2000).
26. Albert Gore, *Common Sense Government: Works Better and Costs Less* (New York: Random House, 1995).
27. See "Bad Justice," editorial, *New York Times*, 21 February 1995, A18; Joe Klein, "The Birth of Common Sense: Bill Clinton Outflanks the Republicans on Regulatory Reform," *Newsweek* 125, 27 March 1995, 31.
28. P. David Marshall, *Celebrity and Power: Fame in Contemporary Culture* (Minneapolis: University of Minnesota Press, 1997).
29. In the 1992 presidential election, Thomas Patterson compared ten questions asked of candidates by citizens with ten questions asked by journalists in campaign debates and press conferences. One of the conclusions he arrives at is that the press conducts its business in a language that is foreign to the concerns of the citizenry. Thomas Patterson, *Out of Order* (New York: Random House, 1993), 55–56.
30. For instance, John Thornton Caldwell quotes a former adviser to the FCC and the White House and board member of the National Association of Broadcasters as saying, "'There will be a plethora of niche [cable] networks responsive to the needs of specific cultural groups within our multicultural society.' In addition to providing 'ownership opportunities' for minorities, 'these culturally specific niche networks will require management teams that are sensitive and responsive to the needs of their target audience.'" John Thornton Caldwell, *Televisuality: Style, Crisis, and Authority in American Television* (New Brunswick, NJ: Rutgers University Press, 1995), 257.
31. A representative work of this utopianism is Howard Rheingold, *Virtual Community: Homesteading on the Electronic Frontier* (New York: Simon and Schuster, 1991). For a critical assessment of the false illusions presented by communication technologies, see Theodore Roszak, *The Cult of Information* (Berkeley: University of California Press, 1994). The polarizations of utopianism and dystopianism became so pronounced by the end of the decade that a group of "middle-of-the-roaders" went so far as to advance what they call a "technorealism" movement, a manifesto grounded in "reality" that should ground us all. See Andrew Shapiro, "Technorealism: Get Real!" *The Nation* 266, 6 April 1998, 19–20.

32. Todd Gitlin, *The Twilight of Common Dreams: Why America Is Wracked by Culture Wars* (New York: Metropolitan Books, 1995).

33. The impeachment and trial of President Clinton were examples of the culture wars for *New York Times* columnist Frank Rich. He argues, "The cultural fault lines of the moment are those of 30 years ago, and potentially just as explosive. The right-wing rage once aimed at long-haired, draft-dodging, sexually wanton hippies (a caricature of the left even then) is now aimed at Bill Clinton, whose opportunistic, split-the-difference politics is actually closer to the old mainstream G.O.P. than to the 60's left but who nonetheless has become the right's piñata for all it hates about the Vietnam era's social and sexual revolutions." Frank Rich, "Let It Bleed," *New York Times*, 19 December 1998, A15.

34. For a representative example of scholarly works focusing on these types of talk shows, see Munson, *All Talk*; Jane M. Shattuc, *The Talking Cure: TV Talk Shows and Women* (New York: Routledge, 1997); Timberg, *Television Talk*; Andrew Tolson, "Televised Chat and the Synthetic Personality," in *Broadcast Talk*, ed. Paddy Scannell (London: Sage, 1991), among others.

35. See Sonia Livingstone and Peter Lunt, *Talk on Television: Audience Participation and Public Debate* (London: Routledge, 1994); Paolo Carpignano, Robin Anderson, Stanley Aronowitz, and William DiFazio, "Chatter in the Age of Electronic Reproduction: Talk Television and the 'Public Mind,'" in *The Phantom Public Sphere*, ed. Bruce Robbins (Minneapolis: University of Minnesota Press, 1993).

36. Doug McIntyre, a writer and guest on *Politically Incorrect*, once called these shows "human cockfighting." See Joshua Gamson, *Freaks Talk Back: Tabloid Talk Shows and Sexual Nonconformity* (Chicago: University of Chicago Press, 1998); Laura Grindstaff, *The Money Shot: Trash, Class, and the Making of TV Talk Shows* (Chicago: University of Chicago Press, 2002); Kevin Glynn, *Tabloid Culture: Trash Taste, Popular Power, and the Transformation of American Television* (Durham, NC: Duke University Press, 2000).

37. See Peter Laufer, *Inside Talk Radio: America's Voice or Just Hot Air* (New York: Carol Publishing Group, 1995), and Howard Kurtz, *Hot Air: All Talk, All the Time* (New York: Times Books, 1996), for accounts of talk radio's success and the personalities that drove it. For an analysis of talk radio's supposed influence on political behavior, see David C. Barker, *Rushed to Judgment: Talk Radio, Persuasion, and American Political Behavior* (New York: Columbia University Press, 2002).

38. Caldwell, *Televisuality*, 292.

39. Caldwell, *Televisuality*, 4.

40. Caldwell, *Televisuality*, 251.

41. Caldwell, *Televisuality*, 256.

42. Carpignano et al., "Chatter."

43. Carpignano et al., "Chatter," 116–17.

44. Livingstone and Lunt, *Talk on Television*, 102.

45. Livingstone and Lunt, *Talk on Television*, 178. They argue that this is occurring in British televised drama, documentary, and current affairs programming.

46. Tolson, "Televised Chat," 198.

47. Munson, *All Talk*, 6.
48. Munson, *All Talk*, 15.
49. Tolson, "Televised Chat," 198.
50. This section is based upon a more complete discussion found in Jeffrey P. Jones, "Vox Populi as Cable Programming Strategy," *Journal of Popular Film & Television* 31 (Spring 2003): 18–28.
51. John Dempsey, "Newest Cable Act Child: America's Talking," *Daily Variety*, 27 June 1994, 32.
52. Rich Brown, "America's Talking Cable Channel Takes Off," *Broadcasting & Cable* 124 (4 July 1994): 16.
53. Scott Williams, "America's Talking–The All-Talk Cable Network–Bows on July 4th," Associated Press, 1 July 1994.
54. Dennis Wharton, "Debuting Cable/Sat Net Tuned to the Right," *Daily Variety*, 29 November 1993, 4.
55. Linda Moss, "'C-SPAN with Attitude' Will Launch December 6," *Multichannel News* 14 (15 November 1993): 14.
56. Phil Kloer, "CNN Interactive Program Will Raise Back Talk to a New Level," *Atlanta Journal and Constitution*, 11 July 1994, A1.
57. Marc Rice, "People, Faxes, Computers Debate the Issues on New CNN Program," The Associated Press, 22 August 1994.
58. Bob Sokolsky, "'TalkBack Live' Touts Town Meeting Format," *The Press-Enterprise* (Riverside, CA), 5 August 1994, B5.
59. Rice, "People, Faxes."
60. CNN cancelled *TalkBack* as America geared up for war on Iraq in 2003. CNN noted the decision for change was based on a "heightened news environment." Yet as America debated the need to go to war when most of its allies did not support such a decision, CNN obviously was uninterested in hearing what viewers and audience members had to say about such a decision. The show averaged between 600,000–700,000 viewers. Caroline Wilbert, "CNN Pulls Plug on Afternoon 'TalkBack,'" *Atlanta Journal-Constitution*, 8 March 2003, 1E.
61. As seen in the analysis in chapter 5.
62. Dan Trigoboff, "3 Nets: News, Views, Confused," *Broadcasting & Cable*, 11 March 2002, 10.
63. Though dipping into overtly political talk on occasion (such as the short-lived *Dennis Miller* in 2004), CNBC largely focuses on business news and talk.
64. Douglas Quenqua, "MSBNC Shifts Focus from Reporting to Commentary," *PR Week*, 10 June 2002, 3; Tim Rutten, "Talk is Cheap, or at Least Cheaper Than Newscasts," *Los Angeles Times*, 7 June 2002, D2.
65. Nimmo and Combs conclude that talk show punditry is persistent in American television because it offers the nation a form of "symbolic healing," providing viewers a therapeutic medicine of symbols and myths in confusing and complex times. Nimmo and Combs, *Political Pundits*, 167–69. The continued prominence of "expert" voices in cable talk programming perhaps reflects this theoretical observation.

66. "Fox News Ratings Show Erosion," *New York Times*, 28 June 2008, http://tvdecoder.blogs.nytimes.com/2008/06/28/fox-news-ratings-showerosion/?scp=2&sq=msnbc%20fox%20news%20ideology&st=cse.
67. Jacques Steinberg, "Cable Channel Nods to Ratings and Leans Left," *New York Times*, 6 November 2007. MSNBC had offered liberal talk show host Phil Donahue at the turn of the century, but quickly dismissed him when patriotic fervor hit the country following 9/11.
68. See, for instance, Jim Rutenberg, "A Surge on One Channel, a Tight Race on Another," *New York Times*, 1 November 2008, A28.
69. Brian Montopoli, "Fox-Backed Democratic Debate Called Off," *CBS News*, 23 August 2007, http://www.cbsnews.com/stories/2007/08/23/politics/main3198082.shtml.
70. David Bauder, "Study: NBC News Doesn't Follow MSNBC's Partisan Drift," *Huffington Post*, 29 October 2008, http://www.huffingtonpost.com/2008/10/30/study-nbc-news-doesnt-fol_n_139162.html.
71. Bill Carter, "Election's Over, So What's Next for the Cable News Channels," *New York Times*, 15 November 2008, C1.
72. Perhaps the best reporting of Fox News's rabid attacks on the new administration was produced by Jon Stewart on *The Daily Show* in a segment called "Fox News Fear Imbalance." See http://www.thedailyshow.com/video/index.jhtml?videoId=216561&title=Fox-News-Fear-Imbalance.
73. Beck even embraced the Beale comparison. See Brian Stelter and Bill Carter, "Fox News's Mad, Apocalyptic, Tearful Rising Star," *New York Times*, 29 March 2009, A1.
74. http://www.huffingtonpost.com/2008/10/30/rachel-maddow-interviews_n_139402.html.

CHAPTER 4

1. Meaghan Morris and Paul Patton, eds., *Michel Foucault: Power, Truth, Strategy* (Sydney: Feral Publications, 1979), 46.
2. For a broader discussion of this challenge, including the role of new media, see Jeffrey P. Jones, "Believable Fictions: Redactional Culture and the Will to Truthiness," in *The Changing Face of Journalism: Tabloidization, Technology and Truthiness*, ed. Barbie Zelizer (New York: Routledge), 127–43.
3. A number of examples could support this claim. For a particularly damning one, see Neil A. Lewis, "Memos Reveal Scope of the Power Bush Sought," *New York Times*, 3 March 2009, A1.
4. For instance, a political sex scandal may produce discussions on issues such as privacy, morality, leadership, individuality and freedom, law and justice, and gender relations. See Michael Billig, Susan Condor, Derek Edwards, Mike Gane, David Middleton, and Alan Radley, *Ideological Dilemmas: A Social Psychology of Everyday Thinking* (London: Sage, 1988); Michael Billig and Jose M. Sabucedo, "The Rhetorical and Ideological Dimensions of Common Sense," in *The Status of Common Sense in Psychology*, ed. Jurg Siegfried (Norwood, NJ: Ablex Publishing, 1994).

5. Lawrence Christon, "Not For the Humor-Disabled: A Talk Show with No Holds Barred," *The Record*, 7 September 1993, D08.

6. Wayne Walley, "NCTA Surfer; Clashing Opinions Fuel 'Incorrect,'" *Electronic Media*, 8 May 1995, 39.

7. Rodney Buxton, "The Late-Night Talk Show: Humor in Fringe Television," *The Southern Speech Communication Journal* 52 (Summer 1987): 377–89.

8. Dennis Miller, *I Rant, Therefore I Am* (New York: Broadway Books, 2000), 56.

9. Alan Wolfe, in a book review in the early 1990s, argued: "Americans are increasingly oblivious to politics, but they are exceptionally sensitive to culture. . . . Politics in the classic sense of who gets what, when and how is carried out by a tiny elite watched over by a somewhat larger, but still infinitesimally small, audience of news followers. The attitude of the great majority of Americans to such traditional political subjects is an unstable combination of boredom, resentment, and sporadic attention. . . . Culture, on the other hand, grabs everyone's attention all the time. . . . Because they practice politics in cultural terms, Americans cannot be understood with the tool kits developed by political scientists." Quoted in Jeffrey P. Jones, "Forums for Citizenship in Popular Culture," in *Politics, Discourse, and American Society: New Agendas*, ed. Roderick P. Hart and Bartholomew H. Sparrow (Lanham, MD: Rowman & Littlefield, 2001), 194.

10. Lawrence Grossberg, *It's a Sin: Essays on Postmodernism, Politics & Culture* (Sydney: Power Publications, 1988), 40.

11. Richard Zoglin, "Politically Incorrect," *Time* 143 (30 May 1994): 67. Not all assessments were so favorable. Indeed, with a format that tended to feature people who were not "experts" in political matters, it attracted its fair share of scorn, typically from those who take their politics very seriously. "Do we really need a panel show in which stand-up comedians, minor former celebrities and the odd political and/or media operative sit around in a circle and say dumb things?", wrote the voice of insider politics, the *Washington Post*. Quoted in Scott Shuger, "Comic Relief: Real Issues, Barbed Wit and Celebrities Galore," *U.S. News & World Report* 122 (20 January 1997): 59–65.

12. Compared with 1992, when neither the political parties nor the networks were interested in Comedy Central's contributions.

13. "Comedy Central Hires Reich for GOP Reports," *Buffalo News*, 14 July 2000, 4c.

14. Phil Rosenthal, "A Comic Koppel," *Chicago Sun-Times*, 15 December 2000, Features section, 65.

15. Caryn James, "They're Celebrities, and You're Not," *New York Times*, 8 February 2004, 2:28. See also Alessandra Stanley, "Dennis Miller: Pranksters, Pundits, Political Animals All," *New York Times*, 30 January 2004, E1, and Rebecca Winters, "10 Questions for Dennis Miller," *Time*, 22 December 2003, 8, where Miller explains how 9/11 changed him and led to his ideologically rightward turn.

16. For the complex array of propaganda employed by the Bush administration, see David Barstow and Robin Stein, "Under Bush, a New Age of Prepackaged TV News," *New York Times*, 13 March 2005, A1. See also "Bush Payola

Scandal Deepens," *Mail & Guardian Online*, 29 January 2005, http://www.mg.co
.za/article/2005-01-29-bush-payola-scandal-deepens.

17. For a nice summary of how competition between the cable news networks affected political reporting and commentary on the Clinton-Lewinsky scandal,
see Eric Alterman, *Sound and Fury: The Making of the Punditocracy* (Ithaca, NY:
Cornell University Press, 1999), 262–78.

18. Theresa Bradley, "Solidly Stewart," *ABCNews.com*, 14 November 2002.

19. John Thornton Caldwell, *Televisuality: Style, Crisis, and Authority in American
Television* (New Brunswick, NJ: Rutgers University Press, 1995); Jean Baudrillard, "Simulacra and Simulations," in *Jean Baudrillard: Selected Writings*,
ed. and trans. Mark Poster (Palo Alto: Stanford University Press, 1988),
166–84.

20. Simon Houpt, "The World According to Stewart," *The Globe and Mail* (Canada), 3 October 2002.

21. Steve Hedgpeth, "'Daily Show's Satiric Eye," *Plain Dealer* (Cleveland), 30 July
2000, 6I.

22. For a detailed examination of the Bush administration's information man-
agement techniques, as well as the press's impotent response, see Frank Rich,
The Greatest Story Ever Sold: The Decline and Fall of Truth from 9/11 to Katrina
(New York: Penguin Press, 2006).

23. Frank Rich, "Jon Stewart's Perfect Pitch," *New York Times*, 20 April 2003, 2:1.

24. Jane Ganahl, "Comic Release," *San Francisco Chronicle*, 23 April 2002, D1.

25. The transcript of the show is available at http://politicalhumor.about.com/
library/bljonstewartcrossfire.htm.

26. Klein was quoted as saying, "I agree wholeheartedly with Jon Stewart's overall
premise." See Bill Carter, "CNN Will Cancel 'Crossfire' and Cut Ties to Commentator," *New York Times*, 6 January 2005, http://www.nytimes.com/2005/01/
06/business/media/06crossfire.html.

27. James Taylor. "Reexamining Same-Sex Marriage in 2004: A Hierarchical
Model of Voter Turnout," Paper presented at the annual meeting of the Southern Political Science Association, New Orleans, 7 January 2009, http://www
.allacademic.com/meta/p277815_index.html.

28. September 1, 2004, ABC News Transcript, *Nightline*, "Democratic National
Convention," http://www.lexisnexis.com.

29. Barbie Zelizer, "When Facts, Truth, and Reality are God-Terms: On Journalism's Uneasy Place in Cultural Studies," *Communication and Critical/Cultural
Studies* 1(1), 2004: 100–19.

30. July 28, 2004, ABC News Transcript, *Nightline*, "Democratic National Convention," http://www.lexisnexis.com.

31. Rich, "Jon Stewart's Perfect Pitch," 2:1.

32. Michiko Kakutani, "Is Jon Stewart the Most Trusted Man in America?" *New York
Times*, 15 August 2008, http://www.nytimes.com/2008/08/17/arts/television/
17kaku.html.

33. July 28, 2004, ABC News Transcript, *Nightline*, "Democratic National Convention," http://www.lexisnexis.com.

34. John Hartley, *Tele-ology: Studies in Television* (London: Routledge, 1992),
52–53.

35. Nathan Rabin, "Interview with Stephen Colbert," *AV Club* (*The Onion*), from http://www.avclub.com/articles/stephen-colbert,13970/.
36. Rabin, "Interview with Stephen Colbert."
37. Charlie Rose, 8 December 2006, "A conversation with comedian Stephen Colbert," http://www.charlierose.com/view/interview/93.
38. http://www.colbertnation.com/the-colbert-report-videos/24039/october-17-2005/the-word---truthiness.
39. Rabin, "Interview with Stephen Colbert."
40. Rabin, "Interview with Stephen Colbert." Original emphasis.
41. Taken from a transcript of the event, http://colbertuniversity.nofactzone.net.
42. Richard Cohen, "So Not Funny," *Washington Post*, 4 May 2006, A25.
43. Dan Froomkin, "The Colbert Blackout," *Washington Post*, 2 May 2006, http://www.washingtonpost.com.
44. Noam Cohen, "That After-Dinner Speech Remains a Favorite Dish," *New York Times*, 22 May 2006, C5.
45. Peter Lauria, "Colbert Soars," *New York Post*, 7 May 2006.
46. Howard Kurtz, *Spin Cycle: How the White House and the Media Manipulate the News* (New York: Simon and Schuster, 1998); Eric Boehlert, *Lapdogs: How the Press Rolled Over for Bush* (New York: Free Press, 2006).
47. Adam Sternbergh, "Stephen Colbert Has America by the Ballots," *New York*, 8 October 2006, http://NYMag.com.
48. Rebecca Ascher-Walsh, "Stephen Colbert, 'Arch Conservative,'" *Los Angeles Times*, 1 June 2009.
49. Sternbergh, "Stephen Colbert Has America."
50. *Real Time with Bill Maher*, Original airdate September 8, 2006.
51. Betsy Boyd, "Cable Is Able Amid Network Laffer Lull," *Daily Variety*, 15 June 2005, A1.
52. Boyd, "Cable Is Able."
53. Michael Learmonth, "FNC Takes Satire Out for Spin," *Variety*, 12 February 2007, http://www.variety.com/article/VR1117959328.html?categoryid=14&cs=1.
54. Charlie Brooker, "Charlier Brooker's Screen Burn," *The Guardian* (London), 24 February 2007, The Guide, 52.
55. Dan Glaister, "One Last Mission for the Man Behind Jack Baur: Make U.S. Right Funny Again," *The Guardian* (London), 17 February 2007, 3.
56. Dave Itzkoff, "For Once, CNN Takes News Less Seriously," *New York Times*, 25 October 2008, C1.
57. Pepper Miller, "What the Hell was CNN Thinking," *Advertising Age*, 3 November 2008, http://adage.com/bigtent/post?article_id=132208.
58. Indeed, many of the features of the show described here were on display at a Huckabee campaign stop the day after he won the Iowa Caucus vote (including an appearance by Chuck Norris and Huckabee playing bass with the rally band). For a full description, see Jeffrey P. Jones, "Pop Goes the Campaign: The Repopularization of Politics in Election 2008," in *The 2008 Presidential Campaign: A Communication Perspective*, ed. Robert E. Denton, Jr. (Lanham, MD: Rowman & Littlefield Publishers, 2009), 184.
59. http://www.comedycentral.com/shows/chocolate_news/about/index.jhtml.

60. Felicia R. Lee, "As Election Nears, A Black Voice Enters Comedy Fray," *New York Times*, 15 October 2008, C1.
61. Leah R. Vande Berg, Lawrence A. Wenner, and Bruce E. Gronbeck, *Critical Approaches to Television*, 2d ed. (Boston: Houghton Mifflin, 2004), 200.

CHAPTER 5

1. Roderick P. Hart, *Campaign Talk: Why Elections Are Good for Us* (Princeton, NJ: Princeton University Press, 2000); David Thelen, *Becoming Citizens in the Age of Television* (Chicago: University of Chicago Press, 1996); E. J. Dionne Jr., *Why Americans Hate Politics* (New York: Simon and Schuster, 1991).
2. Actual broadcast dates are 25 January, 1 February, 16 August, and 23 August 1998. The analysis was conducted from transcripts of these broadcasts.
3. Will's usage of "this man" is similar to the president's usage of "that woman" when referring to Monica Lewinsky in his denial of the affair. Both are semantic moves to distance themselves from the object of referral. In Will's case, he seeks to distance Clinton from any legitimate place in the political system.
4. 23 August 1998.
5. Antonio Gramsci, *An Antonio Gramsci Reader*, ed. David Forgacs (New York: Schocken Books), 360.
6. Of the pundits on *This Week*, for instance, both of Roberts' parents served in Congress. Kristol's father is the conservative intellectual Irving Kristol. Will's wife was a manager in Bob Dole's 1996 presidential campaign. George Stephanopoulos was a senior advisor to President Clinton, and Sam Donaldson has been a senior White House reporter for over two decades.
7. John Dewey and Arthur F. Bentley, *Knowing and the Known* (Boston: Beacon Press, 1949), 270.
8. Dewey and Bentley, *Knowing*, 282.
9. For a helpful summary of opinion polls that demonstrate this see Eric Alterman, *Sound and Fury: The Making of the Punditocracy* (Ithaca, NY: Cornell University Press), 275–76.
10. Gramsci, *Gramsci Reader*; Clifford Geertz, "Common Sense as a Cultural System," *Antioch Review* 33 (Spring 1975): 5–26; Boaventura De Sousa Santos, *Toward a New Common Sense: Law, Science and Politics in the Paradigmatic Transition* (New York: Routledge, 1995).
11. Quoted in Roderick P. Hart, *Seducing America: How Television Charms the Modern Voter* (New York: Oxford University Press, 1994), 15.
12. Michael Billig, Susan Condor, Derek Edwards, Mike Gane, David Middleton, and Alan Radley, *Ideological Dilemmas: A Social Psychology of Everyday Thinking* (London: Sage, 1988), 27.
13. Geertz too notes how intellectual ideas exist in the public imagination as common sense by using the example of science: "The development of modern science has had a profound effect . . . upon Western commonsense views.

... [The plain man] has surely been brought round, and quite recently, to a version of the germ theory of disease. The merest television commercial demonstrates that. But, as the merest television commercial also demonstrates, it is as a bit of common sense, not as an articulated scientific theory, that he believes it" (Geertz, "Common Sense," 19–20).

14. Geerz, "Common Sense."
15. P. David Marshall, *Celebrity and Power: Fame in Contemporary Culture* (Minneapolis: University of Minnesota Press, 1997), 72–73.
16. Marshall, *Celebrity and Power*, 247.
17. Joshua Gamson, *Claims to Fame: Celebrity in Contemporary America* (Berkeley: University of California Press, 1994), 195.
18. When alternative means of making sense were employed, such means were quickly pushed aside. For instance, in a highly unusual moment on the 16 August program, Sam Donaldson offered his reflections on the scandal in what sounded like commentary directly drawn from *Politically Incorrect*. "I'm not as mean a guy as I look, I think," he suggested. "I don't think my heart is as hard as some people think because all of us need some compassion at times. . . . I think the question now is not whether Bill Clinton deserves compassion as a human being, understanding we're all fallen angels. But is he qualified to be, and should he continue to be the leader, the man to whom we look up to in this country, if in fact, he's done these things? I say if he's done these things, he is not qualified to be a leader. Brother, I will help you up, I'll give you a dollar if you need it but you cannot be the president of the United States." The next statement by George Stephanopoulos, however, not only brought this form of analysis and sense making to a close, but reestablished the proper direction and focus of how the scandal should be discussed. "There is a difference between a civil suit that's been dismissed and a grand jury," he quickly intoned. The discussion then careened through issues such as obstruction of justice, subornation of perjury, resolution of inquiry, impeachment, and indictments. This is a vivid, if limited, example of how certain ways of making sense are privileged over others—a privileging that similarly occurs on *Politically Incorrect*, but is based there on common sense.
19. Geertz, "Common Sense," 26.

CHAPTER 6

1. John Doyle, "Will Political Humour Survive the Vote? Oh, You Betcha," *Globe and Mail* (Canada), 12 November 2008, R3.
2. Bruce Fretts, "In Jon We Trust," *Entertainment Weekly*, 31 October 2003, 30–35.
3. Stephen Colbert was asked the same question, and he replied similarly: "People say, 'Aren't you going to be sad when Bush goes?' No. The show is not about that." Jake Coyle, "Behind the Scenes of 'The Colbert Report,'" *SFGate.com*, 8 June 2008.
4. Stewart notes: "I still don't consider myself political. People confuse political interest with interest in current events." Maureen Dowd, "America's Anchors,"

Rolling Stone, 31 October 2006, http://www.rollingstone.com/news/coverstory/jon_stewart_stephen_colbert_americas_anchors.

5. Roderick P. Hart and Johanna Hartelius, "The Political Sins of Jon Stewart," *Critical Studies in Media Communication* 24, no. 3 (2007): 263–272.

6. As Lance Bennett reports, "only 34 of 414 stories told by ABC, NBC, and CBS on the build-up to and rationale for the Iraq War from September 2002 through February 2003 originated outside the White House." W. Lance Bennett, *News: The Politics of Illusion*, 7th ed. (New York: Longman, 2007), 39.

7. Whether Stewart is correct in his assessment of the financial news networks' role in the economic collapse of 2008–2009 is an empirical question, though not one taken up here. What matters, for our purposes, is that Stewart believes they were culpable. *The Daily Show*, March 12, 2009.

8. In Leon Sigal's classic study of news sources, 78 percent of all hard news stories derive from government officials at the federal, state, local, and foreign level. Statistics cited in Bennett, *News*, 113.

9. This, in fact, was a common defense for shoddy reporting in the run-up to the Iraq War, with some reporters contending that it was the Democrats' job (especially those with national security information and clearances) to contest the Bush administration's claims, not the press. For instance, "Washington Post columnist David Ignatius, looking back on the press's failings with regards to Iraq, suggested, 'The media were victims of their own professionalism. Because there was little criticism of the war from prominent Democrats and foreign policy analysts, journalistic rules meant we shouldn't create a debate on our own.'" Quoted in Eric Boehlert, *Lapdogs: How the Press Rolled Over for Bush* (New York: Free Press, 2006).

10. Witness the flak that NBC News received from the Republican Party during the 2008 presidential election. The party maintained that NBC was biased because the commentators who worked at the network's sister cable outlet, MSNBC, were seen as overly critical of Republicans.

11. As Schudson notes, however, interviews were not always a central aspect of reporting. Michael Schudson, *The Power of News* (Cambridge, MA: Harvard University Press, 1995), 72–93.

12. Bennett, *News*, 199.

13. One example of such a critique comes from Arianna Huffington, founder of the new media website, *The Huffington Post*. See "What If Jon Stewart, Instead of John King, Interviewed Dick Cheney," *HuffingtonPost.com*, 16 March 2009, http://www.huffingtonpost.com/arianna-huffington/what-if-jon-stewart-in-ste_b_175503.html.

14. Baym rightly notes the marketplace approach to political discourse that such programming embraces. In it, the model is one of competition and conflict amongst competing interests. He contrasts this with *The Daily Show's* more deliberative form of discursive exchange, one that seeks to achieve "consensus agreement on the common good." See Geoffrey Baym, "*The Daily Show*: Discursive Integration and the Reinvention of Political Journalism," *Political Communication* 22 (2005): 259–276.

15. Frank Rich, "Jon Stewart's Perfect Pitch," *New York Times*, 20 April 2003, 2:1.

16. *The Daily Show* won a Peabody Award two years earlier for its "reporting" and commentary on the 2004 election.
17. Dowd, "America's Anchors."
18. For similar arguments positing *The Daily Show* as an alternative form of journalism, see Baym, *"The Daily Show"*; Dannagal Goldthwaite Young, "The Daily Show as the New Journalism: In Their Own Words," in *Laughing Matters: Humor and American Politics in the Media Age*, eds. Jody C. Baumgartner and Jonathan S. Morris (New York: Routledge, 2008), 241–59.
19. Mark Fishman, *Manufacturing the News* (Austin, TX: University of Texas Press, 1980); Gaye Tuchman, *Making News: A Study in the Construction of Reality* (New York: Free Press, 1978).
20. This is, in essence, what the entire body of journalism studies literature demonstrates. For a primer on the foundational journalism studies texts, see Howard Tumber (ed.), *News: A Reader* (London: Oxford University Press, 1999).
21. See Rodger Streitmatter, *Voices of Revolution: The Dissident Press in America* (New York: Columbia University Press, 2001); Lauren Kessler, *The Dissident Press: Alternative Journalism in American History* (Beverly Hills: Sage, 1984).
22. The various aspects that comprise *The Daily Show* have been examined by numerous authors. See Geoffrey Baym, *"The Daily Show"*; Geoffrey Baym, "Crafting New Communicative Models in the Televisual Sphere: Political Interviews on The Daily Show," *The Communication Review* 10, no. 2 (2007): 93–115; Amber Day, "And Now . . . The News? Mimeses and the Real in *The Daily Show*," in *Satire TV: Politics and Comedy in the Post-Network Era*, ed. Jonathan Gray, Jeffrey P. Jones, and Ethan Thompson (New York: NYU Press, 2009), 85–103; Joanne Morreale, "Jon Stewart and *The Daily Show*: I Thought You Were Going to be Funny!" in *Satire TV*, 104–23; Jamie Warner, "Political Culture Jamming: The Dissident Humor of 'The Daily Show with Jon Stewart,'" *Popular Communication* 5, no. 1 (2007): 17–36; and numerous chapters within the volume Jason Holt, *The Daily Show and Philosophy: Moments of Zen in the Art of Fake News* (Malden, MA: Blackwell, 2007).
23. John Hartley, "From Republic of Letters to Television Republic? Citizen Readers in the Era of Broadcast Television," in *Television After TV: Essays on a Medium in Transition*, ed. Lynn Spigel and Jan Olsson (Durham, NC: Duke University Press, 2004), 386–417.
24. John Hartley, "Communicative Democracy in a Redactional Society: The Future of Journalism Studies," *Journalism* 1, no. 1 (2000): 39–47.
25. Hartley, "Communicative Democracy," 44.
26. "Sarah Palin Gender Card," *The Daily Show*, 3 September 2008, http://www.thedailyshow.com/video/index.jhtml?videoId=184086&title=Sarah-Palin-Gender-Card.
27. Murray Edelman, *Constructing the Political Spectacle* (Chicago: University of Chicago Press, 1988).
28. Michele H. Jackson, "Fluidity, Promiscuity, and Mash-ups: New Concepts for the Study of Mobility and Communication," *Communication Monographs* 74, no. 3 (2007): 408–413; Michael Strangelove, *The Empire of Mind: Digital Piracy and the Anti-Capitalist Movement* (Toronto: University of Toronto Press, 2005).

29. Strangelove, *The Empire of Mind*, 113.
30. Whereas Jamie Warner sees *The Daily Show*, in its entirety, as a form of political culture jamming—that is, a form of critique and resistance to the political branding that seems to dominate modern politics—my reference here is specifically focused on the forms and types of redacted video used on the show that bears direct resemblance, if not relationship, to culture jamming practices. See Warner, "Political Culture Jamming."
31. Aaron Wherry, "News and Laughs at 11," *National Post* (Toronto), 5 October 2002, TO2.
32. Julie Bosman, "Serious Book to Peddle? Don't Laugh, Try a Comedy Show," *New York Times*, 25 February 2007, sec. 4, 3.
33. Bosman, "Serious Book."
34. Baym, "Crafting New Communicative Models," 93.
35. Baym, "The Daily Show," 273.
36. *The Daily Show*, 13 July 2005.
37. Baym, "Crafting New Communicative Models."
38. Although one might argue that Fox News's programs *Hannity* and *The O'Reilly Factor* include formats that would allow for a similar debate, the truth is that neither host is interested in having a conversation with people they disagree with. Instead, their shows are designed around their browbeating and shouting down their guests with whom they disagree, around the agony of conflict and competition between opponents, and the value of that as entertainment (that is, in attracting audiences). MSNBC's Keith Olbermann (*Countdown*) also rarely has on guests with whom he disagrees, and Rachel Maddow is still stuck in the Q&A format of most public affairs programming (such as *Meet the Press* or *Nightline*), choosing to "debate" only other commentators (like Pat Buchanan), not her interview subjects.
39. Numerous references are available for understanding rhetorical fallacies (going back to Aristotle). Those used here include http://www.nizkor.org/features/fallacies/ and http://www.utm.edu/RESEARCH/IEP/f/fallacy.htm.
40. Tom Brokaw, "Jon Stewart: Wickedly Insightful," *Time*, 18 April 2005. Retrieved from http://www.time.com/time/subscriber/2005/time100/artists/100stewart.html.
41. Nicholas Graham, "Tucker Carlson Rips Jon Stewart Repeatedly," *HuffingtonPost.com*, 15 March 2009, http://www.huffingtonpost.com/2009/03/15/tucker-carlson-rips-jon-s_n_175078.html.
42. Eric Deggans, "Jim Cramer finally surfaces on *Today* show," *The Feed* blog, 19 March 2009, retrieved from http://blogs.tampabay.com/media/2009/03/jim-cramer-finally-surfaces-on-today-show-calls-jon-stewart-naive.html.
43. Paul Thomasch, "NBC Boss: Jon Stewart's Criticism Absurd, Unfair," Reuters, 18 March 2009. Retrieved from http://www.reuters.com/article/rbssIndustryMaterialsUtilitiesNews/idUSN1835152820090318.
44. Michael Calderone, "Media Critics Pile on Cramer, CNBC," *Politico.com*, 15 March 2009, http://www.politico.com/news/stories/0309/19997.html.
45. Huffington, "What If Jon Stewart."

46. Isaac Fitzgerald, "Fix CNBC: Jon Stewart Made the Case, Now We're Demanding Action," Alternet.org, 16 March 2009, http://www.alternet.org/blogs/peek/131859/.

47. Andrew Sullivan, "To Catch a Predator," The Daily Dish, *The Atlantic*, 13 March 2009, http://andrewsullivan.theatlantic.com/the_daily_dish/2009/03/to-catch-a-pred.html. Original emphasis.

48. Baym, *"The Daily Show."*

49. Michiko Kakutani, "The Most Trusted Man in America?" *New York Times*, 17 August 2008, AR1.

50. George A. Test, *Satire: Spirit and Art* (Tampa: University of South Florida Press, 1991).

CHAPTER 7

1. Tom Shales, "Michael Moore: Return of a Prank Amateur," *Washington Post*, 21 July 1995, C1.

2. For reference to Moore's relationship to the Yippies, see Larissa MacFarquhar, "The Populist," *The New Yorker* 80, no. 1 (February 16 and February 23, 2004): 132–145.

3. Mike Higgins, "Guys and Dollars," *The Independent* (London), 3 March 1999, 10.

4. Jurgen Habermas, *The Structural Transformation of the Public Sphere* (Cambridge, MA: MIT Press, 1991).

5. Mark Fishman, *Manufacturing the News* (Austin: University of Texas Press, 1980); Gaye Tuchman, *Making News: A Study in the Construction of Reality* (New York: Free Press, 1978).

6. John Hartley, *Understanding News* (London: Routledge, 1982).

7. Moore explains the prominent "use" of public relations people in his work: "I think it's very important that we talk to those PR people, because they're who those of you who work for the newspapers and the TV stations talk to and that's the face of the corporation. That's the person who spends their day feeding the BS line to the media, which then gets repeated as fact six hours later on the news. It's rare that the public gets to see how the PR machine works. . . . Most, if not all, of these PR people are former journalists. They now make three times the money in PR that they made as journalists. Long ago they went to journalism school because they wanted to tell the truth. They found out later that they could make a lot more money to not tell the truth." Kerrie Murphy, "Crimes and misdemeanours," *The Australian*, 13 January 2000, T5.

8. Mike McDaniel, "Humor with a View," *Houston Chronicle*, 19 July 1994, sec. Houston, 1; Chip Rowe, "A Funny, Subversive '60 Minutes,'" *American Journalism Review*, 17 (July–August 1995): 13.

9. Whereas mainstream news media cover white-collar crime as isolated incidents of personal corruption, Moore is intent on showing how corporate corruption is endemic to the capitalist system, as well as how it is generally ignored, if not widely accepted.

10. Murphy, "Crimes and misdemeanours," T5.

11. Moore and producer Kathleen Glynn believe the show invited participation, and were buoyed by the relationship of their website to their show as a means of encouraging participation. As Glynn notes about that relationship during the airing of *The Awful Truth*, "It was a show that was designed to engage the viewer. You wouldn't want it on as a background noise in the house. The people who watched it got involved and wanted to see if there was anything else they could learn about or do." John Silberg, "Moore Is Merrier," *Variety* 382 (26 February 2001): S23. Elsewhere, Moore argued, "We're trying to ignite a spark in a part of the American public that's otherwise very discouraged right now. . . . The nightly news certainly doesn't do much to get people involved." Greg Quill, "Hilariously Subversive Moore Is Coming Back," *Toronto Star*, 14 July 1995, B11.

12. Murphy, "Crimes and misdemeanours," T5.

13. Note the similarity of this rhetoric of populist empowerment to that discussed in chapter 3. Indeed, when *TV Nation* went into production, Moore and Glynn report that they gave the following speech on the first day of shooting: "For one hour each week, we're going to give the average person like ourselves the chance to watch a show that is clearly on *their* side." See Michael Moore and Kathleeen Glynn, *Adventures in a TV Nation: The Stories Behind America's Most Outrageous TV Show* (New York: HarperCollins, 1998), 12.

14. Alan Pergament, "Moore's 'TV Nation,' Still a True Original," *Buffalo News* (New York), 19 July 1995, B12.

15. Ginny Holbert, "Moore Wit on the Way," *Chicago Sun-Times*, 28 December 1994, sec. 2, 39.

16. Jonathan Gray, "Real (and) Funny: Animated TV Comedy's Political Voice," paper presented at the annual meeting of the International Communication Association, 22–26 May 2008.

17. This recounting comes from Moore and Glynn, *Adventures*, 1–5. This original pitch idea was finally shot and aired in the very last episode of *TV Nation* in 1995.

18. The show was always a hit in England, where it eventually made the British Film Institute's list of "Top 100 Greatest British Television Programmes" of all time (ranked number 90).

19. Lizabeth Cohen, *A Consumers' Republic: The Politics of Mass Consumption in Postwar America* (New York: Vintage Books, 2003).

20. Hartley makes this point when he argues that "audiences are understood as 'citizens of media' in the sense that it is through the symbolic, virtualized and mediated context of watching television . . . that publics participate in the democratic process on a day to day basis." John Hartley, *The Uses of Television* (London: Routledge, 1999), 206.

21. Moore says he speaks for the working class: "I want working-class people to know there's someone on TV who's thinking like they do, fighting for them. We can be a surrogate for that America." Quill, "Hilariously Subversive," B11.

22. Joshua Phillips, "Moore Where That Came From," *Newsweek*, 19 October 2000, http://lexisnexis.com/.
23. Patricia Brennan, "Michael Moore: At Large," *Washington Post*, 17 July 1994, Y7.
24. Moore's interest in the prison-industrial complex was first exhibited in *Roger & Me*, where he showed scenes of a new, yet empty City of Flint jail being used for a party, where the guests dressed as guards and inmates.
25. Steve Persall, "Filmmaker Shares View on Ratings," *St. Petersburg Times* (Florida), 27 January 1995, C10.
26. Each rating point represents 942,000 households. The share represents the percentage of television sets in use during that time slot.
27. Moore offered to write Roger Smith a check for some financial hardship in his short follow up to *Roger and Me*, *Pets or Meat: The Return to Flint*
28. "The Insider," *Electronic Media*, 28 August 1995, sec. Biography, 6.
29. Michael Moore, "What You Can't Get Away With on TV," *The Nation* 263 (November 18, 1996): 10; Moore and Glynn, *Adventures*, 196.
30. Several of these episodes were later included in the two-volume videotape releases of the program.
31. Alan Bash, "The Ironic Birth of a 'Nation' on NBC," *USA Today*, 19 July 1994, D3.
32. The lower ratings than on NBC is also related to Fox still being a relatively new network at that time, a consistent fourth in the overall ratings race.
33. Higgins, "Guys and Dollars," 10.
34. In 1999, Bravo was received in 38 million households, yet its prime-time rating was .24, or approximately 66,000 households. During the second season, Moore seemed to realize that the show was really more of a British television program in its popularity, and hence consistently made reference in his introductions to the British viewing audience.
35. Richard Campbell, "Securing the Middle Ground: Reporter Formulas in 60 Minutes," in *Television: The Critical View*, 5th ed., ed. H. Newcomb (New York: Oxford University Press, 1994), 328.
36. Campbell, "Securing the Middle Ground," 327.
37. Michael Kazin, *The Populist Persuasion: An American History* (New York: Basic Books, 1995).
38. Kazin, *The Populist Persuasion*, 1.
39. Rob Owen, "'Truth' in Pittsburgh: Michael Moore Gives City Chance to Show Its Blue-Collar Stuff," *Pittsburgh Post-Gazette*, 22 January 1999, sec. Arts & Entertainment, 36.
40. Some of the writers who worked on his television programs, however, dispute the notion that Moore is a champion of workers or labor. One profile of Moore in the popular press details several claims by former employees who contend that Moore's populist persona is a ruse, nothing more than a construction for entertainment purposes. See Larissa MacFarquhar, "The Populist: Michael Moore Can Make You Cry," *The New Yorker*, 16 February 2004.
41. Charles E. Schutz, *Political Humor: From Aristophanes to Sam Ervin* (Cranbury, NJ: Associated University Presses, 1977), 330.

42. Clifford Geertz, "Common Sense as a Cultural System," *Antioch Review* 33 (Spring 1975): 5–26.

43. Again showing Moore's indebtedness to the Yippies' brand of political critique through public spectacle.

44. Only candidate Alan Keyes takes the show up on the offer. In bestowing the show's endorsement, Moore tells the viewers, "He may be a right-wing lunatic, but he's *our* right-wing lunatic. Alan Keyes—*The Awful Truth* candidate for president of the United States."

45. Other scenarios include "Love Night" (discussed earlier), and "Haulin' Communism," where Moore hires a bright red tractor-trailer rig with a hammer and sickle painted on its side to tour the southern United States for a Communist farewell tour (where the truck cab is eventually firebombed in Alabama).

46. "Duck and Cover" was also featured in *The Atomic Café*, a documentary compilation film about America's ridiculous attempts to discuss and talk about surviving a nuclear attack, a film Moore has admitted to admiring greatly. One of the film's codirectors, Kevin Rafferty, was a cameraman on *Roger and Me*.

47. Industry reports say each episode cost from $350,000 to $550,000 at Fox.

48. Reported in Rowe, "A Funny, Subversive '60 Minutes,'" 13.

49. Bash, "The Ironic Birth," 3D. In a separate interview, Moore boldly stated, "It's its own genre." Mike McDaniel, "Good News: 'TV Nation' is Back," *Houston Chronicle*, 28 December 1994, sec. Houston, 5.

50. Matt Roush, "Newsmag Nirvana, Moore or Less," *USA Today*, 19 July 1994, D3.

51. http://www.thedailyshow.com/video/index.jhtml?videoId=184114&title= The-Best-F#@king-News-Team-Ever---Small-Town-Values. One noticeable difference between Moore and *TDS*'s model, however, is how the latter goes out of its way to critique the idea of "objectivity" in reporting. The *TDS* segments feature the reporter making an idiot of him or herself, getting obsessed with some detail or putting words in the subject's mouth. Moore and his correspondents rarely went that far.

CHAPTER 8

1. Theodore L. Glasser, "Play and the Power of News," *Journalism* 1, no. 1 (2000): 23–29.

2. http://people-press.org/reports/display.php3?ReportID=46.

3. See Michael X. Delli Carpini and Scott Keeter, *What Americans Know About Politics and Why It Matters* (New Haven: Yale University Press, 1996); David T. Z. Mindich, *Tuned Out: Why Americans Under 40 Don't Follow the News* (New York: Oxford University Press, 2005); Jeffrey Scheuer, *The Sound Bite Society: Television and the American Mind* (New York: Four Walls Eight Windows, 1999); Darrell M. West and John M. Orman, *Celebrity Politics* (Upper Saddle River, NJ: Prentice Hall, 2003); William Chaloupka, *Everybody Knows: Cynicism in America* (Minneapolis: University of Minnesota Press, 1999); Roderick

P. Hart, *Seducing America: How Television Charms the Modern Voter* (New York: Oxford University Press, 1994).

4. http://people-press.org/reports/display.php3?ReportID=200.

5. "Jon Stewart," *Inside Politics*, CNN.com, 3 May 2002. Emphasis added.

6. Transcript of *Nightline*, ABC News, 28 July 2004. Emphasis added.

7. Gay Verne, "Not necessarily the news: Meet the players who will influence coverage of the 2004 campaign." *Newsday*, 19 January 2004, B6. Emphasis added.

8. http://www.naes04.org.

9. Transcripts of CNN, October 7, 2004. I analyze three morning broadcasts of CNN to get some idea of the different ways that a news network reports a story, as well as how these brief reports are modified as the morning progresses.

10. Daniel Boorstin, *The Image: A Guide to Pseudo Events in America* (New York: Atheneum, 1960).

11. Thomas E. Patterson, *Out of Order* (New York: Random House, 1993).

12. Steve Hedgpeth, "Daily Show's Satiric Eye," *Plain Dealer* (Cleveland), 30 July 2000, 6I.

13. Gaye Tuchman, *Making News: A Study in the Construction of Reality* (New York: Free Press, 1978).

14. As one news analyst has noted, "Network newscasts hold to standard conventions, and in so doing reduce Bush's sloppy, pause-saturated speech to a tightly constructed set of words that suggest clarity of thought and purpose." Such conventions, therefore, make the news media "susceptible to manipulation by the professional speech writers and media handlers who seed public information with pre-scripted soundbites and spin" See Baym, "The Daily Show," 265.

15. Stephen Armstrong, "I Can Scratch the Itch," *The Guardian* (London), 17 March 2003, 8.

16. Ellen Debenport, "Candidates Try to Cut Media Filter," *St. Petersburg Times* (Florida), 11 June 1992, 1A.

17. William A. Hatchen, *The Troubles of Journalism*, 3rd ed. (Mahwah, NJ: Lawrence Erlbaum Associates, 2005).

18. Mindich, *Tuned Out*.

19. Gene Roberts, Thomas Kunkle, and Charles Layton, *Leaving Readers Behind: The Age of Corporate Newspapering* (Fayetteville: University of Arkansas Press, 2001).

20. Peter Johnson, "Trust of Media Keeps on Slipping," *USA Today*, 28 May 2003, sec. D1; Hachten, *The Troubles of Journalism*, 102–12.

21. Katharine Q. Seelye, "Why Newspapers are Betting on Audience Participation," *New York Times*, 4 July 2005, C1.

22. Gary Younge, "Washington Post Apologizes for Underplaying WMD Scepticism," *The Guardian* (London), 13 August 2004, 2; Katharine Q. Seelye, "Survey on News Media Finds Wide Displeasure," *New York Times*, 27 June 2005, C5.

23. Kristina Riegert, with A. Johansson, "The Struggle for Credibility in the Iraq War," in *The Iraq War: European Perspectives on Politics, Strategy, and Operations*, ed. Jan Hellenberg (London: Frank Cass, 2005).

24. One only needs to look at popular narratives of either news media or the interactions of media and politics to see this recurrent theme. For examples, see films such as *Hero, Power, Broadcast News, A Face in the Crowd, Meet John Doe, The Candidate, Wag the Dog, Bulworth, Bob Roberts,* and *Dave.*
25. Murray Edelman, *Constructing the Political Spectacle* (Chicago: University of Chicago Press, 1988).
26. Michele Foucault, *Power/Knowledge: Selected Interviews and Other Writings, 1972–1977* (Brighton Harvester Press, 1980), 132. Emphasis added.
27. Frank Webster, *Theories of the Information Society* (London: Routledge, 1995), 170.
28. Again, witness the movement toward blogging (and even the news media's embrace of it) as a manifestation of this questioning and reformulation. See, for instance, "'The State' (Columbia, S.C.) Launches Community Blog, Citizen Journalism Push," *Editor & Publisher,* 30 August 2005, and Saul Hansell, "The CBS Evening Blog," *New York Times,* 13 July 2005, C1.
29. Webster, *Theories,* 169–70.
30. Charles Schutz, *Political Humor: From Aristophanes to Sam Ervin* (New York: Fairleigh Dickenson University Press, 1977), 328.
31. Baym, "*The Daily Show,*" 259–76.
32. One might be tempted to assert that this is exactly what competing "news" outlets like Fox News claim—that they are simply pointing out alternative truths. The crucial distinction between a program of political satire and a news organization like Fox that claims to be "fair and balanced," however, is their relationships to power. One is committed to critiquing power wherever it lies, while the other has proven its intentional commitment to supporting the powerful through highly orchestrated and sustained efforts by the media corporation's leadership. See Robert Greenwald's documentary *Outfoxed: Rupert Murdoch's War on Journalism.*
33. Brian Keefer, "You Call That News? I Don't," *Washington Post,* 12 September 2004, B2.
34. *The Daily Show,* 12 March 2009.

CHAPTER 9

1. The pun, of course, is of Al Franken's 1996 book roasting Rush Limbaugh, in many ways the model and early progenitor for bloviated right-wing talk on radio, then television. Al Franken, *Rush Limbaugh is a Big Fat Idiot* (Delacorte Press, 1996).
2. Nathan Rabin, "Interview with Stephen Colbert," *AVClub.com,* 25 January 2006, http://www.avclub.com/articles/stephen-colbert,13970/.
3. "Bluster and Satire: Stephen Colbert's 'Report,'" *Fresh Air with Terry Gross,* WHYY-Philadelphia, National Public Radio, December 7, 2005, http://npr.org.
4. Jonathan Gray, *Watching with* The Simpsons (New York: Routledge, 2006), 45.
5. Gary Saul Morson, "Parody, History, and Metaparody," in *Rethinking Bakhtin: Extensions and Challenges,* eds. Gary Saul Morson and Caryl Emerson (Evanston, IL: Northwestern University Press, 1989), 75.

6. Steven Daly, "Stephen Colbert: The Second Most Powerful Idiot in America," *Daily Telegraph* (UK), 16 May 2008, http://telegraph.co.uk.
7. Rabin, "Interview."
8. This observation comes from Terry Gross in her interview with Colbert, "Bluster and Satire."
9. Gross, "Bluster and Satire."
10. Gross, "Bluster and Satire."
11. Rabin, "Interview."
12. Robert N. Bellah, "Civil Religion in America," in *Religion in America*, eds. William G. McLoughlin and Robert N. Belah (Boston: Houghton Mifflin, 1968), 5.
13. Roderick P. Hart, *The Political Pulpit* (West Lafayette, IN: Purdue University Press, 1977), 58.
14. Daly, "Stephen Colbert."
15. Dan Snierson, "Stephen is King!" *Entertainment Weekly*, 4 January 2007, http://ew.com/ew/article/0,,20006490,00.html.
16. Cognitive psychologist George Lakoff has described this as an authoritarianism he calls the "strong father figure." George Lakoff, *Don't Think of an Elephant: Know Your Values and Frame the Debate* (Chelsea Green, 2004).
17. Morson, "Parody, History," 78.
18. Morson, "Parody, History," 78.
19. Geoffrey Baym, "Representation and the Politics of Play: Stephen Colbert's Better Know a District," *Political Communication* 24, no. 4 (2007): 359–76.
20. *The Colbert Report*, "Supreme Court Press," June 1, 2009.
21. Morson, "Parody, History," 65.
22. Quoted in Gray, *Watching*, 44.
23. Morson, "Parody, History," 66–67.
24. Morson, "Parody, History," 73. Original emphasis.
25. The segments aired on 4 March and 31 March 2009.
26. Morson, "Parody, History," 70.
27. Morson, "Parody, History," 71.
28. Gross, "Bluster and Satire."
29. Definitions taken from Dictionary.com, which lists four definitions taken from *The Random House Dictionary* (2009), *The American Heritage Dictionary of the English Language*, 4th ed. (2009), *The American Heritage Dictionary of Cultural Literacy* (2005), and *The American Heritage Dictionary of Idioms* (1997).
30. Morson, "Parody, History," 71–72.
31. "Captain Kangaroo Court," *The Colbert Report*, Comedy Central, 5 May 2009, http://colbertnation.com.
32. Morson, "Parody, History," 70.
33. Mary Douglas, "Jokes," in *Rethinking Popular Culture*, ed. Chandra Mukerji and Michael Schudson (Berkeley: University of California Press, 1991), 296.
34. As Colbert argues, "Status is always ripe for satire, status is always good for comedy. And [talk show hosts] have the highest possible status." Rabin, "Interview."
35. Heather L. LaMarre, Kristen D. Landreville, and Michael A. Beam, "The Irony of Satire: Political Ideology and the Motivation to See What You Want to See

in *The Colbert Report,*" *International Journal of Press/Politics* 14, no. 2 (2009): 212–31.

36. Jonathan Gray, "Real (and) Funny: Animated TV Comedy's Political Voice," paper presented at the annual meeting of the International Communication Association, Montreal, Canada, 22–26 May 2008. Original emphasis.
37. Gray, "Real (and) Funny."

CHAPTER 10

1. Liesbet van Zoonen, *Entertaining the Citizen: When Politics and Popular Culture Converge* (Lanham, MD: Rowman & Littlefield, 2005), 123.
2. See Schudson for a description of the "Informed Citizen" model of American citizenship that arose in the early twentieth century. See Carey for a critique of this "transmission view" of news and communication. See Jones for a "cultural approach" to moving away from this dominant model of mediated citizenship. Michael Schudson, *The Good Citizen: A History of American Civic Life* (New York: The Free Press, 1998); James Carey, *Communication as Culture: Essays on Media and Society* (Boston: Unwin Hyman, 1989); Jeffrey P. Jones, "A Cultural Approach to the Study of Mediated Citizenship, *Social Semiotics* 16, no. 2 (2006): 365–83.
3. See FCC Chairman Newton Minnow's speech to the National Association of Broadcasters, "Television and the Public Interest," 9 May 1961, Washington, D.C., http://www.americanrhetoric.com/speeches/newtonminow.htm.
4. Thomas E. Ruggiero, "Uses and Gratifications Theory in the 21st Century," *Mass Communications and Society* 3, no. 1 (2000): 3–37; Tony Wilson, *Understanding Media Users: From Theory to Practice* (Malden, MA: Wiley-Blackwell, 2009), 23.
5. Richard Butsch, *The Citizen Audience: Crowds, Publics, and Individuals* (New York: Routledge, 2008).
6. Sonia Livingstone, "On the Relation between Audiences and Publics," in *Audiences and Publics: When Cultural Engagement Matters for the Public Sphere,* ed. Sonia Livingstone (Bristol, UK: Intellect Books, 2004), 17–41.
7. Simon Cottle and Mugdha Rai, "Between Display and Deliberation: Analyzing TV News as Communicative Architecture," *Media, Culture & Society* 28, no. 2 (2006): 168.
8. Cottle and Rai, "Between Display and Deliberation," 171.
9. Nick Stevenson, ed., *Culture and Citizenship* (London: Sage, 2001).
10. Livingstone, *Audiences and Publics,* 21. See also Jones, "A Cultural Approach."
11. John Hartley, *Uses of Television* (London: Routledge), 178.
12. For scholarship on the rational nature of political thinking, see Samuel L. Popkin, "The Reasoning Voter: Communication and Persuasion in Presidential Campaigns (Chicago: University of Chicago Press, 1991). For political psychology and research into the relationship of emotion to political rationality, see W. Russell Neuman, George E. Marcus, Michael MacKuen, and Ann Crigler, eds. *The Affect Effect: Dynamics of Emotion in Political Thinking and Behavior* (Chicago:

University of Chicago Press, 2007); George E. Marcus, W. Russell Neuman, and Michael MacKuen, *Affective Intelligence and Political Judgment* (Chicago: University of Chicago Press, 2000); George E. Marcus, *The Sentimental Citizen: Emotion in Democratic Politics* (University Park, PA: The Pennsylvania State University Press, 2002); David P. Redlawsk (ed.), *Feeling Politics: Emotion in Political Information Processing* (New York: Palgrave, 2006); Drew Westin, *The Political Brain: The Role of Emotion in Deciding the Fate of the Nation* (New York: Public Affairs, 2007). See also George Lakoff, The *Political Mind* (New York: Viking, 2008).

13. Marcus, *The Sentimental Citizen*, 31.

14. Though one might argue that items in this list are actually subsumed under the previous emotional categories (or perhaps don't constitute emotions as much as feelings), the list is offered here to question the broader categories. Is "belonging," for instance, an anxiety or an enthusiasm? Perhaps both, for it depends, of course, on the narrative to which one is reacting.

15. One of the fascinating aspects of my interviews with viewers attending the citizen panelist auditions was how quickly the conversations could turn to discussions of political issues—from the Middle East crisis and abortion to Clarence Thomas and local politics.

16. David Thelen, *Becoming Citizens in the Age of Television* (Chicago: University of Chicago Press, 1996).

17. As one writer argued, "This is yet another letter pleading for the citizen panelist spot on your show. You'll note that your current method isn't exactly giving citizens the good name they deserve. It's too bloody democratic, you'll never get good people that way."

18. As the *Washington Post* levied one version of the criticism, "Do we really need a panel show in which stand-up comedians, minor former celebrities and the odd political and/or media operative sit around in a circle and say dumb things?" Quoted in Scott Shuger, "Comic Relief: Real Issues, Barbed Wit and Celebrities Galore," *U.S. News & World Report* 122 (20 January 1997): 59–65.

19. P. David Marshall, *Celebrity and Power* (Minneapolis: University of Minnesota Press, 1997), 243–44.

20. Marshall, *Celebrity*, 241.

21. Marshall, *Celebrity*, 240.

22. Marshall, *Celebrity*, 246–47.

23. For instance, during the initial phases of the Clinton-Lewinsky scandal, guests on *PI* would regularly intone that Clinton was a "regular guy" (and therefore just like the citizens who supported him) because he liked to "smoke weed and chase women." Indeed, some said he was the kind of guy you would "want to hang out with."

24. Michael X. Delli Carpini and Bruce A. Williams, "Constructing Public Opinion: The Uses of Fictional and Nonfictional Television in Conversations about the Environment," in *The Psychology of Political Communication*, ed. Ann N. Crigler (Ann Arbor: University of Michigan Press, 1996), 160.

25. Nancy K. Baym, "Talking about Soaps: Communicative Practices in a Computer-Mediated Fan Culture," in *Theorizing Fandom: Fans, Subculture and Identity*, ed. Cheryl Harris and Alison Alexander (Cresskill, NJ: Hampton Press, 1998), 111–29.

26. Sonia Livingstone and Peter Lunt, *Talk on Television: Audience Participation and Public Debate* (London: Routledge, 1993).

27. Jake Coyle, "Behind the Scenes of The Colbert Report," SFGate.com, 8 June 2008.

28. Stephen Colbert interview on *Fresh Air with Terry Gross*, 7 December 2005, http://www.npr.org/templates/story/story.php?storyId=5040948.

29. Steven Daly, "Stephen Colbert: The Second Most Powerful Idiot in America," *The Daily Telegraph* (UK), 16 May 2008, sec. 7, 22.

30. Dan Snierson, "Stephen is King!", *Entertainment Weekly*, 4 January 2007, retrieved from http://EW.com

31. Both quotes are taken from the wonderfully informative and thoroughly documented fan site Colbert University (a sister to another fan site, the No Fact Zone, which is featured in the "Community" section of the program's Comedy Central website). For the quotes, see http://colbertuniversity.nofact zone.net/index.php?option=com_content&task=view&id=32&Itemid=54.

32. Gary Saul Morson, "Parody, History, and Metaparody," in *Rethinking Bakhtin: Extensions and Challenges*, ed. Gary Saul Morson and Caryl Emerson (Evanston, IL: Northwestern University Press, 1989), 65.

33. Morson, "Parody, History," 65.

34. Using experimental design and surveying college students who are offered extra credit for their troubles, these researchers' focus is on audience ideology, including questioning whether conservatives who watch the show are actually making resistant decodings of what is supposedly a liberal message (or in the binary thinking of social science, are simply "seeing what they want to see"). See Heather L. LaMarre, Kristen D. Landreville, and Michael A. Beam, "The Irony of Satire: Political Ideology and the Motivation to See What You Want to See in *The Colbert Report*," *International Journal of Press/Politics* 14, no. 2 (2009): 212–31.

35. Adam Sternbergh, "Stephen Colbert Has America by the Ballots," *New York*, 8 October 2006, http://nymag.com.

36. van Zoonen, *Entertaining the Citizen*, 53.

37. Jonathan Gray, Cornel Sandvoss, and C. Lee Harrington (eds.), *Fandom: Identities and Communities in a Mediated World* (New York: NYU Press, 2007).

38. http://www.colbertnation.com/the-colbert-report-videos/72347/july-31-2006/the-word---wikiality.

39. http://colbertuniversity.nofactzone.net/index.php?option=com_content&tas k=view&id=32&Itemid=54.

40. John Cotey, "Conservatives Create Own Wiki Site," *Contra Costa (CA) Times*, 24 March 2007, F4.

41. http://www.wikiality.com/Main_Page.

42. http://www.wikiality.com/Conservapedia.

43. Theodore L. Glasser, "Play and the Power of News," *Journalism* 1, no. 1 (2000): 25–6.

44. Glasser, "Play," 26.

45. As discussed in chapter 2, Ellis describes this process of working through as the way in which television "attempts to define, tries out explanations, creates narratives, talks over, makes intelligible, tries to marginalize, harnesses

speculation, tries to make fit and, very occasionally, anathematizes." John Ellis, "Television as Working Through," in *Television and Common Knowledge*, ed. Jostein Gripsrud (London: Routledge, 1999), 55.

46. Gadamer quoted in Glasser, "Play," 28.
47. Catherine Burwell and Megan Boler, "Calling on the Colbert Nation: Fandom, Politics and Parody in an Age of Media Convergence, *Electronic Journal of Communication* 18, nos. 2–4 (2008).
48. See, for instance, Cornel Sandvoss, *Fans: The Mirror of Consumption* (Malden, MA: Polity, 2005).
49. LaMarre, Landreville, and Beam, "The Irony of Satire."
50. Glasser, "Play," 28. Original emphasis.
51. Jonathan Gray, "The News: You Gotta Love it," in *Fandom: Identities and Communities in a Mediated World*, eds. Jonathan Gray, Cornell Sandvoss, and E. Lee Harrington (New York: NYU Press, 2007), 80.
52. Rebecca Ascher-Walsh, "Stephen Colbert, 'Arch Conservative,'" *Los Angeles Times*, 1 June 2009, http://theenvelope.latimes.com/awards/emmys/env-en-colbert1-2009jun01173713,0,2529447.story.
53. Quote from Colbert speech at Harvard University, December 2006, http://colbertuniversity.nofactzone.net/index.php?option=com_content&task=view&id=32&Itemid=54.
54. For Colbert's segment announcing the results of the "competition," see http://www.colbertnation.com/the-colbert-report-videos/180279/september-02-2008/green-screen-challenge---last-shot. For a user-created compilation of well over 100 entries, see http://makemccainexciting.com.
55. van Zoonen, *Entertaining the Citizen*, 151.
56. van Zoonen, *Entertaining the Citizen*, 3.
57. Glasser, "Play," 24.
58. van Zoonen, *Entertaining the Citizen*, 123.

CHAPTER 11

1. Most of these shows have received awards from critics, including Emmys, TV Critics Association Awards, and Peabodys.
2. Henry Jenkins, *Convergence Culture: Where Old and New Media Collide* (New York: NYU Press, 2006), 227.
3. Although not a television performer, some conservative audiences consider right-wing talk show host Rush Limbaugh a humorous entertainer. For a discussion of Limbaugh and humor, see Paul Lewis, *Cracking Up: American Humor in a Time of Conflict* (Chicago: University of Chicago Press, 2006), 163–69.
4. The show ran from January 2004 to May 2005.
5. Which is similar to the odd amalgam that comprises *Huckabee*, as discussed in chapter 4. This quote is taken from a review of Glenn Beck's Common Sense Comedy Tour performance in Kansas City, Missouri, that was also simulcast to 440 movie theaters. Though Beck's television show is focused

more on populist outrage than humor, it is nevertheless instructive that given the similarity between this comedy performance and *Huckabee* (as well as Limbaugh), these generic characteristics might compose the model of entertaining political talk that works best with conservative viewers. See Mike Hale, "Laughing at Liberals (and Hawking That Book)," *New York Times*, 6 June 2009, C1.

6. Which is not to say that the hosts themselves are not liberal in their thinking.

7. Charles E. Schutz, *Political Humor: From Aristophanes to Sam Ervin* (London: Associated University Presses, 1977), 247.

8. Stephen Colbert makes clear this focus on power (and the necessity of all satirists to do so by using the second-person construction "you're") when he notes in a 2004 interview, "Listen, you're going to attack, or mock, or make fun of anybody who is in power right now, and the Republicans control the judicial, the legislative, the executive branches. So there's hardly another target." Quoted in Lewis, *Cracking Up*, 159.

9. Schutz, *Political Humor*, 322.

10. M. D. Fletcher, *Contemporary Political Satire: Narrative Strategies in the Post-Modern Context* (Lanham, MD: University Press of America, 1987), ix.

11. George A. Test, *Satire: Spirit and Art* (Tampa: University of South Florida Press, 1991), 35.

12. Maher, in fact, proclaimed himself a libertarian at the time, and even a Reagan Republican when it came to fiscal issues.

13. Schutz, *Political Humor*, 299.

14. Tad Friend, "Is It Funny Yet?" *The New Yorker*, 11 February 2002, 28.

15. The free market approach to political discourse is also ensconced in journalism's self-righting principle, as enunciated by John Milton: "Let [Truth] and Falsehood grapple; whoever knew Truth put to the worse, in a free and open encounter?"

16. Greg Mitchell, "Colbert, Mocking Beck, Goes Where 'NYT' Would Not," *Editor & Publisher*, 2 April 2009.

17. With the cancellation of these shows at roughly the same time, the argument I am making did not stop a number of commentators from entertaining the question of whether the failure was more than that. David Zurawik, "What's the Truth about Failed Black Comedy Shows," Z on TV blog, *Baltimore Sun*, 10 March 2009. See also Edward Wyatt, "No Smooth ride on TV Networks' Road to Diversity," *New York Times*, 18 March 2009, C1.

18. Eric Deggans, "Cultural Irreverence," *St. Petersburg Times* (Florida), 1 June 2008, sec. Floridian, 5E.

19. *The Daily Show*, 29 August 2008, http://www.thedailyshow.com/video/index.jhtml?videoId=183521&title=John-McCain-Chooses-a-Running-Mate.

20. Felicia R. Lee, "They Call Me Mister Correspondent," *New York Times*, 2 April 2007, E1.

21. If Clarence Thomas were on television, would we say that the voices or critiques based on the African American experience were well-represented or offered a critical perspective on power?

22. Because HBO is a subscription channel (therefore no advertising), *Real Time with Bill Maher* has not extended far beyond the television screen. Though the program airs repeatedly on HBO across its multiplexed channels (including "on-demand"), the program has gained only limited circulation across the Internet.

23. Stewart and Colbert were even named specifically as infringed parties in the lawsuit.

24. Daisy Whitney, "Comedy Central Heads Miniscule Mobile TV Audience," *RCR Wireless News*, 22 January 2007, 15.

25. For a discussion of the broadcast networks' digital strategies associated with the circulation of morning and late-night talk shows, as well as this concept of the "virtual water cooler," see Jeffrey P. Jones, "I Want My Talk TV: Network Talk Shows in a Digital Universe," in *Beyond Prime Time: Television Programming in the Post-Network Era*, ed. Amanda Lotz (New York: Routledge, 2009), 14–35.

26. Television has always been considered an ephemeral medium. That began to change with DVDs, of course, but more recently, broadcast networks have realized the value of allowing viewers to see entire past seasons of popular programming, as exemplified by their approach in creating Hulu.com and purchasing TV.com as "warehouses" for these materials. But Comedy Central's approach to archiving the entire "back catalog" on-line—ten years worth of programming—is unprecedented.

27. Geoffrey D. Baym, *From Cronkite to Colbert: The Evolution of Broadcast News* (Boulder, CO: Paradigm Publishers, 2009), 164.

28. Christian Christensen, "Jesters and Journalists," *British Journalism Review* 20, no. 2 (2009): 9–10.

29. Test, *Satire*, 4.

30. The differences are stark, with 995,000 men and women aged 25–49 as viewers versus 280,000 viewers aged 18–24. Though networks are interested in the percentage of young people that age, it is nevertheless instructive that so many people outside the "young" demographic are regular viewers. Nielsen Media Research, ratings for the period 31 December 2007–28 December 2008. Ratings supplied to the author by the staff at Comedy Central.

31. See Schutz, *Political Humor*; Jonathan Gray, Jeffrey P. Jones, and Ethan Thompson, "The State of Satire, the Satire of State," in *Satire TV: Politics and Comedy in the Post-Network Era*, eds. Jonathan Gray, Jeffrey P. Jones, and Ethan Thompson (New York: NYU Press, 2009), 3–36.

32. Andrew Sullivan, "To Catch a Predator," The Daily Dish blog, *The Atlantic*, 13 March 3009, http://andrewsullivan.theatlantic.com/the_daily_dish/2009/03/to-catch-a-pred.html.

33. Brian Keefer, "You Call That News? I Don't," *Washington Post*, 12 September 2004, B2.

34. See, for instance, Jedediah Purdy, *For Common Things: Irony, Trust, and Commitment in America Today* (New York: Vintage, 2000).

35. Amber Day, "Earnestly Ironic: Viral Videos for Action," paper presented at the International Communication Association annual conference, 22–26 May 2009, Chicago, Illinois.

36. Jody Baumgartner and Jonathan S. Morris, "*The Daily Show* Effect: Candidate Evaluations, Efficacy, and American Youth," *American Politics Research* 34, no. 3 (2006): 341.
37. Dannagal Goldthwaite Young, "Jon Stewart a Heretic? Surely You Jest: *The Daily Show's* Impact on Cynicism, Political Engagement and Participation," paper presented at the annual meeting of the National Communication Association, Chicago, Illinois, 15–18 November 2007. Original emphasis.
38. Roderick P. Hart and E. Johanna Hartelius, "The Political Sins of Jon Stewart," *Critical Studies in Media Communication* 24, no. 3 (2007): 263.
39. Hart and Hartelius, "The Political Sins," 268.
40. Leave it to scholars to make claims about television by not examining television!
41. Simon Critchley, "Cynicism We Can Believe In," *New York Times*, 1 April 2009, A31.
42. Critchley, "Cynicism."
43. Taken from Jonathan Gray, *Watching with* The Simpsons*: Television, Parody, and Intertextuality* (New York: Routledge, 2006), 153–54. See Peter Sloterdijk, *Critique of Cynical Reason*, trans. Michael Eldred (Minneapolis: University of Minnesota Press, 1987).
44. Sloterdijk, *Critique*, 292. Original emphasis.
45. Gray, *Watching*, 154.
46. See interviews with Stewart in the following: Michiko Kakutani, "The Most Trusted Man in America?," *New York Times*, 17 August 2008, AR1; Jane Ganahl, "Comic Release," *San Francisco Chronicle*, 23 April 2002, D1.
47. Gray, *Watching*, 154.
48. Stewart was tied with "real" journalists Brian Williams, Tom Brokaw, Dan Rather, and Anderson Cooper, http://people-press.org/report/309/todays-journalists-less-prominent.
49. Roderick P. Hart, *Seducing America: How Television Charms the Modern Voter* (Thousand Oaks, CA: Sage, 1998). Of course, Hart is not alone in this regard. See diatribes against television as a cynical agent in: Jeffrey C. Goldfarb, *The Cynical Society: The Culture of Politics and the Politics of Culture in American Life* (Chicago: University of Chicago Press, 1991); William Chaloupka, *Everybody Knows: Cynicism in America* (Minneapolis: University of Minnesota Press, 1999).
50. Hart and Hartelius, "The Political Sins," 264. Emphases added.
51. W. Lance Bennett, "Relief in Hard Times: A Defense of Jon Stewart's Comedy in an Age of Cynicism," *Critical Studies in Media Communication*, 24, no. 3 (2007): 278–83.
52. Bennett, "Relief in Hard Times," 278.
53. Sloterdijk, *Critique of Cynical Reason*, 296.
54. Sloterdijk, *Critique of Cynical Reason*, 101.

Index

About the Author

Jeffrey P. Jones (Ph.D., University of Texas at Austin) is associate professor of communication and theatre arts at Old Dominion University in Norfolk, Virginia. His research focuses on the intersection of popular culture and politics. He is coeditor of *Satire TV: Politics and Comedy in the Network Era* (2009) and *The Essential HBO Reader* (2008), and author of numerous articles and book chapters on media and politics.